GEOGRAPHIES: An Intermediate Series

EDITED BY PROFESSOR R. W. STEEL, M.A., B.Sc.

AFRICA AND THE ISLANDS

The Authors

R. J. HARRISON CHURCH is Professor
of Geography in the University of London
at the London School of Economics,
and is the author of *West Africa* in
the Longmans Series *Geographies for
Advanced Study.*

JOHN I. CLARKE is Professor of
Geography in the University of Sierra
Leone, Fourah Bay, on leave from the
University of Durham.

P. J. H. CLARKE is Geography
Master at Bishop Foxe's School, Taunton, and was formerly Tutor in Geography, Government Teacher Training
College, Kagumo, Nyeri, Kenya.

H. J. R. HENDERSON is Lecturer
in Geography in the University College
of Swansea and was formerly Visiting
Lecturer in Geography at Rhodes University, Grahamstown, South Africa.

All four authors have been in Africa
on many occasions and for long periods,
and know well the areas about which
they have written. Three of them have
taught in varied types of schools in
Africa and Europe, and three again have
held posts in African as well as British
universities or training colleges.

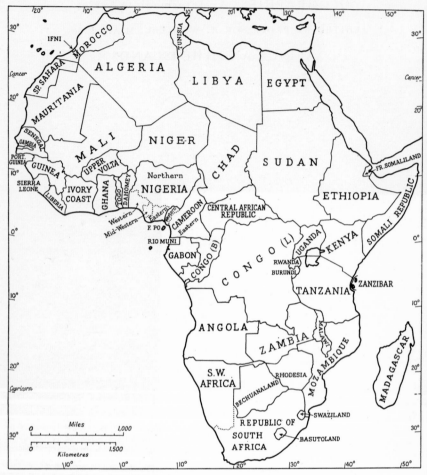

Political Divisions of Africa

Africa and the Islands

by

R. J. Harrison Church, B.Sc.(Econ.), Ph.D.(London)
*Professor of Geography in the University of London at the London School of Economics
and Political Science*

John I. Clarke, M.A., Ph.D. (Aberdeen)
Professor of Geography in the University of Sierra Leone, Fourah Bay

P. J. H. Clarke, M.A. (Cambridge)
*Geography Master, Bishop Foxe's School, Taunton and formerly Tutor in Geography,
Government Teacher Training College, Kagumo, Nyeri, Kenya*
and

H. J. R. Henderson, B.Sc. (Sheffield), M.A. (Liverpool)
*Lecturer in Geography in the University College of Swansea and formerly Visiting
Lecturer in Geography at Rhodes University, Grahamstown, South Africa*

John Wiley & Sons Inc
New York, N. Y.

Published throughout the world except the United States by
Longmans, Green & Co. Ltd.

PRINTED IN GREAT BRITAIN BY
SPOTTISWOODE, BALLANTYNE AND CO LTD
LONDON AND COLCHESTER

Preface

THE new Africa requires books that are modern in approach and are kept up-to-date. The wind—even hurricane—of change that is sweeping through the continent makes difficult the writing of such a book, for no one person can be equally conversant with every part of Africa. When the first author was asked to write this book he immediately realized that it should be a joint effort by specialists in certain areas and aspects. We have been in Africa on many occasions and for long periods, and know well all or most of the areas about which we have written. Three of us have taught in varied types of schools in Africa and Europe, and three of us in African as well as British and other universities or training colleges. We have followed a uniform plan and used common terms, but there is some variation in emphasis where a country or area demands a special approach or attention to a particular aspect. Authorship is noted at the beginning of each chapter.

We have tried to use official names, except where there are recognized English alternatives. Capitals have been used for political names and well-known or important physical features or areas, but complete uniformity is difficult.

Writing about Africa has more pitfalls than writing on any other continent. The facts are not easily ascertained for statistical services are poorly developed, maps are few, and different terms are used by French, British and other writers. In consequence, most British books concentrate heavily on the ex-British areas, but we have sought in text, maps and photographs to counteract this. A special effort has been made to get good and varied photographs illustrating developments and problems, and special journeys were made to Paris and Brussels for this purpose. We are most grateful to the many agencies that have allowed free reproduction.

For our maps our best thanks go to Mr. G. McWhirter (Department of Geography, University of Durham), Miss Glenys Thomas (Department of Geography, University College of Swansea) and to Miss E. Woodhams, Mrs. S. Weston and Mrs. E. Wilson of the Department of Geography, London School of Economics. The last three not only drew their own share of the maps, but made additions to many other maps. Miss B. Powell, Miss J. P. Tagg and Miss M. Austin typed

London-based manuscript and some other parts as well. The patience
and efficiency of our helpers have been of great assistance to us in an
interesting co-operative effort. Lastly, we cannot possibly forget how
much we owe to the eagle eye, editorial skill, African knowledge and
experience of Professor R. W. Steel, whose task has been especially
heavy on a book with four authors.

We are very sympathetic to the aspirations of African peoples and
earnestly hope that we have faithfully interpreted this fascinating
continent in its rapid transformation.

May 1963.

R.J.H.C.
J.I.C.
P.J.H.C.
H.J.R.H.

Editor's Note

IN this reprint recent changes in the names of states have been incorporated in both text and maps: Zambia and Rhodesia respectively for
Northern and Southern Rhodesia; and Tanzania, reflecting the
union of Tanganyika and Zanzibar, though 'Tanganyika' has been
retained where the text refers solely to the mainland territory of the
Republic.

R.J.H.C.

January 1965.

Contents

Contents

Western Central Africa

East Africa

Southern Africa

The African Islands of the Indian Ocean

CONCLUSION

Maps and Diagrams

Plates

For permission to reproduce photographs we are indebted to the following:

Aerofilms Ltd.: Plate 14; Agipan and the Tunisian Embassy: Plates 8, 9; B.O.A.C.: Plate 65; Cie Française des Pétroles: Plates 10, 11 (Sopeg); Cie Fria: Plate 26; East African Railways and Harbours: Plate 55; Fairey Aviation: Plate 13; Documentation Française: Plates 23, 24, 25, 34, 68; Ghana Information Services: Plate 31; Inforcongo: Plates 36 (H. Goldstein), 38 (H. Goldstein), 39 (H. Goldstein), 40 (E. Lobeid), 41 (C. Lamote), 42, 43 (C. Lamote); Kenya Information Services: Plates 47, 48, 50; Public Relations Office, Khartoum: Plate 15; Liberian Information Service: Plates 28, 29; Service Général de l'Information de Madagascar: Plates 69, 70, 71, 72; Ministère de la Co-opération: Plates 27 (Afrique Photo), 30 (Pichonnier), 33; Moroccan Tourist Office: Plates 5 (Souissi Studios), 6, 7 (Flandrin); Niger River Transport: Plate 21; Portuguese State Office: Plate 45; P.A. Reuter Photos.: Plate 54; Satour: Plates 60, 63, 64; South African Information Service: Plate 66; Ministry of Home Affairs, Salisbury, Rhodesia: Plates 56, 57, 58, 59; Taylor Woodrow: Plate 35; Uganda Information Dept.: Plates 46 (David Pasteur), 52, 53; Agência Ceral do Ultramar, Lisbon: Plates 44, 67; David Whitehead & Sons (Nigeria) Ltd. and Kaduna Textiles Ltd.: Plate 32. Plate 49 is Crown Copyright Reserved. Plates 1, 2, 3, 4, 16, 17, 18, 19, 20, 22, 59 are by R. J. Harrison Church; Plate 12 is by John I. Clarke; Plates 61, 62 are by H. J. R. Henderson.

I

AFRICA AS A WHOLE

CHAPTER ONE

Africa in History[†]

MAN himself may have originated in Africa, the Ethiopian Massif was probably one of the world's three centres of seed domestication, Egyptian civilization flourished in the north, and enslaved Africans with free Europeans peopled the Americas.

Although for long retarded by communal and restrictive societies, the physical seclusion of the continent, and the disruption caused by the slave trade, Africa has awakened. The colonial phase is ending, and vast changes are to be seen almost everywhere. Cheap hydroelectric or atomic power may bring much industry to Africa, the source of many minerals. Eradication of the tsetse fly, unique to Africa, and complete control of the malarial mosquito could lead to rapid population growth, more intensive settlement, improved agriculture and stock-keeping. These possible developments can only be understood against the background of history, the physical environment, peoples and their modes of life, which are the subject matter of the general chapters.

The Ancient Empires of North Africa

Ancient Egypt was one of several subtropical empires which developed along rivers but differed from the others in that the source of its wheat cultivation was the Ethiopian Massif. Egypt was also probably the first large country of the ancient world to be under one ruler, which was accomplished as early as 3188 B.C. The desert for long protected Ancient Egypt, while the Nile nourished it with renewable fertility and an assured water supply. The delta of the Nile provided outlets through a short and easily protected coastline on the Mediterranean, an admirable trading area.

The Phoenicians, Carthaginians and Greeks were very dependent upon the sea, limited themselves to coastal cities in North Africa, and made no other impact on the continent. Roman Africa had most of its settlements in what is now northern Algeria and Tunisia, although at

* By R. J. Harrison Church.

† It would be helpful to read this chapter with a copy to hand of J. D. Fage, *An Atlas of African History*, 1958.

its zenith in the third century A.D. Roman rule extended from south-western Morocco along all the North African coast and up the Nile to the first cataract. To all these ancients North Africa appealed strongly as an area of Mediterranean climate, an outlet for traders and emigrants, and as a source of food. Irrigation was well developed by the Romans, and some of their schemes have been renovated for modern use. The Sahara was, however, their frontier, and the rest of Africa beyond their ken.

The Arabs and Islam

The seventh-century penetration of Africa by the Arabs, introducing Islam and Islamic law, Arabic architecture, decorative motifs, thought and culture, was of profound significance to much of Africa, and has remained so. Islam ultimately replaced Christianity in the Sudan and Egypt, and became dominant in all North Africa, coastal East Africa, and in most of the dry lands immediately south of the Sahara, to which it was taken by camel caravans of traders and teachers (Fig. 11). The camel had been adopted in North Africa by about the fourth century, and this remarkable animal permitted another great historical landmark, the crossing of the Sahara. Only small groups of peoples in inaccessible areas remained non-Islamic, for example the Coptic Christians protected by the fastnesses and steep seaward edges of the Ethiopian Massif, the peoples of the Jos Plateau in Northern Nigeria, and those of the forests.

Early States of Interior West Africa

Contemporaneous with these movements was the development of states around the upper or middle Niger, and between that river and Lake Chad. They were probably founded by Hamitic-speaking peoples from north-eastern Africa, who brought camels, horses and donkeys. In an open woodland or savanna environment free of tsetse, cattle could be kept and grain grown. The animals and navigable rivers facilitated extensive rule and commerce. Water was the main physical control, and southern boundaries were determined by tsetse and the forest.

Ghana (in no way coincident with modern Ghana) had its zenith about A.D. 1000, and its capital at Koumbi Saleh 205 miles north-north-east of Bamako (Mali) has been excavated. Mali supplanted Ghana and largely coincided in area with the present state. Ancient Mali was at its zenith in the fourteenth century and once included Timbuktu and Gao. Songhai first developed at Gao in the eleventh century, and it conquered Timbuktu in 1468. The Senegal was reached in 1512. Many of Mali's peoples then moved towards the coasts of what is now the Gambia, Portuguese Guinea, Guinea and Sierra Leone, taking with them knowledge of rice and cotton cultivation; Alvise de Ca'da Mosto, the first to describe the Gambia, saw them growing in 1445. Songhai was conquered by a Moroccan army of 4,000 men who crossed the Sahara in 1591. To the south lay the smaller, purely negro and non-Islamic states of Ouagadougou, Yatenga and Fada N'Gourma (Upper Volta), and the Hausa and Bornu Islamic states in what is now Northern Nigeria, all of which have survived in some form or other.

Trans-Saharan Trade

This was the life blood of all these states, and of their most famous towns, such as Timbuktu (Plate 1), Gao and Kano, which were caravan terminals. By caravans these states received European goods obtained by North African Arabs from such states as the Genoese and Venetian republics, and salt from the Sahara (Plate 2). West African states supplied the caravans with gold then found in Bambouk between the Bafing and Faléme headwaters of the Senegal, and leather, goat and sheep skins which came to be called, erroneously, 'Moroccan leather'. From the forest 'frontier' to the south came more gold, ivory and spices and, above all, slaves.

Slavery was already known in Africa, indeed it prevailed in Ancient Egypt, but a new feature was the great and widespread Arab trade in slaves in North, West, Central and East Africa, which endured for nearly 1,000 years. Slaves were taken to Asia, and even to Iberia where the idea of slavery was implanted, soon to grow into the more formidable proportions of the European slave trade which lasted over three centuries.

Other African States

After the Moroccan conquest of Songhai, no large state survived in West Africa, although several small ones such as Ashanti, Dahomey, Oyo and Benin developed in the forested areas. There were also many states in East Africa, such as Kitwara (twelfth to fourteenth centuries) in what is now Uganda, and later supplanted by the Bunyoro, Buganda, Toro and Busoga kingdoms which are still vigorous, as are Rwanda and Burundi to the south. Among others in Central Africa were Monomotapa, south of the Zambezi, known to have produced gold; Luba, important in the fifteenth and sixteenth centuries in what is now Katanga; and, around the lower Congo a state of that name. From certain of these Central African states the great Bantu migrations into southern Africa took place between the seventeenth and nineteenth centuries.

The Portuguese Sea Route to Asia

The Arab and later the Ottoman Turkish hold on North Africa kept Europeans from trans-Saharan trade, from North and East Africa, and from most overland routes to Asia. There was, therefore, an urge to find a seaway round Africa to the rich commerce of Asia, and to reach the legendary Christian state of Prester John, a confused allusion to Christian Ethiopia. In the latter part of the fifteenth century Portuguese and other navigators were steadily pushing their way along the African coasts, until Vasco da Gama rounded the Cape in 1497, sailed up the east coast where he came upon towns trading with Arabia, Persia and India, and then himself sailed on to India.

At first Africa was significant to Europeans only in relation to Asia. Forts were established by the Portuguese on African coasts for the defence of the Asian trade, and the names Algoa Bay (near Port Elizabeth, South Africa) used by vessels outward-bound for Goa and Delgoa Bay (Lourenço Marques, Mozambique) used by homeward-bound ships from Goa and Asia generally are relic names from that trade. The Dutch soon defeated the Portuguese in most of Asia; thereafter Portuguese forts on the East African coasts were backwaters, and much of the East African trade passed to Omani Arabs. The Dutch used Table Bay as a watering point and established a settlement in 1652. The English first used St. Helena, taken in 1659, but later preferred Cape Town after they captured it in 1806. In the west the French used Gorée, off Dakar, at the most westerly point of Africa, taken in 1658. In the east they took Réunion in 1649, and later on Mauritius, where the Dutch had previously had a port of call and where the British in turn supplanted the French.

The European Slave Trade in Africa

The advanced civilizations of Asia offered greater trading possibilities than Africa, which also presented formidable physical and other difficulties. African footholds for purely African trade were long restricted to those through which compact and valuable commodities could be readily obtained. The earliest was Elmina (Plate 3), still well preserved like some other castles on the coast of Ghana. It was so named because it was supposed to be near a gold mine; in fact, gold was brought by Africans from many workings, nearby and more remote.

Slaves soon came to be the main export from Africa, and remained so for over three centuries. Forts were built along much of the West African and Angolan coasts, at first by the Portuguese (alone in Angola) but later by the Dutch, English, French, Swedes, Danes and others along what came to be known as the Gold Coast. Here there was a plentiful supply of slaves (as well as of gold) from inland Ashanti, climatic conditions were the most pleasant of all the Guinea Coast, slight promontories provided some defence for the castles and shelter for ships, and good water was available.

The coming of Europeans to the Guinea Coast hastened the decline of trans-Saharan trade, which the advent of the Ottoman Turks in North Africa and the Moroccan conquest of Songhai had started. Trade from the rising forest states developed quickly with the European coastal forts, and so diverted supplies from the already deranged Saharan trade. Maritime trade has grown ever since, the coastal areas have prospered and the interior ones declined, until some revival was possible by railways in the twentieth century.

The European slave trade was the greatest affliction Africa has borne. As in the earlier era forts had been established on islands or on the coast to safeguard the lucrative Asian trade, Africa again became subservient to other continents—the Americas, in addition to the Arab slave trade towards Asia already mentioned. It has been estimated that $13\frac{1}{4}$ million slaves were taken from the Congo Basin; if that is correct, between 30 and 35 million may have been removed by Arabs and Europeans from Africa, although many less reached their destinations.

During the centuries of the Arab and European slave trades African states disintegrated as the result of the capture of their political and religious rulers and the dispersion of their peoples. Whole states were destroyed, such as the Congo by the Portuguese in 1665. Trade routes became insecure, and a premium was put on secluded and remote places irrespective of their suitability for agriculture or for settlement. Suspicion of Arabs and Europeans remains among many Africans to this day.

Vast areas were more or less depopulated, like the Middle Belt of West Africa and most of Western Central Africa, although natural conditions always kept some areas thinly peopled. Reduction of the population has usually resulted in the spread of the tsetse fly, because fewer able-bodied persons remain to cut down vegetation which harbours the fly.

Agriculturally, Africa gained something from the slave trade, since the Portuguese found few indigenous crops that would store well for feeding slaves on the long journey to the Americas. They introduced cassava (manioc), sweet potatoes, groundnuts, maize, lima beans, chillies and other crops from the Americas; and they, Arabs, or returning pilgrims introduced Asian yams, cocoyams, bananas, peas, beans and sugar cane. Many of these have become of basic importance to Africa, notably cassava the most widespread food crop (Fig. 15), and groundnuts which are one of the few food and export crops of dry areas.

European Reaction to the Slave Trade

The Mansfield Judgement of 1772 made it clear that domestic slavery was illegal in the United Kingdom, but former slaves became homeless and destitute. Soon after came the far greater problem of resettling slaves who had fought with Britain in the American War of Independence, and were wretched in Britain or Nova Scotia. The Sierra Leone Peninsula was acquired for settlement of a first party from England in 1787; a second arrived from Nova Scotia in 1792, when the settlement was named Freetown. Ex-slaves also came later from Jamaica.

In 1807 Britain abolished the slave trade, and her navy sought to capture all slave ships. Bases were established at Freetown, Bathurst (Gambia), and on the island of Fernando Po leased for a time from the Spanish. Many hundreds of slaves were landed at these places (especially Freetown) from captured ships.

Meanwhile, the American Colonization Society established former American slaves along the coast to the south-east of Sierra Leone, beginning in 1822. In 1847 these settlements declared their independence as 'Liberia', choosing as a state motto 'The Love of Liberty Brought Us Here'. The French Navy was active off the Gabon coast, and slaves it freed from ships were landed at Libreville.

A Creole community grew up in all these settlements, as well as in others where freed slaves gathered, such as St. Louis (Senegal), Ouidah (Dahomey) and Lagos; or on islands such as Fernando Po, São Tomé, Príncipe, the Comoros, Réunion, Mauritius and the Seychelles, where they were later liberated from work on plantations. The term 'creole' has varied meanings in different parts of Africa and the rest of the world. In West Africa it is used to describe a group or a person descended from ex-slaves of varied origin. Such a group or person may also have some European or Asian admixture and much European culture, and this is the main meaning common in the Mascarenes and

outside Africa. The term may also be applied to a variant of English
spoken by such people or by others. With their European culture and
superior opportunities these peoples were early prominent in the
professions, but this often gave rise to a division between them and the
truly indigenous Africans, as in Sierra Leone, Liberia and Gabon, a
rift which is only now being healed.

The Exploration of Africa

The abolition of the slave trade and of slavery led to an economic
hiatus until legitimate commerce could be developed. In West and
West Central Africa trade in palm oil, ivory and wild rubber mostly
took the place of the slave trade. In South, Central and East Africa
there seemed little else to develop except European settlement. In the
plantation isles contract labour was obtained from India and China,
so changing the population structures, and the land-owning and
cropping-systems were ultimately modified as well.

The movement for the abolition of the slave trade and of slavery,
the rise of democratic governments and increased literacy in Western
Europe, and the development of the steamship, all encouraged a
wider interest in Africa, the least known of all inhabited continents,
yet the nearest to the most developed one.

From 1788 until about 1890 there were many European explora-
tions of Africa, especially between 1850 and 1877. Some travellers set
out to resolve the course of rivers, notably Mungo Park's expeditions
to the Niger 1795–7 and 1805–6, and Lander 1830. The sources of the
Nile interested Burton 1854–5, Burton and Speke 1857–9, Speke and
Grant 1860–3, and Baker 1862, while Stanley was concerned with the
Congo between 1874 and 1877. Others crossed the Sahara, such as
Alexander Laing 1823–6, Réné Caillé 1827–9 and Heinrich Barth
1850–6. All these reached the River Niger, Timbuktu and other cities
famed in trans-Saharan trade. Most famous in Britain was David
Livingstone, utterly dedicated to African humanity, who was determined to stop the Arab slave trade and domestic slavery, and wished
to map the Zambezi and Upper Nile. No other explorer spent so
much time walking the continent as did Livingstone from 1841–56,
1858–64 and 1866–73; no one did more to rouse British attention to
the then generally miserable condition of its peoples.

The Advent of European Control

The reasons which led to European occupation of African were
diverse and complex. Many footholds dated from the calling points

of the national maritime routes to Asia, the slave trade bases, the settlements of freed slaves, the older Dutch settlements in Cape Colony, and the nineteenth-century French ones in Algeria. There were a few new trading points concerned with the palm oil trade, such as Calabar. In some cases European occupation took place to safe-guard the freed slaves (Sierra Leone Colony), or to end the slave trade (Lagos and several parts of East Africa).

In many areas advance was for prestige, a telling factor in French areas, as France wished to restore the face she lost in the Franco-Prussian War of 1870–1. In other areas it was the wish of the British to counter such expansion (Sierra Leone Protectorate, Gold Coast Northern Territories and Northern Nigeria). Economic motives, even if at times exaggerated, were important in British Central Africa, sought for its minerals and the possibilities of European settlement. Strategic considerations were significant in all the North African lands, as well as at Dakar, Cape Town, Diego Suarez and Djibouti. Often several of these factors weighed, while trade led on to political control through involvement in inter-tribal rivalry, as in the Gold Coast.

The Conference of Berlin (1884–5) declaration of the need for effective occupancy to sustain title to territory led to the final 'Scramble for Africa' and completion of the political map. In the next five years most of Africa was occupied to secure such title, and the long era of African footholds held mainly in connection with the greater interest and trade with Asia and the Americas was ended. Henceforth, Africa was opened by river transport, railways, roads and, much later, by airways.

To Islamized and Arabic-influenced Africa was added Christianized and Europeanized Africa. The almost incredible mosaic of indigenous political units received an overlay of colonial boundaries, within which diverse and contrasted policies were pursued.

There was fighting in both world wars in Africa. The main result of the first was that ex-German colonies became mandates, with international review of their administration. This was much enlarged by the trusteeship system after the Second World War. That war had other profound effects on Africa. Many Africans fought in Asia and Europe, and brought back nationalist and anti-racialist ideas with them. These were reinforced by the Atlantic Charter and the founda-tion of the United Nations. Massive colonial financial aid vastly increased educational facilities, so producing more national leaders. Also, high prices for raw materials prevailed for many years, so that there was the economic possibility of independence.

1*

From being mainly colonial in 1955, Africa became mostly independent by 1961, only a decade and a half after the independence of
the far more politically and economically evolved countries of
southern and south-eastern Asia. Unlike these, and countries in the
Americas, most African states attained independence with little or
no bloodshed, although the unity of the Congo (Leopoldville) was
not safeguarded without it. But for the problems of the multiracial
countries of European settlement, independence might have come
even more completely and peacefully.

European Settlement in Africa

The Dutch settlement established at Cape Town in 1652 was
probably the first European possession in Africa intended for settlers
since Roman times. By the end of the eighteenth century Dutch settlement had attained the Orange River in the north-west, the Great Fish
River in the east, and to beyond the Great Karoo in the centre. Austere
Afrikaners and Huguenots had penetrated a dry and broken country,
and were increasingly in conflict with the southward-moving Bantu.

The British captured Cape Colony in 1806, and the advent of British
settlers with contrasted political, religious and social outlooks,
together with the abolition of slavery and the method of payment of
compensation, determined the Dutch Afrikaners to move away from
the British. The Great Trek took place in 1836, and British annexation
of Natal in 1844 precipitated a second lesser trek in that year. The
Transvaal and Orange Free State were ultimately established as
dominantly Afrikaner, although wedged in between British- and
Bantu-settled areas.

European settlement also developed in Algeria in the latter part of
the nineteenth century, at the turn of the century (and later) in
Tunisia, Rhodesia and Tanganyika, and almost wholly in the
twentieth century in Angola, Mozambique, Kenya, Morocco and
Libya. In all these lands problems have been created because Europeans have so often acquired exclusive or excessive advantages in the
healthiest and more fertile areas. African farmers are often clustered
in less healthy and more infertile lands, or those that soon became so
because of close settlement (such as many South African reserves or
the former Kikuyu ones in Kenya). Rainfall is frequently less reliable
in these reserves, and they are less accessible, so that economic
development and social welfare have lagged behind.* European

---

* Striking maps illustrating some of these points are in J. D. Fage, *An Atlas of African
History*, 1958, 51–55, and especially in the *Report of the East Africa Royal Commission*,
1953–55, Cmd. 9475 (end maps), and the *Atlas du Maroc*, 1955–date.

settlement led to the greatest problems in devising constitutions for independence in Kenya and Algeria, and racial problems are unresolved in several countries.

The Modern Age

Africa has greatly benefited from the vast range of inventions of the last century and a half. It has been opened up by railways, roads and air services, strikingly so by the latter. Telecommunications have facilitated administration over great distances and appallingly difficult terrain. Cement and steel have made tall buildings possible in a continent often deficient in suitable stone or brick-making materials. Electricity and atomic power have brought industrial possibilities to a continent short of coal, and not rich in petroleum. Africa's hydro-electric power potential is the greatest in the world; that of the lower Congo is said to be greater than that of power already developed in the U.S.A. Tropical medicine and the refrigeration of food have made life safe for those with money and knowledge; while cheap electricity could ultimately provide widespread air-conditioning and so greatly increase human efficiency.

As was pointed out at the beginning, man may have originated in Africa; yet because of historical isolation and formidable physical difficulties, Africa has remained the least developed settled continent, despite its being nearest to the longest developed continents of Asia and Europe. On the other hand, as the nearest tropical land mass to Europe, Africa now has a substantial advantage for the export of raw materials, of which North African natural gas is the most modern example. Can Africa attain the intensive agricultural development of the lands of Monsoon Asia, as well as adequate industrial expansion? Politically, it has been balkanized in independence, just as European countries are coming closer together. The political challenge to Africa is great; the economic and social challenges are immense.

FURTHER READING

The best general studies are J. D. Fage, *An Atlas of African History*, 1958, and R. Oliver and J. D. Fage, *A Short History of Africa*, 1962. E. W. Bovill, *Caravans of the Old Sahara*, 1933, or *The Golden Trade of the Moors*, 1958, vividly describe the early states of interior West Africa and trans-Saharan trade, and Basil Davidson, *Black Mother*, 1961, deals with African history from the first European contacts to European occupation. H. J. Wood, *Exploration and Discovery*, 1951, has a chapter on the explorers.

CHAPTER TWO

The Physical Environment

ONLY Asia of the other continents exceeds Africa in area. Very compact, and almost devoid of peninsulas and major inlets, Africa extends about 5,000 miles from north to south, and a similar distance from east to west. The great size of the continent is emphasized by the fact that several of her individual states are among the largest in the world. For example, the Sudan is nearly a million square miles in area, four and a half times the size of France, or over ten times that of the United Kingdom. Algeria and Congo (Leopoldville) are each nearly as large. That part of Africa south of the Tropic of Capricorn, which appears so small on a map of the whole continent, is nearly 700,000 square miles in extent, and includes almost the whole of the Republic of South Africa.

The area north of Cancer is much larger, because of its greater east–west extent, but Africa is remarkable for its latitudinal symmetry about the equator, reaching to 37° N. and 35° S., so that a very large proportion of the continent lies between the tropics. It is also remarkable for the vast extent of hot desert in the northern hemisphere, which extends tropical conditions over a large extra-tropical area from the Atlantic to the Red Sea, so that temperate conditions are confined to the northern and southern extremities of the continent.

Large mountain ranges are also limited to the north and south, and the predominance of relatively flat surfaces over most of Africa, together with her essentially tropical position, gives a relatively simple distribution of climatic and vegetation types, ranging from equatorial through moist tropical and tropical desert to subtropical or temperate. With such a wide range of conditions, human responses must be expected to vary greatly as well. This chapter gives a reasoned exposition of the physical environment with which man has to work in Africa, paying attention also to the ways in which he has already modified that environment.

GEOLOGY AND STRUCTURE

In many respects the geological structure of Africa is relatively simple when compared with the other continents. Most of Africa has existed

* By H. J. R. Henderson, except for the section on Soils by John I. Clarke.

as a rigid block since Precambrian times, so that strongly folded younger rocks are found only at the margins. The structure of the Basement Complex, as the rigid block of Archaean rocks is often termed, is much more complicated. The details of these ancient structures are the concern of the geographer only where they help him to understand surface features or the occurrence of mineral deposits of economic importance. The rocks concerned are various igneous and metamorphic types, which may be found at scattered places over most of the continent (Fig. 1).

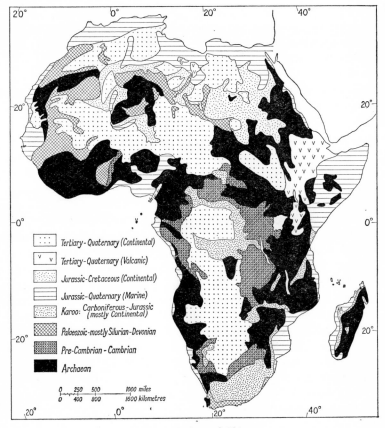

Fig. 1. Geology of Africa
(Simplified from *Carte Géologique Internationale de l'Afrique*)

There is another group of Precambrian rocks, younger than the Archaean, which consists mainly of sediments which have been much less affected by the heat and pressure to which rocks are subjected at times of violent earth movements. These rocks lie on top of the Archaean complex, and are very important economically as they contain some of Africa's richest mineral deposits, including the gold of South Africa and the copper of Zambia and the Congo (Leopoldville).

In some parts of the continent it is not possible to distinguish the upper Precambrian from the lower Palaeozoic rocks that succeed it; in the south this is particularly true. In the Sahara and surrounding areas several outcrops of Cambrian rocks are known, but everywhere the folding of these rocks is surprisingly gentle considering their age. In the northern part of the continent there have been recognized, in more or less normal succession, rocks from the Cambrian through to the Carboniferous, but in the south the situation is different. Along the southern margin of the continent are found the Cape Fold Ranges, a series of typical fold mountains formed of marine sandstones and quartzites thought to be Silurian and Devonian in age. These are the only fold mountains of Palaeozoic rocks in the whole of Africa, and seem to be more closely related to similar folds in Brazil and Australia than to any other part of Africa. The trend of the folds is parallel to the edge of the block to the north, which suggests that they must have been crumpled against the block, although what caused the crumpling is not immediately evident.

The Carboniferous period is represented in southern Africa by a vast extent of almost undisturbed rocks, mostly sandstones, which are typical of 'terrestrial' deposits, formed on the surface of the land and not in the sea. These rocks cover more than half of south Africa and are represented as far north as the Congo Basin. They are the lowest beds of the 'Karoo' series, which includes rocks of Permian and Triassic age as well, and show that continental conditions prevailed over a large part of the continent for most of this time. These rocks also contain Africa's only major coal deposits which are found in South Africa and Rhodesia, showing that swamp conditions also existed at times.

The Trias of the Sahara is lacustrine in origin, and contains deposits of salt and gypsum typical of basins of inland drainage under arid conditions. True marine deposits are unknown after the Devonian until the Jurassic, when we find marine deposits again. These are confined to the northern margins of the continent, the eastern coastal areas from Somaliland to Tanzania, and to Madagascar. None of these now occurs upon the surface of the main block of Africa, all being marginal to it. This marginal distribution of marine beds is emphasized and developed in the succeeding Cretaceous and Tertiary periods, for narrow strips of such rocks are found all around the continent, though more widely developed in the east and the north, where they form the folded Atlas Mountains. Occasionally they are seen to extend up the main valleys, the most notable example being that of the Niger-Benue trough in West Africa.

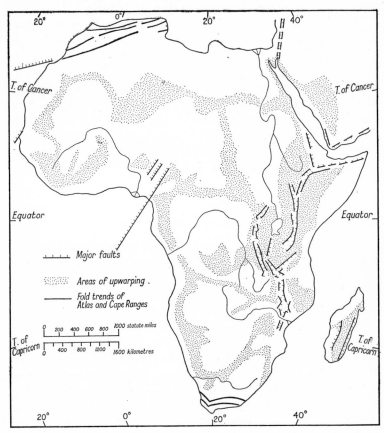

Fig. 2. Structure of Africa. (After Holmes and Furon)

Cretaceous and later deposits in the interior are all continental in type, formed either in shallow inland lakes or of wind-blown sand. Examples of the latter are the Kalahari sand of the south, now largely fixed by vegetation, and the sands of the Sahara, in many places still mobile.

Africa is thus mainly a rigid block of ancient rocks, which appear at the surface over a substantial part of the continent. Much of the block is covered by a veneer of younger rocks, often very thin, and varying in age from late Precambrian onwards. The majority of these have been formed under continental conditions, showing that Africa has maintained its continental nature over a very great span of time. Around the margins are found the only marine deposits of later date than the Devonian, and none of these is older than the Jurassic.

This picture is simplified, and much still remains to be discovered about the geology of Africa. But there is one respect in which the picture must be modified. While folding movements have been rare, it would be wrong to think that there has been no movement at all. Vertical movements have taken place, and warping of the continental block has produced some of the major basins of Africa while elsewhere the block has developed fractures, or faults as they are called. Such faults form the great succession of rift valleys, which run from near the mouth of the Zambezi northward through East Africa, and are continued by the Red Sea and farther north by the Jordan Valley (Fig. 2 and Plate 47).

The Great Rift Valley System

The amazing distance over which features of this system may be traced in Africa indicates a very powerful process which has acted upon the continent to form the rifts. The distance from Beira, near the southern end of the rift system, to the northern end of the Red Sea, is about 3,500 miles, taking no account of the extension of the system into the Jordan Valley and beyond.

In 1921 J. W. Gregory published his study of the rift system. He noticed that the rifts traverse some of the highest parts of the African block, which he supposed to have been warped upwards, just as certain basins have been warped down. He believed that this warping was the result of a lateral compression, and suggested that it occurred during the Cretaceous period, being responsible for the submergence of the Mozambique Channel and thus for the formation of the Cretaceous marine deposits of Madagascar and the Mozambique coast. Subsequently, he suggested, the floor of the Indian Ocean foundered, thus releasing the lateral pressure to which Africa had been subject. This, he maintained, brought about the collapse of the central portions of the up-warped regions of East Africa to form the rift valleys.

The undoubted activity of the faults in late Cretaceous and early Tertiary times also brought about volcanic activity along the rift zone from the Red Sea to Malawi (Nyasaland), producing the extensive lava flows of the Tertiary Volcanics. These are matched elsewhere by volcanic rocks of similar age, for example the Deccan Traps of India. Both are of the same order of age as the folding of the Alps and Himalaya, and of Africa's younger fold belt, the Atlas. It seems reasonable, therefore, to look for processes that will account not only for the rifts, but also for these other phenomena of the same age.

Gregory's theory is essentially that the rifts are due to tension in the crust, bringing about the collapse of the rift floors. This idea has been contested by numerous authorities, of whom Holmes has set out the main arguments involved most lucidly. Holmes prefers to think that the rifts were formed by compression of the crust, resulting in thrust faults. According to this theory, the upthrust mass of the main block would ride up on the underthrust mass, and thereby depress it into the earth. This would tend to produce a second thrust fault parallel to the first, but thrusting towards it. Thus we would have two opposing upthrust masses facing each other across a valley floor formed by a single block which would be bearing the weight of both upthrust masses, and would gradually subside until isostatic equilibrium was regained.

While these two theories, basically opposed to each other, are essentially simple, the great amount of geological mapping and research done since 1945 in Africa has shown that neither theory is really adequate. Whereas it was originally thought that the rifts developed at the end of the Cretaceous period, it has now been shown that they are much older, for the faults follow the line of faults developed in Precambrian times; the Cretaceous and Tertiary faulting is only one stage in the development of these features. According to Dixey, whose study of the rifts appeared in 1956, it seems that the Cretaceous and later movements are due to tension, but that compression caused the earlier faulting. Dixey and other experts believe, as did Gregory, that the vertical movements that have produced the 'basin-and-swell' structure of Africa (Fig. 2) are really the key to the whole problem, but no satisfactory theory has been found to account for these movements.

The Origin of the Continent; Do Continents Drift?

Another group of theories associates the rifts with horizontal movement of the continents, or 'continental drift'. The crust of the earth is believed to consist of two distinct layers: a lower relatively dense layer (sima), and an upper less dense layer (sial). The sial is the material of which the continents are made up, but it is largely absent from the ocean floors, so that it is possible to think of sial continents 'floating' on the sima. If this is accepted, it is possible for the continents to move laterally on the earth's surface.

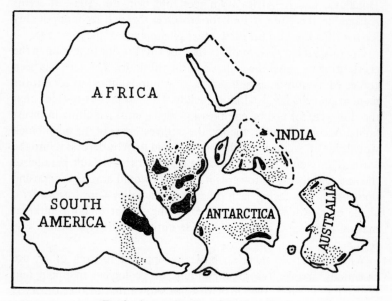

Fig. 3. A reconstruction of Gondwanaland

(After King.) The black indicates the present extent of the continental deposits laid down on the super-continent (Karoo and related series), and the stipple their probable former extent

In 1910 Wegener adduced varied evidence to support his main thesis that all the continents were derived from a single primitive continent, Pangaea. His reconstructions of the distribution of the continents at different periods were based upon the apparent fit of the opposite coasts of the Atlantic Ocean, and the reconstruction was supported by the correspondence of certain structures in South America and southern Africa; for example, the Cape Fold Ranges of South Africa correspond closely in type of rock and nature of structure with the Sierras of Buenos Aires province in Argentina.

There are many flaws in Wegener's theory, but the basic idea has not been discounted. Its significance here is that Wegener, while siding with the supporters of tensional rifting, extended the idea to associate the rifting with the break-up of Pangaea. If this is correct, it is possible that the East African rifts are still widening, and in several million years could become oceanic areas separating parts of East Africa from the rest of the continent.

Du Toit, whose book *Our Wandering Continents* was published in 1937, collected new evidence in favour of the hypothesis, as well as assessing earlier work. He proposed two primitive continents: Laurasia, which is now broken into North America, Europe and Asia; and Gondwanaland, which became South America, Africa, India, Australia and Antarctica. Africa must therefore have been the centre-piece of Gondwanaland, losing the various other blocks from Permian times onwards, as these moved towards their present positions. This thesis has been further developed by King, whose reconstruction of the super-continent was made using curved perspex outlines on the surface of a globe, and taking into account much other evidence (Fig. 3). The central position of Africa in Gondwanaland is important, as it explains the essentially continental nature of most African rocks, and it is also basic to King's theories concerning the major erosion cycles in Africa.

Many geologists, however, do not accept continental drift, pre-ferring to think entirely in terms of vertical movements, despite the many lines of evidence that appear to support the drift hypothesis. Much of their objection rests on the fact that none of the supporters of drift has been able to give a satisfactory explanation of what causes continental drift.

However, the evidence in favour of continental drift is increasing. Several workers have pointed to the diverse climatic conditions that some areas have experienced; for example, the Karoo series of South Africa starts with deposits of tillite, a fossil boulder-clay which clearly shows that in Carboniferous times South Africa underwent an ice age. Similar rocks occur in India, Australia, South America and Antarctica, and these are of about the same age. Some of the most telling pieces of evidence are the glacial striae found on rocks forming the surface on which the tillites lie, and which clearly indicate that at one stage the ice flowed on to the present continent from a main centre off the coast of Natal. It is not unreasonable to suppose that this ice flowed from another part of the super-continent of Gondwanaland. Further favourable evidence comes from the study of the magnetic properties of rocks, but this method is in its infancy in Africa.

It is impossible to say with any certainty what the relationship of the East African rifts may be with continental drift and the break-up of

Gondwanaland, although many sections of the coasts of Africa are closely associated with faults.

The surface form of Africa, as one might expect from its structure, is dominated by great plateaux, often several thousand feet above sea level. In many parts these are so nearly level that the eye can hardly discern any slope in the surface. These plateaux are the product of long periods of erosion uninterrupted by folding. Subsequently, the entire continental block has been uplifted, complete with its near-level erosion surfaces. This uplift has been greatest in the east and south of the continent, where large areas are more than 3,000 feet above sea level, and in Basutoland the plateau surface reaches over 11,000 feet.

The only parts of Africa which are not a part of the plateaux are the two-fold mountain belts, the Atlas in the north and the Cape Ranges in the south, and the few great volcanic cones or masses which have accumulated upon the surface of the continent to give Africa her highest points. Most of these are in East Africa, associated with the rifts; they include Kilimanjaro (19,320 feet), Kenya (17,040 feet) and Elgon (14,176 feet). A notable exception is Cameroon Mountain (13,352 feet) which rises from near sea-level, and, significantly, lies on an important fault line and close to the intersection of the east–west and north–south trending sections of the western edge of the continental block. Other exceptions are the Hoggar and Tibesti Mountains of the Sahara.

The extent of the plateau is so great, and the drop to the coast so sudden in most parts, that there is little coastal plain. A map of the relief of Africa will show how little lowland there is; comparison with a geological map shows the lowland to correspond with the areas of Cretaceous and Tertiary rocks around the margins of the continent. This fits in with the idea of Africa as the central mass of Gondwanaland, from which the other sections have drifted away. At the time of its disintegration Gondwanaland had been eroded down to a peneplain, which was highest in the centre of the super-continent. With the loss of the marginal masses Africa was created with a fairly high and level surface.

This is the basis of the explanation of African land-surfaces suggested by King. He recognizes three main surfaces, of which the highest is the remnant of the surface of Gondwanaland at the time of its break-up (Gondwana surface). The break-up itself initiated a new cycle of erosion, because of the much shorter distances that each river had to cover to the sea; this was the first cycle to develop in Africa as a separate continent, and is called the African cycle. Later cycles were caused by the uplift of the continent, the most important being the Congo cycle. These cycles of erosion were first recognized in southern Africa, but other workers have found similar surfaces further north. The precise mode of origin of the surfaces is debated, but the existence of several distinct surfaces is generally agreed.

A characteristic feature of many parts of Africa is the sharp break between one erosion surface and the next, which often takes the form of a distinct escarpment. One of the best-known is the Great Escarpment which bounds the plateau in South Africa. It is also common to find substantial remnants of an older and higher surface standing above the dominant surface of a particular area. These residual hills have a number of names, for example kopje, bornhardt, inselberg; their form varies according to the type of rock in which they occur. In massive rocks like granite they may rise in sheer rounded forms hundreds of feet above the plains in which they lie (Plate 4); in well-bedded sediments, such as Karoo sandstones, a flat-topped hill with steep even slopes is typical. Both forms are evidence of the vast amount of erosion that has produced the present landscape. Both are of great interest to the student of processes of erosion, for their origins are controversial.

DRAINAGE

According to de Martonne, only 48 per cent of Africa is exoreic, that is drained directly to the oceans by rivers; 40 per cent is without organized surface drainage (areic), while 12 per cent is drained to interior basins which have no outlet to the sea (endoreic) (Fig. 4).

It is remarkable, however, that of those areas which drain to the oceans, a large proportion consists of broad shallow basins with floors between 1,000 feet and 3,000 feet above sea-level, and drained by single outlets, narrowly confined where they break through the basin rims. The outlets of these basins are the great rivers of Africa—Niger, Congo, Orange, Zambezi and upper Nile. The drainage of Africa is thus integrated into relatively few systems, each of large size, except around the margins of the plateau in those parts where rainfall is sufficient to create numerous shorter parallel streams flowing directly to the ocean.

The major divides between these basins are remarkable both for the fact that they are sinuous, and that they are in many places very close to the coasts. The divide between the Indian and Atlantic oceans, for

example, lies first at one edge of the continent and then at the other.
It is also notable that in many parts the divides do not follow any well-
marked relief features.

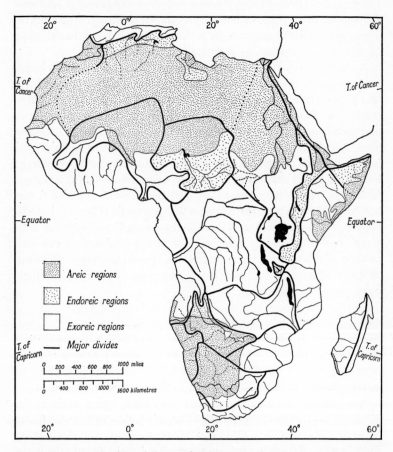

*Fig. 4. Drainage of Africa, following de Martonne's classification, and the major
divides.*

All these facts are consistent with the idea of the break-up of
Gondwanaland, for they fit the concept of a peneplaned super-
continent, with its fully integrated drainage system in which the main
members are interdigitated at their inland or upper ends. The break-
away of the marginal blocks would have led to:

1. The rejuvenation of the existing streams and the creation of new
   marginal streams.

2 Rapid erosion at the new continental edge.
3 Isostatic uplift at the edges of the continent as a result of the removal of much material from these edges.

Thus the seaward ends of the rivers would be cutting down with renewed vigour as the land surface rose to close the basins, producing, where the rivers were able to maintain their courses across the rising land, narrow valley outlets from the basins, characterized by waterfalls and rapids relatively near the sea as the heads of rejuvenation began to move upstream. Above the falls the more mature landscapes of the original upper valleys would survive, modified only by a gentle lowering of the surface by the processes of erosion working down to the base-level provided by the rivers.

The areas of areism are the hot deserts, where present precipitation is insufficient to give rise to an integrated system of drainage, but where past pluvial phases have sometimes produced intricate systems of now dry valleys. Large areas of endoreic drainage are those of Lake Chad, the Makarikari salt pan of Bechuanaland and the eastern Rift Valley. The first two are associated with the downwarped type of basin; the third is the product of rifting.

Perhaps the greatest anomaly is the Nile, with its 4,000-mile course from the downwarped basin of Lake Victoria, situated between the two rifts and in a well-watered region, northward through the eastern Sahara. For the last 1,500 miles the Nile derives no water from its immediate environment, but only from tributaries similarly bringing water from a distance. It, too, has falls in its lower course, the six cataracts of the northern Sudan and southern Egypt. The Nile is everywhere an intruder in an arid landscape, and its course has not been explained satisfactorily.

The Niger rises close to the border of Sierra Leone and only 200 miles from the Atlantic Ocean. It flows north-east into the southern margins of the Sahara, providing irrigation water in the 'inland delta' above Timbuktu, then swings to a south-easterly direction, and reaches the Gulf of Guinea through a great delta 1,200 miles east of its source, having flowed over 2,600 miles to get there. The 'drainage' pattern of much of the areic southern Sahara is 'tributary' to the Niger, the great waterless valleys indicating a moister period when rivers did flow here. The upper part of the valley above Timbuktu is characteristically mature, while the section above Jebba (Northern Nigeria) contains several rapids and falls as the river tumbles from the plateau and heads for the sea. In the part below Jebba the Niger receives its largest tributary, the Benue, which has an unusually large plain section, probably developed along a major fault zone. Its headwaters are vigorously cutting back and have partially captured some of the drainage flowing north to Lake Chad, a process which, if continued, will eventually deprive Chad of much of its water-supply.

Many streams rise in the Fouta Djallon, some flowing inland, others direct to the coast. Of the former, the Senegal is the largest, rising quite close to the Niger, but turning north-west and passing through near-desert to reach the Atlantic well to the north of Cape Verde.

The Congo (Plate 36) has all the characteristics of African rivers: a broad shallow basin nearly 800 miles across both latitudinally and longitudinally, a narrow outlet through the western rim and, associated with this, a series of rapids and falls separating the more mature upper course from the short lower, immature course to the sea. It is atypical only in that it is the one river of Africa with a large navigable estuary, which permits sea-going vessels to reach Matadi, 80 miles inland. Within the basin are several lakes, remnants of a much larger lake of Pliocene or earlier date, and evidence that as the relative height of the basin rim increased, the Congo was not able fully to maintain its course, and that the waters were dammed back (see also pp. 305–307).

To the south, the next major basin is that of the Zambezi, which has similar characteristics to the Congo in its broad upper basin with perennial streams capable of navigation by small craft. From this section the main stream, with a width of over a mile, plunges into the zig-zag gorge below the Victoria Falls, and thence covers another 900 miles to reach the sea, passing over further rapids and through the recently created Lake Kariba on its way. Some of the headwaters above the Falls have in the past fed the interior basin of the Okovango Swamps and the Makarikari salt-pan of Bechuanaland. It may be that the main Zambezi did so too, later being diverted by its own alluvial accumulation through a low part of the divide to form the headwaters of one of the exoreic streams. Certainly, below the Victoria Falls it is of limited use for navigation, and its nuisance value to land transport is well seen from the fact that before the Kariba Dam provided a road crossing, there were only three bridges over the river, one at the Falls, one at Chirundu, and the other at Sena 100 miles from the mouth in Portuguese East Africa where the river is over two miles wide.

On the west is the smaller Cunene River which rises on the plateau, and appears similarly to have pushed itself over the plateau edge in the Rua Cana Falls, on the boundary of Angola and South West Africa, having previously flowed to the Etosha Pan.

The major river of southern Africa is the Orange which, like its tributary the Vaal, rises close to the Great Escarpment of the Drakensberg, and, flowing westward from this fairly well-watered area, traverses the arid areas of the southern Kalahari, drops over the Aughrabies Falls into a gorge which carries it to the edge of the plateau, and so into the Atlantic nearly 400 miles north of Cape Town. Its tributaries, none of which is truly perennial, drain almost the entire plateau area of South Africa, and parts of Bechuanaland and South West Africa where the almost perennially dry watercourses converge on the Orange. Even the main river frequently fails to reach the ocean in a dry season, an event made more frequent by the extensive use of the water for irrigation on the plateau. Apart from this, the Orange has all the typical features seen in the other major rivers.

Lakes

The lakes of Africa are of two main types—those caused by gentle warping of the surface and those occupying rifts, their shape usually being sufficient to show to which group they belong. The lakes of the great rifts of East Africa are mostly long and relatively narrow: Tanganyika and Nyasa are each between 300 and 400 miles long and are also characteristically deep. Most of those of the Western Rift have outlets to the sea, Lakes Edward and Albert through the Nile, Tanganyika through the Congo, and Nyasa through the Shire. Others form centres for areas of inland drainage, for example Lakes Rukwa and Rudolf.

The greatest of the lakes produced by warping is Victoria, which occupies an area warped down between the two great rifts of East Africa. Unlike the rift lakes it is broad, shallow, and has an intricate coastline with many islands, the tops of hills drowned in the down-warping movements. Its outflow to the Nile is over the Owen Falls, where the construction of a power-station has taken advantage of one of the world's greatest natural reservoirs. The Nile then passes into Lake Kioga, a curious conglomeration of finger-like flooded valleys, created by the upwarping of the western end of its basin, with a resultant reversal of the Kafu, and ponding back of the Victoria Nile and other streams to flood their relatively youthful valleys.

Other downwarped lakes, present and past, have been mentioned already. The Congo Basin held one in the past; Lake Chad, in a basin of inland drainage, is much reduced from its former self, and so are the lakes and pans of Bechuanaland—Makarikari, Okovango and Etosha.

WEATHER AND CLIMATE

African weather, like any other weather, may best be understood in terms of air-masses, and the way in which these interact where they meet or converge. The study of air-masses is equally important in the understanding of climate, which is the aggregate of weather conditions over a long period.

The term air-mass is applied to a mass of air which, having lain over a relatively uniform land or sea surface for a period of some days, possesses over large horizontal distances relatively uniform characteristics of temperature, humidity and vertical stability. The plane of contact between two distinct air-masses is called a front. In temperate latitudes a front is usually recognized by the contrasts in temperature between the two air masses involved, but in tropical areas, including most of Africa, there is frequently no such temperature contrast; the only difference being in stability and humidity.

The distribution of air-masses and fronts is closely related to the patterns of distribution of atmospheric pressure, which change from season to season in response to the apparent movement of the sun from Tropic to Tropic.

The pressure distributions discussed here are those based upon surface data, reduced to sea-level. Modern work, based upon upper-air data from radio-sonde balloons, has shown that average pressure distributions and circulation patterns in the free air above the continent is often quite different from that close to the land-surface. It has also been shown that in areas of high altitude, especially during the afternoons, the surface circulation is often much more closely related to upper-air conditions than to the sea-level pressures.

In the light of this, our theories concerning the causes of African weather and climate may need some revision, but until a more complete picture of upper-air conditions over the whole of Africa is available, the earlier theories can still help to elucidate the main features of the climate. The attempt to explain causation can be no more than hypothesis at present, for while the elements of climate can be measured, the processes are complex and at best imperfectly understood.

Pressure

Because of its almost equal extent north and south of the Equator there is a measure of symmetry in the pressure systems of Africa. However, this is somewhat upset by the much greater longitudinal extent of Africa north of the Equator, and by the proximity of the

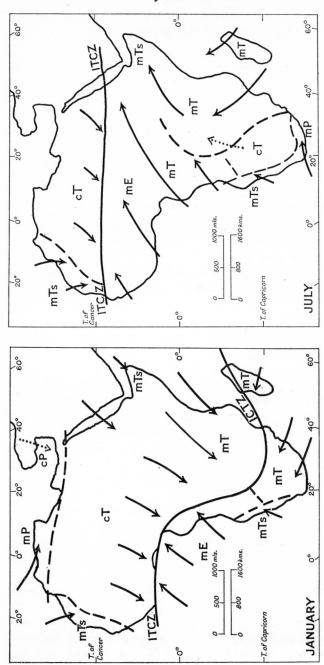

Fig. 5. The dominant air masses over Africa in January and July

Eurasian land-mass, both contrasting with the narrower southern subcontinent, tapering southward between Atlantic and Indian Oceans.

In January the apparent southerly position of the sun causes intense cooling of the northern continents, which intensifies the dynamic anticyclones already over them. The North Atlantic subtropical anticyclone lies between the continental highs of Eurasia and North America, but this high-pressure belt, which affects most of northern Africa, is crossed by a zone of lower average pressure over the warm waters of the Mediterranean Sea, and extending south-eastward in the Red Sea and Persian Gulf. The southern tropical anticyclones are relatively weak in January, and are centred at about 30° S. in the Atlantic and 35° S. in the Indian Ocean. The equatorial low-pressure belt has been drawn south and is linked with the thermal low of the Kalahari, so that the whole of the southern subcontinent is under the influence of a single low-pressure system during the southern summer.

In July the southern subtropical anticyclones are stronger and slightly farther north than in January. The southern hemisphere has no great land-mass to compare with Eurasia in the north, so there is no large thermally intensified anticyclone of the southern winter, but a much smaller anticyclone develops at about 30° S. over southern Africa, precisely between the two subtropical anticyclones, so that high pressure does prevail there from coast to coast.

In the northern summer the Eurasian High of January is dissipated, and an intense thermal Low is created, with its major centre over the Indus valley. This continental Low is so strong that it completely eliminates the subtropical anticyclone that might otherwise occupy the northern Indian Ocean, and low pressures extend right across Africa north of the Equator, where the Sahara also develops a thermal Low. West of this the North Atlantic subtropical anticyclone (Azores High) is strongly established.

Air-masses

In most cases air-masses originate in the high-pressure areas, whence they move towards low-pressure areas. Once they leave their source-regions they are modified according to the conditions in the areas over which they move, but remain recognizable as distinct masses and, at a given place, are characteristic of their particular source-regions in terms of temperature, humidity, stability and wind-direction. The classification of air-masses is based upon the distinction between Arctic, Polar and Tropical air-masses respectively, and their subdivision into maritime and continental types, according to the latitude and nature of the source regions.

Africa never experiences Arctic air-masses; the types which do occur may all be classified as one of the following— polar continental (cP), polar maritime (mP), tropical maritime (mT) or tropical continental (cT).

Polar continental (cP) air can reach Africa only in the northern hemisphere, since Southern Africa is lapped by extensive oceans on its poleward side. The source regions are Siberia and European Russia, and the air leaving these regions is cold, dry and stable. In reaching Africa much of it must cross the Mediterranean Sea, where it acquires some moisture, and this may give rise to precipitation as the air moves south, sometimes as far as Khartoum, but incursions of such air are infrequent. A similar type of air-mass forms in the Atlas in winter, but affects only a small area.

Polar maritime (mP) air reaches both northern and southern Africa from the north and south Atlantic respectively. It occurs frequently over the Mediterranean and North Africa, where it is introduced in the depressions that traverse the Mediterranean in winter. In South Africa it is rarer, but its mode of introduction is similarly in depressions originating on the polar front. In both extremities of the continent this air is typically cool, moist and unstable.

Most of the air-masses affecting Africa are tropical, and it is therefore necessary to subdivide the main types of tropical air, according to whether the air is subsiding (stable), subject to strong upward currents and turbulence (unstable), or neither (neutral). Tropical maritime air may occur in all three forms.

Subsident tropical maritime (mTs) air occurs in the eastern ends of subtropical anticyclonic cells, and thus appears on the west coast of Africa, which is permanently under this type between 15° S. and 30° S. and between 15° N. and 33° N. Stratus cloud and coastal fogs are frequent, but rain never falls from this type of air-mass. A similar mass predominates on the east coast of Somalia, being modified cT air from Asia in the northern winter or from the Kalahari in the southern winter, or modified mT air of the unstable variety which has been stabilized and deprived of its moisture in crossing the continent from the Gulf of Guinea.

Neutral tropical maritime (mT) air, which is characteristic of the western ends of the subtropical anticyclones, is seldom found in the northern hemisphere because there is no permanent anticyclone in the north Indian Ocean, and occurs only intermittently in the region of the Mozambique Channel. It is warm and moist, and requires only slight orographic or frontal lifting to trigger off convectional storms.

The unstable convergent tropical maritime air, often called equatorial (mE) air, is closely associated with the south side of the Inter-Tropical Convergence Zone within the equatorial low-pressure belt, where northern and southern tropical air-masses meet. Originating over the Atlantic and Indian Oceans, this type of air reaches the convergence in Central Africa little modified, and is still identifiable in Ethiopia after crossing the continent from the west coast. It is warm moist air, within which convectional storms develop freely. Similar air occurs off the south-east coasts of Africa and Madagascar during the southern summer.

Tropical continental (cT) air is derived chiefly from the great desert area of Northern Africa, where the air subsides upon a relatively uniform surface, and a dry stable air-mass results. Surface turbulence resulting from intense solar heating by day causes hazy, dusty conditions up to about 5,000 feet. This is the Harmattan of West Africa, and is the principal air-mass on the north side of the Inter-Tropical Convergence. A similar air-mass develops over the Kalahari in much the same way, especially during the southern winter.

Frontal Activity

Fronts are formed where two air-masses converge, usually in one of the major low-pressure systems. A variety of processes can lead to the formation of minor fronts within an air-mass, but most frontal activity takes place within well-marked frontal zones. An individual front seldom remains stationary; it will usually be moving as one air-mass pushes back the other, and may frequently reverse the direction of its movement. Nevertheless the average position of the major fronts can be recognized for a given season.

The most constant frontal zone in Africa is the Inter-Tropical Convergence Zone (ITCZ), at which tropical masses of the two hemispheres meet, within the equatorial low-pressure belt, but little or no frontal rain occurs, as throughout its length dry cT air is being lifted over mT air and the moisture content is insufficient for the condensation level to be reached. However, a great deal of convective activity occurs south of the ITCZ, especially where mE air-masses predominate on the south side, so that non-frontal rains come to various parts of the equatorial belt at different seasons, as the ITCZ sweeps north and south in the course of the year. In January it parallels the West African coast at about 5° N., and beyond 10° E. swings south to about 25° S. in the Transvaal, whence it trends north-eastward across northern Madagascar. In July it is more nearly a parallel of latitude, crossing the continent between 18° N. and 20° N.

The areas commonly affected by true frontal activity are the north-western and southern extremities of the continent. In the Mediterranean area a frontal belt develops during the winter within the low-pressure belt, as polar air from Europe converges with cT air from the Sahara. The north coast of Africa is affected by frontal activity in depressions developed on this Mediterranean Front, and in the north-west in depressions moving from the Atlantic Polar Front, through the Strait of Gibraltar and the Gate of Carcassonne. The Atlantic depressions are the main rain-bearers, for the polar air of the Mediterranean depressions is little modified cP air, and therefore only slightly moist. South Africa lies on the margins of the depression tracks from the South Atlantic Polar Front, and frontal activity here is associated with the introduction of mP air in these depressions.

Rainfall

Practically no part of Africa receives its rainfall evenly distributed over the year; everywhere there are distinct wet or wetter and dry or drier seasons. For this reason average annual rainfall figures have little meaning on their own, since seasonal distribution is so important. The detailed implications of seasonal distribution are discussed in the regional chapters.

The annual rainfall varies from over 100 inches on parts of the West African coast, the east coast of Madagascar, and a few mountain areas of South Africa, to virtually nothing in parts of the Sahara and on the coast of South West Africa. The patterns at the various seasons reflect the migration of the pressure and frontal systems.

In January, with the ITCZ at its furthest south, Africa north of 5° N. is virtually rainless, apart from the Mediterranean coastlands which receive rain from the winter depressions. South of the Equator much of central and east Africa averages over eight inches for the month, and only the western margins of South and South West Africa are rainless.

In April the northward migration of pressure and frontal systems advances the edge of the rain-affected area to about 10° N., but causes a decrease in rainfall over the southern subcontinent. Only north-west Africa is still within the normal range of the Mediterranean depressions.

By July rainfall is virtually confined to the equatorial low-pressure belt between the Equator and 20° N., as the ITCZ advances to its farthest north in the southern margins of the Sahara. Only the south-western Cape Province is an exception, as the depressions in the southern hemisphere westerlies bring frontal rain to the southern tip of the continent.

In October the rainfall distribution has much in common with that of April, as the ITCZ is once more migrating through the equatorial belt. The total for the month tends to be less in Central and East Africa than during April, as the winter anticyclone of the Kalahari is still strong enough to maintain a north-easterly flow of dry mTs and cT air, so that the East African Plateau receives little or no rain at this season.

Temperatures

Africa is essentially a hot continent; if the monthly mean temperatures for July and January are reduced to sea-level values, no part of Africa falls below 50°F in either month. But since much of Africa consists of high plateau, sea-level temperatures have little meaning. Monthly mean actual temperatures below 40°F are found in the Atlas in January, and along the Great Escarpment of South Africa in July, while close to the Equator several East African peaks are high enough to nourish permanent snowfields and glaciers. Even so, temperatures are generally high. In January, only the area north of Cancer is below 60°F, and south of this most of Africa has average temperatures between 70°F and 80°F. In July the average is over 80°F almost everywhere north of 12°N., and large areas exceed 90°F. This great extent of high temperatures is the cause of the thermal low-pressure of the Sahara. At this season only the interior plateau south of the Zambezi–Congo divide, and the south-western coastal districts are normally below 60° F.

CLIMATIC TYPES

The attempt to understand climate and its effect upon the landscapes of the world has led climatologists to propound a number of climatic classifications, each with its particular shortcomings and merits. Figure 6 shows the climates of Africa according to Miller's classification. Seven of Miller's types occur in Africa:

A   Hot climates; no month below 64°F.
     A1   Equatorial; double rainfall maximum.
     A2   Tropical Marine; no true dry season.
     A3   Tropical Continental; winter dry.
     A3m Tropical Continental; monsoon variety.

B   Warm temperate or subtropical climates; no month below 43°F.
    B1   Western Margin (Mediterranean); winter rain.
    B2   Eastern Margin; uniform rain.

F   Desert climates; annual rainfall in inches less than one-fifth of
    mean annual temperature in °F.
    F1   Hot deserts; no month below 43°F.

Each of these may be modified by the effects of altitude.

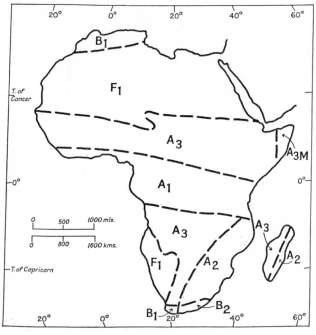

Fig. 6. Climates of Africa. (After Miller)

A division into so few types can give only a very approximate
picture of climatic conditions in an area as large as Africa.

The Equatorial type of climate is experienced in a belt from the
coast of Tanganyika over most of the Congo Basin, and along the
far west as Liberia. Monthly average temperatures
throughout the year, but the extreme tempera-
pical latitudes never occur. The annual range
exceeds 5°, and the diurnal range is normally
figures, especially the annual one, emphasize

the fact that there is little difference in temperature between one air-mass and the next in these latitudes; the greater diurnal range reflects the influence of the sun upon air-temperatures, and the fact that the daily duration of sunlight is almost constant throughout the year.

The double maximum of rainfall is caused by the migration of the inter-tropical convergence across these areas, northward shortly after the March equinox, and southward after the September equinox. Because of the small seasonal differences in temperature, the seasons are thought of as wet and dry, rather than hot and cold. Almost everywhere one of the two wet seasons brings more rain than the other; thus there are distinguished the 'greater' and the 'lesser' rains, to which many local names are given. Entebbe (Uganda) averages 25 inches in the three months March to May, but only 13 inches in October to December. Lagos (Nigeria) receives 39 inches in the greater rains of May to July, and 16 inches in the lesser of September to November. The rain falls typically in heavy convectional showers from the mE air south of the ITCZ, the totals varying according to local circumstances such as distance from the sea, and the direction from which the moist air approaches. Thus Douala, on the Bight of Biafra, receives 159 inches per annum; Mombasa (Kenya), although on the coast, has only 47 inches; most inland stations receive between 60 and 70 inches.

A distinct subtype, the High-altitude Equatorial climate, occurs between about 5,000 and 10,000 feet above sea-level. Temperatures are lower, the annual range extremely small, but the diurnal range tends to be much greater because at high altitudes the rarefied air interferes little with rapid radiation by night or with insolation by day. The rainfall régime is maintained, but the total tends to be less. Nairobi (Kenya, 5,495 feet) has a total rainfall of 39 inches, with maxima in April and November; the average temperatue for the year is 63°F, and for the coolest month 59°F, which should exclude Nairobi from the Equatorial climatic type, but with an annual range of only 6° it has all the other characteristics and must be regarded as an altitudinal modification of the Equatorial type. However, such modifications are limited in their extent in Africa since little of the equatorial belt lies above about 4,000 feet; the Kenya Highlands are the most important area economically. It should be realized also that much of Kenya, Uganda, and northern Tanganyika, while of true Equatorial type, are high enough to have considerably lower temperatures than are typical near the west coast, e.g. Entebbe (U

3,842 feet), coldest month 69°F, annual average 70°F; Tabora (Tanganyika, 4,151 feet), coldest month 70°F, annual average 73°F. The Tropical Marine climates stretch from about 10°S. in Tanganyika to 30°S. in South Africa. They also cover the eastern part of Madagascar. Most of their rainfall comes from the ITCZ during the summer months, but in winter these coasts are affected by easterly winds bringing in mT air. Although moist, this air is relatively warm and usually tends to become more stable once it reaches the land. Thus rain is unusual, except where orographic effects come into play. These produce mist and drizzle in the foothills of the Great Escarpment especially, but heavy rain is rare. Temperatures at the northern end of the belt are very similar to those of Equatorial climates; Lindi (10°S.) has an annual mean of 80°F and a range of only 6°, but further from the equator the temperatures are lower and the range greater until Durban (30°S.) has a mean of 70°F and a range of 13°. In the north, therefore, it is the single rainfall maximum that distinguishes the tropical from the equatorial climates; further south winter and summer become recognizable in terms of temperature differences.

The Tropical Continental climates are the most extensive in Africa, apart from the Desert type. They are found both north and south of the Equatorial belt and, like the Tropical Marine climates, have a summer maximum of rainfall associated with the ITCZ. But in winter they have complete drought, lying permanently under the influence of cT air-masses, since they are too far from the east coast for the mT air of the Trades to penetrate without modification. In the dry season humidity is low, and clear cloudless skies lead to frequent high temperatures. Often these temperatures are higher than those of the cloudier Equatorial climates, to which the summer temperatures approximate more closely. Kayes (Mali) has average temperatures for March, April and May, of 89, 94 and 96°F respectively; but in June, when the rains begin, the average temperature drops to 84°. Of the yearly average of 29 inches of rain, 26 fall in the period June to September, and there is a slight rise in temperatures again as the rains end, from 82°F in September to 85°F in October. This shows how temperature is controlled as much by the incidence of cloud and rain, as by the march of the sun.

Wet season conditions are much the same as those associated with the ITCZ in Equatorial climates. Humidity is high, and the diurnal temperature range is small. As one moves further from the Equatorial belt towards the desert regions both the length of the rainy season and the total rainfall decrease, and the rainfall becomes less reliable.

Annual averages on the margins of the Equatorial belt are about 50 inches, and near the Desert margins 10 inches.

High-altitude Tropical climates, like their equatorial counterparts, differ in value rather than régime of the climatic elements. Single maxima of temperature and of rainfall still occur, but one or more months have average temperatures below 64°F. These conditions apply to much of the plateau of southern Africa; Salisbury (4,856 feet) and Bulawayo (4,435 feet) in Rhodesia both have temperatures below 64° for the four months May to August; Johannesburg (5,925 feet) has only three months above that temperature. While all three thus have temperature regimes that are more typical of warm temperate climates, they are best understood as having modified tropical climates, because of the nature of their rainfall regimes.

The other modification of tropical climates is the Tropical Continental Monsoon type, though this is far more extensive in Asia than in Africa. It is distinctive in that the wind systems are in the nature of land and sea breezes on a huge scale, and with a yearly instead of daily periodicity. The only part of Africa (according to Miller) that has a true reversal of this type is that part of the Somali Republic east of 46°E. During January a north-easterly mTs airstream prevails, but in July the wind is south-westerly although having similar characteristics of dryness and stability. Thus the Somali Republic does not have a monsoon climate of the Indian type, with heavy monsoon rains; it is, in fact, largely arid, the rainfall averaging no more than six inches per annum, almost all falling in heavy showers during the summer months. In this respect it justifies its inclusion in the Tropical Continental climates; it might equally justifiably be classified as a desert climate.

The Western Margin Warm Temperate, or Mediterranean type of climate, is limited to the northern parts of Morocco, Algeria, Tunisia and Cyrenaica, and to the south-western Cape Province. These are the areas of winter rainfall and summer drought, the rain being brought by the influx of mP air and the associated frontal activity in the depressions derived from the polar fronts.

The Eastern Margin Warm Temperate climate is found only in the southern hemisphere, as Africa has no oceanic eastern margin in appropriate northern latitudes. The southern coastal zone of South Africa between 20°E. and 30°E. receives a moderate rainfall the year round, from the depressions in the westerlies during winter, and in summer from the mT air of the south-east Trades, in which orographic lifting is an important factor in causing rain.

The Sahara is the largest area of Hot Desert climates in the world, stretching from the Atlantic to the Red Sea, and continued eastward in the Arabian Desert. The rainfall is low, since the predominant air-mass is the extremely stable cT, derived from subsident upper air over the Sahara itself, and thus dry as well as stable. In the north occasional rain storms are associated with moist air and frontal activity invading from the Mediterranean area in winter, while on the southern edge of the desert the equally infrequent storms are usually associated with the extreme northward extension of mE air behind the ITCZ which reaches farther in to the desert areas in some summers than in others. No part of the desert is completely rainless; indeed, some of the higher ranges in the interior get sufficient rain to support considerable vegetation, and might be termed 'altitudinal oases'. The Hoggar, in particular, may receive rain either from Mediterranean mP air in winter, or from south Atlantic mE air in summer. A much smaller area of hot desert covers most of South West Africa. The coastal strip lies almost permanently under very stable maritime tropical (mTs) air, while farther inland upon the plateau cTs air predominates. Any mT air from the Indian Ocean is thoroughly modified and dry by the time it reaches the desert area. As is usual in arid areas, such rain as does fall is in heavy convectional storms, and the rainfall is extremely variable.

VEGETATION

In as much as industry is little developed in most parts of Africa, the vast majority of the African population depends for its existence upon the land and its products, mostly through pastoralism and simple forms of agriculture. Thus the vegetation of Africa plays an important part in influencing human activity, but it is not always so readily recognized that Man has considerably modified the natural vegetation, through his practices of clearance and burning for cultivation and grazing.

Figure 7 gives a simplified version of the main types of vegetation, as agreed internationally by a group of botanists. The parts north of the Tropic of Cancer have had to be taken from older work, as the map, with its text by R. W. J. Keay, is concerned only with the area south of the Tropic of Cancer. The classification used is physiognomic rather than generic, i.e. it is concerned with the appearance of the vegetation rather than with the species present; the latter criterion is used to subdivide the major groups.

The map shows the existing vegetation, and not the natural climax vegetation that might be expected if the entire continent were left

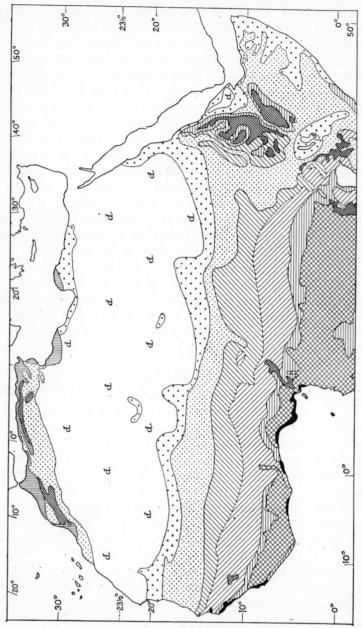

Fig. 7a. Vegetation of Africa (Simplified from Keay and Gaussen)

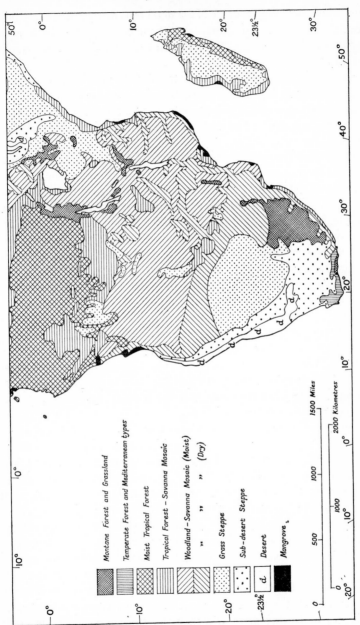

Fig. 7b. Vegetation of Africa (Simplified from Keay and Gaussen)

undisturbed, though because of the small scale many minor differences cannot be shown at all. Indeed, while the boundaries between types appear to be definite on the map, on the ground one type usually grades slowly into the next.

The vegetation types range from true forest through types with both trees and grass in varying proportions to pure grasslands, shrubby vegetation associated with low rainfall, and ultimately to desert. Most of the main groups can be seen in a traverse from the Equator to either Tropic.

The Moist Tropical Forest of this classification is the Equatorial Rain Forest of earlier authors, and corresponds in distribution very closely with Miller's A1 climates, excluding the high altitude modifications. A mature forest of this type consists of several distinct layers, the highest trees being from 120 to 150 feet high. It is evergreen, for although some of the trees are individually deciduous, the forest as a whole is never bare of leaves. In the lower layers woody climbing plants abound.

Most of the area covered by this forest has been or is being utilized for various forms of farming, and in a few places is exploited for its timber resources. Upon abandonment of a clearing, recolonization is effected by species of shrub, tree and climber which are generally absent in the mature forest, but have the ability to establish themselves rapidly. Ultimately these die out as the larger forest species mature and shade them out. Much of the moist forest is therefore secondary rather than primary vegetation, and the popular concept of 'primeval forests' is false for most of Africa.

In a belt surrounding the Moist Forest is the Tropical Forest-Savanna Mosaic. Here patches of moist forest, which are common along streams in savanna areas, are found also on the interfluves. The mosaic thus consists of patches of evergreen forest, and others of savanna, a grass–tree combination in which the trees are deciduous. A patchwork of this kind is characteristic of the boundary zone between two types, but only in this instance does it cover an area large enough to merit mapping as a distinct type. Most of the savanna is burned over annually so that only fire-resistant species of tree survive, for the grass layer is of tall grasses and burns fiercely. Where fires have been excluded from a patch of savanna for several years, invasion by moist-forest species occurs; and since forest-savanna mosaic areas are not noticeably more arid than the moist forest, it is generally believed that the mosaic is a degraded form of the original forest, in which man-made fires have been the chief cause of degradation.

A similar type of vegetation occupies the coasts of Kenya and Tanganyika, where the true forest has disappeared altogether, while a mosaic of Dry Deciduous Forest and Savanna occurs in western Rhodesia, western Madagascar and Ethiopia. In this type the forest trees are simultaneously deciduous for a few weeks each year.

The group of vegetation types which covers the greatest area in Africa is that of the Woodland-Savanna Mosaics. These vary greatly in appearance, but are very difficult to subdivide satisfactorily. All consist of a more or less open cover of deciduous trees, with a ground flora in which grasses dominate, and they are characteristic of areas of moderate rainfall with a marked dry season. The extreme forms are deciduous woodlands in areas of relatively high rainfall, and almost pure grasslands in the drier areas.

Provided that adequate water is to be found most of these types provide grazing and soils suitable for cultivation. Where grazing is the main feature of the economy the savannas are burned frequently to dispose of the old season's growth and to 'bring on' the new, so that only fire-resistant trees survive. Unmolested, the trees will grow to heights of 20 to 80 feet, and a considerable undergrowth may develop; it is therefore thought by most experts that the savannas are largely man-made types of vegetation which would revert to woodland if protected from the burning and cutting to which they have long been subjected. They are divided into Moist and Dry Woodland-Savanna Mosaics, a broad division which reflects climatic rather than soil conditions, being chiefly related to the length of dry season. The moist types tend to be more luxuriant, especially in the grass layer, but as the grass dries out in the dry season the moist types are the more susceptible to modification by fire, since the fires that occur are fiercer.

Adjoining the savannas on their drier margins and separating them from the subdesert areas are large tracts where conditions are too dry for the survival of most perennial grasses; a ground flora of annual grasses and herbs combines with trees, mainly of the genus *Acacia*, to give Grass Steppe. A belt of this type reaches right across Africa at about 15°N., and it is also represented in Algeria, south-east Ethiopia, and on the plateaux of East Africa, Bechuanaland, South West Africa, and the highlands of Madagascar. It provides relatively sparse grazing, but has the advantage that the grasses tend to remain palatable when they die off in the dry season, while the leaves and seed-pods of the trees are also nutritious for stock.

2*

Progressing to still drier areas, the vegetation grades into Sub-desert Steppe, in which perennial shrubs, usually widely spaced, are the only apparent vegetation for much of the time, but after rain, annuals, including grasses and flowering plants, flourish for a few weeks. This type also includes parts of northern Ethiopia, the Somali Republic, northern Kenya and the Karoo Scrub of South Africa. The latter is actively invading the temperate grasslands to the east as a result of over-grazing. A subtype is the Karoo Succulent Steppe along the west coast of South Africa consisting mainly of low succulent plants up to three feet high, many of them bearing beautiful flowers, among which the genus *Mesembrianthemum* is the most frequent. The grazing capacity of these types is very low, and ultimately becomes negligible as the gradation into true Desert takes place. Desert, as shown in Fig. 7, is virtually devoid of all vegetation, except for the occasional solitary plant.

In this traverse from moist forest to arid desert, one cannot take account of all the vegetation types of Africa, for there is a further transition on the poleward sides of the deserts into moister types associated with temperate climates, and within the tropics are parts where special features of the environment such as high altitude, swamp, or a coastal location cause distinctive vegetation to appear.

The high altitude variations are classified as Montane Forest and Grasslands. The forest communities occur in relatively small patches, chiefly in Ethiopia. They are evergreen, but differ from the Moist Tropical Forests in the species present and in height, the trees being smaller. In common with other montane communities this type occurs only above 4,000 feet. Montane Grasslands occur mainly in Ethiopia and in East Africa, especially along the margins of the western Rift Valley. They consist of short grasses, three feet or less in height. Closely related to them, and grouped with them on the map, are the Temperate Grasslands, represented by the South African Grassveld, mostly between 3,500 and 11,000 feet on the plateau and within the summer rainfall area. This includes much good grazing, though the grasses tend to be unpalatable during the dry season, and also includes some of the principal areas of commercial agriculture.

Temperate Forest and Mediterranean Types are here used to cover a wide variety of types in the northern and southern extremities of the continent. True evergreen forest occurs on the south coast around Knysna, and elsewhere in the south-east Cape Province and Natal; it is worked for a wide variety of useful timbers. The remaining types are found in the winter-rainfall areas. In North Africa there are areas of cork-oak forest and argan, a spiny tree similar in appearance to the olive and bearing leathery leaves. Leathery leaves are also characteristic of the shrubs, bushes and small trees that form the Maquis of North Africa and the Macchia or Fynbos of the Cape. In the Cape this is characteristically low shrubby vegetation, but in Morocco and Algeria is generally rather higher, reaching fifteen to twenty feet in places. The natural vegetation has little value, but where water is available, and the ground is suitable for clearing, agriculture under irrigation is usually possible.

Mangrove vegetation occurs in brackish swamps and estuaries, mostly in the zone of Moist Tropical Forests, the most extensive areas being in the Niger Delta. Mangrove of the east and west coasts differs in species composition, the western being similar to that of the Atlantic shores of tropical America, while the eastern species are common to the shores of tropical Asia. In appearance they are identical, consisting of trees with stilt-like roots which support the trunks above water level.

There are also, in various parts of the forest and savanna zones, quite large areas of freshwater swamp. Some of these support swamp forest, others tall grasses and sedges. While the vegetation is distinct from that of the drier land around it, it is the impeded drainage and waterlogged soils that are the barriers to development, rather than the vegetation itself. Examples are seen in the Nile Valley in southern Sudan, and in the Bangweulu swamps of Zambia.

The vegetation is seen to depend upon climate, and especially upon the seasonal variations in climate, but the occurrence of fire, mostly caused by Man, has influenced the vegetation widely. Even in a continent where advanced forms of farming have penetrated to most parts relatively recently, little of the vegetation can be regarded as truly natural.

SOILS

Extensive and intensive soil surveys of African territories have generally occurred only in recent years, so knowledge of the pattern of soils in Africa is fragmentary. There is an immense difference between the detailed work done, for example, in Ghana, Nigeria, the Congo (Leopoldville) and the Republic of South Africa, and the preliminary reconnaissances made in many other countries. In the Congo 250 different soil series have been recognized; in Libya a handful.

Few countries in Africa today are without a provisional soil map, but the quality and intention of the maps vary greatly. Some soil surveys have been made to study soil genesis, some to study erosion, some for irrigation developments, some for crop production. The variety of aims, methods and soil classifications employed render very difficult the task of compiling a detailed soil map for the whole continent. As yet, no such map exists.

Soils, Climate and Topography

Widespread recent work on soil genesis in Africa has revealed the dangers of exaggerating the closeness of the correlation between soils on the one hand, and climatic and vegetational distributions on the other. Soil regions do not coincide precisely with climatic regions; in fact, surprising diversity of soils can occur within a climatic region. One reason is certainly the prevalence of residual or sedentary soils, which demonstrate a close connection between soils and parent material in areas of mature topography as well as in areas which are topographically 'young' or immature. Milne has stressed the influence of local topography on tropical soils through the erosion cycle, suggesting that skeletal soils (young or immature soils) are found on exhumed rock, eluvial soils (leached soils) on freely drained slopes, and colluvial or alluvial soils (soils due to gravity or river action) on lower slopes and valley bottoms. Such a sequence of soils is termed a catena. Milne pointed out that many African soils are the result of extremely long evolution, and reflect past climates rather than present conditions. Much of the land surface of Africa is ancient and has experienced a succession of erosion cycles, each producing soil catenas. Milne concludes that the classification of the Great Soil Groups, which relies heavily on the climatic factor in soil formation, is less valuable in soil mapping in inter-tropical Africa than in temperate latitudes. In brief, climate is accepted as an important factor in the formation of African soils but not to the exclusion of other factors.

Soil Zones

Despite these words of warning, the general influence of climate is apparent in Figure 8, where the broad pattern resembles the generalized patterns of climate and vegetation. In the tropics the rapidity of weathering and leaching is promoted by high soil temperatures which accelerate chemical reactions. Leaching has been so continuous in some soils, especially those termed latosols or latosolic soils, that they are markedly deficient in nutrient salts and silica. This process has been given as the principal reason for their chemical exhaustion as well as for their frequent redness, which results from the prevalence of sesqui-oxides (oxides of iron and aluminium). It must be noted, however, that not all latosolic soils are red—some are yellow, reddish-yellow, reddish-brown or black-red—and that many reasons have been postulated for the formation of latosolic soils. Controversy has been specially acute over the formation of the hard compacted layer

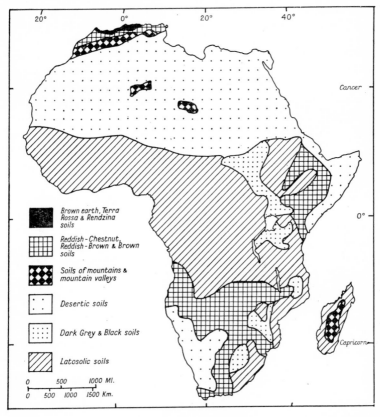

Fig. 8. The soils of Africa

(After *Soil Map of the World* compiled by the U.S. Department of Agriculture, and adopted by the Food and Agriculture Organisation of the United Nations)

known as laterite, which is probably caused by alternate saturation and drying. Laterites are most common in Guinea, Sierra Leone (Fig. 9), Liberia, the Congos, the Central African Republic and Madagascar, where their compaction makes very difficult the use of modern machinery.

One general reason for the low nutrient status of tropical soils may be the immobilization of large stores of nutrients in the abundant vegetation of forest areas. Another feature of tropical soils is the rapid oxidation of organic matter at the surface when the soil is exposed. In these circumstances, forest clearing and ploughing often rob the soil of much of its fertility, and thus shifting cultivation may well be a suitable method of land utilization. Certainly, fallowing and cover crops are beneficial.

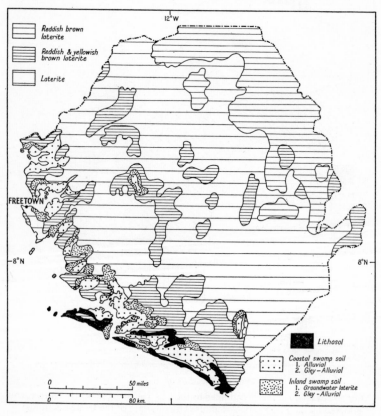

Fig. 9. The soils of Sierra Leone
(After *Atlas of Sierra Leone*)

Common in the upper basin of the Nile, in the lower basins of the Zambezi and Shire, as well as in other parts of East Africa, are dark grey and black soils, sometimes known as black cotton soils or tropical black clays, which are often heavy, sticky or ill-drained. They are the tropical equivalent of the temperate chernozem, and are associated with grass vegetation. Unfortunately, they are less fertile and less easily worked.

In areas of slightly less rainfall is found a group of reddish-chestnut soils which are succeeded in drier areas by reddish-brown soils. The organic matter status of the former exceeds that of the latter, which has a prominent lower horizon of lime accumulation. The distribution of these soils is greatly over-generalized in Fig. 8, and more detailed soil maps of North Africa and South Africa indicate substantial areas of podzolic (leached) soils, sandy soils, solonchak-solonetz (saline) soils, and lime-crust soils. The podzolic and sandy soils occur generally in the wetter and drier areas respectively, while the saline soils are found either along low flat coasts or in interior drainage basins. Lime-crust soils are common in semi-arid areas with a marked seasonality of rainfall; the hard resistant pan, known as calcrete or caliche, may be caused by dry season evaporation and capillary deposition of lime at the surface.

The Sahara and Kalahari deserts are characterized by stony and sandy soils, often with a light, reddish-brown surface overlying a red, heavier horizon. They also include extensive deposits of blown sand, sometimes fixed, as well as saline areas. In many cases, desert soils have revealed surprising fertility on irrigation; even reg sometimes masks quite fertile soil.

In the northern extremity of Africa along the Tellian Atlas of the Maghreb, true Mediterranean soils prevail, notably brown earths and rendzinas, while terra rossas are found in northern Cyrenaica. All three soils are properly termed intrazonal. They are the result of local conditions, and may transgress the boundaries of the main soil belts of the world. Brown earths are typical of the Mediterranean dry forests and exhibit little leaching; in fact they occupy a transitional position between the pedocals (lime-rich soils of dry lands) and the pedalfers (lime-deficient soils of humid lands). Rendzinas are dark grey, dark brown or black friable loams of limestone areas, which, along with terra rossas, are much used for vine and olive cultivation. Like so many pedological terms, terra rossa is ill-defined, but it probably represents the residue after a limestone has experienced prolonged chemical erosion, and thus may be compared with the clay-with-flints of the English downlands. It still contains a valuable proportion of plant nutrients.

These broad soil zones mask a wealth of diversity, depending on the influences of the underlying parent material, topography and the work of man. Although soils of glacial origin are of negligible importance in Africa, Pleistocene aeolian sands are widespread in Central and West Africa far beyond the present bounds of the Sahara and Kalahari deserts.

There are also vast tracts of alluvial soil of great agricultural value, as along the Nile Valley. Numerous swamps and waterlogged soils await drainage and reclamation in many areas. Although it is difficult to imagine much improvement of swamps like Bangweulu in Zambia and the Sudd of the southern Sudan, small swamps can prove to be of great agricultural value, as in Rwanda and Burundi. The extent of swamp soils in Sierra Leone (Fig. 9) gives some indication of the need of a realistic appraisal of their potentialities for African development.

Soil Erosion

Over-cultivation, over-grazing and fire are the three main causes of man-accelerated erosion, which is an extremely serious problem in Africa. It is specially prevalent on areas of present or former grassland, where seasonality of rainfall is marked. It also particularly affects soils of light or medium texture, and slopes which exceed two degrees. But few countries of Africa are unaffected by soil erosion, which occurs in a depressing variety of forms and has greatly diminished the availability of land for agriculture. 'Sheet', 'wind' and 'gully' erosion are all widespread.

It is difficult to determine the relative influences of natural causes and human agencies, but it may be that the sparseness of population in Africa has had a significant effect. Land was once so abundant that no care seemed necessary, but as the population steadily grew, far more attention should have been devoted to the land.

Soil conservation work has been most effective in the Republic of South Africa where erosion has taken a great toll, and in Rhodesia and Kenya, but it began only a few decades ago. In many countries it has been too late to save large areas of fertile soil, and sometimes the soil conservation efforts of European administrators have met with the bitter resentment of Africans, who claim the right to do as they like with their own land. Preventive measures include afforestation, controlled grazing, irrigation, terracing, contour ploughing and cropping, earth dams and stabilization of the soil, along with general improvements in agriculture. Planned rotations of crops, rotational grazing and mixed farming greatly help. But many of these changes are not effective without radical transformations in social conditions.

Soil Fertility

Frequent mention has been made of the low fertility of the tropical soils of Africa. Part of the explanation may be that the clays are largely of a kaolinitic nature, but at the same time the soils are generally low in organic matter. The rapid deterioration of humid forest soils under cultivation, because of leaching and oxidation of organic matter, necessitates fallowing to maintain soil fertility.

One of the major problems of African agriculture is how to extend the period during which the soil remains fertile under cultivation. Chemical fertilizers may have a great future in Africa, although until now their use has been confined largely to the European farms. But application of fertilizer has not always had the desired effect on tropical soils, because it does not always become available to the plant. Even the addition of organic manure, if it were available, is not everywhere of equal benefit to the soil. Although valuable for increasing the plant nutrients and improving the structure of wet soils, manure is only really useful for soils of arid areas when rain has fallen. Unfortunately, the presence of the tsetse fly over much of Africa means that animal manure is rare; furthermore, the African cultivator has no tradition of composting.

There is no doubt that in many parts of Africa (excluding those where population density is high) the introduction of mixed farming would raise soil fertility, as well as facilitate the replacement of the hoe by the plough. Yet mixed farming is only likely outside the tsetse areas, and these are Africa's dry or arid lands. Hence this advance seems to await eradication of the tsetse.

PESTS AND DISEASES

Throughout the realm of nature there exists a state approaching equilibrium, for while one organism preys upon another, seldom does the one become so dominant as to exterminate the other within a short period. Changes in the animal and vegetable populations of an area generally take place slowly, unless one element in the state of equilibrium is disturbed by the introduction of a new organism or a change in physical conditions.

Where a mammal, insect, bacterium or fungus, preys upon man, his animals or his crops, it is regarded as a pest or a disease. So long as both are indigenous to the area, the pest seldom gets out of hand. Indigenous plants, animals and man usually have a certain degree of resistance or immunity against the pests and diseases that have attacked them over a long period. On the other hand, a species introduced to an area may thrive because it finds itself free of any natural enemies, but more usually it will have difficulty in establishing itself because it is not adapted to local climatic conditions, or because it is attacked by some pest or disease against which it has had no opportunity to develop an immunity. Similarly, a disease introduced to an area may have disastrous effects upon an indigenous population which has never before encountered that disease.

In considering the relationship of man, his livestock and crops with the African environment, it is important to keep in mind this distinction between the introduced and the indigenous. For example, the European is often more severely affected by diseases than the African, and it has long been recognized that the European is not well-suited to heavy work under most tropical conditions.

Among the major human diseases that have hampered development in Africa are malaria, yellow fever, trypanosomiasis or sleeping sickness, bilharziasis, tick fever, yaws, leprosy and smallpox. Both malaria and yellow fever are transmitted by certain types of mosquito which are therefore pests in themselves.

Malarial mosquitoes are widespread in Africa, breeding wherever there is stagnant water. Attempts to exterminate them by spraying the swamps and pools in which they breed have been successful in some areas, but this method can hardly be applied to a whole continent. Malaria is seldom fatal but it is debilitating, leaving the victim lacking in stamina. The majority of Africans probably contract it early in life, and thereby acquire an immunity against later infection, but only at the cost of impaired health and reduced activity, which is probably the real basis for the popular belief that Africans are lazy. Moreover, the general weakening leaves the victim more susceptible to other diseases. A European who contracts the disease usually suffers more severe symptoms than an African.

Yellow fever is a more serious disease and causes a high proportion of fatalities among adults, though it seems that many Africans gain immunity through mild attacks in childhood. Inoculation is safe and so effective that the European need not fear the disease, but there is a long way to go before every African is inoculated.

Sleeping sickness is also transmitted by insects, namely by some of the twenty or more species of tsetse fly (*Glossina* spp.) which is unique to Africa. These are blood-sucking flies which act as hosts to the disease-causing *trypanosomes* during one stage of their development. The disease is not always a killer but has accounted for vast numbers of deaths, and even where the best modern medical attention is available mortality is about 20 per cent amongst those contracting it. It is not as widespread as malaria, but occurs in most parts of tropical Africa from Gambia to Mozambique.

Bilharziasis is a disease of the digestive system and bladder, caused by the minute parasite *Bilharzia*, which also has an intermediate host, a water-snail. The disease is contracted through contact with infected water; it can be cured if treated early, but may be fatal if untreated. As with the other diseases named, the most likely means of eradicating the disease is to destroy the intermediate host, but this is not simple.

There are numerous other diseases caused by parasites. Various species of *Spirochaeta* are responsible for tick fever, transmitted by members of the large group of ticks (*Argasidae* and *Ixodidae*), and for syphilis and yaws. All are common in Africa. Larger parasites are also numerous, the most important being the hookworm and various other worms which infest the intestine and other organs of the human body.

While this catalogue might be extended indefinitely, enough has been said to demonstrate the need for effective medical services if Africa is to be more fully developed. Even more pressing is the need for simple preventive measures, such as the provision of clean water supplies, properly isolated sanitation, and the teaching of personal hygiene. All these requirements become progressively more urgent as population densities increase, both in rural areas and in the conditions of the rapidly growing industrial centres.

If the medical man is urgently needed in Africa, so, too, is the veterinarian. The provision of increased supplies of meat and milk to improve the diet of the increasing population has been hampered by the many diseases of domestic livestock. The severity of these is partly due to the fact that the main domestic animals (cattle, sheep and pigs) are not indigenous to Africa, although some types were introduced several thousand years ago. Most domestic cattle are susceptible to nagana, which is carried by the tsetse fly, and is usually fatal. This makes it almost impossible to keep cattle where the tsetse fly is found, which is over much of tropical Africa. Other diseases of cattle include rinderpest and foot-and-mouth disease.

Many of the indigenous antelope and other wild animals are apparently immune from these diseases, but are believed to act as carriers. Attempts have been made to restrict the migration of the wild fauna, and suggestions have been made for the extermination of the wild fauna in certain areas to break the life-cycle of the diseases. Recently, a more enlightened suggestion has been put forward by conservationists, who advocate the use of indigenous species to provide meat by systems of game management and controlled shooting. These animals would not only be more resistant to disease than are imported species, but are also better able to make efficient use of the food resources of the natural vegetation, especially where several species are used, each grazing or browsing at a different level. Experiments are also being carried out in the 'cropping' of the larger animals such as hippo and elephants.

In northern and southern Africa, where conditions permit commercial cattle farming, and where cattle figure in African subsistence farming, efforts are being made to develop breeds which make the best use of the environment by the crossing of indigenous breeds with recognized European or other introduced breeds. The aim is to combine the disease resistance and heat tolerance of the former, with the superior meat and milk production of the latter. Although nagana has been eradicated in South Africa and parts of Rhodesia, and does not occur north of the Sahara, there are still many diseases that attack cattle. These are caused by mineral deficiencies in the grazing, toxic plants and by a host of different micro-organisms often transmitted by ticks. Similar problems face the keeper of sheep.

For any animal-based economy there must be a constant fight against disease, selection of stock to suit the environment, and education of the population to accept the principles of conservation farming, whether of domestic or of wild stock.

The problems facing the agriculturalist are broadly similar. Crops should be those which are not merely able to grow in given climatic conditions, but which are ideally suited, or, failing that, those which will give the best return. Even where these conditions are fulfilled, insect and other pests are numerous enough.

Most spectacular is the locust, whose destructive capacity has been proverbial from biblical times and probably earlier. Three important species occur in Africa: the African Migratory Locust, the Desert Locust and the Red Locust. Swarms of these creatures may reach an immense size and devour every green leaf over many square miles. They can only be combated effectively in the breeding areas; since these are not always the same, and may even be in south-western Asia, some swarms are almost certain to develop. However, all but the Desert Locust are now regarded as being under control.

Other pests are more selective, many insects, bacteria, viruses and fungi confining their attention to one particular crop or group of crops. An example of the insect pests is the maize stalk-borer, a moth larva which infests maize crops in southern Africa and, despite preventive measures, is estimated to reduce yields by at least ten per cent annually. The well-known swollen-shoot disease of cocoa, which has ravaged farms in West Africa, is caused by a virus transmitted by insects. Cutting out of affected trees or spraying with insecticides are methods of control, but both are expensive.

Individual pests can usually be controlled once they are identified and their life-cycles are known, but control measures add greatly to the cost of commercial farming, and are hardly known in subsistence farming, where both the knowledge and the necessary financial resources are lacking.

Governments have the dual problems of finding methods of fighting pests and diseases, and of educating the farmer to make use of modern techniques. There is also the problem, which may be the greatest of all, of finding financial resources to cover the provision of materials and equipment, and skilled men to ensure their correct use.

FURTHER READING

Geology: R. Furon, *Geology of Africa*, 1963, and the *Carte Géologique Internationale de l'Afrique*, compiled under the auspices of the International Geological Congress (with an accompanying pamphlet by R. Furon and G. Daumain).

Structure and geomorphology: L. C. King, *The Morphology of the Earth*, 1962, is a systematic text but bases much of its argument upon African evidence. See also the same author's *South African Scenery*, 2nd Ed., 1951.

Climate: W. G. Kendrew, *The Climates of the Continents*, 4th Ed., 1953, is useful for descriptive climatology, but B. Haurwitz and J. M. Austin, *Climatology*, 1944, especially pp. 325–54, gives a better account of causes. A. A. Miller, *Climatology*, 8th Ed., 1953, gives his climatic classification, and discusses each climatic type, taking examples from each continent.

Vegetation: R. W. J. Keay, *Vegetation map of Africa south of the Sahara*, 1959. J. Phillips, *Agriculture and Ecology in Africa, 1959*, is an interesting study of the relationships of vegetation, climate and agriculture.

Soils: E. B. Worthington, *Science in the Development of Africa*, 1959; E. C. J. Mohr and F. A. Van Baren, *Tropical Soils*, The Hague, 1959, and J. A. Prescott and R. L. Pendleton, *Laterite and Lateritic Soils*, Commonwealth Agricultural Bureau, 1952. For detailed studies, see the Proceedings of the First Commonwealth Conference on Tropical and Sub-Tropical Soils 1948, *Commonwealth Bureau of Soil Science Technical Bulletin*, 46, 1949; *Report of the 2nd Inter-African Soils Conference at Leopoldville 1954*, and *Sols Africains*, a quarterly review published by the Bureau Interafricain des

Sols. Milne's catena concept is seen in G. Milne, 'Some suggested units of classification and mapping particularly for East African soils', *Soil Research*, 4, 1935, 183–98.

Soil Erosion: A. T. Grove, 'Soil erosion and Population Problems in South-East Nigeria', *Geographical Journal*, 117, 1951, 291–306.

Pests and Diseases: L. D. Stamp, *Africa, a Study in Tropical Development*, 1953, 164–81, and G. Melvyn Howe, *Atlas of Disease*, 1963.

CHAPTER THREE*

The Peoples of Africa

THERE is little doubt that Africa has witnessed the whole evolution of man, and that man existed at a very early period. The growing number of finds in East and South Africa demonstrate a succession from anthropoid apes of the Miocene, through the South African *Australopithecinae* (*hominidae*) of the Pliocene, to the East African *Zinjanthropus Boisei* and finally *Homo sapiens* of the Pleistocene. Furthermore, differentiation of human ethnic groups occurred before the Upper Pleistocene, a fact which has increased the diversity of Africa's peoples.

THE DIVERSITY OF PEOPLES

Classification of the diverse peoples of Africa is difficult for several reasons: (*a*) insufficient anthropometric, genetic, linguistic and other data; (*b*) the variety of possible criteria; (*c*) confusing racial, linguistic and cultural terminology and nomenclature; (*d*) the shortage of historical records and the 'darkness' of the African past; (*e*) the frequency of intermarriages, migrations and conquests, and consequent mixing of peoples; and (*f*) the influence of Europeans on patterns of peoples, especially the influence of slavery and the growth of towns.

In the past, ethnic classifications of African peoples have rarely been determined by physical characteristics alone; languages have frequently been employed as additional criteria. However, in recent years a mass of data concerning blood groups has been made available which is helping to clarify the ethnic complexity of Africa. In particular, a study of the ABO blood groups has revealed that Negroes have a high O frequency, and that Bushmen and Berbers have a high A frequency. The Pygmies may also offer a clue to the ethnic evolution of Africa, as they possess a chromosome (cDe) of the rhesus (Rh) system which is uniformly distributed in Africa south of the Sahara, but rare or non-existent elsewhere in the world. It has been inferred that Pygmies or a similar stock constitute a basic component of many African tribes. But the next decade is likely to multiply the volume of

* By John I. Clarke.

blood-group data, and possibly transform traditional concepts of racial development.

At present it is appropriate for our purposes to adopt the simple classification used by Seligman, who was influenced by linguistic studies and distinguishes the following main groups: Negrillos, Bushmen-Hottentots, Negroes, Hamites, Hamiticized Negroes (Nilo-Hamites, Nilotes and Bantu), and Semites (Fig. 10). To these may be added the Asians and Europeans.

Negrillos

The pygmy Negrillos of the equatorial rain forests are certainly among the oldest of African peoples, and their distinctive physical traits justify their consideration as a race separate from the Negroes. The skin colour of Pygmies may be reddish, yellowish-brown or very dark, but their most characteristic feature is diminutive stature. Adult males average 4 feet 9 inches in height, weigh only 88 pounds, and have brown body hair and protruding abdomens. The Pygmies, who live as nomadic hunters and collectors, number 150,000 in all, but estimates are bedevilled by racial mixing with the surrounding peoples, who exercise some control over the Pygmies. The material culture of the Pygmies is small, their condition primitive, and they live in scattered and isolated communities.

Bushmen and Hottentots

The Bushmen are also an old African people, found in the remote parts of South West Africa, Angola and the adjacent countries. Like the Pygmies, they were formerly more widely distributed, and their ancestors may have occupied a large part of northern and eastern Africa as well as the whole of southern Africa. They are a race of nomadic hunters and collectors, driven south by the Bantu and confined to the Kalahari by the northward moving Europeans. The Bushmen nearly suffered extinction at the hands of the Bantu, Hottentots and Europeans, and they now number no more than about 55,000. Bushmen are only a few inches taller than Pygmies, but differ from them by their yellowish wrinkled skin and narrow eye slits. An unusual physical characteristic of the women is their prominent buttocks, or steatopygia. Bushmen practise neither cultivation nor animal husbandry, and have a very low level of culture. Brushwood shelters are their only dwellings, and possessions are few. Yet the ancestors of the Bushmen are famous for their rock-paintings and drawings, which help in the determination of their distribution.

The Hottentots are almost certainly a race derived from the mixing of Bushmen with early Hamitic invaders, perhaps in the Great Lakes area. After moving south they occupied a large area of the western part of South Africa south of the Kunene River. Today, only about 35,000 nomadic pastoralists in South West Africa maintain the old tribal traditions; the remainder have lost their former customs, and many have mixed with Europeans and Asians to form the half-caste peoples known as 'Cape Coloured', 'Griqua' and 'Rehoboth'. The more secure existence of the pastoral Hottentots has probably been the cause of their physical superiority over the Bushmen; they are 4 or 5 inches taller.

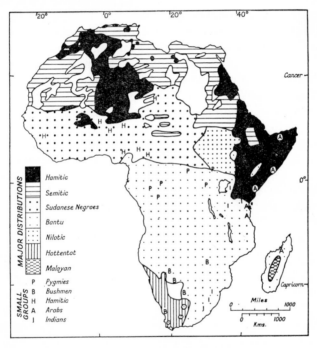

Fig. 10A. Peoples of Africa.

Negroes

Black Africa begins south of the Sahara and Ethiopia, and includes almost three-fifths of the total population of the continent and nearly three-quarters of the Negroes in the world. But the term Negro covers a wide variety of peoples, many of whom have been affected by an admixture of Hamitic blood and an absorption of Hamitic culture.

True Negroes are found in West Africa between the Senegal River and Cameroon. Possibly the purest types of Negroes are found along the Guinea Coast, and are noted for their black skins, moderately tall structure, spiral hair, flat noses, thick lips and lack of prognathism (protrusion of the jaws). They are grouped in a vast and varied array of tribes, which have some common cultural features, notably their gable-roofed huts, types of weapons, secret societies, artistic ability, and former propensity for human sacrifice. These were the peoples who established powerful and extensive kingdoms such as those of the Ashanti, Yoruba and Wolof.

In the savanna zone, which stretches from Senegal in the west to Kordofan in the east, the Sudanese Negroes are much taller, darker and more prognathous. Hamitic influence is still prominent despite continuous negritization. Here, tribal units are almost innumerable, but at the same time the powerful Fulani emirates and Hausa kingdoms once dominated much of the zone. From this zone came many of the Negroes who live in the Saharan oases.

In the Ubangi-Welle Basin, between the Nile and Congo, are found another group of Negroes, distinct from the Nilotic peoples and from the Bantu to the south. They are smaller than the true Negroes, mesocephalic, and usually have a dark reddish-brown skin. Among them are the Azande of the southern Sudan and northern Congo.

Other Negro peoples exist, including the tall Nuba of southern Kordofan and the short Bergdama of South West Africa, who have long been under the sway of the Hottentots.

Hamites

The Hamites are white peoples who are thought to have penetrated into northern Africa from a source area around the Red Sea. They are proud and warlike nomads who have played a very important role in the history of Africa. Their thrusts southward brought them into contact with the other two basic African peoples, the Negroes and the Bushmen, with whom they have greatly mixed. Establishing their superiority, of which they are very conscious, the Hamites founded many of the large African states. The Hamites are properly a linguistic group; but, in general, they are quite tall and light-skinned, and have narrow faces, straight noses and dark wavy hair. They are frequently divided into two branches:

(i) the Northern Hamites, including the Berbers of Libya, the Maghreb and the Sahara and the Fulani of the Sudan;

(ii) the Eastern Hamites, including the Egyptians, the Beja, the Berberines, the Somali and many Ethiopians.

Not surprisingly, these branches embrace a wide range of physical characteristics, despite the common anthropological base.

Hamiticized Negroes

The mixing of Negro and Hamitic blood has varied greatly regionally, and there has arisen an immense variety of peoples who owe their origin to this process. They have been broadly classified, again on the basis of language, into three groups; Nilotes, Nilo-Hamites and Bantu.

The Nilotes live in the basin of the Upper Nile, in the Sudan. They are very tall, slender and dark, but their facial features are more Hamitic than Negro. The pastoral Dinka of the Sudd are an example, although Hamitic features are probably stronger among the Shilluk.

The Nilo-Hamites occur in East and East-Central Africa in Kenya, eastern Uganda and nothern Tanzania. More Hamitic than either the Nilotes or the Bantu, the Nilo-Hamites also speak Nilotic languages with Hamitic elements. Again, tall slender and dark, they have few Negro features. The predominantly pastoral tribes include the cattle-herding Masai.

The Bantu are a broad linguistic group of central and southern Africa, among whom the root -*ntu* means man. Bantu means 'the men (of the tribe)'. Found south of the so-called 'Bantu line', which runs roughly from the Nigeria–Cameroon border east-south-eastwards to the environs of Mombasa, the Bantu have experienced different degrees of infusion of Hamitic blood, producing considerable physical variety. Hamitic features are most obvious among the tribes of East and South Africa. In fact, different linguistic groups of the Bantu tend to have different physical features.

Like the West African Negroes, the Bantu number about 60 million. Despite fairly advanced political and military organization, as seen for example in the Bantu Kingdom of the Baganda, they were, on the arrival of the Europeans in Africa, much less advanced economically than the West African Negroes, as well as in trade, weaving, pottery and metal-work. Most Bantu tribes are pastoral, and place great value on cattle, but many have suffered some disintegration with the movement of people to the towns.

Semites

The Semites are the Arabs, who first entered North Africa from the east as conquerors in the seventh century, but whose main invasions were between the eleventh and fourteenth centuries. They brought Arabic and Islam, and in places mixed so much with the Berbers that tribal origins are confused. Today it is practically impossible to tell Arabs and Berbers apart by physical characteristics alone. Unfortunately, the term 'Arab' is often loosely used to denote a Moslem, a native of North Africa, or merely someone who speaks Arabic. The term now has more of a cultural than a racial connotation, but it would be wrong to assume that Arabs are attached to one mode of life. Although the original conquerors of North Africa were predominantly nomads, their successors also comprise semi-nomads, cultivators and town-dwellers. The purest Arabs tend to be nomads, but they are not exclusively so. They have been active traders along the East African coast, and played a great part in the struggles for its control in the sixteenth, seventeenth and eighteenth centuries. Naturally, they have left their mark in the racial composition.

Asians

Apart from the Arabs, other peoples from Asia have penetrated into Africa, especially into Madagascar and South and East Africa. Madagascar poses a problem of racial origins, for archaeological evidence is lacking to help in deciphering the evolution of the complex mixture of Negro, Caucasian and Malayan peoples. Negroes prevail in the coastal zone and Malayan in the interior, while the smaller Caucasian groups are located wherever there is evidence of European or Arab settlement. The culture and language of Madagascar are principally Malayan, although the culture and language of the Arabs are also strongly represented, far more than those of the Bantu. Theories are numerous about the origins of the Malagasy peoples (Plate 69), but it is likely that the early inhabitants until about A.D. 1000 were almost entirely from Indonesia.

Asia is represented in South Africa by the Indian community, numbering nearly 477,000 in 1961. Unlike the Arabs, the Indians seldom mix with the native peoples. Asians from India and the Levant are found throughout East Africa where they form important urban minorities active in trade and crafts; in 1961, Kenya, Uganda and Tanganyika contained 350,000 Indians, Pakistanis and Goanese as well as 76,000 Arabs. Kenya has over 217,000 Asians, whose numbers have multiplied many times in this century. In West Africa, on the other hand, Asians are mainly restricted to several thousand traders, generally known as Syrians but coming from the Lebanon.

Europeans

There are over $4\frac{1}{2}$ million people of European descent living in Africa. The two largest concentrations occur in the northern and southern extremities where temperate and subtropical conditions prevail: over 3 million in the Republic of South Africa, and about 1 million in North Africa. In the latter the Europeans are mostly from southern Europe, especially Frenchmen (particularly from southern France and Corsica), Italians and Spaniards; in South Africa, the white settlers have been principally Dutch and British. The differences in the origins of the European settlers, and in the period of occupation, have produced contrasts in political evolution, modes of life and cultural values. In both of these regions Europeans are deeply implanted and constitute important minorities with considerable economic power, as they did formerly in the Rhodesias and Kenya, despite their smaller numbers (300,000 and 68,000 respectively in 1960).

North Africa has received European immigrants at least since the second century B.C., although the main waves came in the nineteenth and early twentieth centuries. An important feature of the modern immigrants is that they have mixed very little racially with the native white peoples, despite the lack of ethnic contrasts. On the other hand, in South Africa the mixing of coloured and white peoples has produced a half-caste people generally known as the Cape Coloured, who numbered nearly $1\frac{1}{2}$ million in 1961. Mixing has also occurred in Angola and Mozambique, but has been of little importance in the former Belgian Congo or in the Rhodesias and Malawi, where there were 304,000 Europeans in 1961.

The only other area of European colonization is in East Africa, but the 100,000 Europeans in Kenya, Uganda and Tanganyika are greatly outnumbered by Asians, as well as by the indigenous population. Elsewhere in tropical Africa Europeans were repelled at first, not merely by the climate but also by the difficulties of penetration from the coast into the interior, and by the uncertainty of rich material rewards to be found there. The vast majority of Europeans are town-dwellers; their activities have been largely in administration, commerce and industry, and their numbers in some countries have diminished rapidly after political independence.

LANGUAGES

Languages constitute more reliable evidence of cultural affinity than racial factors, and are being used more and more as a basis for cultural grouping. Linguistically, Africa is extremely complex; there are probably more than 800 separate African languages. Only four, however, are of more than local significance: Amharic, the main language of Ethiopia; Swahili, a Bantu dialect influenced by Arabic and found in East Africa; Hausa, spoken in West Africa and also influenced by Arabic; and Afrikaans, which is spoken mainly in the western part of the Republic of South Africa. It is not surprising, therefore, that these languages, along with Arabic, English and French, are continually gaining ground as lingua francas.

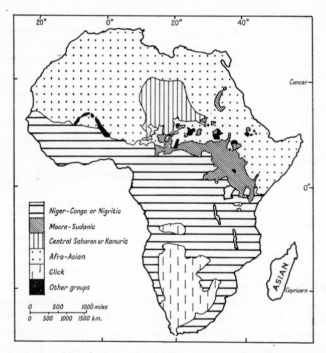

Fig. 10B. Major language families of Africa. (Simplified from J. H. Greenberg, *Studies in African Linguistic Classification*, New Haven, 1955)

  The grouping of African languages has occupied the attention of many ethnologists because, in the absence of other records, linguistic classification throws considerable light on the evolution of settlement in Africa. Greenberg has proposed a classification with twelve distinct language families of which the following five are spoken by the over-whelming majority of the total population: the Niger-Congo, Afro-Asian, Macro-Sudanic, Central Saharan, and Click families (Fig. 10 B). Other families are the Songhai, Maban, Fur, Koman, Kordo-fanian, Temainian and Nyangiya. The distribution of these language families helps to demonstrate cultural groups, although in its *Handbook of African Languages*, the International African Institute has abandoned the term 'language family' in favour of 'dialect clusters', 'language groups', and 'larger language units'.

CULTURE AREAS

Many other criteria may be considered for cultural differentiation, including traditional ways of life, social organization, political

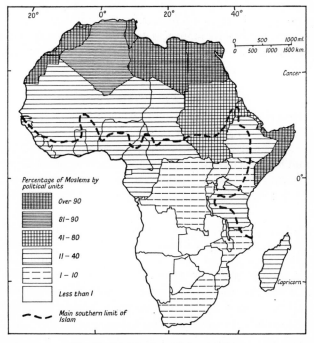

Fig. 11. Distribution of Islam in Africa

organization, religion, types of art and music. On such evidence, attempts have been made to delimit culture areas, which seem to be influenced by environment. Deserts, for example, have acted as obstacles between peoples (e.g. between Black and White Africa), and as conservatories of primitive types (e.g. Tibus and Bushmen). Forests and mountains have often acted as refuges (e.g. Pygmies and Berbers), while grasslands have facilitated extensive migrations. The temperate extremities in the north and south have been the scene of European colonization and close contact with African peoples.

It should be remembered, however, that the limits between culture areas are neither narrow nor rigid, for the factors from which they are derived are dynamic. For example, one of the most significant cultural frontiers of Africa is the moving frontier of Islam (Fig. 11), which, with the exception of European Christian communities in North Africa, Copts in Egypt and Christian provinces in Ethiopia, approximates at present to the tenth parallel. North of this frontier are more than sixty million Moslems. Moreover, Islam is making many converts in Africa, and with the growth of Islamic states the number may well increase still further. To the south animism prevails, but the main progressive influences are from Christianity, which has evolved principally through the educational work of the missions. Christianity now embraces nearly forty million Africans.

THE SPARSENESS OF POPULATION

It has been estimated by the United Nations that in 1960 the total population of Africa was 254 millions, although such an estimate cannot claim an error of less than 5 per cent. In other words, Africa has about $8\frac{1}{2}$ per cent of the world's population on about 22 per cent of the world's land area. The average density is just under 22 per square mile; Australia is the only inhabited continent with a lower density.

The study of the population of Africa is impeded by insufficient accurate data, caused by the dearth of censuses, the prevailing illiteracy, the suspicion and even fear of census enumeration, and the shortage of funds and enumerators. Population data are of five main types: census reports, sample surveys, medical surveys, intensive demographic studies and anthropological monographs. Few are reliable enough for planning and research.

The population map of Africa must therefore be accepted only as a broad approximation. Analysis reveals few general correlations between population distribution and factors of the physical environments; in particular regions, however, such correlations are sometimes more obvious, as for example the large areas of desert, rain forest and swamp which are unsuitable for human habitation.

The patchiness of African population distribution is frequently explicable only with reference to social, historical and political factors. The desire for refuge and defensive sites has caused the higher densities of the Fouta Djallon and the Atlas Mountains. Political stability has

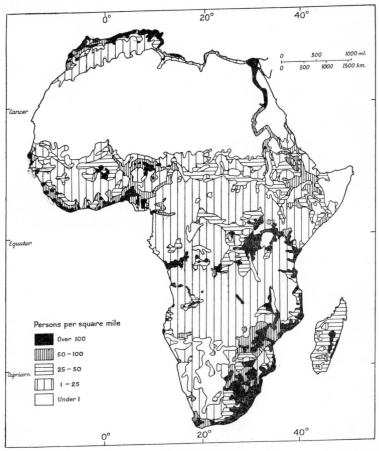

Fig. 12. Distribution of population in Africa
(Simplified from *The Times Atlas of the World*, Vol. I, 1958, plate V.)

assisted population growth in parts of Ethiopia, Uganda, southern Nigeria, Rwanda and Burundi. Migrations between territories occupied by different European powers can also explain some of the disparities of population distribution.

3

While the bulk of the continent is sparsely populated, there exist islands of overpopulation where the local resources and systems of agriculture are incapable of adequately supporting dense populations. Nowhere is overpopulation so obvious as in the Nile Valley of Egypt. In some cases, such as Rwanda, Burundi and southern Malawi, soils are suffering from intensive utilization, and alleviation of population pressure is sought through migration to other areas.

Present political boundaries pay little heed to population distribution or composition; they traverse populous and uninhabited areas alike, and frequently dissect tribal groups. Only Nigeria has a population comparable with the larger countries of Europe, Asia and the Americas. In 1960, only three countries (Nigeria, Egypt and Ethiopia) had more than 20 million people, and only five (Republic of South Africa, Congo (Leopoldville), Sudan, Algeria and Morocco) had between 10 and 20 millions. At the other end of the scale, a number of independent and colonial countries had well below one million people: Mauritania, Spanish Sahara, Fernando Po and Rio Muni, Gambia, Portuguese Guinea, Gabon, Congo (Brazzaville), French Somaliland, Zanzibar, South West Africa, Swaziland, Basutoland and Bechuanaland.

Some environmental problems

There is no simple explanation of the sparse population of Africa but a great variety of environmental, biological and social reasons. Certainly, the continent as a whole is not hospitable. Its position alone is enough to ensure difficulties in the diffusion of population. Africa straddles the equator and over two-thirds of it lies within the tropics, without an extensive mountain mass to mitigate the climate. As a result, over one-third of Africa experiences a hot, wet climate, with which one associates not merely the luxuriance of tropical forests but also the prevalence of diseases, the rapid exhaustion and erosion of soils following forest clearing, and a sparse population. The exhaustive agricultural practices and the lack of fertilizers indicate that the cultivated area and the population density are smaller than they might be.

Furthermore, the east–west width of Africa at the Tropic of Cancer is great, and so is the Sahara. Fortunately, south of the equator the Kalahari is not a mirror image, as the width of Africa at Capricorn is small. Nevertheless, three-eighths of the continent suffers from some degree of aridity. Whereas profusion of water was perhaps the main limiting factor of population growth in the equatorial forests, scarcity of water is the key factor in the deserts. Even abundant underground supplies will enable only local expansion of population. The moister grasslands of Africa offer much better conditions for agriculture and pastoralism, but the prevalence of pastoral nomadism does not encourage high population densities.

The most favoured locations for the establishment of population are undoubtedly the lower Nile Valley and the northern and southern extremities of the continent, where there are some similarities in climate and European colonization. The similarities can be exaggerated, because not only are their reliefs entirely different, but so are the native populations and their cultures, as well as the nature of European settlement.

Slavery

The slave trade certainly contributed to the sparseness of population. Estimates of the volume of this trade vary, but it is possible that 20 million Negroes were exported to the Americas between the sixteenth and nineteenth centuries, and that many millions more were massacred in the process. The Europeans were not first in the field; Romans, Arabs, Turks, Persians and Indians all used black slaves. Moreover, the trade in Negro slaves to the Islamic countries has been estimated at 10 to 15 millions. It may be that over 50 million persons were exported or killed by the slave trade, and therefore millions of births prevented. The worst affected were the Sudanese Negroes and the Bantu. Kuczynski, writing in the nineteen-thirties, believed that the populations of many West African territories were lower than before the European slave trade; but tribal warfare and disease were also to blame.

Hunger and Disease

Associated with the inherent environmental difficulties of Africa are the multiplicity and variety of microbes and parasites which attack animals, crops and men. Locusts, mosquitoes, tsetse flies, hookworms and water-borne disease organisms have greatly influenced the growth and migrations of population in Africa. So also have diseases such as typhus, smallpox, plague, trachoma, leprosy, tuberculosis and the venereal diseases. Unfortunately the incidence of many of these diseases has increased during this century, and many have spread through the greater mobility of population in Africa brought about by European intervention. Diseases of more temperate lands, such as influenza, have been introduced, and have spread rapidly among fairly segregated populations with no immunity.

Widespread malnutrition helps the spread of disease. Lack of protein is specially noteworthy, owing to the low consumption of animal products. Deficiency diseases, such as beriberi, kwashiorkor and pellagra are common in certain parts. The worst diets are often found amongst the new town-dwellers, who cannot afford to eat enough food of the right types. They are also sometimes guilty of excessive consumption of alcohol, which has become a social disease in many non-Islamic countries.

Disease and hunger ensure high mortality, and sometimes reduce the average expectation of life to well below 30 years. They also cause high sickness rates, as well as debility, apathy and fatalism. Great efforts have been made to combat disease, especially in those countries colonized by Europeans, but the real disorder is malnutrition which, in turn, depends on the social and economic advancement of the African peoples. Backwardness and superstition are closely related to the frequently appalling conditions of hygiene, the inadequate and unbalanced diets, and the high pre-natal and infant mortality. A great increase in education is necessary to ameliorate these conditions.

Low Negro Fertility

The sparseness of population may also be partly attributed to the fact that the fertility of African Negroes is not as high as that of many peoples in other underdeveloped areas of the world, including North Africa. The causes are not clear, but certainly include venereal disease, labour migration and abortion. The insufficient consumption of vitamin E, which assists fecundity and is present in cereals and fish, may also be instrumental.

Other causes may be seen in the matrimonial systems and the concept of the family. Contrary to common belief, polygamy has a lowering effect on general reproduction. The reasons for this are complex and variable but the most important is that in a population of an equal number of females and males, the polygamy of a minority of males enforces celibacy among an equivalent or larger number of other males. The result is that less children are born to a society which is polygamous than to a similar one in which monogamy prevails. Polygamy is very common in Africa, especially south of the Sahara, where according to estimates by Dorjahn about 35 per cent of the males are polygamous and that 100 of these polygamous males have about 245 wives. In Islamic countries, on the other hand, polygamy is much rarer than often supposed.

In Bantu Africa, the occurrence of matrilineal descent minimizes paternal authority, and tends to produce less paternal interest in the family and its growth. Often there is tension between the father and the wife's brother, in whom authority over the children is frequently vested.

GROWTH OF POPULATION

It is generally agreed that between 1650 and 1850 there can have been little increase in the population of Africa. In the hundred years which followed, the population may have doubled, if the estimates by Willcox and Carr-Saunders of early population numbers are accepted. United Nations experts believe that the earlier estimates are low and that the increase of population is slower. As mortality declines the population of Africa is growing much more rapidly.

POPULATION ESTIMATES FOR AFRICA
(in millions)

Year	Willcox	Carr-Saunders	Year	United Nations
1650	100	100	1920	136
1750	100	95	1930	155
1800	100	90	1940	177
1850	100	95	1950	199
1900	141	120	1960	254

The regions which are in the process of most rapid demographic growth are the northern and southern extremities of Africa: the Maghreb, Egypt and the Republic of South Africa. In 1904 the Republic had 5,176,000 inhabitants; in 1961, 15,841,000. In 1856, Algeria had about $2\frac{1}{2}$ million people; in 1960, 10,095,000. In 1897, Egypt had 9,715,000 people, and in 1960, 26,059,000.

It seems fairly certain that although early European occupation often arrested population growth, it has more recently been an important cause of the accelerated population growth, through the reduction of mortality and the increase in the demand for labour. The death rates of those countries with relatively good medical facilities are in the order of 15–20 per thousand, in comparison with rates exceeding 20 per thousand and even 30 per thousand in the rest of Africa. The expectation of life is slightly longer and generally exceeds 40 years, but the structure and growth of the European populations of these countries differs markedly from those of the African populations.

As a result of higher fertility and lower expectation of life, there is a far greater proportion of children among African peoples than among Europeans in Africa, although the latter have a higher proportion of children than equivalent populations in Europe.

APPROXIMATE AGE-COMPOSITION OF EUROPEANS
IN AFRICA AND AFRICANS

Population groups	Europeans (per cent)	Africans (per cent)
Young (less than 20)	30–40	45–55
Adult (20–59)	50–60	40–50
Aged (60 and over)	7–12	5–10

The proportion of young Africans is probably higher in tropical Africa than in the northern and southern countries, although population structure and growth undoubtedly vary considerably within tropical Africa. There the rate of population growth may be correlated to some extent with the degree of European influence and with the density of the indigenous population; densely peopled areas are registering the greatest gains. Average mortality is about 20–25 per thousand, and fertility 30 to 35 per thousand, but there are wide local deviations from these means. In general, West and East African countries experience more favourable demographic conditions than those of Central Africa.

It seems, however, that we should not expect a massive population increase in Black Africa in the near future, because although mortality will certainly decline, there is no reason to expect any immediate change in fertility. Will the development of the natural resources of Black Africa be retarded by lack of population? This question cannot be answered easily, but certainly there is a chronic shortage of economically productive manpower, as in Liberia. The situation differs greatly from that in Egypt and the Maghreb, where the labour-supply is already excessive and increasing fast.

MIGRATIONS

Africa has long experienced tribal migrations, especially in its grasslands, but in recent decades shortage of manpower in the industrial centres and large towns established by Europeans has led to the migration of large numbers of unskilled labourers over vast distances. Africans are accustomed to subsistence economies, and were not easily persuaded to become wage-labourers. Moreover, they were not adept at regular employment in large organizations.

Initially, migrants set off with the intention of obtaining enough money to maintain their families for a short period, and then of returning home. Consequently, this labour force is unstable, and the great majority of migrants are males. The effects on the social structure and economy of the tribal village are sometimes disastrous: lack of manpower, later marriage and lower fertility. Now, the desire to

Fig. 13. Labour routes in Africa
(Partly after Prothero and Dresch)

return home is disappearing. Industries and the towns are exerting a growing attraction, and the process of migration is gathering momentum. More and more migrants are breaking the ties with their tribes and homelands, and are being rapidly but inadequately assimilated

into the swollen cities of Africa, where they usually live in sordid evil-
smelling shanty towns which spring up in the suburbs. In many
countries urban populations have multiplied several times since 1940,
and nearly all the major cities of Africa are growing very rapidly,
presenting almost insoluble problems to the authorities.

Much of the movement is between countries. The Republic of South
Africa draws most migrants; the Portuguese overseas provinces
of Mozambique and Angola alone authorize between 100,000 and
200,000 migrants to enter it each year. Other sources of labour are
Malawi, Swaziland, Basutoland and Bechuanaland. Katanga also
attracts migrants from Malawi and the Portuguese provinces. Many
migrants leave densely populated Rwanda and Burundi for Uganda.
In West Africa there is a fairly constant drift from the rural north to
the more urban south, and from the more arid former French territories to the richer former British ones. In North Africa, the movement
is again from the interior to the coastal towns. In Algeria, rural–
urban migrations have reached a further stage, for about 320,000
Algerians, mostly from rural areas, are now living in France: 280,000
are males.

It is not easy to enumerate the many millions of Africans who have
migrated within the past decade, but the net effect has been the
heightening of density contrasts. The question is whether these
migrations will continue, or whether they will dwindle. It seems likely
that the breakdown of tribal systems, the desire for higher living
standards, the growth of industries, and improvements in agriculture
will ensure that Africans remain on the move.

FURTHER READING

Prehistory: L. S. B. Leakey, *The Progress and Evolution of Man in Africa*,
1961.

Peoples of Africa: G. P. Murdock, *Africa: Its Peoples and their Culture
History*, New York, 1959: W. R. Bascom and M. J. Herskovits (Eds.),
Continuity and Change in African Cultures, Chicago, 1959; C. G. Seligman,
Races of Africa, 3rd Ed., 1957; C. Daryll Forde (Ed.), *Ethnographic Survey
of Africa*, International African Institute; L. H. Gann and P. Duignan,
White Settlers in Tropical Africa, 1962; L. W. Hollingsworth, *The Asians of
East Africa*, 1960; G. Delf, *Asians in East Africa*, 1963; H. J. Greenberg,
Languages of Africa, Indiana, 1963.

Distribution and growth of population: K. M. Barbour and R. M. Prothero
(Eds.), *Essays on African Population*, 1961; F. Lorimer and M. Karp (Eds.),
Population in Africa, Boston, 1960; International Union for the Scientific

Study of Population, *Problems in African Demography*, Paris, 1960; J. Beaujeu-Garnier, *Géographie de la Population*, tôme 2, 1958, 9–167; R. W. Stephens, *Population Pressures in Africa South of the Sahara*, Washington, 1959; R. W. Stephens, *Population Factors in the Development of North Africa*, 1960; G. H. T. Kimble, *Tropical Africa*, Vol. 1, New York, 1960; Lord Hailey, *An African Survey*, 1957.

Migrations: R. Mansell Prothero, 'A Geographer with the World Health Organization', *Geographical Journal*, 1962, 489–93; I. Schapera, *Migrant Labour and Tribal Life*, 1947; R. Mansell Prothero, 'Continuity and change in African population mobility', in R. W. Steel and R. Mansell Prothero (Eds.), *Geographers and the the Tropics*, 1964.

CHAPTER FOUR*

Modes of Life

MUCH of Africa is still cut off from the world economy and most Africans live in independent tribal units which rely on the local environment for subsistence and barter. It was reported in 1954 that in nine countries of tropical Africa between 65 and 75 per cent of the total cultivated area and about 60 per cent of the total male population over fifteen years old were engaged in subsistence production. In former French West Africa the respective percentages were as high as 77 and 81. The vast majority of Africans make their living from the land as cultivators and pastoralists, and to a lesser degree as hunters and collectors or mixed farmers. These economies are both a reflection of the environmental possibilities and of cultural influences and traditional modes of life. Although the subsistence economies are broadly related to environmental patterns (see Fig. 14), cultural bias may lead to varied uses of similar land.

The impact of Western civilization and colonization has drastically affected native economies in northern and southern Africa; elsewhere, economic changes are more localized and less profound. Tribal wars have virtually ceased, livestock numbers have increased, larger areas are cultivated, more cash crops are grown, new means of transport and communication are available, and modern mines and industries have appeared.

Yet Africa is still not a very productive continent. It plays only a small part in international trade. Although a money economy has reached all corners of Africa, many of the newly independent countries have limited modern economic activities. A few have substantial contacts with the world economy but, in general, these contacts depend on specialized exports from specific localities, notably mines. Minerals yield high money incomes, and account for the importance of the Republic of South Africa, the Congo (Leopoldville), Zambia and Rhodesia in the table of African exports. Mines also have far-reaching social and economic repercussions, often well beyond the boundaries of the countries in which they occur. Industry in Africa largely means processing for export, and is mostly confined to the main towns, which are experiencing unprecedented growth.

* By John I. Clarke.

HUNTING AND COLLECTING

From Palaeolithic times until quite recently, hunting and collecting were the prevalent forms of economy over the whole of southern and eastern Africa. Today they survive only among widely scattered remnant peoples, inhabiting remote or environmentally unattractive

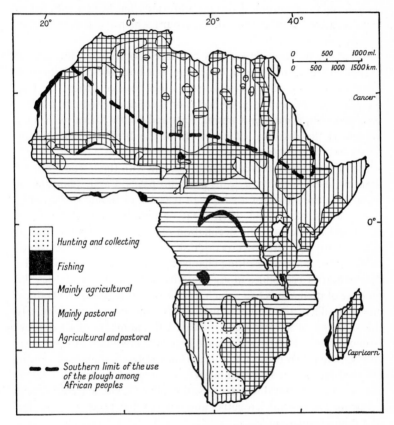

Fig. 14. The distribution of types of subsistence economy
(After Murdock)

areas and numbering in all no more than a few hundred thousand. They include the Bushmen of the Kalahari Desert, the Pygmies of the Congo Basin, and very small groups of East African peoples such as the Dorobo and Sanye of Kenya, the Kindiga and Sandawe of Tanganyika, and the Majo of southern Ethiopia. In North and West Africa hunting and collecting groups were replaced by Neolithic food producers.

Despite local differences, there is a striking uniformity of culture among these primitive peoples. They are remarkable, for example, for their use of bows and poisoned arrows and dome-shaped shelters, for the absence of slavery and social classes and for common features in their social organization. Cultural uniformity has been attributed to local exogamy (marriage outside the group), which assists the diffusion of customs.

Reference has been made only to those peoples who derive their livelihood from hunting and collecting, but both these activities are common in a subsidiary way in many other parts of Africa; the vast quantity of game and natural vegetation is conducive to both. Indeed, the profusion of game in Central, East and South Africa must have influenced the dispersal of ancestors of the Bushmen, the Nilotic tribes and the southern Bantu.

Hunting of game altered entirely in scale with the introduction of firearms, used both by Africans and Europeans. Large quantities of game have been shot for a variety of reasons, including sport, ivory, horns, hides, skins, and dried meat or biltong. One of the great ecological problems is the decimation of certain species for foreign demands of, for instance, crocodile skins, elephant tusks and rhinoceros horns, and the resulting change in the balance of species. The destruction of crocodiles along the Nile, for example, increases the number of predacious fish, which are the preferred diet of crocodiles, and thus affects the number of fish of economic importance. Similarly the shooting of leopards has increased the numbers of their prey, baboons and wild pigs, which have become a great pest in some agricultural areas. To protect wild life from wholesale slaughter, certain reserved areas have been established. In order of decreasing control they are Strict Natural Reserves, National Parks, Game Reserves and Controlled Areas which together amount to well in excess of a quarter of a million square miles.

CULTIVATION

For ease of study, agriculture in Africa may be arbitrarily divided into cultivation and pastoralism. In some ways an equally satisfactory division would be that between subsistence and commercial production, although again the categories are not entirely exclusive of each other; subsistence farming often includes small sales to markets, while commercial farming rarely omits the production of some crops for local subsistence. Generally speaking, whilst African farming is still primarily for subsistence, European farmers have been largely interested in commercial farming. However, the dichotomy is less and less rigid as increasing numbers of Africans devote themselves to cash crop production.

Land Tenure and European Alienation

The varied indigenous systems of land tenure in Africa were appropriate to subsistence economies and to societies dominated by kinship. As a member of a social group an individual had the right to utilize land necessary for the subsistence of his family. Land had no exchange value. It could be allotted to an outsider, but this was not regarded as an economic transaction. Where occupation was stable, ownership of land was normally acquired; where shifting cultivation or nomadism prevailed, no permanent rights existed, only rights by usage.

With the introduction of money, land is becoming negotiable. The growth of commercialized agriculture and improved techniques have put more land under cultivation; certain types of good quality land are in heavy demand, as, for example, the cocoa lands of West Africa and the cotton lands of East Africa. Sometimes a right-holder has ousted a tenant in order to grow a cash crop. In other words, the traditional attitudes towards land are declining in the face of a new commercial attitude. One of the great problems is that loss of land in African rural society means dependence upon others, or migration to the towns.

The whole process has been accelerated by the introduction of European legal forms, and aggravated by European alienation of land. European settlers or planters, invited by their governments or by concessionaire land companies, found Africa sparsely populated and primitively farmed. Its land rights also seemed to be of questionable validity according to European concepts. In some cases, it can be said justifiably that the Europeans arrived before the native peoples; in others, excuses were found for land appropriation, such as native resistance to European domination. The acquisition of land by Europeans caused considerable resentment among Africans, not merely because of their prevailing sense of communal right over land, but also because many of the alienated lands were selected because of their physical advantages for cultivation.

Climate and soils have had great influence on European farming, which is mainly concentrated in the more temperate northern and southern parts of the continent, where the problems of racial contact are most acute.

PERCENTAGE OF LAND ALIENATED OR RESERVED FOR
EUROPEAN OCCUPATION
(*c.* 1950)

Republic of South Africa	89	Tunisia	6
Southern Rhodesia	49	Bechuanaland	6
Swaziland	49	South West Africa	5
Algeria (excluding Sahara)	13	Malawi (Nyasaland)	5
Congo (then Belgian)	9	N. Rhodesia (now Zambia)	3
Angola	Not available, but significant	Morocco	2
		Rwanda and Burundi	2
Kenya	7	Tanganyika	0·9

Traditional African Cultivation

The stages of the development of cultivation in the various parts of Africa have depended upon a number of factors including soil, climate, the density of settlement and traditions of the peoples. Tradition plays an important role in agricultural practices, which are frequently well adapted to the local environment and have proved worthy of analysis before attempts are made to introduce new methods or crops. Innovations have been most successful where they have been adapted to existing systems; from the sixteenth century onwards the Portuguese successfully introduced a number of Latin American crops into West Africa (cassava, sweet potatoes, groundnuts, paw-paws, tomatoes) which incurred no drastic changes in indigenous systems of cultivation.

One of the great barriers to innovation has been the small scale of agriculture practised by indigenous peoples. Despite the vastness of the continent and the overall sparseness of population, there is excessive congestion and pressure on the land in certain areas. The Nile Valley, the fertile uplands of Rwanda and Burundi, adjacent south-western Uganda, the Kenya Highlands, and the Kabylie Mountains of northern Algeria, are all obvious examples. In these areas of fixed or stable cultivation, parcellation and fragmentation of land hinders agricultural progress, while the growing populations demand more and more from the soil, often seriously reducing the fallow period. Soil exhaustion, erosion and insufficient land cause migrations to the towns.

In the more thinly populated areas, the main system of agriculture has been that of bush fallowing. It entails the cultivation of a patch of land for a period of years (usually 3 or 4) until the soil shows signs of exhaustion, followed by departure to another patch. The original patch is left to natural vegetation but may be used again later when the soil has recovered its fertility. Bush fallowing is associated with land abundance and low soil fertility which is rapidly worsened by cultivation. Over vast areas, therefore, agricultural improvements depend upon methods of maintaining and, if possible, increasing soil fertility.

The practice of bush fallowing varies from savanna to forest, but one universal feature is the use of fire for clearing. In forest areas, mature forest is preferred to regenerated bush for clearing, as the soils are likely to be more fertile and the forest more likely to contain straight timber suitable for house building. Bush fallowing is consequently largely responsible for the reductions in the extent of high forest. Firing destroys weeds, and the wood ash increases the fertility by adding potash. The stumps are invariably left in the ground because they do not hinder cultivaton by hoe. By the wasteful chitemene system employed in Zambia the timber and brushwood of a large area is burnt on a small part of it; sometimes the area cleared is ten times the size of the area cropped. In savanna areas short periods of cropping are separated by long periods of repose. In some cases villages are never permanently established, but are moved every few years. The Lozi of the plain of the upper Zambezi practise this mode of life. In North Africa many of the semi-nomads of steppe and semi-desert areas may be considered as shifting cultivators as they sow cereals in moist hollows and wadi beds which are not delimited, and vary from year to year.

The mode of life of the North African cultivator has long differed substantially from that of the Negro cultivator, owing to his possession of the plough (Fig. 14) in contrast to the prevalence of the hoe in Negro Africa. The use of the plough, whose distribution is possibly linked with the spread of Islam from the north-east, engenders not only a different economic system, but involves men in a greater proportion of the agricultural activities. Whereas in areas of hoe cultivation the social status of women is high, it is the reverse in areas of plough cultivation.

Staple Subsistence Crops

Cultivated plants in Africa are bewildering in their profusion, and include about nine-tenths of all the known varieties. Many were introduced by Arab and Indian traders, by the Portuguese or by later European settlers. They originate especially from South-West and

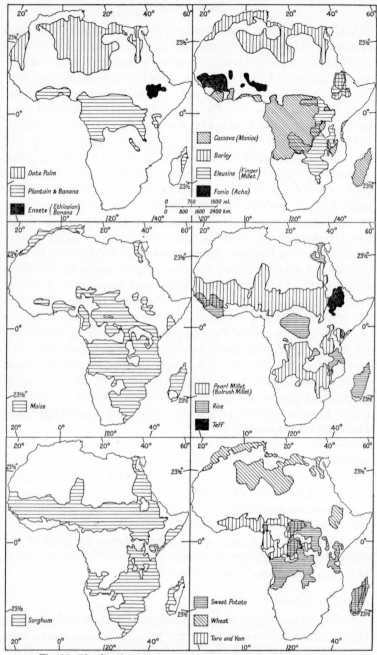

Fig. 15. *The distribution of sixteen staple subsistence crops in Africa*
(After Murdock, Johnston and Jones)

South-East Asia and America, and they provide valuable evidence for historical reconstructions.

In Fig. 15 the distributions of sixteen important staple subsistence crops of indigenous societies are represented, including nine cereal grains, five tubers or root crops and two fruit trees. In the table below they are listed in approximate order of general importance and by place of origin:

Type	Place of Origin				
Cereal grains	*W. Africa*	*Ethiopia*	*S.W. Asia*	*S.E. Asia*	*America*
Sorghum (Guinea corn)	X				
Pearl Millet (Bulrush millet)	X				
Maize					X?
Wheat			X		
Barley			X		
Rice				X	
Eleusine (Finger millet)		X			
Fonio (Acha)	X				
Teff		X			
Tubers or root crops					
Cassava (Manioc)					X
Yam				X	
Taro (Coco-yam)				X	
Ensete (Ethiopian banana)		X			
Sweet potato					X
Fruit trees					
Banana				X	
Date			X		

Sorghum is possibly the main crop of Africa and is very widespread. It was probably first cultivated by Negroes of the western Sudan five thousand years before Christ. Some introduced crops also have a wide distribution, notably cassava and maize, though some say maize was grown in West Africa in pre-Columbean times. In contrast, three indigenous staple crops (fonio, teff and ensete) have only a restricted distribution. Unfortunately, many of the staple crops are poor in proteins: cassava, maize, millet, sorghum, bananas and yams. A large number of other crops are grown to supplement and diversify the staple foods: beans, peas, peppers, onions, tomatoes, pumpkins, cucumbers, gourds, melons and many others.

African Commercial Agriculture

There is clearly a growing tendency among Africans to produce cash or exchange crops. These crops are exceedingly varied, and are both indigenous and exotic (Fig. 16). They include cereals (wheat, barley, maize, rice), condiments and indulgents (coffee, cocoa, sugar cane, tobacco, ginger, khat, hemp or hashish, opium poppy), oil plants (oil palm, castor, olive, clove, sesame, cottonseed), fruits (date, banana, pineapple, coconut) as well as cotton, groundnuts (Plate 24) and wattles (from which are extracted tanning materials).

Inherent problems in cash crop production are remoteness and poor transportation facilities. Cash crops therefore tend to be grown near towns, road or rail routes, or the coast. In many areas where cash crops are now produced they were first grown alongside subsistence crops, sometimes causing acute soil exhaustion. Share-cropping by kinsmen or partners of the owner has also been important in the extension of cash crops; the share-croppers cultivate part of the owner's land for a portion of the produce. In this way cocoa-growing in Ghana and adjacent countries developed into an important world industry in a few decades, and reduced the extent of shifting cultivation in West Africa. In some cocoa-growing areas the native system of mixed cultivation has been almost abandoned in favour of a system akin to monoculture. One result of this type of development is the dangerous deficiency in food production. The situation can become very serious when a small country depends excessively on the production of one or two export crops; Gambia and Senegal, for example, rely too much on groundnuts.

One reason for the entry of African cultivators into cash crop production has been their acquisition of European properties in certain countries; this is the case in Morocco and Tunisia. Whatever the reason, commercial agriculture is bringing the African cultivator considerable wealth as well as closer contact with world affairs.

Agricultural Schemes and Co-operatives

The need for a rapid agricultural revolution has seemed so vital to African governments that many new colonization, settlement and irrigation schemes have emerged to facilitate and guide the transformations. They have varied greatly in size, aims, methods and results, from small pilot projects intended to test the use of machinery in African conditions to the grandiose and calamitous East African Groundnut Scheme undertaken by the British Overseas Food Corporation in 1946.

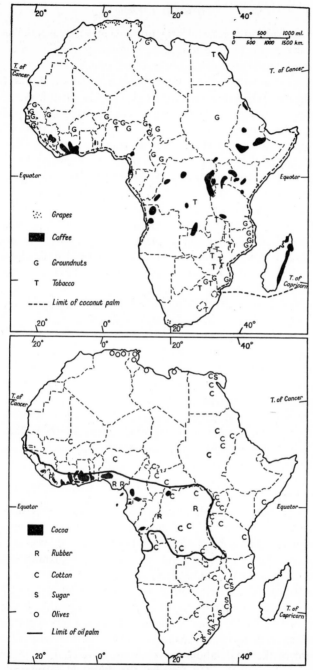

Fig. 16. *The distribution of eleven cash crops in Africa*

Among the most successful irrigation schemes has been the Gezira Irrigation Scheme in the Sudan, based on the production of cotton. Also based on the production of this crop is the Zande Development Scheme in southern Sudan, employing the backward Zande tribe. The Belgians in the Congo and the French in their territories put into operation many *paysannat* settlement schemes designed to stabilize peasant cultivation and to develop exchange crops. In British territories considerable support was given to group farming schemes aimed at settling independent peasant cultivators or providing group services, particularly machinery, to owner-farmers. The Bamenda-Cross River Calabar Scheme in Eastern Nigeria began in this way, and specializes in the cultivation of oil palms. The Uganda Development Corporation has also been instrumental in this type of work, taking over areas of coffee and tea plantations to settle native farmers under technical supervision. Resettlement schemes have also been successful in Northern Nigeria (Anchau), Tanganyika (Sukuma), Rwanda and Burundi. In many parts of Africa, more and more control has been assumed by public corporations and governments in an effort to guide agricultural development along the right lines.

At the same time, the growth of co-operative movements in Africa has greatly stimulated agricultural improvements through self-help and individual initiative. Co-operatives proved of great value, for example, in the evolution of native cocoa-growing in Ghana and coffee-growing in Tanganyika, by providing among other things marketing, storage, pulping, transportation and credit facilities. In French territories, membership of *sociétés de prévoyance* was usually made compulsory.

Plantations

It is no longer appropriate to divide cultivation in Africa into 'peasant' and 'plantation' systems, because African peasants are producing crops formerly confined to plantations, and because newly independent African governments are establishing plantations, e.g. Eastern Nigeria, Ghana and Sierra Leone.

Plantations are not widespread in Africa. In North and South Africa European plantations have been less important than European private settlers. On the other hand, plantations are very significant in East Africa; in Kenya and Tanzania (Tanganyika) they employ about one-third of the total labour force. Sisal production is the main industry of Tanganyika. On Zanzibar the clove and coconut plantations are owned by Arabs and Indians. Other East African plantation products are coffee, tea, rubber, sugar, tobacco and pyrethrum. In West Africa plantation products are few, mainly rubber in Liberia and some coffee in the Ivory Coast. In the Portuguese provinces of São Tomé and Príncipe the crop is cocoa, and in Angola and Mozambique plantations produce coffee, sisal and sugar. In the Maghreb vines and olives are the main plantation crops. Some plantations reach gigantic proportions; the Firestone Company's concession in Liberia amounts to a million acres, of which about 100,000 have been planted, employing a labour force of 30,000. Even larger was the concession for oil palm development obtained in 1911 by *Les Huileries du Congo Belge* which amounted to 1,875,000 acres.

More often owned by companies than by individuals, plantations are noted for their efficient production and research. After the Second World War a new development in the plantation system occurred, namely farming by public corporations. Examples are the work of the Cameroon Development Corporation in taking over the banana estates of German settlers, that of the Colonial Development Corporation on the tung and tobacco estates of Malawi, and that of the production of groundnuts and rice in Senegal by French government sponsored companies.

Farming by Europeans

Farms owned by Europeans in Africa have been acquired and worked in diverse ways. In general, however, they are larger than African farms, more mechanized and fertilized, employ more labour and concentrate on cash crop and/or livestock production. Furthermore, as European colonization has prevailed in areas experiencing low to medium rainfall, it is natural that cereals and livestock should be basic to farming.

Yet farming by Europeans in Africa varies not merely with the environmental conditions but also with the country of origin of the colonists. Thus the scale of European farming in the Republic of South Africa and the ex-British countries of Central and East Africa is much greater than in the Maghreb, where in some areas European farming is no more than an extension of the peasant tree cultivation of the Midi. In the Maghreb, vines, olives and citrus dominate in the Mediterranean zone, and give way southward to cereals. French colonists have never shown the same interest in livestock production as South Africans, who possess a very large livestock population. Fodder crops occupy the largest part of the non-cereal land of the

Republic, and on the vast farms, exceeding 1,000 acres on the average, cereals are also important.

European farming is diminishing in many African countries, especially those recently or about to become independent. Insecurity during struggles for independence and subsequent political pressure have induced many colonists to leave. In some countries, notably Libya and Tunisia, governments have difficulty in replacing colonists by trained farmers.

PASTORALISM

While pastoral nomadism has developed only over the past thousand years in Africa, it seems that, like hunting and collecting, it is diminishing in importance in various parts of the continent. Indeed, even among sedentary pastoralists there appears to be a growing tendency to place less reliance on livestock and to look more to cultivation for subsistence needs. Moreover, it is generally agreed that the development of mixed farming would have a beneficial effect on the soils and also open the way for the replacement of the hoe by the plough. A few examples of indigenous mixed farming occur in Africa, but they are rare.

Pastoralism is still the dominant subsistence economy over large areas of grassland and desert. In some countries, as in Niger, it is the main economy and animal products figure high in the list of exports. But pastoralism varies in character from region to region according to the type of livestock, the degree of nomadism, the prevalence of the tsetse and animal diseases, and the scale of European influences.

Cattle

Africa is rich in variety and numbers of domestic animals, although only the ass, ostrich and, perhaps, the Arabian camel were first domesticated within the continent. The main types of livestock are cattle, camels, sheep, goats and pigs. Cattle are dominant among all pastoralists south of the Sahara, the Galla of Ethiopia, the Baggara Arabs of eastern Sudan, the Fulani and the Hottentots, and their distribution owes much to the wanderings of Hamites (see Fig. 17). African varieties of cattle are derived from three main species: (*a*) *Bos taurus*, the long-horned Mediterranean cattle, themselves descended from *Bos primigenius* which appeared in Egypt in the early Neolithic period and spread southwards and westwards with the migrations of the Hamites; (*b*) *Bos indicus*, the hump-backed zebu which have spread over East, Central, West and South Africa, but rarely in the forest zone; (c) *Bos brachyceros*, small shorthorn cattle, derivative breeds of which are common in West Africa.

African cattle are of relatively low economic value, with small meat and milk yields. Among many peoples of West Africa and northern Angola they are not even milked. Dairy products such as cheese,

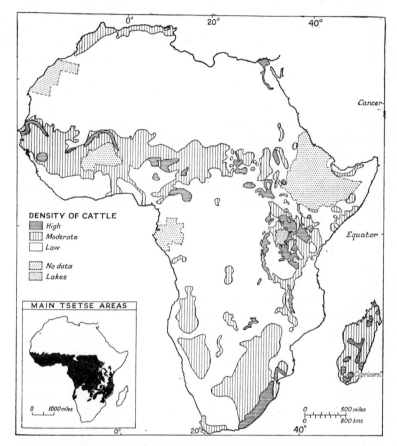

Fig. 17. *The distribution of cattle in Africa. Inset of main tsetse areas.* (Simplified from map by W. Deshler and J. C. Thomas in *Geographical Review*, January, 1963)

curds, fermented milk and butter are unknown in large areas; elsewhere, however, the manufacture of ghee (clarified butter) is the main dairy industry. A localized use of cattle is the extraction of blood by the Masai and Fulani, who mix it with milk in their traditional diet. The main economic use of cattle is for meat and hides; they are rarely used, for example, as beasts of burden, though some peoples, including the Swazi, have given up the hoe for the ox-drawn plough.

The fact is that cattle play a special role in the social customs of many African peoples, especially in East Africa, where they contribute greatly to the character of a large culture area. They are of particular significance in marriage and sacrificial ceremonies, and have great prestige value; the wealth of an individual or a tribe is usually measured in terms of the number of cattle owned. Furthermore, they have long been the basis of commercial transactions, the quality of cattle and value for consumption mattering little. Cattle are capital. It was natural, therefore, when cattle raids and diseases diminished in destructiveness that overstocking should soon become a serious problem. Frequently it has been a cause of severe soil erosion.

Cattle rearing in East Africa is rarely nomadic in the true sense of the word, as animals are usually returned to kraals at night. Pastoralism and cultivation frequently exist side by side without fusion; sometimes, as in Baganda, fusion takes place. In West Africa, the Hamitic Fulani exhibit only isolated cases of fusion of agriculture and herding. On the other hand, in many parts of Africa cattle-keeping, a male occupation, is becoming more closely associated with cultivation, in which women often do more work.

Over large areas of southern Africa and in the Mediterranean littoral of the Maghreb European breeds of cattle prevail, and indigenous breeds have to some extent been ousted. The level of stock-rearing is much higher than in native herds, although it is not without problems of breeding, nutrition and disease.

Pigs, Camels, Sheep and Goats

Pigs, once important in North Africa, are now almost non-existent owing to Moslem prohibition of the consumption of pork. They are reared, however, by the Nuba in the Sudan, by tribes of Portuguese Guinea, and are numerous in all the southern zone of West Africa, and on European farms in South Africa, Rhodesia and Kenya.

The camel is the dominant animal in the Sahara, among both Arab and Berber tribes, and also along the Red Sea margins and in the Horn among the Beja, Afar and Somali. Camels are the nomadic beasts *par excellence*, their annual cycle of movement being determined partly by the availability of pastures and water and partly by tribal customs. Along the northern fringes of the Sahara camels are invariably associated with sheep (especially the Barbary fat-tail) and goats. All three are milked and provide other valuable products, but they suffer severely during the periodic droughts. At these times many North African nomads have traditionally practised transhumance into the more humid Atlas mountain zone. In general, such pastoralists are more properly termed semi-nomads, for they usually sow some cereals, possess some fruit trees, are mobile for only part of the year and are based on permanent villages. All forms of pastoral nomadism, however, are declining in the face of modern transport, urbanization, oil exploitation and agricultural improvements.

Sheep and goats, especially the latter, are widespread in Africa. In South Africa, where sheep-farming is an important industry, merinos are numerous, as well as crossbreeds coming from local ewes and Southdown, Dorset Horn and Leicester rams. Goats, like camels, have not been regarded as profitable by European farmers, although they constitute the major source of meat supply of Africans. Indeed, they warrant closer attention for they have several distinct advantages. They replace themselves more rapidly than cattle, survive in tsetse-infested areas, and are rarely infected by either rinderpest or tuber-culosis.

Development of the Livestock Industry

Animal diseases have exercised a serious control on the spread and evolution of animal husbandry in Africa. The most severe are trypanosomiasis, rinderpest, East Coast fever and contagious pleuro-pneumonia. Trypanosomiasis, caused by the tsetse fly, is prevalent in West, Central and East Africa, where 65 to 75 per cent of the area is infested. Great strides have been made towards its elimination, but complete success has been prevented by the presence of large numbers of wild animals, and by the traditional habits and social customs of pastoralists. Such habits have greatly hindered scientific improve-ments of pastoralism. Native farmers are not alone to blame; despite high standards of livestock farming, overgrazing on European farms has caused severe erosion over large areas. The widespread introduc-tion of rotational grazing would greatly reduce this danger. Other needs for native livestock farming are improved breeds and water supplies, and better methods of treatment and preservation of animal products, notably of skins, meat and dairy products. The last two are in short supply in many towns of Africa because of inadequate storage and transport.

FORESTRY

Between one-fifth and one-sixth of Africa is forested, no accurate percentage being possible because of the difficulty of defining forest in areas where it is intimately associated with grassland. Although more than two million square miles are forested, few people derive their livelihood entirely from forest products; in fact, forests are cleared more for cultivation than for timber.

During historic times there has been continuous reduction of the forest cover, notably of the 'high forest' of Central Africa, much of which has been transformed into secondary bush. Reduction has been attributed to climatic change, commercial forestry, bush fallowing, and to destruction by animals, both domesticated and wild. It is now widely realized that forests are valuable not merely for their commercial timber and other materials (nuts, gums, resins, fibres, oil seeds, tan stuffs, palm oil, bees wax and drugs), but also for their protection of water supply and soils, as well as their influence on climatic conditions. Reserved and protected forests have therefore been established in numerous territories in order to control clearing, while forestry services are increasingly widespread and efficient. Fast-growing exotic species, especially pines, eucalyptus and mango, have been introduced in many countries to replace the slow-growing indigenous species, but it is sometimes thought that they exhaust African soils and intensify fungus and pest problems.

Types of Forest

Broadly, there are three main types of forest in Africa (Fig. 7):

(*a*) Moist Tropical Forest;

(*b*) Woodland-Savanna;

(*c*) Temperate Forest.

Only the Moist Tropical Forest is capable of contributing much timber for export. It is indeed one of the largest timber reserves in the world and may be divided into four masses—the Guinea forest, Nigerian forest, Equatorial forest and the scattered patches along the East African coast—some of which comprise both primary forest as well as secondary forest, which includes cleared patches. The West African forests produce most timber for the export trade because of their accessibility from the coast. Commercial production is generally hampered by inadequate communications, small local demand, lack of soft woods, great variety of species as well as the scatter and low density of marketable species. These are primarily cabinet woods including several mahoganies, red timbers such as makoré, the white avodiré and the brown iroko. Other species, notably okoumé and limbo, are felled for the veneer industry (Fig. 18). Some forty species are exported, although only fifteen regularly, a very small proportion of the total number of species. The markets for most African woods are in Europe, South Africa and America, but areas such as the Copper-belt have growing demands for timber.

The Woodlands are floristically less varied and commercially less important. Their main functions are as a protection for the soil, and as a basis for bush fallowing. But, as already indicated in an earlier chapter, there exists a complete gradation of forest types between

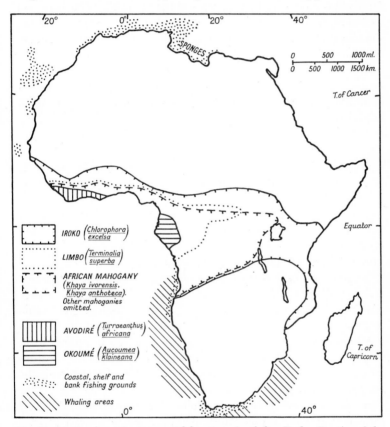

Fig. 18. Limits of certain commercial forest species, (after Haden Guest) and the main fishing and whaling areas

Moist Tropical Forest and Desert, depending on the relative influences of climate, soil, relief and man. In general, they vary from dense stands through Forest-Savanna and Woodland-Savanna mosaics to Grass Steppe and Steppe. In detail, however, the patterns are more intricate. Unfortunately, there is a constant tendency towards the degradation of woodland into savanna, particularly through the disastrous effects of bush fires which ravage such large areas of Africa during the dry season. They greatly reduce the quantity and quality of timber available, so that woodlands are cut mostly for local fuel needs.

The scattered patches of Temperate Forest found in North and South Africa are the surviving remnants of much larger forests which suffered ruthless clearing, mishandling and fires. In North Africa the forests also experienced severe depredations by charcoal burners, and by the incursions of nomadic flocks anxious for fodder during the summer droughts. In both extremes of the continent, forest production is small, and far-sighted conservation and plantation policies are being implemented. At the same time there are interesting developments in the fixation of sand dunes, especially with acacias. There is no doubt that forestry is worthy of the closest attention, and should occupy more people.

FISHING

Despite the immense length of its seaboard, and the vast extent of its lakes and rivers, the fisheries of Africa are of small importance in the economy of the continent. Africa accounts for only 6 per cent of the world's catch of fish, and many countries import fish from the northern hemisphere. In view of the inadequacy of agricultural production and protein consumption in most African countries, this is an unfortunate situation, for which immediate remedies are required.

A number of reasons can be suggested for the small catch, including the usually limited extent of the continental shelf, the excessive variety of fish in tropical waters, and the lack of large shoals. These factors account for the prevalence in African waters of pelagic species (fish which are not limited to shelves): anchovy, pilchard, sardine, shad, mackerel, tuna and many other species. Tropical waters are unimportant for fishing in comparison with the cooler waters of the Benguela and Canaries currents and of the Mediterranean Sea; at the same time, the fisheries of these latter waters have developed largely through European capital and enterprise. Many African peoples practise fishing, but few regard it as their dominant subsistence economy. Exceptions are found along the Congo and Niger rivers, the lagoons of Dahomey, Togo and the Ivory Coast, and the coasts of Mauritania and Angola. Unfortunately, Africans have usually employed ingenious but inefficient methods not conducive to large-scale production. Storage and transport of fish have been particularly poor.

Marine Fishing

By far the most important marine fishing area off Africa is on the Agulhas Bank between Walvis Bay in the west and Durban in the east (see Fig. 18). Fishing is for both pelagic (especially pilchards and sardines) and demersal (Cape hake, sole) species, and there is both line and trawl fishing. Crawfish, or spiny lobsters, are also exported in large numbers, and whaling takes place, particularly off the Natal and Zululand coasts. South Africa is one of the ten largest fish-producing countries in the world and produces over one-third of the catch of the continent. South West Africa and Angola follow in importance and, because of their small populations, export the bulk of their productions, which play a large part in their economies. Improved techniques of refrigeration, packaging and canning have greatly helped exports. Fishing in these areas, as off the Moroccan and Mauritanian coasts, is assisted by upwelling currents maintaining the nutrient content of the water. Morocco is Africa's fourth fish producer, catching mainly sardines and tuna. Here and in Mauritania French capital has greatly encouraged development, as in the other countries of the Maghreb. Libyan and Egyptian fisheries have been stimulated by Italian and Greek enterprise.

Of the tropical fisheries of the Atlantic and Indian oceans, the former are more important. Fisheries of the coasts of West and Central Africa are predominantly inshore and in the hands of native fishermen, who use nets, seines or baskets, from the beaches or from dugout canoes. The scarcity of good harbours, save in Sierra Leone, hampers the use of large modern boats. Ghana has the highest production, followed by the Congo (Leopoldville) and Nigeria, but all import substantial quantities. The East Coast of Africa is specially poor for fisheries, perhaps because of the excessive purity of the water, the low coastal population and poor communications. There is scope for improvement, particularly with the construction of sardine and tuna canneries.

Inland Fishing

The inland waters of Africa exceed England and Wales in area. Their productivity, though not as high as African marine fisheries, is significant because they are situated close to centres of population. Africans use traditional fishing methods. Europeans saw great possi-bilities of increasing the yield of inland fisheries, and are making scientific studies of the great variety of indigenous species of fish; the inland waters of Africa contain about 2,000 separate species in comparison with about 50 found in Europe. Nevertheless, some waters have been naturally almost devoid of fish, and have presented challenging problems in the introduction of exotic species. Trout, for example, have been introduced successfully into all suitable waters in East and South Africa.

Fish farming developed rapidly under the impetus of Belgian initiative in the Congo, where, before independence 122,404 fish ponds covering 10,091 acres had been established. Production, mainly of a species of tilapia, amounts normally to approximately one ton of fish per annum per acre of water. It is therefore an important supplement to diets, and experiments are taking place in several countries.

It should be noted that the small high class fish market for which most modern developments cater is quite different from the native market. Fish for the latter are usually either sun-dried or partly smoked, and processing and marketing methods leave considerable room for improvement.

MINING

Although gold, tin and other deposits have been worked in many parts of Africa for centuries, large-scale production began only after European conquests. The mining of iron ore and phosphate rock in Algeria dates from 1865 and 1886 respectively; elsewhere the large extractive industries commenced mainly within this century (Fig. 19). Systematic searches for oil awaited the nineteen-fifties.

Slow uneven and superficial exploration of mineral resources during the first few decades of the twentieth century were partly responsible for the delayed expansion of mining; other reasons are high transportation costs, problems of foreign investment, fluctuations in the world market, rapid depreciation of machinery and shortages of skilled labour. Since the Second World War there has been a great impetus in mining developments and oil exploration, stimulated partly by new knowledge and techniques and partly by the desire of the new African nations for some measure of economic viability. The iron ore of Mauritania is one example. Unfortunately, despite rich and varied reserves, progress has resulted in 'haves' and 'have-nots'.

Large foreign companies, with or without financial ties with African countries, have been mainly responsible for extractive industries, and non-Africans still occupy most of the managerial and technical posts. However, Africanization is increasing. Mining in Africa provides full-time employment for well over one million persons, about half of whom work in South Africa, where, apart from gold and diamonds, large quantities of uranium, coal, asbestos, iron ore, manganese and chrome are mined. In the 'fifties, South Africa accounted for over two-fifths of the gross value of mineral output in Africa.

The other major mineral producing region is the Katanga–Zambia copper region, which also contains cobalt, uranium, silver, gold,

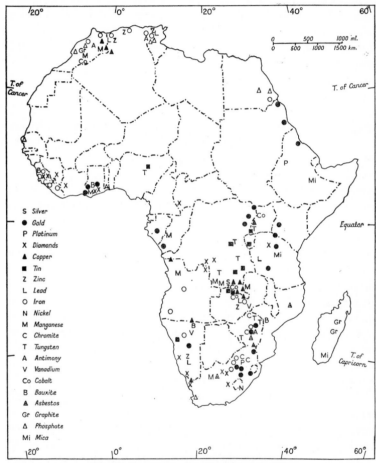

S   Silver
●   Gold
P   Platinum
X   Diamonds
▲   Copper
■   Tin
Z   Zinc
L   Lead
O   Iron
N   Nickel
M   Manganese
C   Chromite
T   Tungsten
A   Antimony
V   Vanadium
Co Cobalt
B   Bauxite
△   Asbestos
Gr Graphite
△   Phosphate
Mi Mica

Fig. 19. Important mineral workings in Africa

cadmium, platinum, palladium, zinc, germanium etc. The Congo (Leopoldville) is also rich in manganese, tin and gold.

Important producers in recent decades have been the Maghreb (iron ore, phosphates, lead), South West Africa (diamonds, lead), Rhodesia (gold, asbestos, coal), Ghana (gold, diamonds, manganese), Nigeria (tin), Sierra Leone (iron ore, diamonds), Angola and Tanzania (diamonds); but new producers enter the field every year.

Until the massive exploitation of oil resources after 1956, gold, copper and diamonds represented more than 60 per cent of the gross value of mineral output in Africa. Most minerals mentioned so far occur in the Basement Complex; oil reserves are now being rapidly located in interior sedimentary basins, especially in the northern Sahara, or in coastal fringes and deltas, as in Nigeria. Much greater diversity and quantity of mineral production should be expected during the next few decades.

INDUSTRY

It is not easy to distinguish between crafts and industries, but while the latter are generally a recent introduction into Africa the former are traditional and found throughout the continent. Inevitably certain tribes, groups or villages specialized in individual crafts, becoming smiths, weavers, potters, carpet and mat makers, leather-dressers, boat-builders and even jugglers, musicians and story-tellers. Many congregated in the markets and bazaars of towns, but rarely was production large or organized.

Factory industries are largely concerned with the processing of minerals and agricultural products. The location of raw materials and the degree of European impact have therefore caused the great measure of localization of industries, which are most developed in the major cities of the Maghreb, Egypt, South Africa, Zambia, Rhodesia and the Congo (Leopoldville). Elsewhere manufacturing is characterized by the small scale of production, the local market having less influence on manufacturing, which is primarily for export. Consumer industries financed by European capital and producing soap, cigarettes, cottons, fish oil and the like are growing, but slowly. Colonial governments usually relied on non-African private investment which was inadequate, but in recent years there has been increased government participation in manufacturing, especially in Egypt and the Republic of South Africa.

The previous lack of industrial and urban traditions in Africa meant that the introduction of modern industry involved much greater economic and social transformations than in Europe. Africans had no experience of regular paid labour; services had been rewarded rather than paid. The relative positions of Europeans and Africans in manufacturing have not been everywhere the same. In West Africa, for example, Europeans have held technical and supervisory capacities

. Timbuktu (p. 4), once a famous
rans-Saharan terminal on the Niger, and a
reat commercial and cultural centre, is now
ar from West Africa's main routeways.
n the distance is one of its ancient mosques,
n the foreground a well and some of the
nany trees planted by the French.

. A camel caravan at Bamba, on the
Niger (Mali). The camels in the background
ad brought the slabs of salt, each worth
bout £1 10s., from Taoudenni (northern
Mali, Sahara), for loading on a river steamer
ound for Gao, a town of the ancient Mali
nd Songhai states.

3. Elmina (p. 5) castle built
by the Portuguese in 1481–2
by assembling stone blocks
previously numbered in Portugal and taken out in many
vessels. The castle is in excellent preservation and serves
as a Police Training College.

4. An 'inselberg', near Abuja, Northern Nigeria. A remnant of an older and higher surface, its hard granite has enabled it to resist erosion, in contrast to surrounding rocks which have been weathered away. It has the characteristic sheer but rounded form of a granite mass.

5. The western part of the High Atlas, near Iger, Morocco. The road rises to 6,825 feet. Cultivation terraces are visible.

whereas in North, Central and South Africa they have sometimes worked alongside Africans as skilled or even unskilled workers, not always without racial tension or for equivalent wages.

Growing industrial centres soon suffered a shortage of manpower, caused not merely by the subsistence nature of native economies and the low levels of education, health and technical skill, but also by the youthfulness of the population and the small number of adults. Industrialization therefore necessitated migrations of labour from areas of high rural population density (Fig. 13). Sometimes colonial governments mistakenly took advantage of the African custom of communal work for the chief or tribe in order forcibly to secure manpower, and forced labour has been, for example, a characteristic feature of Portuguese territories. The import of indentured Indian labourers to South Africa and East Africa also caused considerable social and political problems. Although the great majority of wage labourers in Africa are immigrants to the areas in which they are working, a stabilized labour force is emerging.

Regional Developments

In North and West Africa the main concentrations of wage earning urban populations tend to be located in the ports, which in exporting raw materials have become the foci of processing and secondary industries. Examples are Alexandria, Tripoli, Tunis, Algiers, Oran, Casablanca, Dakar-Rufisque, Abidjan, Takoradi, Tema, Lagos, Port Harcourt and Douala. Interior towns are more often administrative and trading centres which have been less industrialized; they include Kairouan, Constantine, Fez, Marrakesh, Kumasi, and Kaduna. The Nile Valley is, of course, exceptional. Usually in North and West Africa mining townships are small. The presence of large numbers of Europeans in the Maghreb has greatly stimulated the growth in the number of wage earners, who are much more numerous than those in West Africa. In the latter, mining and lumber workers account for a considerable proportion of the total number of wage earners.

As mining, industries and towns are not extensive in East Africa, the proportion of wage earners is not high. Large scale migration of labour is therefore not so vexing a problem; most of the labour for plantations and African cash crop cultivation is drawn from local sources.

Wage earners are much more numerous in the Congo where plantations and mining assume a marked importance. Their proportion is highest in Katanga where copper and other metals are the foundation of modern developments. Such features are repeated in the

4

great mining centres of South Africa, Zambia and Rhodesia, but European farming and manufacturing have also contributed to the increase in wage earners. Together they have engendered massive labour migrations in a part of Africa which was formerly sparsely populated (Fig. 13). Malawi, Mozambique and Angola, less colonized and little industrialized, have become labour reservoirs for the more developed parts of southern Africa.

TOWN LIFE

Large parts of Africa had no towns until recent times. Among the reasons for the lack of urban life are the absence of industry, the prevalence of pastoral nomadism and fallow farming, as well as the habit of establishing new capitals with each new ruler. Notable exceptions to this generalization are found in parts of West Africa— especially the Yoruba cities (e.g. Ibadan, Lagos, Ogbomosho, Abeokuta, Ilorin, Oshogbo) —along the Swahili coast of East Africa, the Nile Valley and the Maghreb. Even in these regions large cities were rare, for unlike the towns of Europe they were not based on industrialization. Although Yoruba cities were important craft and trading centres, their inhabitants were mainly farmers who were organized socially on the basis of kinship. These towns were without imposing public buildings, and the most impressive sights were the markets. The walled towns of the western Sudan, like Timbuktu and Kano, were primarily trading centres for trans-Saharan traffic and for the forest areas to the south. As for the old Arab towns of the Maghreb and coastal East Africa, they were small and functioned as markets, ports, craft and religious centres.

The tendency towards modern urbanization is largely a result of contact with the West, especially through the arrival of European town dwellers, the advent of modern communications, the export of raw materials, and the growth of commerce and industry. Towns are attractive to migrants for other reasons, such as their cinemas, cafés and bars. Urbanization has greatly accelerated with increased investment and development plans.

Old and New Towns

In general two types of towns may be distinguished in Africa: old established towns, such as the majority of those in the interior of West Africa, Tanzania, Uganda and Ethiopia; and new towns growing rapidly like many of those in North Africa, coastal West Africa, South Africa, Zambia, Rhodesia, Kenya and the Congo.

These two classes may tend to veil a complete range of towns, but will facilitate understanding of the processes of urbanization.

The old towns are closely associated with agriculture and have grown out of distinctive cultures. Many of their residents have originated from the immediate environs and are engaged in a wide variety of occupations. Much of the housing development has been uncontrolled, and ranges in character from slums to mansions. Unless they have been almost completely Europeanized, as in the case of Algiers, few of the old towns grew rapidly; Ibadan is an exception. Some have been scarcely affected by European contact.

On the other hand, the new towns have grown out of a relationship to Europe, rather than to their surrounding areas. Growth has been so rapid in some cases, such as Leopoldville, Nairobi and Casablanca, that they may be justifiably called mushroom towns. Some have exceeded the capacity of their hinterlands to support them, and must rely on imported foodstuffs. Occupations have been dominated frequently by large business organizations, so that it is fairly easy to classify new African towns according to their primary function. This task will become more difficult as manufacture of consumer goods increases and functions diversify.

Europeans have greatly influenced the forms of these new towns, as well as the styles of housing and shops. This accounts for some of the architectural differences between, say, Tunis and Tripoli, or between Abidjan and Accra. But, on the whole, new towns exhibit remarkable monotony of layout, and are mainly noteworthy for their sharp distinctions between European, African and, sometimes, Asian quarters. In Algeria, Tunisia and Morocco, the nature of this distinction was determined by the policy for urban expansion in each of these territories of former French North Africa. Europeans have controlled housing in many new towns in Africa, and Africans have often been confined to special areas. Examples are seen in Zambia and Rhodesia, and in the mining towns of the Congo (Leopoldville), where housing is institutional.

In Kenya, African residential housing has been provided by the local authorities. Although the quality of this housing is usually higher than that of African constructions, the amount is often insufficient to meet the growing demand. The result is that a large proportion of African urban populations live in the grossly over-crowded conditions of suburban shanty-towns. On the other hand, in providing housing facilities the authorities could not ignore the fact that the new townspeople of Africa are essentially a labour force, comprising a great majority of young men and small proportions of women, children and old people. The newer the town the more abnormal the age and sex composition of the population. Housing has, therefore, often been provided for individuals rather than families.

African urban populations are characterized by poverty, malnutrition and disease. They are also heterogeneous and temporary. One reason is undoubtedly the character of industrialization, involving a small degree of mechanization and a large quantity of unskilled labour. The towns have become poles of attraction, especially for those areas suffering from overpopulation.

Degree of Urbanization

It would be wrong to exaggerate the degree of urbanization in Africa. While Europeans and Asians are mostly concentrated in

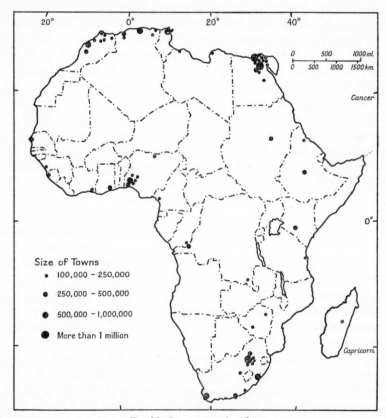

Fig. 20. Large towns in Africa

towns, Africans are still primarily rural. In the Republic of South Africa about one-quarter of Africans live in towns, in Egypt over one-third, and in the countries of the Maghreb from one-fifth to one-quarter, but in other territories, especially in East Africa, the proportion may be less than five per cent. Egypt has thirteen towns with more than 100,000 people and South Africa has ten, and both countries have conurbations numbering over one million people; in East Africa however, the largest town is Nairobi (300,000) on a site which was uninhabited at the beginning of the century.

Broadly speaking, urbanization is greatest where European influences are most profound. Towns are mainly road and rail centres, and ports. Few large towns are remote from the coast, and so to some extent they are an index of economic development. Large towns in Africa (Fig. 20) form well-marked clusters in the Maghreb, Egypt, Nigeria and South Africa. Isolated exceptions are Dakar, Khartoum-Omdurman, Addis Ababa, Leopoldville and Brazzaville—large capitals of states which are feebly urbanized. At the same time, a number of African countries, such as Mauritania, Spanish Sahara, Niger and Chad, have little experience of urbanization.

FURTHER READING

Valuable general texts are: Lord Hailey, *An African Survey*, 1957; G. H. T. Kimble, *Tropical Africa*, Vol. 1, New York, 1960; E. B. Worthington, *Science in the Development of Africa*, 1959; G. P. Murdock, *Africa: Its Peoples and their Culture History*, New York, 1959; D. Westermann, *The African Today and Tomorrow*, 3rd Ed., 1949; International African Institute, *Social Implications of Industrialization and Urbanization in Africa South of the Sahara*, UNESCO, 1956; *The Sociological Review*, New series, Vol. 7, no. 1, July 1959, Special number on 'Urbanism in West Africa'; W. O. Brown (Ed.), 'Contemporary Africa: Trends and Issues', *Annals of the American Academy of Political and Social Science*, 298, 1955, 1–179; J. Phillips, *Agriculture and Ecology in Africa*, 1959; E. J. Russell, *World Population and World Food Supplies*, 1954, 174–317; W. Hance, *African Economic Development*, 1958; United Nations, *Economic Survey of Africa since 1950*, New York, 1959; S. Haden Guest, J. K. Wright and E. M. Teclaff (Eds.), *A World Geography of Forest Resources*, New York, 1956, 341–91; L. P. Green and T. J. D. Fair, *Development in Africa*, Johannesburg, 1962. Several contain extensive bibliographies. Two useful articles (with maps) are G. P. Murdock, 'Staple Subsistence Crops of Africa', *Geographical Review*, 1960, 523–40, and W. Deshler, 'Cattle in Africa: Distribution, Types and Problems', *Geographical Review*, 1963, 52–8.

II

REGIONAL STUDIES

NORTH-WEST AFRICA

CHAPTER FIVE

The Maghreb

DJEZIRA EL MAGHREB, 'the Western Isle', is the name given by the
Arabs of the Middle East to those parts of Morocco, Algeria and
Tunisia which are dominated by the Atlas Mountains. Germans have
called it Africa-Minor, Frenchmen know it as *l'Afrique du Nord*, and
Englishmen often refer to it as the Barbary States. The adjective
'Barbary' exaggerates the importance of Berber influence, so 'The
Maghreb' is the best term, because the region is at the western
extremity of the Arab world and an island between the Mediterranean
and the Sahara. Furthermore, in many ways it is a zone of contact and
transition between Europe and Africa, as well as between nomad and
cultivator, between the desert and the sown.

The transitional nature of the Maghreb has impeded the political
unity which its mountain ranges, Mediterranean influences and
physical separateness would seem to suggest. Although the Maghreb
has never achieved political unity, it justifies general treatment before
consideration of the three individual territories. All three have
Saharan sectors, but these will be examined in Chapter Six.

THE PHYSICAL ENVIRONMENT

The Regions

The group of mountain chains which are collectively known as the
Atlas Mountains are the result of Tertiary orogenesis of marine
sediments deposited in the Tyrrhenian geosyncline. They incorporate
only isolated fragments of the Primary Basement which prevails farther
south. Broadly speaking, the Atlas Mountains bear structural resem-
blances to the Alpine mountain chains on the northern side of the
Mediterranean, although the nature of the structural links across the
Straits of Gibraltar and the Sicilian Sea is a matter of considerable
speculation. Evidence of the structural instability of the Maghreb is
found in the appallingly destructive earthquakes at Orléansville
(Algeria) in 1954 and at Agadir (Morocco) in 1960.

* By John I. Clarke.

The Atlas system falls into three distinct entities:

(*a*) The Coastal Mountains of the Rif and Tellian Atlas;
(*b*) The High Atlas and Saharan Atlas;
(*c*) The Middle Atlas.

The Coastal Mountains are represented at their western extremity by the wild, wooded Rif, a structurally simple mountain chain rising to over 7,300 feet. Unfortunately, it hinders east–west communications, and was partly responsible for the backwardness of the former Protectorate of Spanish Morocco, which was largely confined to it. Eastwards, in Algeria, the complex series of coastal ranges, plateaux and plains known as the Tellian Atlas determines the alignment of the coastline. It contains several highly individual Primary massifs, including Great and Little Kabylie between Algiers and the Tunisian boundary, where sedentary village life is traditional. The Northern Tell of Tunisia, like the bulk of the Tellian Atlas, is composed of limestones, sandstones and clays, but changes direction to south-west–north-east as if to indicate possible structural connexions with Sicily.

The High Atlas and Saharan Atlas, along the northern fringes of the Sahara, stretch about 1,250 miles from Agadir on the Atlantic to the Cape Bon Peninsula in north-east Tunisia. In general, their altitude increases westward. The High Atlas rises to over 13,000 feet (Plate 5) and for 500 miles presents steep walls to north and south: to the plain of the Haouz of Marrakesh, and to the synclinal basin of the Sous between the High Atlas and the Anti-Atlas. The latter is really an uplifted edge of the Saharan platform and is, therefore, geologically distinct from the rest of the Atlas Mountains, although its human occupation is not unusual. East of the High Atlas is a long series of limestone and sandstone escarpments and plateaux—the Mountains of the Ksours, the Amour, the Ouled Naïl, the Ziban and the Aurès—which together form the Saharan Atlas. They are lower than the High Atlas, and appear to be in a more advanced stage of erosion; viewed from the air they look buried in their own debris. In eastern Algeria and central Tunisia the main mountain chain turns north-eastward and converges on the Northern Tell. In Tunisia it is called the High Tell or Dorsale (French: 'backbone'), as it forms a diagonal barrier across the country dividing the Mediterranean north from the Steppe and Desert south. However, one or two east–west mountain ranges occur south of the Dorsale and, separated by high plains, they constitute a region known as the High Steppe.

The Middle Atlas is a formidable barrier linking the High Atlas and the Rif in eastern Morocco. It is a regularly folded chain with summits

4*

nearly 10,000 feet high, separating Atlantic Morocco from eastern Morocco. At its northern extremity is the Col of Taza, the main route between Morocco and Algeria.

Three areas of plateaux and plains are defined by the mountain chains:

  (i) The Plateaux and Plains of Atlantic Morocco;
 (ii) The High Plateaux of the Shotts;
(iii) The Low Steppe of eastern Tunisia.

The Plateaux and Plains of Atlantic Morocco are surrounded by the Rif, the Middle Atlas and the High Atlas, and include not merely the basin of the Sebou, the sedimentary plains of the Chaouïa, the Tadla, the Haouz of Marrakesh and the coastal plains, but also the Primary massifs of the Moroccan Meseta, namely the Central Massif, the Massif of the Rehamna and the Djebilet.

The High Plateaux of the Shotts stretch almost 500 miles from east to west, from the Middle Atlas in Morocco to the convergence of its northern and southern barriers, the Tellian Atlas and the Saharan Atlas, in western Tunisia. The plateaux are extremely monotonous expanses of thick alluvium. In eastern Morocco they are 100 miles wide and 3,500–4,000 feet high, but they become narrower and lower towards Tunisia. Their name is derived from the presence of several vast saline mud flats, known as shotts, which are the result of internal drainage. The Low Steppe of eastern Tunisia, south of the Dorsale, is another semi-arid alluvial plain. The occasional torrential flows of *wadis* (usually written *oueds* in North Africa, and meaning watercourses) descending from the Dorsale across the Low Steppe sometimes reach the sea; more often they fan out and evaporate in *Sebkhas* (salt-marshes). Indeed, the flow of all wadis in the Maghreb is very irregular, and none is naturally perennial. In south-eastern Tunisia, the Low Steppe is prolonged by a coastal plain known as the Jefara, back on the southern side by a Cretaceous and Jurassic escarpment, which dips southwards under the dunes of the Grand Erg Oriental. Both plain and escarpment continue into Tripolitania.

Climatic Zones

The importance of climatic zonation is paramount in geographical study of the Maghreb. Rainfall is perhaps the key environmental influence on human activity. Two isohyets are often taken as the arbitrary boundaries between the major climatic regions; the 16-inch isohyet corresponds roughly with the limit between the Mediterranean

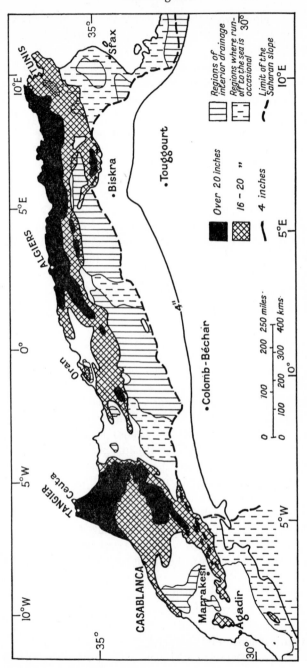

Fig. 21. Rainfall and run-off in the Maghreb

and Steppe regions, while the four-inch isohyet is accepted by many French authorities as the best climatic approximation to the boundary of the Sahara (Fig. 21).

The Mediterranean region experiences winter rainfall and three to four months of summer drought. Cereals (wheat and barley) can be cultivated without irrigation, vines, figs and olives generally bear fruit, and animals are rarely entirely without pastures. Variety of relief and of disposition to westerly winter depressions naturally induce regional differences in annual rainfall; some of the coastal ranges receive over 40 inches, others less than four inches. These differences join with geological influences in determining the main types of soils and vegetation. In the moister areas podzols on sandstones, and terra rossas and rendzinas on limestones are found clad with cork oaks, evergreen oaks and Aleppo pines. In the drier parts, crustal soils may develop and the two prominent trees, both coniferous, are Barbary thuya and juniper. However, much of the forest cover has been destroyed by the depredations of nomadic flocks (the goat is a special menace), as well as by clearing for cultivation. Consequently, bush vegetation reminiscent of the *maquis* and *garrigue* of southern France is very common.

The Steppe region, on the other hand, suffers from summer drought of five to six months duration. Rainfall tends to occur in spring and autumn rather than in winter, but its unreliability makes the cultivation of cereals without irrigation a real gamble. Figs and olives which are not irrigated can only be regularly harvested in western Morocco and eastern Tunisia where maritime influences bring beneficial humidity. All reliable cultivation without irrigation becomes impossible where annual rainfall is less than eight inches. The soils are thin, light coloured and humus deficient, and the sparse vegetation is dominated by esparto grass and artemisias, with jujube-trees and dwarf palms along the wadis. On the uncultivable saline soils around the edges of the sebkhas, saltbush is common. The Steppe region is primarily the domain of pastoralism, especially of semi-nomadism, although its utilization is not wholly determined by climate. Much depends, as we shall see, on the traditions, aims and resources of man.

The presence of these two distinct zones in the Maghreb has meant that nomad and cultivator have always been in close juxtaposition. The nomads dominated the sedentary peoples for centuries and prevented political unity and stability. Nevertheless, the zones were complementary, because nomads and cultivators were able to exchange products. With the French occupation of the Maghreb in the nineteenth and early twentieth centuries the two zones evolved disharmoniously; the Mediterranean zone was heavily colonized and cropped and experienced an economic revolution, while the Steppe zone remained largely neglected and its nomadic inhabitants were often deprived of seasonal access to pastures in the former zone.

This dual division of the Maghreb is naturally a simplification of complex regional environments, as well as of seasonal and annual climatic variations. In winter, the whole of the Maghreb is influenced to some extent by Mediterranean climatic conditions. Yet winter is not a prolonged rainy season; rains are often torrential and provoke heavy soil erosion and flooding. In summer, Saharan conditions prevail and temperatures and evaporation soar, especially during a *Sirocco*, the hot, dusty blast from the Sahara which drastically reduces humidity, withers crops and causes much discomfort. It has many other names: *Chergui* in Morocco, *Chehili* in Algeria, *Ghibli* in Tripolitania, and *Khamsin* in Egypt.

INVADING PEOPLES: AN HISTORICAL RÉSUMÉ

One of the most interesting aspects of the historical geography of the Maghreb is the way in which each invading people has viewed the environment through different eyes and from different points of view, with the result that economy and settlement patterns have varied through the ages.

Berbers and Phoenicians

Prehistoric peoples occupied several parts of the Maghreb, but the basic autochthonous element today are the Berbers. The word 'Berber' is derived from the Latin *barbari*, which meant all people foreign to the Romans. The Berbers have an individual language but no literature or homogeneous racial characteristics; they include Mediterranean, Alpine and even Nordic types. Today, the Berbers are chiefly concentrated in the mountains of Morocco and Algeria, where they retain their complex family and political systems as well as their rural customs. They were hunters, cultivators and nomads when Phoenician traders established posts along the coasts between 1200 B.C. and the third Punic war (149–146 B.C.). Carthage, near Tunis, was the focus of Phoenician activity, but although better methods of olive cultivation were taught to the natives little colonization took place.

Romans

The Romans also settled the Maghreb in small numbers, but they extended cultivation by dry-farming and irrigation techniques, exported oil and wheat to Rome, built towns and strategic routes, created four provinces, and transformed the eastern Maghreb. Splendid amphitheatres, coliseums, aqueducts, triumphal arches and other Roman remains are still visible in many places in North Africa. In southern Tunisia the Roman *limes* (frontier) extended to the limit of the desert, to which nomadism was repelled. Even the Vandals could not entirely destroy the Roman works, and later the French were to learn much from Roman agricultural methods in semi-arid areas.

Arabs

The greatest destruction of Roman efforts was wrought by invading Arab tribes from the east. The first wave came in the seventh century A.D., and brought the Islamic religion. Islam, with observances such as purdah and the Friday visit to the mosque, is deeply rooted in the towns, in which mosques are prominent features. Some mosques, indeed, became Islamic universities (Fez, Tunis and Kairouan). However, the main Arab invasions came in the eleventh century, when the warlike nomads of the Beni Hillal and Beni Suleim tribes descended upon the Maghreb 'like a wave of locusts'. Agriculture dwindled and retreated before the nomads. Cultivators found security only in mountain fastnesses, where their castellated *ksours* (fortified granaries) are picturesque sights today. Here the Berber language survived, whereas on the plains Arabic became dominant, although it would be wrong to believe that all Berbers are cultivators and all Arabs nomads. The nomads brought a new tribal system, which emphasized the authority of the sheikh and contrasted with the more democratic Berber system, and also brought the Islamic system of land tenure. They scorned sedentary cultivators, and often reduced them to serfdom by enforcing their 'protection' at a heavy price. Wars and internecine troubles among the nomads, and later piracy, produced internal anarchy, which only subsided when tribal groups united to form confederations, captured an important town, and achieved political supremacy. This was invariably short-lived, because nomads seemed to lose their strength and cohesion in urban life.

Town and country were alien elements, and each town (*medina*) had high surrounding walls and a fortress (*kasbah*) for defence against nomadic marauders. Within the walls, the labyrinthine street pattern was partly caused by the absence of wheeled traffic and the prevalence of camel transport.

Turks

From the sixteenth century onwards the Turks were masters of the central and eastern parts of the Maghreb. Only the western Maghreb remained independent. New administrative boundaries were established, but the rule of the Turks was military and fiscal, and thus they had little influence on the racial and linguistic composition of the population. The Maghreb remained backward and decadent; piracy was rife, the nomads maintained their internal supremacy at the expense of the cultivators, and widespread urban life was mainly restricted to eastern Tunisia. Elsewhere, agriculture was localized on mountain slopes and valleys. One of the few happy features of the period was the immigration of 'Andalusians', Moslems expelled from southern Spain, who brought craft trades to some towns (e.g. Tetuan and Tunis) and established peasant villages in north-east Tunisia.

THE EUROPEAN TRANSFORMATION OF THE MAGHREB

The French occupation of the Maghreb brought rapid political and economic transformation. France did not occupy the Maghreb all at once. Algiers was taken in 1830, but other parts of Algeria, in particular Kabylie, were not subdued until 1857. For a long time Algeria was a military colony, but after 1870—when the policy of Assimilation came into vogue—it became part of France, and that part of Algeria within the Maghreb became three *départements*. On the other hand, the Saharan lands stayed under military rule. The administrative framework remained virtually unchanged until 1959 when twelve *départements* were established. Independence came in 1962 after eight years of war with France. Tunisia, occupied in 1881, and Morocco, divided between France and Spain in 1912, were Protectorates, a fact which facilitated their independence in 1956. Tunisia later deposed its Bey and became a Republic, while the Sultan of Morocco assumed the title of King. The shorter and less intensive occupation of the two Protectorates by France has added to the variety of economic and social progress in the Maghreb.

Following the independence of Morocco, the only remaining footholds of Spain in North Africa are the enclave of Ifni and the *Plazas de Soberanía* (fortified places of Spanish sovereignty') including the garrison towns (Presidios) of Ceuta and Melilla, and a few islets off the northern coast of Morocco.

The impact of European culture on this corner of the Moslem world has led to great material changes: order and regular administration, fixation of boundaries, European colonization, evolution in agriculture and land tenure, increase in population, industrialization, growth of towns, and the construction of roads, railways, ports, airports, hospitals, schools, hotels and many other facilities. In much of the Maghreb French culture has been superimposed on Moslem culture, with the result that there are many striking contrasts in ways and standards of living. It is true that many Moslems speak French, wear European clothes, and are no longer fervently religious, but they remain attached to Arab civilization and have strong national feelings.

Growth of Population

The European population of the Maghreb reached its peak in 1956 when there were more than one and three-quarter millions, of whom about 56 per cent lived in Algeria, about 30 per cent in Morocco and 14 per cent in Tunisia. Even then, Europeans constituted only a small minority of the total population of 22 millions. By 1963 the total population had risen to 27 million, but the European population had fallen to less than one million as the result of hasty departures for Europe from all three countries of the Maghreb. Apart from Frenchmen, there are also important minorities of Italians in Tunisia (45,000 in 1961), and of Spaniards in north-western Algeria. Maltese, Greeks and Jews form other minorities.

The Moslem population has doubled in the last 25 years, largely owing to the great reduction in mortality; the introduction of modern medicine by the French has eliminated cholera and pest, and greatly reduced typhus and many former killing diseases. Unfortunately, malnutrition and deficiency diseases are still common. On the other hand, in a population with a youthful age structure, fertility remains high and large families are still a matter of pride. Polygamy is less important than generally imagined, but divorce, which is very easily acquired, especially if the wife does not bear a son, leads to the establishment of successive families.

Urban Growth and Morphology

Four out of five Europeans live in towns, especially the ports, like Casablanca, Tangier, Oran, Algiers, Bône, Bizerta, Tunis, Sousse and Sfax, where they are professional men, skilled workers and traders. The towns in which Europeans have settled have become magnets for the native population, who have been attracted by the opportunities for employment and the social amenities; they have also been repelled from rural areas by drought, poverty and hunger, by the expansion of European colonization, and by the over-population in those mountain massifs which were formerly regions of refuge from nomads (for example the Anti-Atlas, the western High Atlas, the Rif and Kabylie). The result is that many towns have grown at an astonishing rate. Casablanca, a tiny village in 1912, had 965,000 inhabitants in 1960, when Algiers had grown to 884,000 inhabitants and Tunis to 680,000.

The morphology of the towns has naturally changed. The old crowded *medinas*, with their narrow streets, closed courtyards, bustling bazaars (*souks*) and poor sanitation, presented an unattractive prospect for European residents, who found various solutions to the problem. In Algiers, for example, the old medina was opened up by new roads, at Tunis a 'grid-iron' European town was built alongside the medina (Fig. 26), and at Fez a twin town was constructed some distance away. On the outskirts of many of these growing towns are large, sordid shanty-towns (*bidonvilles*), which are scenes of great poverty. Sometimes the Europeans created entirely new towns, like Sidi bel Abbès in Algeria. Those traditional Moslem towns which proved unsuitable to European settlement, such as Kairouan, Monastir and Mahdia in Tunisia, and Tlemçen in Algeria, have tended to stagnate.

The medinas have also experienced some changes of character. Artisans once formed about one-third of their inhabitants, and congregated in separate streets according to their craft: artisans of the quieter and nobler trades—perfumers, incense makers, book-sellers and goldsmiths—in the centre of the medina alongside the mosque; and those with the noisier, dirtier crafts near the walls. In the face of competition from European mass production the number of artisans has declined, and although each street in the souk has its special trade, many of the goods are imported and shoddy.

Industrialization

In the early stages of European occupation there was little indus-trialization in the ports, little processing of the raw materials exported, and all manufactured goods were imported. There were several reasons. Local power resources seemed scanty. Saharan oil and natural gas were discoveries of the mid-1950s, and even today the Maghreb has only a few small oilfields, the most important being near Souk el Arba in northern Morocco, and near Relizane in Algeria. There are only two coalfields, each producing one-half million tons per annum, and located at Djerada (Morocco) and Colomb-Béchar (Algeria), 75 and 350 miles respectively south of the port of Nemours. There were the usual difficulties associated with hydro-electric power stations in semi-arid areas, namely irregular river flow and rapid silting of reservoirs. At the same time, skilled labour was very short and the market poor; so there was little investment in industries until after the last war. Since then, investment has greatly increased, and many industries have grown up on the outskirts of the major ports, especially of Casablanca, Algiers and Tunis: engineering and the production of olive oil, flour, jams, beverages, canned foods, textiles, leather and chemicals (superphosphates, copper sulphate and soap) are noteworthy. Moreover, despite the natural difficulties, many hydro-electric installations have been established, especially in the Mediterranean zone.

Mining

Phosphates and iron ore have been the two principal mining products of the Maghreb (Fig. 22). The total annual production of phosphate rock exceeds seven million tons, sixty per cent of which comes from the great deposits of Khouribga and Louis Gentil in Morocco, and the remainder from a zone along the Algerian–Tunisian boundary—particularly from the four mines near Gafsa in central Tunisia. These latter deposits have a lower percentage of phosphorus than those of Morocco, and mining suffers from keen competition.

The same zone is also important for iron-ore production, but in this case mining is greater in Algeria than in Tunisia. The Ouenza and Bou Khadra mines in the Tebessa area now produce over three million tons of ore annually, whereas the Djerissa mine in Tunisia produces only just over one million tons. The other significant orefield is at Kelata near the port of Melilla in Morocco, where annual production is one and a quarter million tons. Phosphates and iron ore are mined by large foreign companies which have constructed railways and mining towns, but have exported most of the production.

Other minerals, mined in smaller quantities, include lead, zinc, manganese, cobalt and molybdenum, but production depends on world prices. The lead mines at Bou Bekker in eastern Morocco produce about 70,000 tons a year.

Fishing

Fishing was for long a local and neglected industry, but has taken a new lease of life since the war owing to the infusion of European

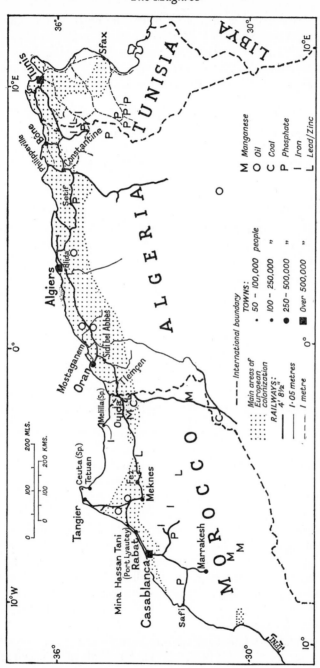

Fig. 22. Towns, railways, mining and colonization in the Maghreb

capital, particularly in Morocco, where the ports of Casablanca, Mogador, Agadir and Safi have developed many sardine factories. In Algeria and Tunisia, Italian, Greek and Maltese fishermen are prominent, although some come only for the season. Two special types of fishing off the Tunisian coast are for tuna and sponges.

European Rural Colonization and Traditional Agriculture

Europeans settled mainly in the Mediterranean and Atlantic zones of the Maghreb, in northern Algeria and Tunisia and western Morocco (Fig. 22). Colonization, both private and official, that is, state-directed, has transformed the aspect of the plains, formerly the scene of insecurity, pastoralism and, sometimes, of pestilence. Nearly eleven million acres were colonized by Europeans by 1950, who then occupied a considerable proportion of the total cultivable area. Since then this figure has been greatly reduced. Although some of the colonized land had previously been almost neglected, much was very fertile.

EUROPEAN COLONIZATION
(*c.* 1950)
Area in Acres

	Official	*Private*	*Total*	*Number of Farms*
Algeria	4,250,000	2,500,000	6,750,000	26,000
Tunisia	687,500	1,437,500	2,125,000	4,000
Morocco (excluding ex-Spanish zone)	998,750	927,500	1,926,250	6,000
	5,936,250	4,865,000	10,801,250	36,000

European and native agricultural production contrast greatly. Europeans are mainly interested in cash crops for export and generally pay scant attention to livestock; while local farmers are more concerned with crops and stock for local consumption. European crop yields are higher and more regular than those of natives; they occupy larger and more fertile farms in areas of fairly reliable rainfall, invest more capital, and buy more fertilizers and machinery. Native agriculture relies more on the vagaries of rainfall and on the will of Allah, and suffers from disastrous annual vicissitudes which affect the whole life of rural areas; marriages, house construction, nutrition and health all depend on the bounty of nature.

Wheat and barley are basic cash crops for the European farmer and subsistence crops for the Moslem (Fig. 23). While the Moslem relies

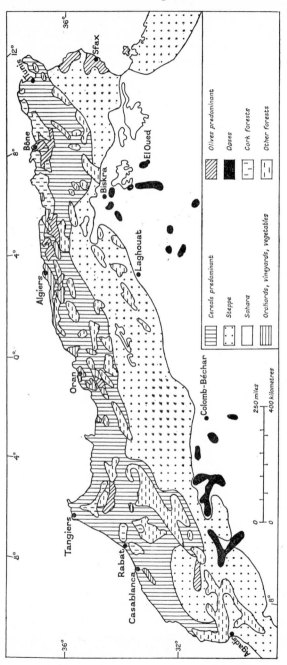

Fig. 23. Land use of the Maghreb

mainly on hard wheat, Europeans use special drought-resisting varieties of soft wheat. They also employ dry-farming techniques in regions of less than 20 inches of rainfall per annum. Some of the richer Moslem farmers have copied the new methods and have succeeded; other poorer peasants with a more fatalistic approach to farming were unable to compete, sold their lands and migrated to the towns.

In the moister regions some European farms practise mixed farming, but the main attention is devoted to the vine, especially in Algeria. The vineyards of Algeria now cover one million acres and, until the export of Saharan oil, wine provided well over one-half of the value of Algerian exports; 40–60 thousand million francs worth go annually to France, herself the world's largest producer. Vines are a rich crop, and are associated with much more intensive exploitation and denser settlement than cereals. Like many of the vineyards, market gardens were often developed by Italians and Spaniards, and are found around the principal towns. Market gardens permit an even denser colonization than vineyards, as two crops (potatoes, tomatoes, peas, beans, artichokes etc.) are grown every year.

Not all regions of the Mediterranean zone have been densely colonized; some well peopled areas, especially mountain massifs, remain in the hands of North Africans. In Kabylie, for example, native arboriculture, including olives, figs, peaches, apricots, almonds and grenadines, enables a dense population to survive, but not without considerable periodic migration to the towns and to France. Thousands of Kabyles are found in Paris.

European colonization has penetrated the Steppe zone in several places, in particular the Low Steppe of eastern Tunisia around the port of Sfax. Here, millions of olive trees are arranged geometrically and were established by a small number of Frenchmen, some of whom were not resident in the area. The development has taken place by contracting out the work to native tenant-farmers (*mgharsa*), and by copying Roman cultivation methods. It has led to little European settlement.

NATIVE NOMADISM AND CULTIVATION ON THE STEPPES
Nomadism

The Steppes of the Maghreb are still primarily the domain of pastoral nomads who migrate with their sheep, goats and camels (dromedaries in North Africa) in search of pastures. Pure nomads are rare in the Steppe zone; most are semi-nomads who also sow cereals in moister hollows and along wadi beds, and live several months of the year in villages or fixed encampments. The time spent with the flocks, their size and composition, and the distances of migration vary from tribe to tribe. There are numerous grades and types of semi-nomadism, which depend to some extent on the terrain (Fig. 24). Although the majority of semi-nomads inhabit the plains, some live in the mountains of the Middle Atlas, the eastern High Atlas, the eastern Rif, the Aurès, and the Mountains of the Ksours in southern Tunisia, where they cultivate irrigated crops in the valleys and practise a form of transhumance.

The scene on most of the Steppes has changed little in comparison with the agricultural revolution in the Mediterranean zone, although horses are rare as raiding is no longer permissible, and fewer camels are required for caravans. The pulling of esparto grass (used for making fine paper) has become an important supplement, huts and small houses have appeared near many winter camps, and large tribal units have become less integrated following the increased importance of migrations for work, but on the whole the Steppes are very backward in comparison with the Mediterranean zone. The nomads have also suffered from developments in the north, where there used to be ample summer pastures for Steppe and Saharan flocks, as well as harvest work for the nomads. It was a region of refuge during summer drought. Now these northward migrations are anachronistic and sorrowful because there are fewer pastures available and the harvesting is mostly done by combine-harvesters.

Steppe Cultivation

The Steppes are therefore in urgent need of development before depopulation takes place. The environment is marginal for agriculture, but in certain areas cultivation and village life have persisted for centuries, despite the surrounding nomads. Tunisian examples are the coastal zone of native olive cultivation known as the Sahel of Sousse, the small densely populated island of Djerba (sometimes called 'the Island of the Lotus-eaters'), and the Jebel Matmata in the south, where troglodyte villages, fortified granaries and valley cultivation prevail. The sedentary peoples of these regions now practise a very profitable form of periodic emigration to the major towns, where they have established quasi-monopolies of certain crafts and trades. Djerbian grocers, for example, are so common all over Tunisia that the words Djerbian and grocer are almost synonymous.

Elsewhere in the Steppe zone there are possibilites of extending the cultivated area, especially in Morocco, where arboriculture should

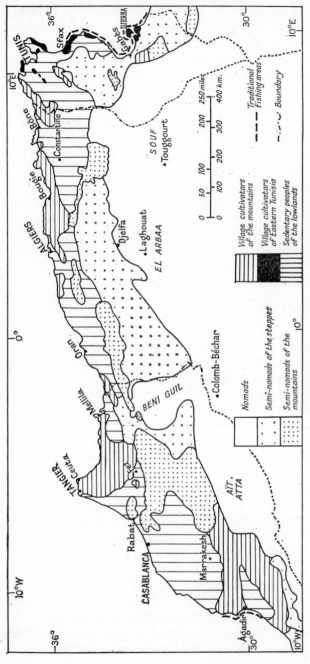

Fig. 24. Rural modes of life in the Maghreb (After Despois and Dresch)

develop. Its extension, however, depends on the settlement of the nomads, a difficult task involving numerous social, financial, legal and educational problems. Moreover, there is also a great need for forage crops to provide feed for stock in times of drought. Successful settlement of nomads has been achieved in certain localities, in particular among the Ouled Sidi Ali ben Aoun, a tribe of some 4,000, who have been settled on a small part of the High Steppe of central Tunisia. The main difficulty is water. Although large dams have proved successful for hydro-electricity and irrigation in the Mediterranean zone, they are of little value on the Steppes where the flow of wadis is too capricious. Smaller more temporary dams are here more adequate. Fortunately, oases along the desert margins benefit from artesian water located in Tertiary and Cretaceous aquifers, as well as in the Inter-Calary Continental Albienne nappe which offers so much hope in the Sahara.

POLITICAL UNITS

The boundaries of the three countries of the Maghreb—Morocco, Algeria and Tunisia—were established by the Turks and fixed by the French. They reflect the more traditional division of the Maghreb into western, central and eastern sectors, a division based not merely on physical characteristics but also on cultural traditions. The three countries have different personalities; Morocco has been likened to a lion, Algeria a bear, and Tunisia a woman.

ALGERIA

Algeria north of the Sahara covers about 125,000 square miles, and has a Mediterranean coastline of nearly 600 miles. In many ways it occupies the most unfavoured part of the Maghreb. The Mediterranean zone is narrow and has a vigorous relief, while the Steppe and Desert zones have smoother landforms and push farther north than in Morocco and Tunisia. The disposition of these climatic zones has enabled pastoral nomads to dominate most of the country in the past, and cultural life has been largely confined to a few northern towns. Accordingly, Algeria knew little political stability.

One important consequence of French rule is the rapid growth of the Moslem population. In 1836, Algeria had about $2\frac{1}{2}$ million Moslems; in 1960 it had $10 \cdot 2$ millions. The main causes of this growth are the decline in mortality and the youthful age-structure; over half of the Moslem population is less than twenty years old. About seventy per cent of the Moslems speak Arabic, and the rest are Berber speakers, who are localized in the mountains of Kabylie, Miliana, Aurès and Namemcha.

Despite great efforts to encourage French settlers during the nineteenth century, the total European population of Algeria only rose to one million by the mid-twentieth century, and no more than half were of French stock (mainly from southern France and Corsica). The remainder were from other parts of the Mediterranean, especially Spain, Italy and Malta. As a 'colonie de peuplement', Algeria was not a great success; four-fifths of the Europeans were town-dwellers. Since independence was granted in 1962, many hundreds of thousands of Europeans have departed.

Although in the 1950s there were less than 20,000 European farmers, they occupied one-third of the cultivated land, and their farms averaged over 260 acres, compared with the average of 15·6 acres of Moslem farms. Moreover, their distribution has accentuated inherent differences between western and eastern Algeria.

The narrow Tellian zone of north-western Algeria is lower, more fragmented and contains longer longitudinal plains than the eastern Tell. In the north-west, Moslem shifting cultivators on the low plains were almost entirely replaced by colonists, especially Spaniards, who have transformed the landscape by the creation of vineyards. Colonization has been restricted almost entirely to the plains, which farther south are used for cereals. Southward again, pastoral nomadism and shifting cultivation of cereals prevail on the Steppes, which also provide esparto grass in plenty, while in the massifs of the Saharan Atlas perched villages and fortified granaries indicate the location of summer pastures.

Oran (393,000) is the principal port of western Algeria, exporting wine, grain, esparto and sheep, and importing manufactured goods. It is the most European town in Algeria and is mainly a product of this century; in 1831 it had 3,000 inhabitants. It has no monopoly of the maritime trade of western Algeria, as Mostaganem also exports agricultural products, while Nemours and Beni Saf export coal and iron ore respectively.

Eastern Algeria is more mountainous and more Berber. The dense populations and traditional cultivation of tree crops, especially olives, in the coastal massifs of Great and Little Kabylie restricted colonization to isolated coastal plains and wider valleys. European farmers are fewer southward across the high plains of Constantine, and their cereal cultivation is replaced by Steppe. Beyond, in the Aurès Mountains, are the Berber Chaouia, who include groups of sedentary cultivators as well as semi-nomadic pastoralists practising summer transhumance to the high pastures.

In eastern Algeria, the presence along the frontier zone of phosphate deposits at Le Kouif and Jebel Onk, and of iron ore at Ouenza-Bou Khadra, attracted other colonial enterprises and caused the expansion of the port of Bône (164,000) which, like Oran, is a French creation. Exports include agricultural products, as well as minerals, but Bône has never had a great import trade. Until 1959, the trade of Bougie was similar to that of Bône on a much smaller scale, but in that year the 400-mile oil pipeline connected Bougie with Hassi Messaoud, and it began a new life as an oil terminal. Philippeville (88,000), between Bougie and Bône, fulfils the function for which it was founded in 1838, a port for the region of Constantine. Unlike most of the old towns of the interior of Algeria, Constantine (223,000) has grown as a trading centre, and its magnificent site overlooking the gorges of the Rummel is a valuable tourist attraction.

Algiers serves the transitional zone between eastern and western Algeria. The town is built on the slopes of the small massif of Bouzarea, below the old Turkish Kasbah, but the urban area now extends about 8 miles round the Bay of Algiers, and includes some 900,000 inhabitants. It is the capital, cultural, industrial and commercial centre, as well as the principal port. As the main link with Europe it has much of the character of a French city. To the south lies the plain of the Mitidja, one of the great feats of colonization; formerly an unhealthy marsh, it is now a maze of vineyards and market gardens.

Algeria did not produce untold wealth for France. Wine was for long its main export, often accounting for more than half of the total export trade, followed by iron ore, cereals, fruit and vegetables, all of which are produced in France. Moreover, despite the predominance of French goods among Algerian imports, they often amounted to less than one-fortieth of total French exports.

Algeria is primarily an agricultural country, native agriculture being largely concerned with cereals, livestock, olives and collected crops like esparto and cork, while Europeans have devoted their attention to vines, early vegetables, citrus fruits, industrial crops (tobacco, cotton), as well as cereals. The extension of the vine over one million acres is excessive, as the native majority of the population are forbidden on religious grounds to consume wine, and France is the world's largest producer. Yet France is committed to import substantial quantities of Algerian wine, although much is transformed into industrial alcohol. Other serious agricultural problems include the annual vicissitudes in production caused by variation in rainfall, soil erosion resulting from the devastation of forest and bush land, the shortage of adequate irrigation on the Steppes, and the overpopulation of the northern mountain massifs which suffer from fragmentation of property.

Algerian industrial development since the Second World War has been essentially concerned with the transformation of agricultural products—flour milling, distilling, jam and tobacco manufacture, preparation of cork and so on—and the industries are principally at the ports. The bulk of the iron ore and phosphates are still exported, and there is little heavy industry. Nevertheless, factories have appeared producing chemicals, cement, clothing, sugar, household equipment and miscellaneous other products. One of the reasons for the dearth of industry in the past was the shortage of power, but the post-war development of hydro-electricity in various parts of the Tellian Atlas, especially west of Algiers, and the discoveries of oil and gas in the Algerian Sahara, offer considerable hopes for the future (Chapter Six). Will sufficient industries be created to cope with the great demand for employment, or will Algerians continue to emigrate to France in large numbers ? Algeria needs great investments to develop her resources, especially in view of losses in war.

MOROCCO

The Kingdom of Morocco possesses stronger individuality than the other countries of North Africa, for which many reasons can be given. Although it has a double maritime façade, to the Atlantic and the Mediterranean, Morocco has been more open to Saharan influences. Tucked away in a corner of Africa, on the edge of both the Mediterranean and Arab worlds, Morocco has been far less influenced by Romans, Arabs and Frenchmen than either Algeria or Tunisia. To the north the mountain barrier of the Rif restricts the infiltration of Mediterranean influences, while off-shore bars and few maritime interests have in the past curbed port development on the Atlantic. There is also a greater contrast between mountain and plain which, along with the Atlantic façade, has provided Morocco with more beneficial watercourses and greater opportunities for agricultural expansion than are found further east. The mountains of Morocco are higher than elsewhere in North Africa (Tubkal in the High Atlas is 13,694 feet), and have acted both as a barrier against outside penetration as well as a refuge for the Berber way of life. Berber-speaking peoples constitute about 35 per cent of the total population of 11,599,000 (1960), and probably only ten to fifteen per cent of the tribes are of Arab origin. Arab influences have been greatest in the towns of the plains, where the number of Arabic speakers has continually increased.

During the period 1912–56, Morocco was divided into northern and southern Spanish Protectorates and the much larger French Protectorate, but pacification was only completed in 1934. Although modernization and development have been very rapid, there was little time available for a consolidation of European colonization. In 1951, there were 363,000 foreigners (83·7 per cent French) in the French zone, and in 1955 there were 91,000 Spaniards in the northern Spanish zone. Since independence in 1956 these numbers have greatly diminished; in particular, there have been many departures of European officials.

Morocco is a varied country, with diverse modes of life, which cannot always be explained by reference to environmental conditions; tribal traditions are often instrumental. The valleys of the western High Atlas and Anti-Atlas, for example, are inhabited by numerous sedentary cultivators of the Berber Chleuh tribes, who live in fortress-like villages; because of the density of population many of the Chleuh are forced to migrate to Casablanca and other towns in order to survive. On the other hand, the eastern High Atlas, the Middle Atlas and the Moroccan Meseta are more sparsely populated by semi-nomadic peoples who practise summer transhumance to high pastures, but usually pass the winter in fortified villages in the valleys. Environment has had more influences over the Berber peoples of the Rif; while the dry eastern Rif has a small population of pastoralists, the humid western Rif has a dense population of village cultivators. Wheat and sorghum are the principal cereals in the western Rif, but each farmer possesses some olive and fruit trees, as well as a small flock of sheep and goats. This economy does not suffice for the numerous inhabitants, and so emigration is very common.

In the far north-west of the Rif is the former International Zone of Tangier (142,000) which was integrated into Morocco in 1957. For long a financial and tourist centre, it was in 1962 declared the summer capital of Morocco and a 'free zone' for commercial purposes. It has a growing number of industries, and its port serves as a normal outlet for northern Morocco. There are plans to transform the harbour area into a free port, with an industrial zone for processing raw materials.

The position of the Spanish *Plazas de Soberanía* is delicate. The ancient port and walled city of Ceuta (60,000), which faces Gibraltar across the straits, developed as a military and administrative centre, but is now a bunkering and fishing port. It is smaller than Melilla

(80,000), the remote and more Moorish port of north-eastern Morocco, which annually exports over one million tons of the iron ore of Kelata. Tetuan (101,000) is the one large town in the north which is not a port, and it is the centre of the only extensive cultivated zone.

The plains of Morocco also offer considerable contrasts. The eastern high plains of the Dahra are merely a continuation of the Plateaux of the Shotts, and their alfa Steppes are pastured by nomadic tribes of the Beni Guil who penetrate far north, and crossed by the railway line connecting the coalfield of Colomb-Béchar with that of Djerada, Oujda (129,000), and the port of Nemours. On the other hand, the valley of the Moulouya, fed by the High and Middle Atlas, is aligned by oases of fortified villages.

The plains of western Morocco are far more intensively peopled. In the north, along the valley of the Sebou between the Col of Taza in the east and the coastal plain known as the Rharb, is a varied but generally fertile, densely colonized and highly developed zone, where cereals, vines and citrus fruits are the important crops and where good pastures are available. Inland from Mina Hassan Tani (86,000), the port of the Rharb and formerly known as Kenitra and Port Lyautey, are several important towns located along the east–west routeway to the col of Taza including the old cities of Fez (216,000) and Meknes (177,000). Fez, the larger, is a Moslem holy city, as well as a traditional centre of trade and crafts, and its unspoilt medina is one of Morocco's great tourist attractions (Plate 6).

The fertile coastal plains further south also produce wheat and vines, but although colonists are common in the north around Rabat and Casablanca they diminish southwards. The mushroom growth of Casablanca (965,000), the largest city in North-West Africa, the economic capital and chief port of Morocco (Plate 7), overshadows the smaller administrative capital, Rabat (227,000). Casablanca attracts migrants from all over the country, especially from the overpopulated mountain massifs, and its several contrasting concentric zones of European and indigenous housing, and its slums, pose great problems to the planners. The city is surrounded by an extensive zone of market gardens.

In contrast, the drier (less than 10 inches) interior high plains at the foot of the Atlas ranges and the Moroccan Meseta are partly pastoral, partly cultivated, and rarely colonized; cultivation is mainly limited to irrigable areas. The limestone plateaux are, however, covered in places by rich phosphate deposits, which are mined and quarried on a large scale. Along the base of the High Atlas, in the Haouz of Marrakesh, the wadis have been captured in several ways for irrigation, on which the oases depend. The great native city of Marrakesh (243,000) dominates the whole of southern Morocco. The port for the southern plains, for agricultural products, phosphates and fishing, is Safi. On the Steppes of the Sous, between the High and Anti-Atlas, cultivation and colonization have occurred where irrigation has been possible. Although shattered by earthquakes in 1960, Agadir is the regional capital, a fishing port and tourist centre.

Agriculture is still Morocco's principal activity and employs nearly three-quarters of the population. There is a great contrast between, on the one hand, the modern European type of farming and the best Moroccan-owned farms which often rely on irrigation and produce cash crops (citrus fruits, grapes, tobacco); and, on the other, the traditional agriculture which depends on cereals and livestock and is more reliant on natural conditions. The better farms are principally located on the more fertile parts of the Atlantic plains. At the moment, great efforts are being made to increase the irrigated area, which amounts to less than 4 per cent of the total cultivated area. Irrigation works are found especially along the river systems of the Sebou, Moulouya and Oum er Rbia. At the same time, gradual progress is being achieved in the settlement of nomads and the consolidation of fragmented properties.

Phosphates are the largest single item of export, reaching $7 \cdot 6$ million tons in 1961, and among other things provide much of the export trade of Casablanca and Safi. Kelata is the only large iron working, and the exports of manganese, cobalt and zinc tend to oscillate annually. With only small productions of coal and oil, Morocco is short of sources of energy, although since the Second World War there has been a great expansion in hydro-electric power development. It is not surprising that Morocco feels jealous of Algeria's possession of so much of the Sahara and its oil.

Moroccan industries are in need of greater dispersion, for, stimulated by foreign capital and staff, they are over-localized at Casablanca. They include industries based not only on the national resources, for example, flour milling, canning, the preparation of leather and skins, the manufacture of cement and superphosphates, but also on imported raw materials (sugar refining, the manufacture of textiles, soap, tobacco).

Fishing is mainly based on the ports of Casablanca, El-Jadida (Mazagan), Safi and Agadir, and is largely in the hands of French companies. Sardines and tuna provide the bulk of the catch.

Morocco has adequate bases for considerable economic development. She has a slightly more varied economy than the other countries of North Africa—even tourism is more favourably placed—and with the injection of further capital she should become a prosperous nation.

TUNISIA

Tunisia is the smallest country in the Maghreb—it has only 48,195 square miles—and its population is but 4,168,000 (1961). These facts did not prevent Tunisia from gaining independence from France; nor from gaining an international influence far in excess of its numbers. Its recent measures curbing the influence of Islam over the individual (control of polygamy and divorce, reduction of purdah and religious fasts) are revolutionary in the Moslem world, and indicative of Tunisia's initiative. One reason for her prominent position is that she possesses a distinct national unity which owes much to her strong cultural and urban traditions; a contrast with her eastern and western neighbours. Tunisian cities show signs of Phoenician, Roman, Arab, Turkish, Spanish and French culture; in the case of Tunisia, the sea has favoured foreign incursions. Roman, Arab and French rules made great impressions on the country and brought the expansion, the recession and the re-expansion of agriculture. In particular, Tunisia was the first country of the Maghreb to receive the Arabs and was almost completely Arabized; Berber-speakers are confined to a few isolated localities in the south and number only about one per cent of the total population.

The route into Tunisia was easy for the Arabs, because the southern coastal plain (the Jefara) funnelled the nomads through the gap between the shotts and the sea at Gabès and then on to the eastern Low Steppe. South of the shotts, nomads are preponderant, except on the densely peopled island of Djerba (noted touristically for its beauty), the peninsula of Zarzis (where olive cultivation is dominant), the Djebel Matmata (home of troglodytic peoples), and the small oases of the Nefzaoua.

Pastoral nomadism also prevails on the High Steppe of central Tunisia. Many of the Hamama and Fraichiche migrate northward in summer into the moister mountain lands of the Tell, the blessed lands where crops ripen and pastures are rarely parched, in order to find pastures for their flocks and work as harvesters, although there is a gradual tendency towards settlement on the Steppes by means of the expansion of arboriculture. The oases of the Djerid, especially

6. A view from the north over the medina of Fez (p. 126), the Karaouyine (ancient Islamic university), the Kouba (tomb of Idriss 1st, founder of the town), with the Middle Atlas in the distance.

7. Casablanca (p. 126), a tiny village when the French declared a protectorate over Morocco in 1912, now has about a million inhabitants. It is the largest city in North-West Africa and the economic capital and chief port of Morocco.

8. Harvesting Deglat en Nour dates at Tozeur, Tunisia (p. 130).

9. Sousse (p. 130), Tunisia. In the foreground esparto grass is awaiting export to Scottish paper mills, the 14 small tanks on the quay on the right store olive oil, and phosphates are loaded at the inner right-side quay. Beyond are the walls and the old city, with newer areas in the trees.

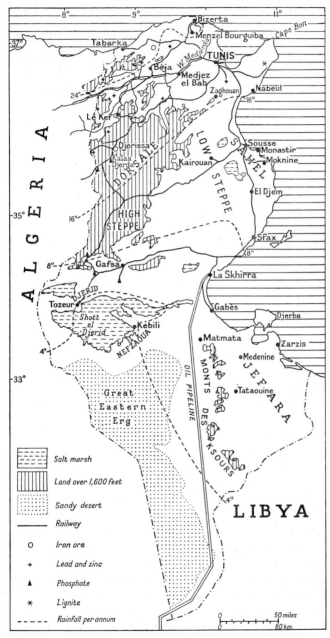

Fig. 25. Tunisia

Tozeur, are the home of 'Tunis Dates', the fine variety known as *Deglat en Nour* (finger of light), exported in substantial quantities to Britain for the Christmas market (Plate 8). The dates of the oasis of Gafsa are much inferior. In the isolated mountain chains east and west of Gafsa are some cultivators, while in the vicinity are located the four large phosphate mines of Metlaoui, Moularès, Redeyef and M'Dilla.

On the Low Steppe the traditional olive cultivation of the Sahel of Sousse, and the modern olive cultivation of the Sfaxian region, have both expanded greatly and have induced the settlement of semi-nomadic tribes. The contrast in the character of the two regions is marked. On the low undulating hills of the Sahel, olives benefit from adequate rainfall and humidity, and settlement is in the nature of a number of large old walled villages, which have long resisted the encroachments of the nomads: Monastir, Mahdia, Moknine, M'saken, and Kalaa Kebira. On the other hand, the magnificent geometrically arranged Sfaxian plantations have been developed by dry farming techniques and most of the farmers live in Sfax itself. Sousse (48,000) and Sfax (66,000), both walled cities (Plate 9) with adjacent European towns, export the olive oil of the Low Steppe, and the phosphates and esparto grass of the High Steppe; they are also fishing ports. In the interior of the Low Steppe the walled and minaretted holy city of Kairouan (40,000) receives pilgrims and tourists and produces carpets, but has escaped modernity.

Tunisia north of the Dorsale is known to the people of the south as the Tell or Friguia; it is mountainous, moister, more cultivated and more colonized. In the High Tell, to the south of the Medjerda, the mountain ridges are forested, while the plateaux produce cereals, but the region is also noted for iron ore (Le Kef and Djerissa) and phosphates (Kalaa Djerda and Ain Kerma) as well as lead and zinc. These scattered mineral deposits are connected by railway with Tunis. Wheat and barley are also the main crops along the valley of the Medjerda, where colonization was dense and where major works for irrigation, drainage, soil conservation, flood control and reclamation affecting nearly 700,000 acres are now in progress. Where irrigation has been developed in the lower valley, the larger farms of ex-colonists have been sub-divided, and the tiny holdings of Tunisians consolidated for intensive production of vegetables. The Northern Tell is humid (Ain Draham at 2,200 feet receives 60 inches per annum), and forested with evergreen and cork oaks. Cultivators and pastoralists eke out a meagre existence. Bizerta

(45,000) was for long an important French naval base at the mouth
of the lake of the same name.

In the plain of Tunis, there is greater emphasis on vines, olives,
market gardening and cattle, and European colonization was particularly intensive. Tunis (680,000) is sited on an isthmus between the
Lake of Tunis and a sebkha; the main port of Tunisia, it is linked by

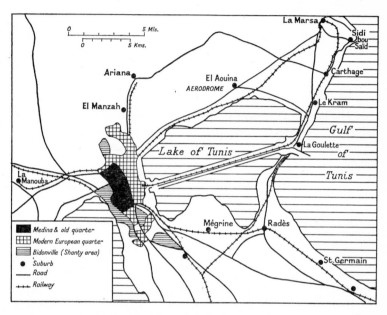

Fig. 26. The site and form of Tunis

canal (a deep controlled channel) across the Lake of Tunis to the
outport of La Goulette not far from Carthage (Fig. 26). Tunis contains
nearly one in six of the total population of Tunisia, although its
industrial development, similar to that found in Algiers and Casablanca, is insufficient to employ the vast surplus labour. Its morphology—a modern European town alongside an interesting old Arab
town, surrounded by attractive modern suburbs and appalling modern
shanty-towns—is symptomatic of the social contrasts, and of the clash
of old and new in the Maghreb.

The French, who ruled Tunisia as a Protectorate from 1881 until
1956, created a modern state without effacing its personality, but the
economic advance was not revolutionary. Only about one-eighth of
the country is cultivated, and of this area about one-fifth, much of the

best land, was colonized by Europeans. Since independence, this latter proportion has much declined, although Italians as well as Frenchmen are found especially in north-eastern Tunisia. Despite impressive efforts along the Medjerda, only about one per cent of the cultivated area is irrigated, and rainfall remains the key to prosperity in the country. After wheat or barley, olives follow in importance, and about 27 million trees make Tunisia the world's largest exporter of olive oil. Like so many Mediterranean countries, Tunisia has a problem in the development of the centre and south, where olives, almonds, apricots and dates may well be instrumental in agricultural improvements.

Industrialization has progressed rapidly since the last war, but progress is hampered by insufficient sources of power and capital. It is certain that much of Tunisian labour is capable of adapting itself to industrialization, but it is doubtful if this small country has sufficient natural resources of major significance to meet the problem of a rapidly growing population. Above all, she needs the investment of foreign capital.

FURTHER READING

The bulk of the literature is in French. The three best general geographies are J. Despois, *L'Afrique du Nord*, 1949, J. Dresch, *Afrique du Nord* in P. Birot and J. Dresch, *La Méditerranée et le Moyen-Orient*, vol. 1, *La Méditerranée Occidentale*, 1953, and J. M. Houston, *Western Mediterranean World*, 1964. See also J. Célérier, *Le Maroc*, 1948, M. Larnaude, *Algérie*, 1950. J. Despois, *La Tunisie*, 1961, and S. E. Tlatli, *Tunisie Nouvelle*, Tunis, 1957. In English, a good general volume is N. Barbour (Ed.), *A Survey of North-West Africa*, 1959; L. Laitman, *Tunisia Today*, New York, 1954, and R. Landau, *Morocco Independent*, 1961, are balanced accounts. Useful atlases are the Oxford Regional Economic Atlas, *The Middle East and North Africa*, Oxford, 1960, and *The Times Atlas of the World*, vol. 4, *Southern Europe and Africa*, 1956. A most valuable analysis in historical geography is J. Despois, 'Development of Land Use in Northern Africa', in L. D. Stamp (Ed.), *A History of Land Use in Arid Regions*, UNESCO, 1961, 219-38.

CHAPTER SIX

The Sahara

THE Sahara is the largest and driest desert in the world. It covers nearly four million square miles, almost one-quarter of Africa, and extends 3,500 miles from the Atlantic to the Red Sea and 1,100 miles from the Atlas Mountains to near the northern bend of the Niger River. No sharp line distinguishes the Sahara from surrounding environments, although for convenience French geographers normally consider the 100 mm. isohyets (c.4 inches) as its approximate boundaries (Fig. 27). In the north this line coincides roughly with the northern limit of oases in which dates ripen, and in any case the desert is curtailed by the long chains of the Atlas Mountains as well as by the southward penetration of the Gulf of Syrte. On the southern side of the Sahara, the desert grades imperceptibly into Grass Steppe and Sub-Desert Steppe which together form a belt several hundred miles wide.

The essential physical unity of the Sahara necessitates its separate treatment, despite its political fragmentation. However, the distinctive social and economic conditions which occur in the countries of the Nile Valley justify their exclusion from this chapter.

THE PHYSICAL ENVIRONMENT

Climate

The main characteristics of the Saharan climate are aridity, temperature ranges and wind. Nowhere in the Sahara does average annual rainfall exceed five inches, and some central parts receive less than one-half of an inch; the average for Reggane, near the atomic bombing range, is actually less than one-quarter of an inch. In general, the amount diminishes towards the heart of the desert, but the mountain massifs receive more than the basins. Rainfall varies greatly from year to year and may be torrential; cases can be cited of the fall of 12 inches in one day followed by up to four years of drought. Moreover, the long hours of sunshine and little cloud cover ensure very dry air and rapid evaporation. Annual temperature ranges are about 45°F, but daily ranges reach 90°F. Absolute maxima have risen over 135°F, although shade temperatures have little meaning in a desert. Very high temperatures are rarely attained in the western and southern Sahara.

* By John I. Clarke.

The early belief that the great contrast between day and night temperatures is the principal cause of the exfoliation of rocks has been disproved experimentally; other causes now invoked are chemical weathering, and the effect of the change in pressure conditions when deep-seated rocks are exposed by erosion. Sometimes excessive temperatures and aridity are associated with high winds bearing large quantities of sand and dust, which have erosive power and also greatly restrict human activity. Such climatic conditions pose physiological difficulties to man and the desert is, by definition, sparsely populated by flora and fauna. However, it has not always been so, for during the course of the Quaternary the desert benefited from humid phases which brought conditions much more favourable than those experienced at present. Archaeological studies, in particular those of flora, fauna and cave-paintings, have revealed flourishing prehistoric periods.

Major Relief Regions

Contrary to popular conception, the Sahara has varied relief features. The northern Sahara is a vast trough of recent composition, which gently descends and widens to the east, and is known as the Saharan Piedmont. It is a region of oases and numerous nomadic flocks, and extends southward by way of a Secondary trough containing low plateaux and further oases: the Mzab, Tademaït, Gourara, Touat and Tidikelt.

The western Sahara has the aspect of an immense flat plain gently inclined towards the Atlantic. The crystalline plateau of the Eglab rises only 1,500 feet above the monotony of sand and gravel, separating two large sedimentary basins with peripheral escarpments: the basins of Tindouf to the north and of Taoudenni to the south. South-east of the Eglab are the gravel wastes of the plain of Tanezrouft, probably the most desertic region in the whole of the Sahara.

The central Sahara is dominated by the vast massif of the Hoggar, whose lunar landscape was caused by erosional effects on volcanic and crystalline forms. Volcanic plugs and cones are frequent, and the highest rises to over 9,000 feet. The southward extensions of the Hoggar are the Adrar des Iforas and Aïr, of which only the latter is much affected by vulcanicity. North-east of the Hoggar is the Tassili des Ajjer, famous for its cave-paintings; it is a sandstone plateau eroded into a labyrinth of wadis and buttes.

The eastern Sahara, in contrast, is a vast plateau 1,500–3,000 feet high, from which rises the volcanic and crystalline massif of the

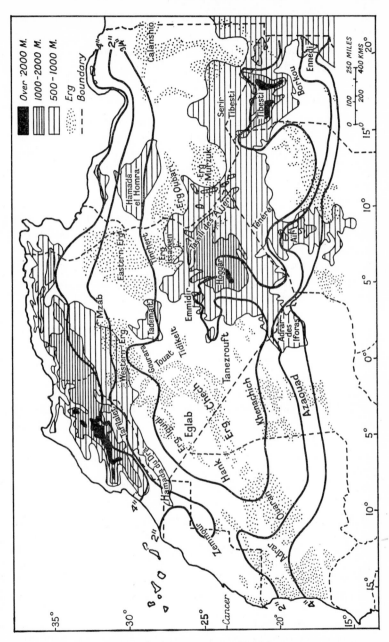

Fig. 27. Relief and rainfall of the Sahara

Tibesti, whose highest peak, the gigantic volcano Emi Koussi, is over 11,000 feet. The Tibesti and the sandstone plateau of Ennedi to the south-east separate the great depression of Lake Chad from the basins of the Fezzan and Kufra.

Morphological Features

The abrupt break of slope between mountain and plain, the sparseness of vegetation, and the obvious influence of structure upon relief strike the newcomer to the Sahara. At the same time, there are a number of morphological features which constantly recur: *erg, reg, hamada, wadi, grara* and *sebkha*.

Ergs, or sand seas, are frequent but they cover only about one-seventh of the Sahara. The dunes have a great variety of forms, but in general they are aligned from north-east to south-west following the direction of the trade winds. Those in the northern Sahara (Erg Iguidi, Erg Chech, the Great Western Erg, the Great Eastern Erg, and the Calanshio sand sea) are best known because they affect the north-south routes. Unlike these ergs, some of those in the southern Sahara are fixed by vegetation.

Reg is a bleak, interminable plain, such as that of Tanezrouft, from which the wind has removed all the finer particles and has left only gravel and coarse sand. Sometimes this covers fertile fossil soil. Regs are devoid of pastures and waterholes, but may have thorn trees and are easily crossed by vehicles. In the eastern Sahara this landscape is called *ténéré* or *serir*. Hamadas of the northern Sahara are desert plateaux of bare rock dipping gently southwards (e.g. Hamada of Dra, Hamada el Homra).

Wadis (called *oueds* in the western Sahara) flow only after rare downpours. The flow is sometimes astonishingly persistent; the Wadi Saoura has been known to flow 500 miles south from the High Atlas. The flow from the central massifs is naturally shorter, but some of these watercourses are so deep, large and long that they give rise to the opinon that the Sahara must have enjoyed greater humidity at an earlier period. Graras, or closed basins into which wadis flow, have great accumulations of alluvium. Where the waters evaporate in salt-marshes or salt-flats, they are known as sebkhas.

THE PEOPLES OF THE SAHARA

The total population of the Sahara is probably no more than 2,500,000, an average density of less than one per square mile. The concept of density of population has little value, however, because while enormous areas remain uninhabited some oases teem with life. Four-fifths of the population live in the northern margins of the desert; the only comparatively populous parts of the interior are the Tibesti and Hoggar Mountains and some groups of oases (Fezzan, Touat and Tidikelt).

Despite small numbers, there is ethnic variety. Negro peoples form the oldest elements: the Tibu of the Tibesti, and the Haratin, descendants of slaves formerly taken from West Africa. Even today, many Haratin cultivate in the oases for Berber and Arab overlords. The population is, however, greatly mixed and it is difficult to distinguish peoples according to their physique.

Distinction by language is clearer. The Berber-speaking peoples are found mainly in southern Algeria, in the oases of Mzab, Gourara and the Oued Rhir, they also include the famous black-veiled Tuareg tribes of the Hoggar and the region to the south. Originally white-skinned, the Tuareg have been greatly affected by mixture with Sudanese Negroes. The Tibu of the Tibesti have their own language, but in their mountain refuge they now number no more than 10,000. Renowned for their fortitude and endurance, they are nomadic pastoralists who possess gardens in the mountain valleys, cultivated by negro vassals. Berber- and Tibu-speaking peoples are partially surrounded by Arabic speakers in the eastern, western and northern Sahara. In the western Sahara, although not confined to Mauritania, are about 40,000 Moors, who are of very mixed origin (Arab, Berber, Negro and possibly Ethiopian), but are proud pastoralists.

Nomads and Cultivators

Modes of life offer the clearest contrasts. Two are traditionally imposed by the Sahara, pastoral nomadism and sedentary cultivation, which are contrasted socially and economically.

Pastoral nomadism, based on the herding of camels, sheep and goats, occurs in various forms, of which the following are the most important:

(a) Nomads who move outside the Sahara in summer, such as the Arbaa of the Laghouat area, who migrate northwards in small groups with their sheep and camels to the Tellian Atlas. Unfortunately, the development of northern Algeria has made it increasingly difficult for them to find pastures for their flocks, and seasonal work for themselves as harvesters.

(b) Nomads who spend the whole year in the Sahara, and depend largely on their camels; the Rgueibat and Chaamba of Algeria, and many Libyan nomads fall into this group. The Rgueibat are a large tribal confederation of about 50,000 people with common economic and political interests, and a patriarchal social organization.

(c) Semi-nomads who periodically engage in the cultivation of cereals, along wadi bottoms and in moister hollows when conditions are favourable. They include many peoples of the Saharan periphery, among whom are the Duri-Meni of the Colomb-Béchar area, the Merazigue of southern Tunisia, and the Zintan and Orfella of Tripolitania.

The traditional social structure of the Sahara was based on the pre-eminence of the nomad over the cultivator, for whom the nomad had nothing but scorn. This structure has been greatly upset by foreign rule which greatly reduced tribal raiding, the 'protection' of oasis cultivators by nomads (which implied the exaction of tribute for little protection), and the caravan traffic of gold and slaves. The income and prestige of the nomads have accordingly suffered. However, salt continues to be transported over long distances in the southern Sahara. Enormous caravans (*azalaïs*) containing as many as 25,000 camels make the two to three week journey to the salt deposits of Taoudenni (Plate 2), Tisemt and Bilma. Moreover, some richer nomads still own date-palms in the oases; others settle in the oases only when they are at the point of starvation.

The main oases are found in the northern Sahara, where underground water is more abundant and shallower. In southern Morocco they are found along the upper reaches of the Wadi Dra and the wadis of the Tafilalet. In central Algeria there is a line of oases along Wadi Saoura, to which are joined those of Touat and Tidikelt. Some of these oases are watered from *foggaras*, underground tunnels often several miles long which tap water-tables in neighbouring mountains. Farther east in the Mzab, over 3,000 wells 100–250 feet deep have been dug into the hamada by a local Moslem sect in order to supply the oases with water. Wells also supply the oases of the Wadi Rhir. Nearer the Tunisian frontier in the Souf, which extends over part of the Great Eastern Erg, circular hollows have been excavated in the sand to enable the roots of the palms to reach the groundwater level. The oases of the Fezzan are much more widely scattered, and are often formed by springs and wells at the foot of escarpments. Southern

Cyrenaica has only one important oasis, Kufra, which is among the more remote in the Sahara; much further north are Jalo and Jiarabub. In the south-eastern Sahara the principal oasis is Bilma in Niger.

The oasis-dwellers are freer and more numerous than formerly. Now they may comprise two-thirds of the total inhabitants of the Sahara, although there is a considerable emigration from the Algerian oases to the towns of the Maghreb. Emigration from the Fezzan and the oases of southern Cyrenaica is increasing as northern Libya offers more opportunities for employment. Apart from dates, the main food of the Sahara, oasis cultivators produce a few other tree crops (figs, apricots, grenadines), vegetables, cereals (especially wheat and barley in the north, sorghums and maize in the south), and peppers in astonishing quantities. Cultivation is on a pocket handkerchief scale, and revenues, especially for the share-croppers (*khammes*), are often minimal. But the northern oases are more geared to the commercial production of dates than those found in the heart of the desert, which often suffer from excessive diversity of palm species.

Everywhere the villages are compact, and are often rectangular in arrangement with narrow streets, closed courtyards, and vaulted rooms. Many are walled or contain fortified granaries (*ksours*).

ECONOMIC DEVELOPMENT

Oil and Minerals

The traditional economies and ways of life are being rudely shattered by the discovery of underground resources (Fig. 28). The surprising lateness of the oil discoveries can perhaps only be explained by the lack of prospecting, the interruption of the Second World War, and the long held belief that the Sahara was entirely crystalline. In fact, it contains over three-quarters of a million square miles of sedimentary rocks, which are fairly undisturbed and therefore favourable to the concentration of oil.

In 1956 two important discoveries of oil were made by French companies in Algeria: at Hassi-Messaoud (Plate 10), 60 miles east-south-east of the oasis of Ouargla, and at Edjelé, 300 miles further south-east across the Great Eastern Erg. Many other fields have been located in the Edjelé area not far from the Libyan boundary, and at points between Edjelé and Hassi Messaoud. These oilfields have immense reserves and are connected by 24-inch pipeline to the port of Bougie in Algeria; the fields near Edjelé are also linked to the port of La Skhirra in southern Tunisia. Extensions of pipelines are in progress. Algerian production was 23·6 million tons in 1963. Latest estimates suggest an output of 50 to 60 million tons in 1965. The oil fields have been developed at great expense; they were considered of supreme importance to France, not merely for saving foreign exchange but also for reducing her dependence on Middle East supplies.

Intensive exploration has followed in Libya by American, British, French and Italian companies. Gushes have occurred at many places in all three provinces, but especially at Zelten, Dahra and Beida, all south of the Gulf of Syrte. A pipeline network connects the oil-fields to three terminals on the Gulf of Syrte at Marsa Brega, Sidra and Lanuf, and a fourth terminal is expected near Tobruk. Exports began in 1961, amounting to 22 million tons in 1963. Half of the profits go to the Libyan Government and greatly multiply the revenue of the country. In 1959 the oil fever extended to the Spanish Sahara, when the doors were opened to foreign oil companies. With searches also proceeding in the Western Desert of Egypt, southern Tunisia, southern Morocco and Mauritania, there is no doubt that a North African oil province is emerging.

Natural gas in sufficient quantity to enable an annual production of 50 thousand million cubic metres has been found at Hass R'Mel, about 40 miles north-west of the oasis of Ghardaïa and 280 miles south of Algiers. The gas, which is a bright hope for Algerian industrialization is taken to the Mediterranean coast at Arzew by pipeline (Plate 11). It may be taken to Europe by submarine pipeline, and is already sent by methane tankers. Other deposits of natural gas have been discovered near In Salah, about 600 miles from the Mediterranean.

On the matter of power we should remember the coalfield at Colomb-Béchar, and the prospects of the development of solar energy—the subject of intensive investigation by the French.

Almost eclipsed by these dramatic finds have been the discoveries of other minerals, which are principally although not exclusively found in primary rocks. Work has begun on two large iron-ore deposits which occur at Gara-Djebilet in Algeria, 75 miles south-east of Tindouf and 250 miles from the Atlantic coast of the Spanish Sahara, and at Fort Gouraud in Mauritania, linked by a 400-mile long railway with Port Etienne on the Atlantic (see Chapter Thirteen). Copper has been found at Akjoujt in Mauritania, 250 miles south of Fort Gouraud, and is also to be worked and linked by road and rail to Port Etienne. At Djebel Guettara, 95 miles south of Colomb-Béchar, are over one million tons of manganese, while at Taouz, 110 miles west of the same town, are extensive deposits of lead ore. Many rare metals have been found in the Hoggar and Aïr massifs.

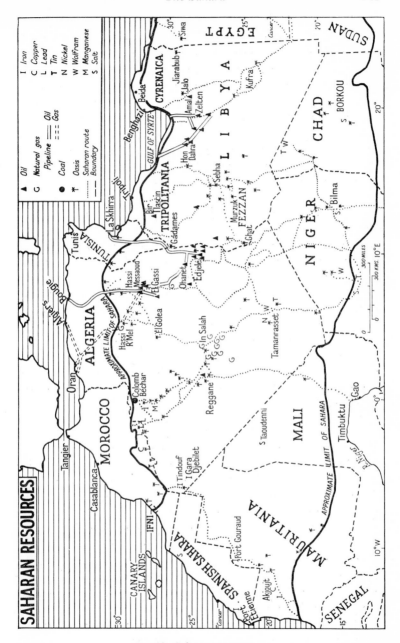

Fig. 28. Saharan resources

Development Problems

Severe transportation problems are encountered in all Saharan mineral development which, apart from pipelines, has necessitated the rapid construction of hundreds of miles of road in difficult conditions. The aim in southern Algeria has been to improve greatly the main north–south axes: the Oran–Colomb-Béchar–Reggane axis; the Algiers–Laghouat–El Golea–In Salah axis; and the Biskra–Touggourt–Hassi Messaoud–Fort Flatters axis. Connections also exist with El Oued and Souf, and between Ghardaïa and Ouargla. In Libya a road links Tripoli with Sebha, the capital of the Fezzan, and another joins Jiarabub with Tobruk. At the same time there has been an enormous increase in air traffic, especially of passengers and expensive equipment, and by 1960 there were at least 40 airports in the Sahara.

Until recently, life in the Sahara concentrated along wadis and around springs and shallow wells; so the successful exploration of deep artesian water has been essential for mineral exploitation. The most prolific aquifer discovered is in the Inter-Calary Continental Albienne nappe of Jurassic to Cretaceous age. Other underground water supplies have been located in deep Palaeozoic sandstones in the In Salah region, as well as in shallower recent deposits in various parts of the northern Sahara. The Saharan inland sea project, which dates back to the 1880s and involves the drowning of Shotts Melrhir and el Rharsa in eastern Algeria, has not been shelved entirely despite the fabulous cost.

THE SAHARA TODAY

When underground resources were found during the 1950s there was a complete reappraisal of the value of the Sahara. For long regarded by the European powers as a romantic waste of little economic value, they did little to ameliorate the conditions of the inhabitants, especially in the Spanish Sahara. Carved up by these powers into geometrical shapes, the Sahara now has boundaries of little significance to the Saharan peoples themselves. Morocco and Tunisia are especially embittered about the slight extent of their Saharan territories. The political fragmentation is largely a relic of the European conquest of the desert, which took place from the north and the south. Algeria and Libya obtained the greatest shares.

Until 1957, the Algerian Sahara was administered as Military Territories, but in that year it became two départements of France called Oasis and Souara. In this same year an attempt was made by the French Government to unify the whole of the French Sahara for social and economic development by the creation of the *Organisation Commune des Régions Sahariennes* (O.C.R.S.), which originally included the Saharan territories of Soudan (now Mali), Niger and Chad, as well as southern Algeria. Mauritania, the sole unified Saharan province, held aloof. Southern Algeria and Mali have since withdrawn but Niger and Chad are receiving grants and technical assistance.

The future of the Algerian Sahara, and that of French oil production there, is uncertain. Morocco claims part of Algeria's western Sahara, Spanish Sahara and Mauritania. The Sahara is in a revolutionary phase, and it is difficult to forecast either its economic or its political future.

FURTHER READING

The best general volumes are in German and French: H. Schiffers, *Libyen und die Sahara*, Bonn, 1962; R. Capot-Rey, *Le Sahara Français*, 1953; R. Furon, *Le Sahara*, 1957; and B. Verlet, *Le Sahara*, 1958. Works in English include G. Gerster, *Sahara*, 1960; L. Cabot Briggs, *Tribes of the Sahara*, Princeton, 1960; B. E. Thomas, Trade Routes of Algeria and the Sahara, *Univ. of California Publications in Geography*, 1957; J. I. Clarke, 'Economic and Political Changes in the Sahara', *Geography*, 1961, 102–19; A. T. Grove, 'Geomorphology of the Tibesti Region with special reference to Western Tibesti', *Geographical Journal*, 1960, 18–31; T. Monod and C. Toupet, 'Land Use in the Sahara-Sahel Region', in *A History of Land Use in Arid Regions*, UNESCO, 1961, 239–53.

CHAPTER SEVEN

Libya

ALTHOUGH the United Kingdom of Libya measures nearly 680,000 square miles, it contains only 1,200,000 people, about 1·8 per square mile. Unlike the countries of the Maghreb, Libya has an almost entirely Saharan environment. Structurally it is outside the chaos of Tertiary orogenesis; geologically and morphologically it is more uniform than the Maghreb. Furthermore, it possesses only a narrow fringe of Mediterranean climate, cleft into two by the southward thrust of the Gulf of Syrte into the heart of the desert. Libya's vast desert contains a mere 65,000 people: 55,000 in the Fezzan, especially in the three oases of Sebha, Brak and Murzuk, and about 10,000 in the four Cyrenaican oases of Jiarabub, Jalo, Marada and Kufra. The desert and the Gulf of Syrte have separated the two moister and comparatively populous areas: northern Tripolitania, with over two-thirds (800,000) of the Libyan population, and northern Cyrenaica, with under one-third (350,000). Libya has therefore widely spaced nuclei, with separate outlooks, although the importance of these was reduced in the change of constitution in 1963 from a federal to a unitary state by the abolition of the three provinces and their substitution by ten administrative units. The construction of a new capital at Beida in the Jebel Akhdar of northern Cyrenaica is partly aimed at reducing provincial rivalry, epitomized by periodic migrations of the government between Tripoli and Benghazi.

HISTORY

Independence is a new experience for Libya. Her history is one of intermittent domination by Egyptians, Phoenicians, Greeks, Romans, Vandals, Byzantines, Arabs, Spaniards, Turks and Italians, several of whom have left lasting marks. Cyrenaica was colonized by the Greeks who founded, among other settlements, the magnificent city at Cyrene; while in Tripolitania the Phoenicians established three trading settlements at Sabratha, Oea (Tripoli) and Leptis Magna. Later, Rome rebuilt these cities, whose majestic ruins remain today. As in the Maghreb, the Romans also developed irrigation systems and

* By John I. Clarke.

arboriculture, revealing the agricultural potentialities of the Steppe zones.

Following the glories of classical times, Libya suffered as a routeway and 'no-man's land' between the ethnic reservoir of the Middle East and the zone of immigration and implantation in the Maghreb. Arabs moving westward displaced or assimilated the indigenous Berbers, who all eventually adopted Islam and many also adopted the Arabic language. The Arabs ensured the predominance of pastoral nomadism (Plate 12) and the tribal system, as well as the restriction of cultivation to a thin discontinuous coastal strip, a few mountain plateaux and valleys, and some scattered oases. Urban life was confined to Tripoli, which was ruled by corsairs and collectors of taxes and lacked culture.

During their short occupancy of the country from 1911 to 1943, the Italians attempted to emulate the agricultural and architectural achievements of Rome. Aridity inevitably restricted colonization efforts to the two northern zones, which offered the greatest possibilities for development. Mussolini aimed at the creation of a 'little Italy' containing 300,000 Italians. By 1939, there were 110,000; but during and since the war large numbers departed for Italy and by 1960 no more than 35,000 remained, all in Tripolitania and most of them in Tripoli. The Italians poured money into their colony, built towns, harbours, roads (especially the coastal road from Tunisia to Egypt) and railways and transformed the moister regions. Italy received little in return. It was a militaristic, fascist colonization, which suppressed the Libyans, who derived little benefit during the period of Italian rule. They were thus ill-equipped for independence, when this was achieved in 1951.

It was realized that this poor and backward country could not be viable without liberal foreign aid, received mainly from the United States and Britain in return for military establishments, and from the United Nations. However, it is confidently expected that oil will balance the budget; the expenditure of the numerous oil companies and many geological and geophysical parties is about £80 million a year. Oil exports, which amounted to 22 million tons in 1963 (see p. 140), should brighten Libya's future. Fishing, industry and tourism bring little revenue, while agriculture is confined to small areas and is too subsistent and too influenced by the whims of rainfall. Less than one per cent of Libya is potentially productive land, and only one-quarter of that is available for cultivation; the rest is suitable only for grazing or forests. Conditions differ between northern Tripolitania and northern Cyrenaica.

NORTHERN TRIPOLITANIA

Tripolitania is the richest and most prosperous part of Libya. Most of its people are concentrated primarily in the coastal oases of the Jefara, the boomerang-shaped plain of Quaternary deposits which is bisected by the Tunisian–Libyan boundary, secondly along the eastern coastal zone between Homs and Misurata, and finally on the Cretaceous and Jurassic escarpment to the south of the Jefara. The escarpment is known as the Jebel (locally Jebel Nefousa, Jebel Garian or Jebel Tarhuna), and rises to 1,000 feet above the plain. Aridity increases rapidly away from the coast, and only a few wadis of the eastern Jebel manage occasionally to reach the sea.

The native coastal oases between Tunisia and Misurata are discontinuous because they are interrupted by salt marshes (*sebkhas*) and sand dunes. Cultivation is subsistent and depends on rains in winter and shallow wells in summer. Dates are the principal crop, but although there are millions of palms they are too mixed and the dates too poor in quality to command an export market. Many of the palms suffer from the scars caused by the extraction of palm wine (*lagby*). Other crops are olives, citrus, almonds, pumpkins, watermelons, vegetables and barley, but again only small quantities are produced commercially. The inhabitants, mainly Arab-Berbers, live in large villages, one of which, Zuara, is entirely Berber. At Zuara and Zavia sponge and tunny fishing are prominent, but are mainly in the hands of Greeks and Italians.

A typical example of a small native farm, known as a *sanyah*, in Tripoli oasis covers $3\frac{3}{4}$ acres, all of which are irrigable, and has 80 date palms, 40 olive trees, 15 pomegranates, 4 apricots, and 2 figs; the rotational system lasts $2\frac{1}{2}$ years during which one-third to one-sixth of the farm lies fallow. In the first summer lucerne is grown, followed by wheat in the winter, then tobacco or peanuts, and in the second winter vegetables.

Italians occupied large parts of the coastal strip and of the Jefara to the south of Tripoli (Fig. 29 and Plate 13), especially areas with more than 8 inches per annum. Their agricultural methods were much more modern than those of the Libyans, and they concentrated on profitable tree crops (olives, almonds and citrus), vines, cereals and, latterly, groundnuts. The increased cultivation of the latter was made possible by the use of artesian water, discovered by the Italians in the Miocene deposits. The exports of groundnuts rose fairly steadily during the 1950s to a total of about 10,000 tons per annum. There is, however, a danger of overpumping.

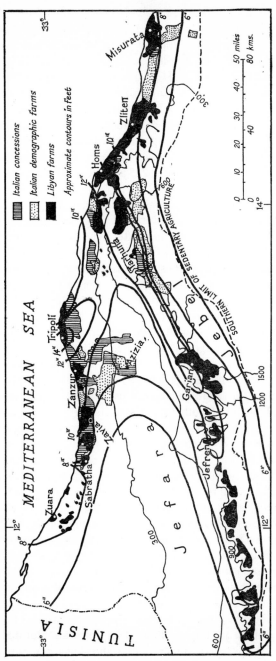

Fig. 29. Distribution of Libyan and Italian sedentary agriculture in northern Tripolitania, about 1950

Italian holdings were of two types: private concessions, usually large estates specializing in tree crops; and smaller demographic settlements, established only a few years before 1939 to boost the numbers of Italians, the capital being provided by three Italian government agencies (ENTE, INPS and ATI). Demographic holdings averaged 60–75 acres, and were grouped together to form communities of peasant farmers, who were given all facilities. A typical demographic farm of 75 acres at Bianchi south-west of Tripoli is largely irrigated and normally operates a rotation of cereals (wheat and barley), groundnuts and then forage, although tree crops are the basis of the economy (575 olives, 235 almonds, 185 citrus and 1,000 vines).

Both types of Italian farm are still operative, although many of the Italians who succeeded in paying for the demographic farms have sold them to Libyans and have returned to Italy. Some former Italian settlements were almost entirely Libyan-owned by 1960. Others which had little time to become well-established before the war are deserted and uncultivated. Money and water are not the only requirements for the extension of Tripolitanian agriculture; one of the major problems of the Libyan Government is the settlement as peasant farmers of people accustomed to nomadic life and tribal organization. The discipline of irrigated agriculture is alien to the nomad's mentality.

Much of the Jefara is either too sandy or too dry (the western half has less than eight inches per annum) for reliable cultivation, and remains a zone for semi-nomads who usually sow cereals along the wadis. The Jebel, on the other hand, is moister (up to twelve inches) and many parts are traditionally cultivated by Berbers, some of whom live in villages largely composed of underground dwellings carved vertically or horizontally into the soft limestones and marls. In several localities Italian colonization demonstrated the possibilities for arboriculture; but by 1960 few Italians remained. Elsewhere on the southern dip-slope, known as the Dahar or the Ghibla, semi-nomads are widespread and esparto grass collection a minor industry. Southward down the Dahar, steppe merges imperceptibly into desert.

Tripoli (184,000) is located in the moister middle of the Jefaran coastal strip, and is the only large town in Tripolitania; Zuara, Zavia, Homs, Misurata and Garian are small market towns and administrative centres. At Tripoli, the Italians constructed a large and beautiful modern city, confining the old medina to a small peninsula. Thousands of Italians remain in Tripoli, where they form an educated class, employed as shopkeepers, traders, clerks and skilled tradesmen. The city contains a number of small industries processing agricultural products and fish, as well as some traditional industries (e.g. weaving and leatherwork); like most African towns it also contains hordes of unemployed and underemployed. The large port built by the Italians had little use after the war until supplies for the many oil companies began to be imported. No other port in Tripolitania can receive cargo vessels. Tripoli's airport, named after King Idris, is 17 miles south of the city beyond a belt of dunes in process of fixation. The airport has a fair traffic, but is much smaller than the huge American air base of Wheelus Field, just east of the city.

NORTHERN CYRENAICA

Northern Cyrenaica is dominated by the Jebel Akhdar, the Green Mountain, which rises over 2,600 feet above sea-level. It is a limestone plateau 150 by 45 miles, severely affected by three north-facing fault-

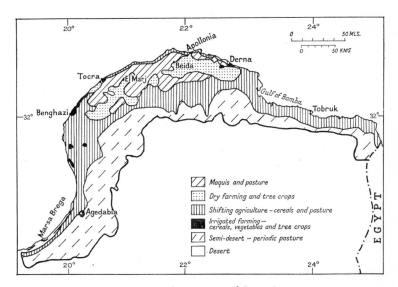

Fig. 30. Land-use regions of Cyrenaica

scarps which restrict the development of a coastal plain and provide only one extensive area really suitable for cultivation, the plain of Barce (or El Marj, as it is called today). Unfortunately, this small town was destroyed by earthquake in 1963. In the eastern part of the Jebel, the scarps are also deeply gouged by wadis which impede communications. However, altitude reduces temperatures, ensures an average annual rainfall ranging from 8 to 24 inches, and enables the formation of terra rossa soils and scrub-oak forest.

Until the Italian colonization in the 1930s very little land in northern Cyrenaica was used for cultivation (Fig. 30); livestock raising was the main occupation of the Senussi, the members of the religious sect who dominate Cyrenaica and whose hereditary leader, the Emir Idris el Senussi, became the first King of Libya. The Senussi fiercely resisted the Italians for many years and were severely suppressed; in revenge they permitted no Italians to return to Cyrenaica. The demographic farms which the Italians established on the plain of Barce and elsewhere are now occupied by Libyans, many of whom do not farm in the same way or with the same efficiency, partly because of their lack of experience and partly through lack of credits. The Italian farmers, heavily sponsored by their governments, grew wheat, barley, vegetables and vines, and planted olives, apricots and other fruits; after their evacuation the vines (a crop anathema to abstaining Moslems) and trees were left untended and much of the land reverted to pasture and the cultivation of barley.

Agricultural development offers good hopes in certain localities, but some authorities lament the remoteness of the major springs from the fertile soils and the difficulties of damming wadis in limestone areas. They stress the need to rationalize the livestock industry rather than to introduce alien agricultural practices. Livestock herding is the main economy of Cyrenaica, provides the principal agricultural exports, and is found all over the country. Goats and cattle prevail in the wooded areas of the north; sheep and camels are more numerous in the steppe and semi-desert further south. Flocks usually spend the summer in the Jebel where water and pasture are available, but migrate southward to the steppe in November or December. Essential needs are the provision of adequate forage reserves, veterinary services, washeries for the wool, marketing facilities, and increased standardization of breeds. In other words, the standard of living of the nomad can best be raised by the commercialization of livestock farming.

The classical sites of Cyrene, Apollonia, Tocra and Tolmeita are only small Arab villages today, and attract far fewer tourists than they deserve. Benghazi (120,000) contains over one-fifth of the total population of Cyrenaica, although it has few industries and is in a semi-arid zone. Both the town and the port of Benghazi were badly damaged during the war, but they have been rapidly reconstructed since oil development has taken place. The airport of Benghazi is at

Benina, 12 miles east at the foot of the first escarpment. Derna (16,000) is in an attractive position touristically, but is too hemmed in by unproductive escarpments to develop as a port. It exports only livestock to Malta and Sicily; the local catches by Greek fishermen are merely weighed, not imported. Derna oasis is interesting as one of the few in North Africa which grows bananas in quantity (Fig. 31).

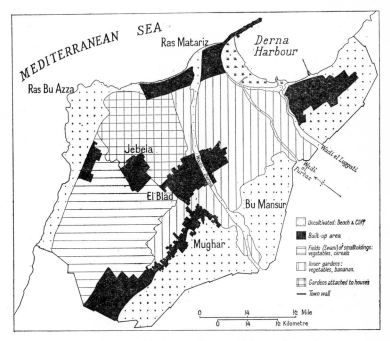

Fig. 31. Types of farming in the oasis of Derna, Cyrenaica
(After Buru)

Between Derna and the Egyptian frontier is a lower region known as Marmarica, which is in the lee of the Jebel Akhdar as far as eastward moving depressions are concerned, and is therefore more arid. Settlement is coastal; Tobruk (5,000) is of local importance only as a port, but serves the military airport of El Adem, 19 miles to the south.

A series of wadis carve their way down the southern slopes of the Jebel Akhdar and eventually terminate in salt-lakes, locally called *baltes*. It is a semi-arid steppe belt occupied by pastoralists, who frequent a number of markets. Agedabia is one, and is located on the road between Tripoli and Benghazi; it may well grow in importance if the Syrte oil discoveries fulfil expectations (see p. 140).

Libya is an arid country and all hopes rest on oil. Despite excellent technical assistance by the missions of the United Nations, the United States and of Britain, the agriculture of Libya has not been revolutionized, and the desert has not receded. The mammoth task of modernizing the country needs enormous sums of money and cannot be accomplished in a decade. Apart from its economic problems, Libya may have considerable difficulty in reconciling regional interests, especially if oil royalties are, or appear to be, unequally distributed between them.

FURTHER READING

The best general volume is International Bank for Reconstruction, *The Economic Development of Libya*, Baltimore, 1960. See also E. E. Evans-Pritchard, *The Sanusi of Cyrenaica*, Oxford, 1949; H. S. Villard, *Libya, the New Arab Kingdom*, 1956; S. G. Willimott and J. I. Clarke (Eds.), *Field Studies in Libya*, Durham, 1960; *Libya* (Overseas Economic Survey, H.M.S.O.); J. I. Clarke, 'Oil in Libya: Some Implications', *Economic Geography*, 1963, 40–59; H. Schiffers, *Libyen und die Sahara*, Bonn, 1962.

NORTH-EAST AFRICA

CHAPTER EIGHT

The Nile

THE Nile is 4,160 miles long and stretches over 35 degrees of latitude from its source on the East African Plateau near Lake Tanganyika to the Mediterranean. With a basin extending over 1,100,000 square miles and containing some 45 million people, the Nile is the dominating fact of north-east Africa. Its influence over the distribution and activities of the population increases northward as rainfall diminishes. To the peoples of Egypt and the Sudan the Nile's habit of regular flooding has long been essential; elsewhere in the basin the demands upon the river are less vital. The economies of Egypt and the Sudan depend upon the river, yet these two countries contribute hardly anything to the volume of the Nile; most of the Nile water comes from the Ethiopian Highlands and from the East African Plateau. Unfortunately, the political division of the Nile Valley has greatly complicated the utilization of the water. The Nile has become a source of rivalry between nations.

The size of the Nile Basin, the diversity of its rainfall régimes, and the importance of the tributaries provoke considerable complexities in river flow. No great river has been studied as much as the Nile, but while the broad pattern of flow is well known, the details of flow of some tributaries, especially in Ethiopia, have not been fully investigated.

The mountainous upper course of the White Nile—known initially as the Victoria Nile, then as the Albert Nile and later the Bahr el Jebel (River of the Mountains)—has a regular flow owing to the steady discharge from lakes Victoria and Albert amounting to about 25–26,000 million cubic metres per annum. Even as the river wanders slowly northward across the vast clay plains of the Sudan the influence of the lakes is still paramount. Unfortunately, half of the volume of the Bahr el Jebel is lost by evaporation and transpiration in the interminable swamps and intricate channels of the Sudd of southern Sudan; one important side channel, the Bahr ez Zeraf (River of Giraffes), leaves the main river and follows a more direct course. Losses of water in the Sudd are redressed by the river Sobat which comes down from the highlands of Ethiopia to join the White Nile

* By John I. Clarke.

above Malakal. Most of the flow of the Sobat comes in the latter half of the year, but is substantially diminished by swamps. So, also, is the flow of the Bahr el Ghazal (River of Gazelles), which rises on the Congo–Nile divide and contributes only a small outflow to the White Nile. As no further significant change in river flow occurs until Khartoum, the annual discharge of the White Nile is not appreciably different from that of the Albert Nile.

At Khartoum, however, the White Nile is joined by the Blue Nile, which rises above Lake Tana in Ethiopia, issues from that lake at over 6,000 feet, and follows a tortuous and often inaccessible course until reaching the Sudan where it is swollen by two other important Ethiopian rivers, the Rahad and Dinder. Consequently, the Blue Nile's contribution to the annual discharge of the Nile below Khartoum is twice that of the White Nile. As the rainy season in the Ethiopian Highlands begins in March or April the Blue Nile at Khartoum is on the rise by June. August and September are the months when it is in spate; this is true also for the Nile throughout the Sudan and Egypt. The flood discharge of the Blue Nile is about forty times as great as its minimum discharge in April. In other words, the Blue Nile largely determines the annual cycle of river flow below Khartoum. The only important subsequent change is the addition of the Atbara, another river from Ethiopia, which merely emphasizes the cycle established by the Blue Nile, with an annual discharge about one-quarter of the latter. Like the rivers Rahad and Dinder, the Atbara is a torrential stream which is tremendous in summer flood but only a series of stagnant pools in winter.

For the remainder of its course the Nile flows through desert terrain which provides no significant tributary. Its flow is interrupted by cataracts which impede navigation, and its volume is determined by irrigation and, to a lesser degree, by percolation and evaporation.

CONTROL OF THE NILE

In its natural state the flow of the Nile is too irregular to permit a large population. To reduce the annual oscillations in river flow and to make the maximum use of the Nile waters, a system of dams and barrages has been developed. It is important to note that a dam is built to store water and often to produce hydro-electric power, while a barrage is designed to raise the river level to the height of irrigation canals above its emplacement. Two problems render difficult the task of providing adequate annual storage: the large quantities of silt in the flood waters of the Blue Nile, and the occurrence of very low years. Both can be overcome by overall development of the basin, a dire emergency in view of the rapid growth of population and the need to increase the cultivated area.

The basin of the Nile should be considered as a geographical whole, but its political division has prejudiced the chances of attaining the optimum control over the river. Schemes for a 'century of storage' have been thwarted by the fear and suspicion of both Egyptians and Sudanese. The British-initiated Nile Waters Agreement of 1929 was denounced in 1955 by the Sudan, which was receiving only 8 per cent of the total water supplies. This agreement also provided that the Sudan might not construct, without Egypt's consent, works which would affect the amount of water flowing into Egypt, and that Egypt might not undertake conservation works without the Sudan's prior consent. Fortunately, the two countries came to a measure of agreement in November 1959, when they decided that new storage for national requirements should be constructed on the land of the beneficiary. It is a pity that earlier schemes have been rejected for ones which satisfy national aspirations.

Whereas rational hydrological development of the Nile Basin would necessitate storage and drainage works mainly outside of Egypt, she has persisted with the construction of the High Dam at Aswan (H in Fig. 32), which will cost about £400 million and be completed by 1974. This project is more expensive than the excavation of the proposed Jonglei Canal (Q) to by-pass the swamps of the Sudd, a project postponed indefinitely, although it would increase the water available by an amount equal to the loss sustained by evaporation from the new reservoir above the Aswan High Dam. Furthermore, the High Dam means the flooding of a long stretch of the Nile Valley above Wadi Halfa in the Sudan, displacing population, and inundating archaeological treasures in Egypt (Plate 14). On the other hand, the Jonglei Canal scheme is not without social and economic difficulties: it has been estimated that it would directly affect 600,000 and indirectly another 400,000 Nilotic pastoralists, through the loss of pasture and fisheries.

The system of control developed until the middle of this century is theoretically simple. Water for Egypt is stored by the Jebel Aulia Dam (L) on the White Nile above Khartoum, and by the Aswan Dam, in order to increase low water discharge in Egypt by fifty per cent. The Nile in flood cannot be restrained; at other times storage can take place. Jebel Aulia Dam, built by the Egyptian Government in the 1930s, stores water from August until March; the Aswan Dam stores the falling flood of autumn after the main silty flood has refertilized the soils of Egypt. The stored water enables perennial irrigation to occur, and it increases the productive capacity of the land.

The distribution of water is regulated by the series of barrages: Isna (G), Nag Hammadi (F), Asyut (E), at the head of the delta at Mohammed Ali (C), and along the Rosetta and Damietta branches at Edfina (A) and Zifta (B). These last two barrages also serve to prevent sea water from encroaching too far inland. Before the construction of barrages the various irrigation canals had to be deep enough at their heads to take in water from the river at its low stage. In the nineteenth century, under Mohammed Ali Pasha, huge canal digging efforts were made by hundreds of thousands of labourers committed to a period of sixty days unpaid work, the *corvée*.

In the Sudan, the Sennar Dam has long stored the water of the Blue Nile after the main flood has passed in late August and early September. It is not merely an important storage reservoir, but maintains levels necessary for the irrigation of the Gezira scheme, the life blood of the Sudanese economy. In 1961, work commenced on two different dams in the Sudan: the Roseires Dam, with three times the capacity of the Sennar Dam to provide additional water for irrigating the Manaqil extension of the Gezira scheme and later the Kenana scheme; and secondly, the Atbara Dam at Khashm el Girba to irrigate an area of 500,000 feddans (feddan = 1·038 acres) on the west bank of the Atbara.

Progress was made in the control of the upper Nile in 1954 when the Owen Falls Dam in Uganda converted Lake Victoria into a vast reservoir. It also provides hydro-electric power for use in Uganda. A dam at Mutir would have a similar effect on Lake Albert, as would one below Lake Tana in Ethiopia; both lakes would be invaluable long-term storage reservoirs. Other possible projects for the Nile include:

(a) Masindi Port Barrage, to speed the flow of water through Lake Kioga;

(b) Nimule Dam, to ensure navigability of the river when the Mutir Dam lowers the water level;

(c) Dams at the fifth and sixth (Sabaloka Gorge) cataracts for hydro-electric power;

(d) Semna Dam, to provide 25 milliard cubic metres for irrigation and hydro-electric power.

The Wadi Rayan scheme for water storage during exceptional floods has been made unnecessary by the construction of the High Dam at Aswan.

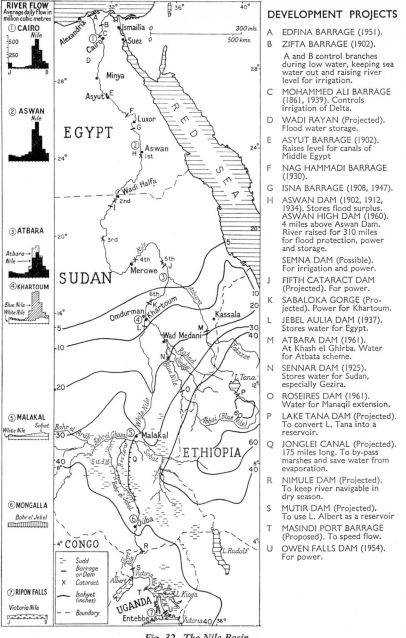

RIVER FLOW
Average daily flow in million cubic metres

① CAIRO *Nile*
500
250
J   D

② ASWAN *Nile*

③ ATBARA
Atbara →
Nile →

④ KHARTOUM
Blue Nile →
White Nile →

⑤ MALAKAL
White Nile   *Sobat*

⑥ MONGALLA
Bahr el Jebel

⑦ RIPON FALLS
Victoria Nile
J   D

Key:
≈ Sudd
— Barrage or Dam
× Cataract
— Isohyet (inches)
-- Boundary

DEVELOPMENT PROJECTS

A   EDFINA BARRAGE (1951).

B   ZIFTA BARRAGE (1902).

     A and B control branches during low water, keeping sea water out and raising river level for irrigation.

C   MOHAMMED ALI BARRAGE (1861, 1939). Controls irrigation of Delta.

D   WADI RAYAN (Projected). Flood water storage.

E   ASYUT BARRAGE (1902). Raises level for canals of Middle Egypt.

F   NAG HAMMADI BARRAGE (1930).

G   ISNA BARRAGE (1908, 1947).

H   ASWAN DAM (1902, 1912, 1934). Stores flood surplus. ASWAN HIGH DAM (1960). 4 miles above Aswan Dam. River raised for 310 miles for flood protection, power and storage.

     SEMNA DAM (Possible). For irrigation and power.

J   FIFTH CATARACT DAM (Projected). For power.

K   SABALOKA GORGE (Projected). Power for Khartoum.

L   JEBEL AULIA DAM (1937). Stores water for Egypt.

M   ATBARA DAM (1961). At Khash el Ghirba. Water for Atbata scheme.

N   SENNAR DAM (1925). Stores water for Sudan, especially Gezira.

O   ROSEIRES DAM (1961). Water for Manaqil extension.

P   LAKE TANA DAM (Projected). To convert L. Tana into a reservoir.

Q   JONGLEI CANAL (Projected). 175 miles long. To by-pass marshes and save water from evaporation.

R   NIMULE DAM (Projected). To keep river navigable in dry season.

S   MUTIR DAM (Projected). To use L. Albert as a reservoir

T   MASINDI PORT BARRAGE (Proposed). To speed flow.

U   OWEN FALLS DAM (1954). For power.

Fig. 32. The Nile Basin
(After Hurst and *Oxford Regional Economic Atlas: The Middle East and North Africa*)

METHODS OF IRRIGATION

The Nile waters have been used in a variety of ways for the purpose of cultivation:

    (*a*) Seluka irrigation;
    (*b*) Basin irrigation;
    (*c*) Traditional lift irrigation;
    (*d*) Pump irrigation;
    (*e*) Perennial irrigation by gravity flow.

The word 'seluka' means digging-stick with a foot-rest, as well as the land cultivated by this tool. Seluka cultivation takes place on the moist and fertile land which has been inundated by the Nile flood. This is the traditional method of farming along the lower land.

Seluka irrigation led naturally to basin irrigation, in which the flood plain is divided into basins ranging from 400 to 40,000 feddans each, by the construction of banks along the river and cross banks to the valley sides. Basins are flooded to a depth of one to two metres for 40 to 60 days in August and September, when much silt is deposited. This method of irrigation has been practised since time immemorial in Egypt, but is now prevalent only in upper Egypt. Basin irrigation was not introduced in the northern Sudan until the early part of this century, as the areas capable of flooding are restricted; only the Kerma basin is comparable to an Egyptian basin. In areas of basin irrigation villages are on mounds above flood level, and no elaborate system of ditches is necessary. Basin irrigation is generally diminishing in extent and changing in character with the introduction of summer cultivation from wells sunk in some of the basins. There is an attempt to intensify production and to counteract the effects of variations in the irrigated area caused by oscillations in the height of the Nile flood.

The traditional water-lifting devices in use along the Nile Valley are the *shaduf* (the counter-balanced dipper), the *saqia* (water-wheel or Persian wheel turned by an ox), and the *Archimedean screw* (a screw in a cylinder turned by a handle). The saqia is still the basis of agriculture in the Northern Province of the Sudan, and is associated with an individualistic approach to farming.

Pump irrigation schemes first developed before the First World War, but the main progress has been since the Second World War. Diesel-driven pumps have enabled the irrigation of the areas formerly too high for irrigation by primitive lifting devices. Pump irrigation schemes may be private, co-operative, or government controlled. They are specially frequent in Upper Egypt and in the Sudan, where, until recently, adequate finance has not been available for large barrages, and where the area of land in the north at least has not justified large expenditure. In the Sudan, therefore, individual initiative has been prominent and private capitalists have invested large sums in irrigation. There are now many thousands of pump schemes in the Sudan, affecting an area well over ten times that under basin irrigation. The main crops grown are cotton, dura (sorghum), wheat, beans, peas and animal fodder.

A large part of the Nile Valley in Egypt, and an increasing area in the Sudan, has been converted to perennial or gravity flow irrigation. Perennial irrigation enables two or three crops on the same area of land each year, and thus permits the commercialization of agriculture through the growth of cash crops, especially cotton. Four-fifths of the cultivated area of Egypt is under perennial irrigation, the proportion increasing as one proceeds down the Nile. The delta is the principal area and is fed by three main canals. Above the delta there are complex irrigation systems based on the Asyut barrage for Middle Egypt, and the Isna and Nag Hammadi barrages for Upper Egypt. The Sudan, through the Gezira scheme, the Manaqil extension, the Kenana extension and the Atbara scheme, is making rapid progress in extending perennial irrigation. The outstanding success of the Gezira scheme is a great inducement.

We should note that two other methods of irrigation occur in Egypt and the Sudan: irrigation from wells, and flush irrigation. The Sudan has examples in the Gash and Tokar deltas of flush irrigation, by inundation canals in the former and by natural flooding in the latter.

The need for drainage to accompany irrigation works was inadequately realized until after the First World War, when it was seen that continuous irrigation without drainage led to a toxic accumulation of salts. Now drainage works are being rapidly extended.

TRANSPORT

Steamship transport of passengers on the Nile is relatively more important in the Sudan than in Egypt, where alternative land routes are available and where international tourism has greatly diminished. The importance of the Nile between Khartoum and Juba is particularly noteworthy, as this section is navigable at all seasons and it is the main artery for southern Sudan. The cataracts naturally restrict navigation below Khartoum, and the Nile no longer serves as an export route for the Sudan, the traffic being diverted by rail to Port Sudan.

In Egypt, below Aswan, the Nile becomes an important highway for goods, and use is also made of the canal Bahr el Youssef. Steamships, tugs and barges are common, but are greatly outnumbered by the slow sailing boats known as *felukas*. Using the prevailing wind from the north they sail upstream with manufactured products, fertilizers and petroleum, and then drift gently downstream with agricultural products and building materials. In the delta, the canals are the traditional arteries of trade and passenger traffic.

FURTHER READING

H. E. Hurst, *The Nile*, 1952; J. Besançon, *L'Homme et le Nil*, 1957; K. M. Barbour, 'Irrigation in the Sudan', *Trans. and Papers, Inst. British Geographers*, 1959, 243–63.

10. A small part of the Hassi Messaoud oil fields in the Sahara (p. 139). Mud, used in drilling, is prepared in the nearby building. Three wells are burning in the distance and near them, and to the far left, are tanks indicating producing wells.

11. The 320-mile long natural gas pipeline (diameter 24 inches) which crosses the Atlas Mountains to Algiers, Arzew (where this photograph was taken), and Oran.

12. Watering sheep and goats in northern Libya. Water is lifted in a goat-skin bag. Vegetation is sparse near waterholes.

13. Libyan and Italian agriculture near the Tripolitanian coast (p. 146). The orderly arrangement of olives and vines planted by the Italians during their occupation of Libya, contrasts with the patches of Arab date palm groves and tiny gardens.

CHAPTER NINE

Egypt

EGYPT forms the north-east corner of Africa. Roughly rectangular in shape, its boundaries are mostly straight lines. It comprises 386,200 square miles and is therefore larger than Nigeria but only two-fifths of the size of its southern neighbour, Sudan. The value of the Egyptian land area is very unequal; $96\frac{1}{2}$ per cent is almost uninhabited desert and so 99 per cent of the 27 million inhabitants (1962) live on only 13,500 square miles in the Nile Valley and the delta, one of the most densely peopled areas in the world. As the majority of the rapidly growing population live directly from agriculture, and industrial development is limited, the man–land ratio is a serious fact in Egypt. Agricultural expansion is difficult because, apart from along the Mediterranean coast, where rainfall ranges from four to eight inches, and interior Sinai where the total exceeds ten inches, all water comes from the Nile. Upper Egypt receives only about one-tenth of an inch of rainfall per annum. No wonder that Egypt is often called the 'gift of the Nile'.

HISTORY

In one sense the history of Egypt has been the taming and utilization of the Nile. The earliest phase of economic development, the transition from food-gathering to food-producing, is the subject of conflicting opinions. It has long been held that the beginnings of agriculture and the domestication of animals occurred during the upper Palaeolithic, and coincided with the movement of hunters from the drying up steppes of the Sahara into the marshlands of the Nile Valley. Now it is postulated by Butzer that Palaeolithic man migrated into the Valley 10,000–20,000 years before the development of agriculture about 5,000 years ago. Villages are assumed to have existed some 2,000 years before the dawn of agriculture.

The basin system of irrigation evolved gradually, but its widespread extension required a more advanced social and political organization, such as that provided by Menes (3400 B.C.). The success of this system was the economic basis of Egyptian civilization. The extent of cultivation in ancient Egypt is estimated at 6 million acres, not substantially

* By John I. Clarke.

6

lower than that of today, but during the late Roman and early Arabic periods 1½ million acres were lost to cultivation because of increased salinity in the Berari belt of the delta. Cereals were the backbone of ancient agriculture, so much so that the Greeks called the Egyptians the Artophagoi. Barley was the main crop of Pharaonic Egypt, but was overtaken by wheat in the Middle Ages. Pulses, onions and flax, the main fibre, were also important. Pastures were never adequate, so fodder crops such as fenugreek, vetch, beans and bersim (clover) were grown. Later the Arabs introduced new cash crops—sugar, rice, cotton, tobacco, indigo and saffron—which were grown on areas perennially irrigated by primitive methods.

Not all foreign influences were beneficial. From 525 B.C. until A.D. 1936 Egypt was ruled without interruption by foreign conquerors: Persians, Greeks, Romans, Arabs, Turks, Mamelukes, British. Until the mid-twentieth century the ruling classes were invariably alien. Modern Egypt began with Mohammed Ali (1805–49); he introduced modern methods of perennial irrigation which have revolutionized the Egyptian economy by increasing the crop area and enabling extensive cash crop production. Massive growth of population and towns ensued, and Egypt began to rely on the world market. With the opening of the Suez Canal in 1869, Egypt became of great interest to the European powers, notably Britain. From 1882 until independence in 1936 Egypt was occupied by British troops, who retained a garrison along the Suez Canal until the disastrous Suez campaign of 1956.

The most significant event in the recent history of Egypt was the coup d'état by a group of army officers on 23 July 1952 and the abdication of King Farouk. Since 1952, Egypt has gained the Suez Canal, started the High Dam at Aswan, made substantial social and economic reforms, as well as achieving greater national identity. Egypt has become one of the most socialist countries in the world. Apart from land, the government now runs all the basic enterprises: banking, insurance, foreign trade, transport, broadcasting, the press and the main industries, mines, constructional enterprises, and hotels. Ambitions to lead a united Arab world crystallized in the formation of the United Arab Republic (U.A.R.) on 1 February 1958. Dreams of its extension were halted in 1961 by Syria's decision to secede.

THE PHYSICAL ENVIRONMENT

From Wadi Halfa to the Mediterranean, a distance of over 900 miles, the Nile carves the deserts of Egypt into two unequal parts. In the far south the river is deeply entrenched with precipitous cliffs on the eastern side and a lower escarpment on the west. North of Aswan the valley widens, but it is never much more than 12 miles across. This is the main belt of basin irrigation, although perennial irrigation is gaining ground. The delta begins north of Cairo; one-half is perennially irrigated, and one-half is occupied by lakes, swamps and cultivable desert areas awaiting reclamation.

Apart from dependence upon the life-giving waters of the Nile, agriculture in the valley and delta is closely related to the quality of the soils. The majority of valley soils are heavy or light loams, but thick black clay soils (*ard soda*) occur in the delta, and sandy soils (*ard sofra*) prevail along the desert fringes and towards the south. Fertility is generally high, but increased salinity has rendered some soils useless for cultivation, especially in those parts of Upper Egypt where perennial irrigation has replaced basin irrigation.

The Western Desert is a vast arid treeless plain composed of limestones and sandstones of Jurassic to Miocene age. Over half the plain is below 1,000 feet, the southern part being generally above this level. The only highland is in the extreme south-west, the Gilf Kebir, but along the western boundary with Libya massive sand-dune formations make an effective barrier. A number of depressions with steep limestone edges are characteristic of the Western Desert, and as underground water comes to the surface they are the sites of oases: Siwa, Bahariya, Farafra, Dakhla and Kharga. Most of the soils are sandy, many are saline, but in general they are related to the geology. The oasis of Siwa, where the water is distinctly saline, and the Qattara Depression are well below sea-level, the lowest point of Qattara being minus 440 feet. The other four oases lie along a line about 125 miles west of the Nile and are higher in the south than in the north. About 40 miles south of Cairo, the Fayum Depression is about 150 feet below sea-level; as Lake Qarun in the depression is markedly saline, the Fayum receives its fresh water from the Nile by canal.

The Eastern Desert, bounded by the Nile and the Red Sea, is a highland zone ranging from 1,000 to 7,000 feet. Limestones predominate in the north-west but elsewhere are the igneous and metamorphic rocks of the Basement Complex, along with Nubian Sandstones. Wadis running east and west dissect the plateau; the exception is the southward-flowing Wadi Qena. No extensive plain fringes the Red Sea coast, and, as drinking water is lacking, settlements are rare.

The Sinai Peninsula linking Africa with Asia may be divided into two regions. In the north there is a large dissected limestone plateau which is tilted northward and descends gently from the mountains of El Tih at about 5,000 feet towards the broad coastal plain. Covered with sand dunes, the plain is fringed by the salt-water lagoon of Lake Bardawil. In the south is a highland composed of granitic and meta-morphic rocks, dominated by Gebel Katherina (8,644 feet) in which locality is St. Catherine's convent. To the east the highland plunges into the Gulf of Aqaba; to the west it is bounded by a series of step-faults and the narrow coastal plain of El Qa'a.

PEOPLE AND LAND

Unlike most African countries, Egypt has no problem of ethnic diversity. Most Egyptians are of an almost pure Hamitic type, and, apart from about 2 million Coptic Christians and a small number of Jews, they are all Moslems. All Egyptians speak Arabic. The Copts and the Jews are mainly town-dwellers in Middle and Lower Egypt and work in trade and crafts.

More important than the composition of population is its growth (see Fig. 33). It has risen from about 10 millions in 1900 to 27 millions in 1961, and the rate of growth is now as high as 2·4 per cent per annum. At this rate the population will double again within 35 years. The reason is that while death rates have steadily declined through improved medical services, birth rates have remained high.

Unfortunately, there has been no corresponding increase in either agricultural land or crop production. The cultivated land per head has actually declined; and while yields have risen through greater use of fertilizers and better strains, crop production has increased at a slower rate than population. So Egypt still imports substantial quantities of foodstuffs; nevertheless, large numbers go hungry. The excess of rural population ensures low wages, low standards of living, inadequate and unbalanced diets, low productivity of workers and migration to the towns. The energy-sapping worm diseases bilharzia and ankylostoma have increased with the spread of perennial irrigation, particularly in Lower Egypt. Malaria and trachoma affect the majority of the rural population. Hygiene is primitive. Though much progress has been made during recent years, it is difficult to do more than prevent further decline in living standards.

Population densities in the delta and the valley increase from the northern and southern extremities towards the head of the delta. Density has considerable influence upon land use; the importance of maize, the main food crop, closely follows population density. The densities have nearer parallels in the Far East than in Africa, and they have sharp boundaries along the valley edges. Land is so valuable that even the area occupied by settlements, about one million feddans (1 acre = 1·038 feddans), is considered grossly excessive.

One of the main causes of poverty in Egypt has been the unequal distribution of land ownership. Before the Agrarian Reform Law of September 1952, over 70 per cent of land owners had less than one feddan, and occupied in all only 13 per cent of the cultivated area;

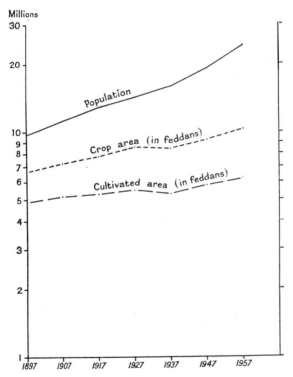

Fig. 33. Semi-logarithmic graph showing rates of change of population in Egypt (1897–1957) in comparison with crop and cultivated areas

while 6 per cent of the owners had five feddans or more, and accounted for nearly two-thirds of the cultivated area. There were also about 2 million landless labourers. The multiplication of minute holdings reflected the desire of the Egyptian *fellah* to possess land, as well as the Moslem law of equal inheritance which accelerates division of property. Disparities in land ownership tended to produce two classes of society; the very rich absentee landlords living grandly in Cairo and Alexandria, and the mass of the poor *fellaheen*. Few of the landowners felt responsibilities to the fellaheen. The Agrarian Reform Law was designed to redistribute about 565,000 feddans, just under 10 per cent of Egypt's farmland. All landowners were permitted to retain 200 arable feddans for their own use, and up to 100 feddans for their children. The land held in excess was to be requisitioned within a five-year period, unless the large landholders sold their surplus in two to five feddan lots to farmers with less than ten feddans. By June 1959 only 295,000 feddans had been redistributed, of which a large proportion was confiscated royal estates.

Several projects for agricultural extension are in progress, especially in the delta. The main project is the High Dam at Aswan, which will allow an extra 2 million feddans to be cultivated. The conversion of 700,000 feddans from basin to perennial irrigation will also become possible, and a minimum rice area of 700,000 feddans will be guaranteed. Apart from providing enough water for all the agricultural needs of the country, the High Dam will generate hydro-electricity to be utilized for the production of iron and steel and chemical fertilizers. With Russian aid and equipment, work on the High Dam began in January 1960; it should be completed by 1974.

Expansion of the cultivated area is unlikely to provide a permanent solution. The area may be doubled from 6 million to 12 million feddans, but no more than 10 million feddans may be available by A.D. 2000 even if the most ambitious projects are completed. The Egyptian deserts cannot be extensively cultivated. More significant is the transfer from basin to perennial irrigation, which greatly increases the crop area.

ECONOMIC DEVELOPMENT

Agriculture

Perennial irrigation has enabled Egypt to grow a wide range of crops more effectively than by former irrigation techniques. It has meant the rediscovery and rise of cotton, rice and sugar cane, the introduction of maize and the decline of wheat, flax, indigo and saffron. Summer cash crops have become dominant at the expense of food crops. Dangers are overcropping, soil exhaustion, soil salinity (caused by excessive watering), and 'red water famine' or the lack of silt-laden red water so beneficial to the fertility of basin irrigated lands.

Maize, bersim, cotton and wheat are the four main crops. Wheat has a widespread distribution, but the other three all require moderate temperatures and a humid atmosphere, and thus diminish southward even within the delta. Maize and bersim have had more regular acreages, and each occupies more than one-fifth of the crop area. Maize is slightly more important and is the staple food of man and animal. Bersim (lucerne) is grown as a fodder crop because of the lack of natural pasture, and has permitted an increase in the number of animals. It is also invaluable as a green nitrogen fertilizer.

Cotton is the main cash crop and is of primary importance in the Egyptian economy. It provides international credit, but its acreage varies annually under the influence of world prices and crises. Restrictions have rarely been effective. Cotton occupies from $12\frac{1}{2}$ to 25 per cent of the crop area, and is favoured most by large landowners and their tenants. Because of the dangers of reliance upon one cash crop, the present government is making great efforts to diversify production as well as to maintain high yields and quality. Unfortunately, pest attacks have drastically reduced production in recent years. Egypt produces about two-thirds of the world's long staple cotton (over $1\frac{3}{8}$ inches: Karmak) and one-third of the long/medium staple ($1\frac{1}{8}$–$1\frac{3}{8}$ inches: Giza 30 and 23). The long/medium and medium staples prevail on the black soils of the delta; while the long staple is found in Middle Egypt. Exports are no longer mainly to Britain; the U.S.S.R., Spain, Czechoslovakia, China, India, France, Yugoslavia and the U.S.A. are now the main importers. Cotton is sown between February and April and is picked between August and October.

Secondary crops tend to be more localized in distribution. They include rice, beans, vegetables, barley, sugar cane and fruit; while beans and barley are declining, rice, vegetables and fruit are gaining ground. Rice has transformed agriculture in the northern part of the delta, and is widespread in the Fayum. It now accounts for about eight per cent of the crop area of Egypt. Water demands are at least twice those of cotton. Rice, which is quite salt tolerant, is used as a reclamation crop, permitting numerous washings of the soil to leach out surplus salts, and is often subsequently replaced by bersim and animal husbandry, and later by cotton. Barley is generally found on inferior sandy soils on the delta margins or in the southern part of the valley. Fruit is also associated with sandy soils. Sugar cane is a valuable industrial crop, though small in area, and is largely confined to the Minya and Kena–Aswan areas of Upper Egypt. Kena and Asyut grow lentils.

Minor crops include onions for export, sesame and groundnuts for vegetable oils, and lupins, chick-peas and fenugreek as substitutes for bersim; all are grown on the poorer valley soils.

Agricultural Regions

The valley and delta fall into four agricultural regions: the delta, the metropolitan triangle, Middle Egypt and the south. The delta is not one of the most densely populated areas. Land use is extensive, holdings are large and production is for cash. Variations exist within the delta:

(*a*) the central area, Gharbiya, concentrates on cotton;

(*b*) the sectors along the distributaries, Kafr El-Sheikh and Dakahliya, are important for rice;

(*c*) the eastern and western areas of the delta, Sharkiya and Beheira respectively, have sandier soils and more diversified crops, including sesame and groundnuts, as well as crops destined for the markets of Cairo and Alexandria;

(*d*) the Berari swamp and marsh land in the northern part of the delta awaits reclamation, except around Alexandria where 25,000 acres of swamp land were reclaimed during the 1950s;

(*e*) the northern dune belt between Lake Burullus and the sea is sparsely populated, but is used for vegetable and fruit production because of its higher rainfall (9 inches);

(*f*) the province of Tahrir on the west of the delta, where about 30,000 acres of desert land are in process of reclamation and colonization.

The metropolitan triangle includes Munufiya and Kaliubiya provinces at the head of the delta, as well as Giza in the lower part of the valley. This region has more sandy soils, very high population densities, and a dominance of food crops rather than commercial crops. Maize, bersim and wheat are more extensive than cotton. Local specialities are milk products in Munufiya, fruit in Kaliubiya, and vegetables in Giza.

In Middle Egypt, which comprises the Fayum, Beni Suef, Minya, Asyut and Sohag, the same food crops predominate, with a southward diminution of bersim and increase of wheat and beans. In addition, the Minya–Asyut sector is noted for cotton, Minya for sugar-cane and onions, and the Fayum for rice and fruit.

In the south, more marginal soil and climatic conditions occur and basin irrigation prevails. Although maize and wheat are still important, sugar and lentils largely replace cotton and bersim as cash crops, and barley assumes more importance than elsewhere in the valley.

The coastal zone of Marmarica and Maraeotis receives five to eight inches of rainfall along a belt twelve to twenty miles wide. Known as

Dera'a Bahari, it had more productive cultivation in Roman times than now. Vines, olives, fruit and grain were grown, and wells, cisterns, tanks and aqueducts were widespread. Neglect of water supplies and the prevalence of nomadism reduced the value of this zone until recently, when repairs to water systems and dry-farming techniques have been accompanied by some settlement of nomads. Barley is the main crop now. No large-scale migration from the valley can be envisaged, as the zone has restricted supplies of underground water and unreliable rainfall.

Fig. 34. Egypt; economic
The towns are numbered thus: 1. Tanta, 2. Mahalla el Kubra, 3. Mansura, 4. Damanhûr, 5. Zagazig, 6. Shibin el Kom.

In northern Sinai, the arid Jeffar is pastured by nomads who also cultivate patches of wheat and barley. Along the valleys of the Wadi al-Arish some irrigation occurs. About 50,000 acres in north-western Sinai may be irrigated by the transfer of fresh water from the Ismailia Canal under the Suez Canal.

The only other cultivated areas are the oases, whose romantic attraction should not exaggerate their small agricultural significance. Their cultivated area is only 30,000 feddans. In Roman times they were undoubtedly more productive, but their water supplies have deteriorated through neglect and choking. Grain, olives, figs, dates and pomegranates are the principal crops.

The Western Desert is sparsely inhabited by pastoral nomads, who probably number no more than 25,000. They are mainly sheep-herders of the Awlad Ali clans, who come from Libya. Only the camel-herders of the south practise extensive nomadism. Development projects for the Wadi el Natrun, Qattara Depression and Fuka–Ras el Hikma region are designed to establish forage reserves, cultivation and industry, to improve water supplies, and to settle the nomads. In the Eastern Desert rainfall is slightly more generous, and nomadic tribes can often find good grazing.

Industry and Mining

The development of industry is frequently mentioned as a means of reducing rural over-population and raising standards of living. Such a solution is doubtful, although the government is encouraging rapid and substantial development through import measures, tax reliefs, new businesses, and state participation in large enterprises. The local market can grow considerably only if the national income rises. Much recent industrial expansion has not been the result of a national income rise, but of the acquisition of large foreign loans, especially from the U.S.S.R., U.S.A. and World Bank. Industries are still largely concentrated in Cairo and Alexandria. Moreover, the main industries are still textiles, tanning and leather goods (especially shoes), foodstuffs (especially sugar refining and oil-seed crushing), tobacco and cigarettes and construction materials (especially cement). The textile industry includes cotton, wool, rayon, jute, linen, carpets, clothing and hosiery. Factories are either small or very large; large mills occur at Mahalla el Kubra and Kafr el Dawal in the delta.

Great priority is now being given to the development of heavy industries: iron and steel, fertilizers and oil refining. Egypt's only large iron and steel plant at Helwan, south of Cairo, has an estimated annual capacity of 220,000 tons of iron and steel products. Yet Egypt possesses important deposits of iron ore about 30 miles east of Aswan which have remained unexploited since their discovery in 1937 because of the lack of fuel resources. She also produces limestone, manganese (200,000 tons) and feldspar, other requirements of an iron and steel industry. The fuel problem will be overcome by the completion of the Aswan High Dam, which should produce 2·4 million kW or 10,000 million kWh per annum. This power will also provide for the fertilizer industry already established at Aswan, now utilizing electricity from the existing Aswan Dam.

Egypt has no coal, but commercial production of oil began as early as 1911. Unfortunately her production and reserves are negligible in comparison with other states of the Middle East; in 1961 production was 3,671,000 tons, about a million tons less than internal consumption. Nearly two-thirds came from the developing field of Belayim in western Sinai, where offshore drilling has proved fruitful. All the other oilfields (see Fig. 34) are along the Red Sea coasts, though there is some renewed interest in the Western Desert. Increased investments are going into refineries and petrochemical plants, localized at Alexandria and Suez, while pipelines are to connect these installations with the major cities of the interior.

Unfortunately, Egypt is not rich in mineral wealth in commercial quantities, and few minerals are regularly exploited. Apart from those mentioned, gold, lead, zinc, copper, gypsum and chromium are all exported in small amounts. Phosphate reserves are estimated at 179 million tons of rock, and are developed at Safaga and Quseir along the Red Sea coast, and at Siba'iya in the upper Nile Valley where there is a superphosphate plant. Limestone production is the basis of the growing cement industry, centred on Tourah and Helwan.

The expansion of the electric power grid is likely to assist dispersal of industry. Small village and cottage industries, such as rugs, carpets, spinning and weaving, and jam and fruit preserving are being encouraged. Despite these measures, the drift into the cities continues, causing low wages and persistent unemployment.

URBANIZATION

At the census of 1960 it was found that 35·4 per cent of the population of Egypt were living in towns, compared with 30·1 per cent in 1947, and 24·3 in 1937. More than 8 million people were town-dwellers. The rapidity of recent urbanization has meant that many of the new town-dwellers are inadequately assimilated and live only as beggars, boot-blacks, pedlars and the like. Slum conditions are common, as many Egyptians prefer urban poverty to rural poverty.

Cairo and Alexandria are the great foci of attraction. Cairo (3,346,000 in 1960), or El Kahira, is the largest city in Africa and in the Arab world, and has great influence throughout the latter. Located at the head of the delta, Cairo lies mainly along the eastern flood plain of the Nile, although it spreads on to the bluffs. Well connected by railways with all the other towns of the delta and the Nile Valley up to Aswan, Cairo predominates in nearly all political, social and economic activities, except maritime trade. Alexandria (1,513,000) is the main port of Egypt. Founded by the Greeks in 332 B.C. away from the mud of the Nile, Alexandria lies along a narrow isthmus backed by Lake Mariut. Imports of machinery, iron and steel, wheat, petroleum, vehicles and fertilizers are largely balanced by exports of cotton. Trade is now mainly with U.S.S.R., U.S.A., West Germany, Czechoslovakia, China, East Germany, Italy and the United Kingdom, but that with the latter has been drastically reduced since the Suez crisis. Industries are mainly concerned with cotton, although Alexandria has a growing number of other manufactures. It is also a summer resort.

Of the eleven other towns with populations exceeding 100,000 (1960), three groups may be distinguished:

(*a*) Suez Canal ports: Port Said (244,000), Ismailia (111,000) and Suez (203,000);

(*b*) Industrial centres in the delta: Tanta (184,000), Mahalla el Kubra (178,000), Mansura (152,000), Damanhûr (126,000), Zagazig (124,000) and Giza (250,000).

(*c*) Valley centres: Asyut (122,000) and Fayum (102,000).

Most of the towns with populations between 50,000 and 100,000 are along the valley.

THE SUEZ CANAL

Opened in 1869, the Suez Canal stretches 101 miles from Port Said on the Mediterranean via Lake Timsah and the Bitter Lakes to Suez on the Red Sea. In 1956 Egypt nationalized the European-dominated Suez Canal Company, whose concession was due to expire in 1968. Three years later the World Bank granted a loan to Egypt in order to improve the Port Said harbour and the canal which permits the passage of vessels of up to 37 feet draught. Egypt has successfully managed the increased traffic of the canal.

Although the volume of traffic passing through the canal has oscillated according to the economic state of the world, there has been a great increase since 1942. In the mid-thirties traffic amounted to 30–40 million tons; by 1962 it was over 197 million tons. Daily transits now exceed 50 vessels. Much of this increase has resulted from the growing dependence of Europe upon Persian Gulf oil, which accounts for three-quarters of the heavier northbound traffic. Ores, raw materials, and bulk foodstuffs also move north; while machinery, manufactured goods and fertilizers move south. The British share of shipping passing through the canal has declined from three-quarters in the late nineteenth century, to 21 · 7 per cent in 1962. Larger tankers and Saharan oilfields may eventually diminish Egyptian revenues from shipping using the canal, but at present there are few indications of that.

FURTHER READING

The most valuable general texts are J. Ball, *Contributions to the Geography of Egypt*, Cairo, 1939; J. Besançon, *L'Homme et le Nil*, 1957; G. L. Harris (Ed.), *Egypt*, New Haven, Human Relations Area Files, 1957; H. E. Hurst, *The Nile*, 1952; C. Issawi, *Egypt in Revolution: an Economic Analysis*, 1963; J. and S. Lacouture, *Egypt in Transition*, 1958; and R. R. Platt and M. B. Hefny, *Egypt: a Compendium*, New York, 1958. More specialized works include G. Hamden, *Studies in Egyptian Urbanism*, Cairo, 1959 and 'Evolution of Irrigation Agriculture in Egypt' in L. D. Stamp (Ed.), *A History of Land Use in Arid Regions*, UNESCO, 1961, 119–42; A. B. Mountjoy, 'The Suez Canal at Mid-Century', *Economic Geography*, 1958, 155–67; and D. Warriner, *Land Reform and Development in the Middle East*, 2nd Ed., 1962.

CHAPTER TEN

The Sudan

WITH an area of 967,500 square miles, the Sudan is the largest country in Africa, yet its population numbers only 12 million (1961 estimate), most of whom are concentrated along the Nile Valley. On 1 January 1956 the Sudan became an independent republic after 57 years of rule by the Anglo-Egyptian Condominium. This form of government, though in some ways unsatisfactory, gave efficient administration and justice, and spared the Sudan the problem of European colonization. It also introduced parts of the Sudan to world trade, and gave political identity to a part of Africa with little physical individuality, diverse in races and religions, and for long the prey of numerous outside powers and peoples.

THE PHYSICAL ENVIRONMENT

The Regions

Much of the Sudan is composed of a huge clay plain of aggradation surrounded by uplands. The clay plain is down-warped and so flat that rivers crossing it relinquish their loads and generally overflow their banks whenever their volumes rise. The only diversity of relief is provided by a number of inselbergs, remnants of a former surface, now in the process of gradual burial under alluvium. During the rainy season the southern half of the plain (south of latitude 10°N.) becomes a swamp, to be replaced in the dry season by a parched wilderness blackened by fires. The swamps are termed *sudd* (Arabic 'obstruction'), because of the large masses of floating vegetation which impede navigation. Permanent marshes are restricted, however, to the courses of the main rivers.

The eastern edge of the clay plain is not entirely coincident with the Sudanese–Ethiopian boundary, and massifs and spurs of the Ethiopian Mountains project into the Sudan. Some are composed of the Basement Complex, others of Tertiary lavas.

To the south of the clay plain is the Ironstone Plateau, 1,500–2,500 feet above sea-level, and drained by numerous streams flowing down

* By John I. Clarke.

from the Nile–Congo divide. Composed of the Basement Complex, it is the prevalence of red laterite on the interfluves between the streams which has given the plateau its name. Sporadic inselbergs (cp. Plate 4)

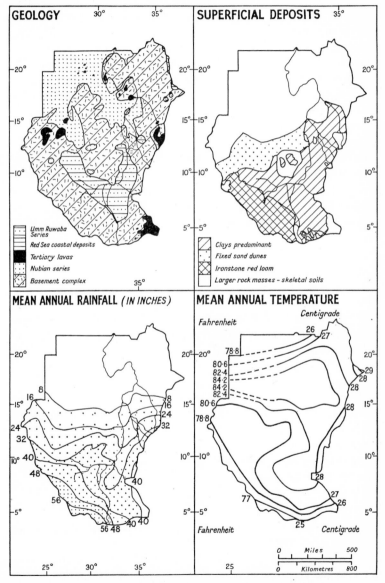

Fig. 35. Some physical features of the Sudan. (Partly after Lebon)

rise 500–1,000 feet above the general level, and towards the border with Uganda higher massifs occur, especially the Imatong Mountains.

Two other areas of exposed Basement Complex, massifs and inselbergs are the highlands of western Darfur and the Nuba Mountains in the heart of Kordofan, but these two areas receive no more than one-half the rainfall of the Ironstone Plateau. Furthermore, rising up above the Basement Complex in Darfur is the volcanic massif of Jebel Marra, whose summit on the edge of an extinct volcanic crater is at nearly 10,000 feet. The Jebel Marra has a rugged 'badland' topography, caused by the erosion of lavas and tuffs. A similar but smaller massif is found to the north-east, the isolated Meidob Hills.

Between the Jebel Marra and the Nuba Mountains stretching for over 600 miles from east-north-east to west-south-west is a long belt of sand dunes. Formed during an arid phase of the Pleistocene, they are now fixed by acacia trees and savanna. Known in Arabic as *qoz*, the sand sea has been a hindrance to communication between Khartoum and Darfur.

Northward the fixed dunes region gives way to desert, which varies from rocky and gravelly plateaux, massifs, mesas and buttes, to vast expanses of live sand dunes. The latter are most frequent west of the Nile in the Libyan Desert (which covers large areas of Egypt and the Sudan as well as Libya), in contrast to the Nubian Desert east of the Nile which is more rocky and mountainous. Between the two deserts the Nile winds northward through areas of increasing desiccation. Its restricted and incised valley, sometimes fringed by flood-plain terraces, is generally too narrow for large-scale irrigated agriculture.

Along the eastern edge of the Nubian Desert are the rugged Red Sea Hills, which rise to over 5,000 feet, and are again composed of Basement Complex. To the east they are represented by a dissected fault-line escarpment 2,000–4,000 feet high, marking the western edge of the Red Sea rift valley. The escarpment overlooks a coastal plain 10 to 25 miles wide festooned by dunes and coral reefs.

Climatic Transition

More significant economically than the relief regions is the climatic transition from north to south, in particular the gradual increase in the total annual rainfall (Fig. 35). North of latitude 20°N. little or no rain falls and perpetual drought prevails. Southward, rain falls and is increasingly reliable. As far south as 6°N. there is an almost imperceptible gradation of the Tropical Continental climate. Most important is the cleavage of the year into two distinct seasons: (*a*) a hot summer or high sun period during which torrential showers or thunderstorms are experienced—mainly in the afternoon and evening—this season is called, perhaps inappropriately, the rainy season; (*b*) a dry and, for at least a few months, cooler season. Southward the rainy season increases to over eight or nine months of the year until an attenuated Equatorial climate is reached, where no month is completely without rainfall. Along the southern boundary with the Congo (Leopoldville) and Uganda, about 60 inches are received annually.

The Sudan is a very hot country, for temperatures are rarely mitigated by altitude. Cloud cover in the south is largely responsible for the reversal from summer to winter of the average monthly temperature gradient: the mean monthly temperature of January rises from 60°F in the north to over 83°F in the south, but in June it declines from over 90°F in the north to about 78°F in the south. Consequently, central Sudan experiences the highest mean annual temperatures (Fig. 35); at Khartoum more than 100°F can be recorded during any month of the year. The highest temperatures in most parts of the Sudan normally occur just before the rainy season.

A region with climatic conditions distinct from the north–south sequence is the Red Sea coast and the eastern slopes of the Red Sea Hills. Here the main rainfall occurs during the winter months of November and December, while the summer heat of May to October is partially attenuated by sea breezes.

Vegetation

The vegetation of the Sudan is closely dependent upon the régime and distribution of rainfall. All vegetation is tropophilous—or adapted to the contrast between the two seasons, in particular to a period of drought. Throughout most of the Sudan there is a period of growth and greenery, followed by a period of withering, burning and browning. The increase in the length of the growing period is the cause of the sequence of vegetation types encountered from north to south across the Sudan (Fig. 36). Desert in the north gives way gradually to Semi-desert (Sub-desert Steppe), which is replaced by Grass Steppe first with acacia and short grass and then with acacia and tall grass. Farther south the proportion of semi-deciduous woodland increases to form a belt of Woodland-Savanna.

Only in a few highland areas is the general sequence disturbed, notably in the Jebel Marra, the Nuba Mountains, the Imatong

Mountains and Boma Plateau in the far south, where there is Montane vegetation.

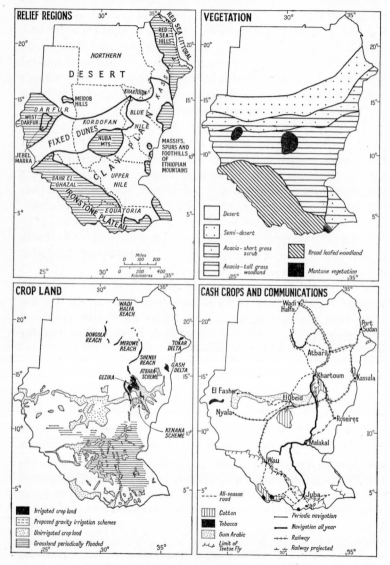

Fig. 36. More geographical features of the Sudan
(Relief regions after Lebon, Vegetation after Andrews and Tothill, and Crop Land and Crops after Barbour)

PEOPLES

The varied conquests and reconquests of different parts of the Sudan have produced considerable ethnic diversity. Most significant is the cultural divide which occurs approximately along latitude 12°N. The name Sudan is derived from the Arabic term *Bilad-es-Sudan* meaning 'Country of the Blacks', but, in fact, the essentially negroid, pagan and socially backward peoples found south of latitude 12°N. account for only one-quarter of the total population. To the north the peoples are largely of mixed negroid-white descent, Arabic in culture and Moslem in religion.

Significantly, the line dividing these two major cultural zones is not very far from the boundary between the deserts and semi-deserts of the north, and the savannas and woodlands of the south. Although Sudanese nationalists, anxious to spread national consciousness, have accused British imperialists of fostering and exaggerating this cultural divide, it is a reality caused by the centuries of stagnation and isolation experienced in the south, in contrast with the continuous contact of the north with Egypt. Sudanese are now anxious to point out that the closeness of this contact may be over-emphasized, as it has been shown genetically that the ethnic ties between Egyptians and Sudanese are not as close as those between Sudanese and other neighbours. As the northern Sudan has few extensive areas available for irrigated agriculture, nomadic pastoralism is more prevalent than in Upper Egypt, where sedentary cultivation is prominent, and Egypt offers no attractions to Sudanese pastoralists. Contacts are therefore mainly through trade.

A synopsis of the peoples of the Sudan can only be schematic. The peoples of northern Sudan, apart from the town-dwellers, belong to several district groups: the Beja of the Red Sea Hills, the Nubians of the northern Nile, the Arabs of the Central Rainlands, and the Nuba of the hill masses. The Beja are fairly typical Hamites, and have been called Fuzzy-Wuzzies because of their unruly shocks of dark frizzy hair. They resisted the incursions of Arab nomads, although there has been some admixture of Negro blood. Nubian cultivators have more Negro blood, revealed in rich chocolate-brown skins. Nubia has been arbitrarily dissected by the Egypto–Sudan boundary. The tribes revealing the largest proportion of Arab or Semitic blood are undoubtedly the camel breeders of the desert and semi-desert zones; including the Kababish, Ja'aliin, and Kawahla. The Baggara cattle-owners have more negroid features but not as many as the very dark-skinned Nuba cultivators inhabiting the hills of central Sudan. The

Fur of Darfur are also negroid, but there tribal complexity is acute. Although many tribes of northern Sudan have retained their own language, they are largely agreed upon the use of Arabic as the *lingua franca* and Islam as the faith.

The peoples of southern Sudan are even more complex. Linguistically they comprise three broad groups: the Nilotes of the upper Nile, Nilo-Hamites of the far south, and the Sudanic tribes west of the Nile. The Nilotes include the Dinka, Shilluk, Nuer, Anuak, Burun and other tribes. Nearly six feet tall on the average, naked, spindle shanked, long-headed and elaborately coiffured, they are famous as cattle-breeders. Nilo-Hamites are shorter, have flatter noses, wear clothes and breed goats. Among the more prognathous Sudanic tribes, who closely resemble West African Negroes in physique, are the Azande and Moru-Madi of the south-west. In general, the peoples of the south do not exhibit any great affection for the Arab peoples of the north: they retain bitter memories of the slave trade.

Except along certain stretches of the Nile, around the Nuba Mountains and among the Aweil Dinka, the density of population is everywhere low. The reasons vary from region to region and include prolonged traffic in slaves, the lack of public security, poor agricultural techniques, and the shortage of drinking water, as well as the prevalence of nomadism and the occurrence of sleeping sickness. On the other hand, a very high birth-rate (over fifty per thousand) and a declining death-rate (under twenty per thousand) suggest a doubling of population by 1980.

SETTLEMENT

Rural settlement is invariably clustered, partly because of water supply and partly for security. Along the northern Nile villages are often linear and parallel to the river. In the extreme south, however, dispersed settlement is favoured by the Azande.

House-types vary from north to south. In the north, flat roofs and sun-dried bricks daubed with clay or dung prevail; in the centre and south, round huts are built with thatched conical roofs made of grass, millet stalks and wood poles. In Islamic central Sudan compounds made of millet stalks surround the houses, but in the south houses and villages tend to be more rudimentary.

As industries are rare, towns are few and far between. Khartoum was founded on a defensive site by the Egyptians in 1824, was destroyed by the Dervishes of the Mahdi, and subsequently rebuilt by Kitchener. It is now the seat of government and the University, as well as the main commercial centre. Neighbouring Omdurman contrasts with Khartoum in being an essentially Sudanese city, while Khartoum North has a more functional atmosphere. Together, the three towns contain about 312,000 inhabitants (1961)—between one-quarter and one-third of the total urban population of the Sudan. The other towns of the Sudan have grown very slowly, and most appear as overgrown villages with only administrative functions. Most of the other main towns are also found within the Central Rainlands: El Fasher, El Obeid, Kosti, Wad Medani, Kassala, Atbara. Elsewhere towns are rare; a few are located along the northern Nile, while the southern provinces each have one important centre with between eight and ten thousand inhabitants and a total urban population of less than two per cent. Along the Red Sea littoral, Port Sudan is expanding rapidly as the Sudan's only modern port (Plate 15).

ECONOMIC DEVELOPMENT

Agriculture

The Sudan is almost entirely an agricultural country; its most important crop is cotton, which is the backbone of the Sudanese economy. Long-staple cotton is chiefly grown in irrigated areas, while short-staple cotton is grown in areas of rain cultivation. The production of the irrigated areas accounts for over three-quarters of the total cotton crop.

The staple food crop almost everywhere is common millet (*Sorghum vulgare*) or *dura* in Arabic. Irrigated cereals include wheat—which is also grown without irrigation in the Jebel Marra—barley and maize. Dates are the principal crop of the irrigated areas of Northern Province. Groundnuts are also widely grown as a food crop, and sesame as a source of vegetable oil. Other less widespread crops which are gradually gaining in significance are coffee, tobacco, sugar, rice, citrus, mango and guava.

Pastoralism and cultivation are both prominent, and occur together —a rare feature in Africa. Few families are without livestock, which are valued not merely for food, manure and labour but also for prestige. Rain-fed and irrigated cultivation exist. Although the latter is commercially more vital, rain cultivation plays a very important role, and until recently it accounted for four-fifths of the Sudan's crop production.

Rain Cultivation and Pastoralism

Once again there is a succession of types of agriculture and land use from north to south across the Sudan, disturbed only by the occurrence of the Nile and its belt of irrigated agriculture. In the far north vegetation is sparse, but camels, sheep and goats graze on the scrub, and milk forms a basic item in the diet of their Arab nomadic herders. Better grazing is found on the plateau of northern Darfur, where *gizu* grazing occurs, in which plants are dried before consumption. Vegetation is more plentiful further south in the zone of acacia-grass scrub, which is the zone most frequented by Arab nomads. Cultivation in the north is virtually confined to the Nile Valley.

Rain cultivation is possible as far north as latitude $16\frac{1}{2}°$N., but the principal area of rain cultivation lies between latitudes $10\frac{1}{2}°$N. and 15°N. (Fig. 36), between the 8- and 24-inch isohyets. This zone is often called the Central Rainlands. It is the principal area of land rotation. The length of the rotation depends on the proximity of the village; near the village the land has only short rest periods, but further away the number of rest years is more than double the years of cultivation. Most cultivated areas under land rotation are also used as pastures, because the livestock belonging to cultivators graze upon the stubble and on the regenerating vegetation. The environs of villages are grazed intensively by livestock of the cultivators, but further afield the pastures are frequented by the flocks of nomads and semi-nomads. Unfortunately, local over-grazing and over-cultivation are real dangers and may lead to serious degradation of vegetation and soil erosion. Cultivated lands not used as pastures are mainly those managed by *hariq* or fire cultivation, in which controlled burning clears the ground of weeds before cultivation takes place. Common millet (*Sorghum vulgare*) and bulrush millet (*Pennisetum typhoideum*) are the main crops; sown after the early rains of July they are harvested in December. In this region gum arabic is tapped from the wild *Acacia senegal* and *Acacia seyal*; most of the world's supply comes from the province of Kordofan. The only exceptions to this traditional pattern of land rotation in the Central Rainlands are the small areas of terrace cultivation found in the Nuba Mountains and the Jebel Maraa.

Before the Condominium the wells, cisterns and curious reservoirs hollowed out of baobab trees provided insufficient water supplies for the region. During times of drought pastoralists and cultivators alike migrated towards the Nile, Bahr el Arab or Sobat. The Condominium and the Republic have both stimulated general economic improvement in several ways. Railways were built from Atbara to Port Sudan and Suakin (1905), and from Khartoum to Sennar and El Obeid (1911). Subsequently, a line was opened from Sennar to Kassala and beyond to join up with the line from Atbara to Port Sudan. More recently, there have been further railway connections to Roseires (1954), Nyala (1959) in Darfur, and Wau (1962) in Bahr el Ghazal. This last line may stimulate meat and gum exports. Certainly the lines to Kassala and Roseires have assisted the semi-mechanized cultivation of millet at Jebel Dali, Jebel Mazmum and Gadaref. Secondly, deeper wells were dug along railway lines and in towns, as well as in the piedmont zone of the Nuba Mountains. In this zone a large number of small reservoirs (*hafirat*, sing. *hafir*), which capture rainwater and the flow of intermittent streams, have greatly encouraged settlement and agricultural extension. Formerly dug by hand, they are now dug by machines especially to foster cotton growing. Thirdly, the great Gezira Irrigation Scheme, its extensions, and the flush irrigation schemes of the Gash and Tokar deltas have greatly stimulated development. Finally, the presence of the three towns (Khartoum, Khartoum North and Omdurman), which form a conurbation remarkable for its nodal position, has also been instrumental in helping the Central Rainlands to become the progressive nucleus of the Sudan.

Immediately south of the Central Rainlands is a zone in which cultivation is unimportant. It is an irregular east–west zone across southern Darfur and southern Kordofan, which is the grazing area of the cattle-owning Baggara. They migrate southward to the clay plains during the dry season, but retreat northward from the mud and flies in the rainy season.

On the southern clay plains are found scattered patches of cultivation along the slightly elevated interfluves above the floodable marshlands. Along these interfluves, and along the northern edge of the Ironstone Plateau, are the permanent villages and conical thatched huts of the Nilotic tribesmen: Dinka, Nuer, Shilluk and Murle. Here dura is grown under a system of land rotation during the rainy season when the surrounding areas are inundated. But the Nilotes are mainly cattle-owners and keep their cattle tethered during the rainy season. At the beginning of the dry season the tribes migrate ten to fifty miles from their villages to set up cattle camps in the heart of the dry plain near a river course, where fires are lit to eliminate the rank grass of the rainy season. Food supplies are supplemented by fishing. Slight variations to this prevailing pattern are found around Aweil among the western Dinka, who are so congested that they practise permanent cultivation, and among some of the northern Dinka and Shilluk, who produce some millet and cotton for sale.

Slave-raiding in the nineteenth century drastically reduced the population of the Ironstone Plateau, so that large expanses are very sparsely inhabited. Less than 2 per cent of the province of Equatoria is cultivated, although it is estimated that about 87 per cent is potentially cultivable. Moreover, infestation by the tsetse fly prevents livestock farming. Shifting cultivation is practised, but annual burning undermines soil fertility. The local negroid tribes include the Azande, a large tribe of mixed Bantu and Sudanic stock, for whom a development scheme known as the Zande Scheme (Azande is the plural of Zande) was initiated in 1945. The first major agricultural scheme implemented in the southern Sudan, it has proved successful in establishing a cotton industry based on local short-staple cotton production. The method adopted was to re-organize the native practice of shifting cultivation and resettle tens of thousands of the backward Azande in elongated villages. Apart from cotton, cash crops include millet, sesame, palm oil, sugar cane and groundnuts, while cassava, maize and bananas are grown as subsistence crops. Expansion of tobacco, coffee and tea cultivation is likely, as these commodities figure high in the list of Sudanese imports. Perhaps the key problem is the cost of transport from this exceedingly remote region. Exports will be greatly assisted by the railway from Wau to Juba, scheduled for completion in 1965.

Irrigated Agriculture

Although rain-fed cultivation is increasing in the Sudan, irrigated agriculture provides the bulk of the commercial crops. The irrigated area doubled during the 1950s, and there is no reason to believe that there will be a slowing down of the rate of progress. Irrigation has been vital to the development of northern and central Sudan, where rainfall is meagre and unreliable. As there are few minerals and industries in the country, irrigation schemes have attracted both private and public investment on a large scale. The nature of the investment, the density of population and the relief have all influenced the methods of irrigation adopted.

Below Khartoum the Nile is incised, and only discontinuous alluvial terraces are available for irrigation. They are wider where the Nile crosses the sandstones of the Nubian Series than where it crosses the Basement Complex, but altogether their areas are insufficient to warrant large barrages and gravity flow irrigation. Traditional methods of irrigation (seluka, basin, primitive lift) are gradually being replaced by pump irrigation, especially in the Merowe-Dongola and Shendi-Berber reaches of the river, where, apart from numerous small private schemes, there are several large government pump schemes. Unfortunately, many individuals have refused to participate in new schemes. Dates are the principal crop grown by irrigation in the north, but wheat, barley, millet and maize are also common. Lubia (hyacinth bean) is grown as a fodder crop for the bullocks which work the *saqias*. Cotton is only grown on the private scheme at Zeidab.

The north has long been overpopulated, and there is little room for expansion of irrigation. Thus there is a migration southwards to central Sudan, where a large part of the sparsely populated clay plain is suitable for irrigation. The problem is further aggravated by the need to resettle in the central Sudan the peoples displaced by the flooding above the High Dam at Aswan. Accordingly the Sudan Government began work in 1961 on the Atbara Dam at Khashm el Girba, where it is intended to settle people from Wadi Halfa on 500,000 feddans. Some of the land will be devoted to sugar-cane, and a large sugar refinery has been constructed.

On the triangular plain between the White Nile and Blue Nile the great Gezira Irrigation Scheme came into operation in 1925 with the completion of the Sennar Dam. It has become a model for the economic development of backward regions. The plain of the Gezira, which in Arabic means 'island', slopes gently from the Blue Nile to the White Nile and northward towards Khartoum. With very heavy clay soil suitable for keeping water at the surface and for growing long-staple cotton the plain proved ideal for irrigation. The Manaqil Extension to the Gezira Scheme, completed in 1961, brought the total irrigated area to 1,800,000 feddans. This extension was developed in four phases and draws water from the new Roseires Dam, begun in 1961, which will also eventually irrigate a further scheme of 1,200,000 feddans in the Kenana Extension.

The Gezira Scheme (Plate 16) is famous for creating the richest peasantry in Africa. Tenants have forty feddans each, split into four fields, although some tenancies are being divided. A four course rotation over eight years is used, with cotton, the cash crop, grown one in four years on each field. The heavy clays are of low fertility, and at least half of the land is always under fallow. Cotton is sown in August, watered at fortnightly intervals for about 28 weeks and picked between early January and early May. The scheme is operated on a partnership basis, the Sudan Government and the tenant each receiving 42 per cent of the cotton crop, the Sudan Gezira Board 10 per cent, and the Tenant Reserve Fund, Local Government, and Social Development Departments each 2 per cent. On the Manaqil

Extension farms are smaller (15 feddans), and a three year rotation is in operation. Other crops grown are dura, lubia for fodder and beans, all of which are kept by the tenant. Animal fodder is always needed, because of the Sudanese practice of keeping cattle, sheep and goats for home milk and meat supply.

Central Sudan is also the principal part of the country for pumping schemes, which have developed so extraordinarily since the war. Around Khartoum these schemes tend to be small, and are mainly fruit and vegetable gardens supplying the Khartoum market. On the other hand, most of the pump irrigated lands along the White Nile and Blue Nile are occupied by schemes of more than 1,000 feddans, initiated largely by private enterprise. Nearly all irrigated land along the White Nile is used for cotton, but along the Blue Nile some fruit is grown alongside the cotton fields. It is hoped that eventually some 2,550,000 feddans will be irrigated by pumps, and that this figure will include some schemes along the Rahad and Dinder rivers.

In view of all these potential demands upon the waters of the Nile, it is not surprising that agreement between Egypt and the Sudan has been difficult. The Sudan seems to have more irrigable land than she has water to use upon it, hence the apparently lavish acreage per tenant on the Gezira and high proportion of fallow.

Mention must here be made of the two flush irrigation schemes under government control utilizing the flood waters of the rivers Baraka and Gash. These two Ethiopian rivers flow for 70 to 110 days in summer, soak their deltas, and cover them with a fine layer of silt. They are unfortunately irregular, and the areas irrigated for cultivation vary from 40,000 to 75,000 feddans a year in the Gash Delta, and from 32,000 to 136.000 feddans in the Tokar Delta (of the Baraka River). High-grade cotton is sown soon after the flood subsides, and crops can be excellent.

ECONOMIC DIVERSIFICATION

The Sudan is too dependent on cotton; for years nearly half of its revenue has been derived from the Gezira alone, and much of the remainder from the Sudan Railways which transport the cotton to Port Sudan (Plate 15). Unfortunately, fluctuations in the production and price of cotton give grave concern to the government, which is now making great efforts to diversify the economy. Encouragement is being given to the production of sugar cane at Guneid on the Blue Nile, castor oil seed in the Kassala area, wheat along the Shendi reach, tobacco in Equatoria, and to other crops.

Apart from a little mining of gold, copper, mica and manganese, and the widespread production of salt, mineral extraction is negligible; and as yet the Sudan has neither coal nor oil. Manufacturing industry depends upon imported petroleum, and is still of small importance. Cotton is the basis of development; several large mills and many small works in the Khartoum conurbation are engaged in cotton ginning, spinning and weaving. Khartoum also has the usual simple processing and consumer-good industries. Until recently the only other factories of note were salt works at Port Sudan, a cement factory at Atbara, cotton mills at Nzara and a meat cannery at Kosti. New industries are being encouraged, such as a cigarette factory at Wad Medani, a pulp and paper mill at Malakal, cement works at Rabak and Kosti, sugar refineries at Guneid and Khashm el Girba and a cardboard factory at Aroma.

The economic dilemma of the Sudan is aggravated by rapid population growth and by regional disparity in economic development. The concentration of population, wealth and opportunity along the Nile contrasts with the multiplicity of human and economic problems in southern Sudan. Gradually a more even spread of agricultural and industrial activities is being achieved as the result of government policy and of improvements in communications.

The latter are vital in a country so vast, where deserts and swamps create such physical difficulties. Asphalted and all-season roads are rare, partly because of the lack of stones, but extensions are in progress. The government has favoured railways rather than roads for inter-regional communications (Fig. 36). The new railway links with the three southern provinces (Bahr el Ghazal, Upper Nile and Equatoria) are of political as well as economic significance, for communications with the south have depended upon Nile steamers or, latterly, upon the Sudan Airways. Juba is always accessible by steamer from Khartoum, but Wau only seasonally. The Blue Nile steamers from Khartoum up to Roseires were replaced by the railway in 1954. Another railway is projected along the east bank of the White Nile from Khartoum to Rabak, a continuation of the line from Wadi Halfa.

Like many countries in Africa, the Sudan faces a severe problem of developing an immense area thinly populated by diverse human groups at low standards of living.

Further Reading

K. M. Barbour, *The Republic of the Sudan*, 1961, is a valuable regional geography, and J. D. Tothill (Ed.), *Agriculture in the Sudan*, 1948, is still indispensable. See also M. Shibeika, *The Independent Sudan: The History of a Nation*, New York, 1960; K. J. Krotki, *21 Facts about the Sudanese*, Khartoum, 1958; P. de Schlippe, *Shifting Cultivation in Africa*, 1956; and A. Gaitskell, *Gezira: a story of development in the Sudan*, 1959. Noteworthy articles include J. H. G. Lebon, 'Land-use mapping in the Sudan', *Economic Geography*, 1959, 60–70; J. H. G. Lebon and B. C. Robertson, 'The Jebel Marra, Darfur, and its Region', *Geographical Journal*, 1961, 30–49; and G. Hamdan, 'The Growth and Functional Structure of Khartoum' *Geographical Review*, 1960, 21–40; K. M. Barbour, 'North and South in Sudan, a Study in Human Contrasts', *Annals of the Association of American Geographers*, 1964, 209–26.

CHAPTER ELEVEN

Ethiopia and the Horn of Africa

THE Horn of Africa thrusting out into the Indian Ocean is fringed with desert lowlands mostly inhabited by the Somali peoples, and is virtually sealed off from the rest of Africa by the high dissected Ethiopian tableland which stretches from the Red Sea to the East African Plateau about Lake Rudolf. Ethiopia, formerly called Abyssinia, and the Horn together form a clear sub-unit of Africa, which remained very isolated from European influences after the Middle Ages and developed a distinctive identity; only the Portuguese, searching for Prester John, made any contact. Despite the legendary renown of Ethiopia, Europe and Egypt did not penetrate into this part of Africa until after the opening of the Suez Canal (1869). Italy, France, Britain and Ethiopia then divided up the lands of the Somali, and Italy occupied Eritrea, but Ethiopia under Emperor Menelik II fiercely resisted foreign invasions, especially by the Italians, and managed to preserve her independence.

However, isolation was no longer possible. The initial step in its reduction was taken by the Emperor, who in 1894 granted a concession for the construction of a 486-mile railway from Djibouti in French Somaliland to Addis Ababa, the new Ethiopian capital founded in 1878. Between 1897 and 1908, Menelik extended, consolidated and delimited his territories, taking in Somali and other lands. Haile Selassie became Prince Regent in 1916 and Emperor in 1930, and has advanced the process of modernization, but in 1936 the Italians conquered the country and ruled it as a colony until the liberation of Italian East Africa in 1941. The extent of Ethiopia has since been changed by the addition of Eritrea, the former Italian colony to the north along the Red Sea, which joined the Ethiopian Federation as an autonomous state in 1952 and was fully incorporated into Ethiopia in 1962. Italian Somaliland was under British control from 1941 until 1950 when it became a United Nations Trust Territory known as Somalia. In 1960 it achieved independence just after the British Somaliland Protectorate, and both joined to form the Somali Republic, also known as Somalia. French Somaliland remains, while other areas inhabited by the Somali people are ruled by Ethiopia and Kenya.

ETHIOPIA

Ethiopia comprises some 395,000 square miles. Compactly situated within 15 degrees of latitude and 15 degrees of longitude, Ethiopia lies astride routes connecting Africa with Asia, routes which are regaining their former significance with the increase of air traffic. In few parts of Africa is there such extensive highland or such environmental and human diversity.

Physical Regions

Ethiopia consists of a huge tableland of the Basement Complex capped by sedimentary deposits (limestones and sandstones) and by vast areas and great thicknesses of lava, known as plateau basalts. The volcanic activity was associated with the faulting which created the great north-east to south-west Rift Valley (Plate 17). Minor volcanoes, earthquakes, recent lava flows and hot springs bear witness to continued structural instability.

During pluvial phases of the Pleistocene period many Ethiopian lakes were much more extensive than they are today. Together with continued uplift of the highlands, these phases were responsible for the frequency of gorges and the deposition of large quantities of alluvium and gravel on the margins of the highlands.

The Rift Valley is generally above 5,000 feet and is floored in its southern part by many lakes (Fig. 37). The northern part comprises the inland drainage basin of the Awash River, which ends in Lake Abbe. Further north the Rift Valley opens out to the Danakil plains of Afar, the Kobar Sink (a fault basin below sea-level), and the Afar Alps (a horst parallel to the Red Sea).

The valley divides the western highlands and plateaux from the eastern ones. Both mountain masses are greatly faulted, extremely varied in geological composition, and rugged in relief. Steepness of slopes is a great hindrance to agriculture, settlement and transportation (Plate 18).

Striking features of the western highlands and plateaux are the Semien Massif which rises to 15,158 feet, small tablelands (*ambas*) isolated by river gorges, and the impressive Abbai Gorge which cuts down more than 6,000 feet below the plateau level. The River Abbai (Blue Nile), with its origin in Lake Tana, is the largest of the Ethiopian rivers in the Nile catchment area; others are the Takazze (Atbara) and

Baro. These rivers carry away about half of the total outflow of water from Ethiopia. The Omo system drains southward to join Lake Rudolf, a small portion of which lies within Ethiopia. In the far west there is a fringe of eroded remnants of the plateau, giving way to the Sudan Plains.

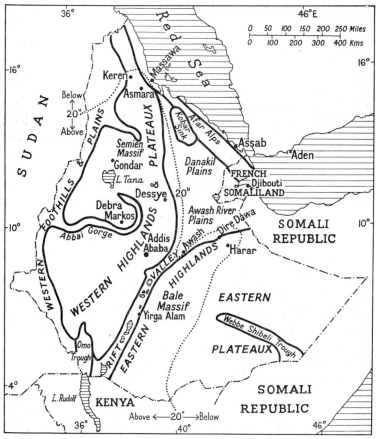

Fig. 37. Major relief regions of Ethiopia. (After Last)

The eastern highlands and plateaux present a high scarp face to the Rift Valley, but in general they descend gradually south-eastward to the Indian Ocean. The most extensive highland in Ethiopia is the Bale Massif east of Yirga-Alam, most of which is about 10,000 feet high. The northern parts of the eastern highlands are drained by the headwaters of the Webbe Shibeli, and the southern parts by the headwaters of the Juba.

Climatic Zones

The great influence of altitude on climate and vegetation was realized long ago by the Ethiopians who distinguish three types of climate. The first is the *Kolla*, found up to 6,000 feet with average temperatures of 79°F and dry (less than 20 inches annually). This climatic region (Fig. 37) has desert, thorn shrub or savanna vegetation, and is sparsely inhabited by pastoral nomads herding sheep and camels. The kolla zone includes the Danakil Plains, the Awash Valley and the lower slopes of the Somali Plateau. *Woina Dega*, between 6,000 and 8,000 feet up, is sub-tropical (72°F average) and moist (20–60 inches annually). This zone, called 'the wine highlands', includes most of the plateau country, that is, most of the cultivated and populous areas. Coffee, cotton, millets and sorghums for local consumption, and some Mediterranean fruits, including grapes and olives, are the principal crops. *Dega*, above 8,000 feet, has an average temperature of 61°F and is humid (50–70 inches annually). This high mountain zone is mainly grassland with bushes, and is devoted to livestock raising (Plate 19). Cereals, among which are wheat and barley, are grown in some localities, as well as many varieties of beans and temperate fruits. Afro-Alpine vegetation, including coarse grasses, red hot pokers (*Kniphophia*) and giant lobelias, occur above the tree-line (about 10,000 feet).

It should be stressed that there are two distinct seasons: the wet Tropical Monsoon season, the 'big rains', lasting generally from mid-June till September; followed by the dry season, often broken in February or March by the 'little rains'. Aspect greatly influences the amount of local rainfall, which is not altogether a blessing in Ethiopia. Along with bad farming, torrential monsoonal rainfall is responsible for marked erosion and leaching of the highland soils, now acid and of low fertility in crystalline areas; volcanic soils are much more fertile. The seasonal distribution of rainfall is also a principal reason why only about 7 per cent of Ethiopia is forested; other reasons are the unrestricted cutting and the lack of conservation. In this century, however, eucalyptus has been widely planted and has pushed back the indigenous juniper.

Peoples

Ethiopia has a total population estimated at 21·8 millions (1961), with a density of 55 per square mile. Population density varies with altitude (the Woina Dega having the highest densities) and also with the road pattern as the roads facilitate movement to markets.

Tiny irrigated fields, de-
sand and the Temple of
Simbel (c. 1290–1224
cut in Nubian sandstone,
t—Sudan border. The
ple is being moved to a
above to save it from in-
tion in the artifical lake
nd the Aswan High Dam.

Port Sudan (p. 181), built
ng British administration
place the shallow port of
in.

16. Gravity irrigation of the Gezira (p. 185), with the main canal in the
lower right-hand corner and the dark fields under cotton. The Blue Nile
is in the centre and the Guneid pump irrigation scheme on the right bank.

17. Recently extinct volcanoes at Bishoftu, south-east of Addis Ababa and near the Rift Valley. Teff (a poor millet) is growing in the foreground.

18. A 6,000-foot cleft in the 11,000-foot high eastern fault edge of the Ethiopian Western Highlands. Below are foothills and the Awash River Plains. Basalt is evident on the left.

19. Dega country (p. 192) near Debra Birhan, at nearly 10,000 feet, north-east of Addis Ababa. There is quite intensive cereal cultivation, and cattle are kept.

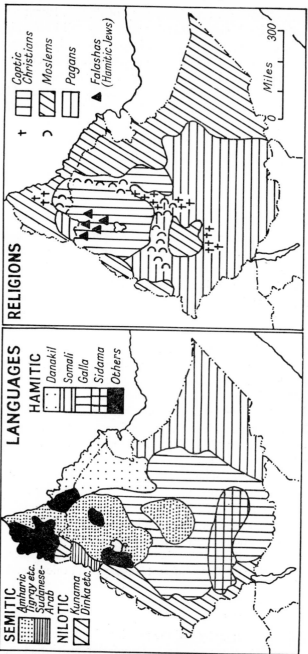

Fig. 38. *Languages and religions of Ethiopia.* (After Kuo)

7

The peoples have such a wide variety of origins, languages and religions that it is astonishing that they have been politically united as a nation for centuries. Ethiopian civilization probably originated in the assimilation of basically Hamitic peoples by an influx of Semitic tribes sometime in the first millennium B.C. They are both Caucasian peoples with European-type features, and became consolidated in the Kingdom of Aksum (first to seventh centuries A.D.). This achieved quite a high degree of civilization, and was converted to Christianity in the fourth century. Negro features are common in southern Ethiopia, however, and it is thought that they derive from a very early element pushed southward by a Hamitic race. Cut off from the sea in the seventh century by the rise of Islam, Ethiopia remained isolated for centuries, during which time she extended her influence southward. Semitic languages were imposed over large parts of northern Ethiopia, but even here pockets of primitive Hamitic peoples remained, some pagan, some Islamic and some Christian. In the south, there are many Hamitic and Negro tribes which have never been assimilated.

Two racial and linguistic groups are outstanding: the Amhara and the Galla. The Amhara number about 2 millions and are descendants of the northern Semitized aborigines. They have usually been the ruling class; Amharic is the official language, and their religion, Coptic Christianity, is the state religion. The Galla number over half of the total population, and are racially closely allied to the Somali. They are pagan or Islamic and speak a Hamitic language with many different dialects. They are generally found south of and at lower altitudes than the Amhara, but some have penetrated into the northern part of the Ethiopian Highlands. Most Galla are farmers or labourers, and, unlike other sedentary Ethiopians, live in isolated houses and small family groups.

Other ethnic groups of numerical if not cultural importance are the Falasha, the so-called 'Black Jews' of Ethiopia found north of Lake Tana, the Sidama, a Hamitic race in the south, the Danakil, fierce tribesmen of the north-east, the nomadic Somali of the eastern frontier zone and the Nilotic Negroes of the western frontier regions. Within all these and other ethnic groups there are substantial tribal differences. It is said that there are forty different languages in Ethiopia and eight in Eritrea.

Society and Settlement

The difficult topography and the paucity of outside contacts have helped to isolate ethnic groups and to foster provincialism, self-sufficiency, superstition and illiteracy. Some 95 per cent of the population are uneducated, although schools are increasing quite rapidly. The church and the monarchy are the unifying forces in a society in which rank and status play a prominent part. The system of land tenure is still largely feudal in character and dominates the lives of the people. The landlords have had such power over the peasant tenants (*gabars*) that the latter, who constitute the majority of the population, have been virtually serfs who owe dues to the central government, and pay rent (in tribute or in services) to the landowners. Individual ownership of land is still rare; most land is owned by the emperor and his family, the State, the Church, or by absentee land-lords. In recent years the worst features of the gabar system have disappeared and the government has announced its intention of abolishing it. Slavery, which was formerly of great importance, was abolished only in 1942.

The influence of the Ethiopian Church is enormous, despite the large number of Moslems. Unfortunately, the wealth of the Church contrasts greatly with the poverty of the people. The number of priests is exceptionally high; one estimate is that they number one-fifth of the total male population. Churches dominate the villages, in which live most Ethiopians. Apart from the capital, Asmara (120,000) in Eritrea, and Dessye, many of the towns (for example Gondar, Harar, Debra Markos, Dire Dawa and Aksum) have less than 50,000 people and are usually old, walled regional- and market-centres. They contrast with the semi-modernity of the capital, Addis Ababa ('new flower'), which has in part a more cosmopolitan atmosphere. Nearly 8,000 feet above sea level, in the heart of a rich agricultural region, and near the geographical centre of the country, Addis Ababa has grown rapidly. Its population is now about 450,000. Improved communications have greatly assisted this growth, and that of several other towns (e.g. Dessye, Awash, Keren).

Church and State are closely linked, but the power of the emperor is supreme. Haile Selassie is an absolute monarch who has ruled since 1930. All progress must receive his sanction. He has given the country a constitutional government, has modernized many of its institutions and has opened it up to agricultural and industrial development.

Agriculture

Some nine-tenths of the population of Ethiopia are dependent upon agriculture, but only a small proportion of the total area is utilized: about 9 per cent is arable and some 30 per cent pastoral.

Arable and mixed farming are especially important in the Ethiopian Highlands; in the semi-arid and arid areas of the east they depend largely on opportunities for irrigation. It is primitive subsistence cultivation, using crude implements and techniques; wheeled transport, for example, is almost unknown on farms, and pack animals are much used. Modernization presupposes widespread education and a complete change of outlook and system.

The main cereals are teff (a type of millet), which is one of the bases of the diet, dura (sorghum), bultuk and dagussa (drought-resistant cereals), wheat, barley and maize. The land-use of Gende Hogalo, a small village (pop. 138 in 1953) in the Central Highlands, studied by C. Brooke, illustrates the importance of cereals (see Fig. 39).

Coffee (of the mocha variety) is increasing in importance as a cash crop and represents 55–65 per cent of the total exports, much going to the United States. Plantations are mainly in the south-west, but many 'coffee forests' grow wild and untended, and production could be greatly multiplied. Many areas have black and dark brown clay soils, and a climate suitable for cotton, the cultivation of which is increasing. Nevertheless, cotton is still imported to supply Ethiopia's textile mills at Asmara, Dire Dawa, Addis Ababa and elsewhere. Sugar is no longer imported, as cane sugar is now produced in large quantities by the plantation and factory at Wonji, fifty miles south-east of Addis Ababa. Commercial production of fruit and vegetables is small but increasing, especially on irrigated farms in Eritrea, where vineyards are also noteworthy. Oilseeds are produced in large quantities, and form the second largest item in the export trade. It is thought that exports could be considerably expanded. Oil is extracted from the seeds of rape, sesame, sunflowers, cotton, pumpkins, mustard, cabbages and flax, as well as from peanuts and castor beans. Other crops include koba, a fibre crop for ropes and food, and khat, the leaves of which are chewed as a stimulant.

Animals, however, are still a sign of wealth, especially among the nomads of the dry lowlands and the settled pastoralists of the foothills. FAO estimates of livestock give 20 million cattle, 20 million sheep, 15 million goats, 3 million horses, mules and donkeys and 600,000 camels. Overgrazing and the resultant soil erosion are great problems in the drier areas. Unfortunately, the quality of the meat and the quantity and quality of milk are low, and diseases prevalent. A million and a half cattle die annually of rinderpest, and other regular diseases include contagious pleuropneumonia, anthrax, black leg and tick fever. No European and few Middle Eastern countries will accept

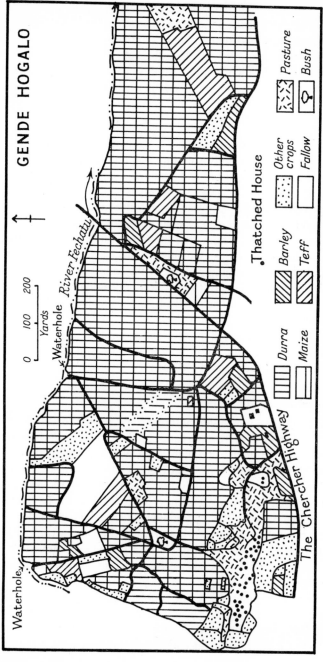

Fig. 39. Land use of Gende Hogalo, Ethiopia. (After Brooke)

Ethiopian meat, although hides and skins are the third largest export; their annual value reaches the equivalent of nearly £2 million.

It is sometimes said that Ethiopia's agricultural potential is great enough for her to become 'the breadbasket of the Middle East', but this would necessitate enormous capital investment and a complete social revolution; both seem unlikely in the immediate future.

Industries and Mining

Manufacturing and mining play a relatively unimportant part in the economy. There are only a few hundred small industrial enterprises in Ethiopia, processing food and producing simple consumer goods. Most are located in or near Addis Ababa and Asmara. The total employed is probably between twenty-five and thirty thousand. Ethiopian investments are very small; most of the capital is foreign. Moreover, Ethiopians show little liking for trade, most of which is in the hands of numerous Armenians, Greeks, Indians and Arabs.

No agreed estimates are available of the country's mineral wealth. Various deposits are known to exist, but only gold (in the far south), potash, platinum and salt are worked. Neither coal nor oil is available in significant quantities. Ethiopia's rivers have immense hydro-electric power potential, although projects have been delayed by lack of hydrological data. The power station at Koka on the Awash has more than doubled output of electricity.

Development

Economic development and internal trade depend to a large extent on the improvement of transport and communications. Until recently, the 486 mile Franco–Ethiopian Railway from Addis Ababa to Djibouti carried 40 or 50 per cent of the country's freight. Now the road from the capital to Assab is of growing importance. The Italians built many excellent roads, but these fell into disrepair. In 1950, the International Bank for Reconstruction and Development made a loan for their reconstruction and for the construction of new roads. Many radiate from Addis Ababa. Ethiopian Air Lines have a good internal system, operating from over 30 provincial towns, as well as a number of international routes.

Shortage of capital is a major problem. Italian reparations have enabled some development, especially the Koka power plant. The International Bank made other loans to establish the Development Bank, and to improve the telecommunications network. But money does not mean automatic progress; training of personnel is vital, and in this connection the Point Four Programme, operating under the United States International Co-operation Administration, and various specialized agencies of the United Nations have made valuable contributions. Progress also depends upon the wills of the people and the Emperor, and upon reform of the social and land-owning systems.

Eritrea

Eritrea is worthy of special mention, first because it was, until 1962, an autonomous unit federated with Ethiopia, and second because it experienced a half century of Italian rule (1890–1941) when it developed far more rapidly than Ethiopia. After the departure of the Italians development practically ceased, and Eritrea has lost its identity.

Eritrea had an area of 45,000 square miles, comprising a narrow and arid coastal plain, the central Eritrean Plateau (6,000–8,000 feet) a prolongation of the Ethiopian Highlands, and gentle western slopes towards the Sudan. Much of the plateau receives more than twenty inches of rainfall per annum, but the rest suffers from aridity.

The 1,100,000 people (1950) belong to various groups: the nomadic Arab Beja tribes of the west, the Negro cultivators of the south-west, the Tigrinya-speaking Coptic highlanders, the Arab Afar nomads of the southern coastal plains, and the urban Eritreans of Asmara, Massawa and so on. Although 80 per cent of the population are dependent upon agriculture, only three-fifths of these are settled agriculturalists who work the 3 per cent of Eritrea which is cultivable; the remaining two-fifths of the agricultural population are nomads.

Farming is poor and backward, and has to contend with the difficulties of monsoonal rainfall, stony soils, insufficient underground water, communal land ownership and banditry. The Italians, who numbered 60,000 in 1941, attempted to develop irrigated agriculture on the coastal plain, especially for cotton and cereals. They also established industries, and constructed 224 miles of railway, two seaports (Massawa and Assab), a good road system and several towns. Only 17,000 Italians remain, and general economic activity has declined. Asmara (120,000) was the capital of Eritrea and is connected by railway with the port of Massawa (17,000). Since 1952 the port of Assab has grown much more rapidly than either Massawa or Djibouti. Both Massawa and Assab have salt industries and together they control the maritime trade of Ethiopia.

THE HORN OF AFRICA

The dominant people in the Horn of Africa are the Somali, who are classed as Eastern Hamites, both linguistically and ethnologically, like most of the peoples of North-East Africa. They claim, however, to be of Arab (i.e. Semitic) origin, because they invaded Africa from Arabia, and have also adopted the Sunni form of Islam. They have no great racial purity, but are generally tall, robust and militant. One of the most important features of the Somali nation is its division into tribal groups (Fig. 40), tribes, sub-tribes and clans (*rers*). This structure in

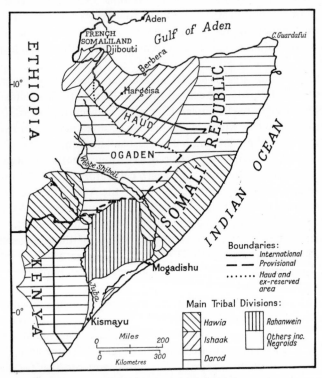

Fig. 40. The lands of the Somali

the form of a family tree lends emphasis to nationalist claims. There is also, however, a system of class and caste, the lowest of which are the smiths, leather-workers and hunters. Apart from the prevailing illiteracy and pressing need for education, one of the great impediments to development is the attitude (like that of other African pastoralists) that manual work is degrading.

The only other peoples in the Horn are a few Arabs in the coastal towns, and some Negroes in the river valleys. But the boundaries of the Somali Republic, created in 1960 following the independence of the British Somaliland Protectorate and the Trusteeship Territory of Somalia, do not coincide with the limits of the Somali people, who are numerous in the three surrounding territories.

NUMBERS OF SOMALI
(Estimated, 1959)

Somali Republic		1,900,000
Former Italian Trusteeship	1,300,000	
Former British Protectorate	600,000	
Ogaden Province of Ethiopia		300,000
Northern Frontier Province of Kenya		70,000
French Somaliland		30,000

The presence of Somali in Ethiopia and the provisional nature of the border between the two countries are the causes of much tension. There are also movements for the incorporation of French Somaliland and the Somali areas of Kenya into the Somali Republic.

FRENCH SOMALILAND

French Somaliland is the only part of the Horn remaining under European control, and is an Overseas Territory of the French Community comprising only 9,071 square miles with a population of about 80,000 (1961). There is only one town, Djibouti (41,000), which is a strategic port and calling point on an inlet of the Gulf of Aden, and the terminus of the railway to Addis Ababa. It is consequently also a transit port for Ethiopia.

THE SOMALI REPUBLIC (SOMALIA)

With 262,000 square miles, the Somali Republic is well over twice as large as the British Isles, but it has only 2 million people (1962). Most of the country is semi-arid or arid, especially the north, where there is usually less than 10 inches of rainfall and many parts have less than 5 inches. Rain falls there mostly in the *gu* season (April–June), and more lightly in the *dhair* season (October–December). Four main physical regions can be distinguished in the north-western sector. First is an open alluvial coastal plain, less than half a mile wide in the east and 60 miles across in the west. Hot and dry, it is known as *Guban*, the 'Burnt', and supports frankincense and myrrh

7*

trees, the Islamic peoples of the Horn producing nine-tenths of the Christian consumption of incense. Inland is a slightly higher plain with occasional limestone ridges and igneous hills, ranging from one to thirty miles wide, where acacias are common and watercourses invariably dry. This plain is backed by a high vertical limestone escarpment rising to 7,894 feet in the eastern part of the former Protectorate. Box-trees are common up to 6,000 feet, and cedars at greater altitude where rainfall exceeds 20 inches. Finally, there is a vast featureless plateau gently sloping south-eastward, and note-worthy for its aridity, high grass, thorn bush and euphorbia, and nomadism.

In the southern part of the republic, rainfall increases to 16 inches along the coast at Mogadishu and to over 20 inches in the south-west, but generally diminishes inland. Unlike the north, the heavy rains fall in the *dhair* season (October–December), and the light rains in the *gu* season (April–June), but these two seasons are still separated by two dry seasons: *jilal* (January–March), and *hagai* (July–September). Most of the country is low plateau or plain fringed with extensive coastal dunes, which have diverted southward the perennial flow of the Webbe Shibeli for several hundred miles until it peters out in sands and swamps. South of the Juba the bush becomes very thick with much mangrove and wild life abounds: lion, leopard, lynx, elephant, rhinoceros, hippopotamus, zebra, buffalo, gazelle, crocodile and many other species.

Livestock and Nomadism

Livestock are dominant in the economy, for most Somali are nomadic, as the following figures show:

SOMALI NOMADS*

Territory	Percentage of Somali nomadic	Estimated number nomadic
French Somaliland	20	5,000
Former Protectorate	85	514,000
Former Trusteeship	66	867,000
Ethiopia, Ogaden Region	85	257,000
Kenya	80	56,000
Total	74	1,699,000

* L. Silberman, 'Somali Nomads'. *International Social Science Journal*, 1959, p. 560.

Somali are mainly dependent upon camels, especially for milk, hides and transport; Somali families usually have 10–100 camels, but the richest have up to 1,000. Sheep and goats are also numerous, especially in the northern zone. Cattle are quite common in the settled agricultural areas of the south.

The movements of tribes are determined particularly by the availability of seasonal grazing and water (wells are more frequent in the south than the north), but other factors such as salt-licks, diseases, river crossings and inter-tribal disputes are also important. The tribes generally follow elliptical routes from the coast into the interior and back, and there is a natural tendency to press into the moister regions of Ethiopia and Kenya. By an agreement of 1897 between Britain and Ethiopia the Haud was ceded to Ethiopia, but the right was reserved for British Protectorate tribesmen to graze their flocks on the pastures which they traditionally used. About a quarter of a million Somali tribesmen are permitted to cross into Ethiopian territory every year to graze, mainly in the Haud, but there are interminable disputes. European administration has unwittingly intensified the problem of pressure on resources by reducing human and animal diseases without adequately improving grazing, water supplies and settled agriculture. This situation applies especially to former British Somaliland, from which the push of Somali migration into Ethiopia is most apparent.

Other Resources

Cultivation is confined to a few scattered areas, especially in the south; only 150,000 acres are cultivated in the former Protectorate, and 418,000 acres in the former Trusteeship. Water is the major problem, and cultivation is localized in the valleys and moister zones. The main crop is millet, but maize, sugar, bananas, rice and cotton are grown along the Webbe Shibeli and Juba rivers, where the Italians established plantations. Only bananas are grown in sufficient quantities for profitable export. There are, however, many schemes for dams, storage, new crops and other improvements when money is available.

More aggravating is the fact that there are no important minerals. Industry is slight and largely restricted to the processing of a few agricultural products, especially sugar. The Societa Agricola Italo-Somala factory at Villabruzzi along the Webbe Shibeli, daily processes about 600 tons of cane sugar. Another factory at Merca makes rope from banana-leaf fibres. Even the abundant fish resources off the coasts have not been commercially exploited, and fishing is carried out by 'outcast' tribes. An Italian tuna cannery was a casualty of the last war, and, like several other Italian enterprises, has not been restarted. On the other hand, many Somali become sailors, and communities of them can be found in many of the great ports of Britain and the Indian Ocean.

One-tenth only of the people live in the towns, which are few and isolated. Mogadishu (90,000) is the capital and main port and was sold by the Sultan of Zanzibar to Italy in 1905. In the northern zone, Hargeisa (40,000), the former capital of British Somaliland, and Berbera (40,000), a port trading with Aden, are the principal towns. Transport between the towns is difficult as there are no railways and most of the roads are rough cleared tracks used only in the dry season.

The Somali Republic is poor and has little with which to pay for her necessary imports; the main exports are livestock and skins. Both Italian and British Somalilands were financial liabilities to their European rulers, and it seems that external financial aid will long be vital. Her physical conditions and social and economic structures are not unlike those of Libya, but she is without oil. It is difficult to envisage economic viability.

FURTHER READING

Ethiopia: E. W. Luther, *Ethiopia To-day*, 1958, is a good account by an economist, G. C. Last, 'The Geography of Ethiopia', *The Ethiopia Observer*, 1962, 82–134, also has a comprehensive bibliography. Other useful works are E. Ullendorff, *The Ethiopians*, 1959; D. A. Talbot, *Contemporary Ethiopia*, New York, 1952; L. T. C. Kuo, 'Ethiopia', *Focus*, June, 1955; C. Brooke, 'The rural village in the Ethiopian Highlands', *Geographical Review*, 1959, 58–75; Y. Abul-Haggag, *Physiographical aspects of Northern Ethiopia*, 1960; and F. J. Simoons, *Northwest Ethiopia; peoples and economy*, Madison, 1960; C. Jesman, *The Ethiopian Paradox*, 1963.

Somalilands: International Bank for Reconstruction and Development, *The Economy of the Trust Territory of Somaliland*, New York, 1957; M. Karp, *The Economics of Trusteeship in Somalia*, Boston, 1960; J. A. Hunt, *A General Survey of the Somaliland Protectorate 1944–1950*, 1951; C. Robequain, *Madagascar et les bases dispersées de l'Union française*, 1958 (for French Somaliland); H. Deschamps et al., *Côte des Somalis, Réunion, Inde*, 1948; I. M. Lewis, *A Pastoral Democracy*, 1961.

WEST AFRICA

CHAPTER TWELVE

The Environment and Resources

WEST Africa is a clearly defined part of Africa. The Sahara separates it from North Africa, although political boundaries extend into the desert, and the Cameroon–Bamenda–Adamawa Mountains have kept it apart from Western Central Africa. West Africa is as extensive from west to east as the United States, whose area it almost equals. This area also constitutes one-fifth of Africa, yet has 30 per cent of its peoples. If, more appropriately, we consider only tropical Africa, then West Africa has 30 per cent of the area, 40 per cent of the people, and nearly the latter percentage of the external trade. West Africa traded across the Sahara with North Africa for some eight centuries and has been in contact with Europe for longer than any other part of tropical Africa, of which it is also the nearest area to Europe.

HISTORICAL OUTLINE

The camel brought Islam (Fig. 11) Arabic culture and trade to West Africa, the peoples of the drier areas are dominantly Islamic, and Arabic culture is especially evident in Mauritania, Northern Nigeria and Niger. Until the late fifteenth century all external trade from West Africa (mainly in slaves and gold) was with North Africa and Arabia via the Sahara, and this lucrative trade sustained the ancient states of West Africa (pp. 3–4).

Gorée islet, at West Africa's most westerly point, was alone important in West Africa to the Asian sea route. On the other hand, West Africa was the main centre of the European gold and slave trades, especially between Cape Three Points and the Volta Delta in the fifteenth to eighteenth centuries; and, for slaves alone, from 'the Slave Coast' between the Volta and Niger deltas from the seventeenth century until 1885 when the last slave ship sailed from Ouidah (Dahomey). West African religious and art forms survive in north-eastern Brazil, Trinidad, Haiti and elsewhere, while American food crops, introduced by the Portuguese, are especially important in West Africa (Fig. 15).

* By R. J. Harrison Church.

Abolition of the slave trade led to settlements for freed slaves in and around Freetown (Sierra Leone) and at many points on the Liberian coast; while St. Louis, Bathurst, Ouidah (Dahomey) and Lagos have quarters originally settled by freed slaves, sometimes from Brazil. Legitimate trade replaced the slave trade very slowly. Nineteenth-century trade was mainly in palm oil and kernels from Calabar and the Niger Delta ('Oil Rivers'), Dahomey, the Ivory Coast and Sierra Leone; gold from the Gold Coast; and groundnuts from Senegal. Vegetable oils were sought for lubricants (as mineral oil was almost unknown), for candles (then a main illuminant), and for soap (as the rising populations of Western Europe learned the advantages of frequent washing). Cocoa was introduced from the Amazon to São Tomé in 1822, from there to Nigeria in 1874, and to the Gold Coast (Ghana) in 1879. It has since become a main article in West African trade, and Ghana's leading export.

Starting from the old bases of Gorée and St. Louis, French advance was mainly up the Senegal and down the Niger rivers, as part of a grand plan to link North, West, Central and East Africa. It failed at Fashoda (1898) but the first three were joined at the price of occupying most of the Sahara and other poor lands. British areas developed from legacies of the slave trade (Cape Coast), the settlement of freed slaves (Freetown), action against slave areas (Lagos), later legitimate trade (Oil River Protectorate), and from countering the French (Sierra Leone Protectorate, Gold Coast Northern Territories and Northern Nigeria).

Small tribal units were grouped in larger colonial territories. To the great indigenous differences were added those of the European official language, contrasted administrative methods and education, land and other laws, economic policies, French conscription and the British lack of it: to say nothing of the differences between the four separate British colonies. No settlers were permitted in British West Africa, which was saved the complications of multi-racial societies of most other areas of Africa. Settlers were permitted in French West Africa but only a few went to the Ivory Coast and Guinea, and most have left.

The almost entirely colonial West Africa of 1957 became virtually independent by 1961. The great federation of French West Africa broke up in 1959. West African countries are now grouped in the Union of African States (Ghana–Guinea–Mali), a loose association; in the Benin–Sahel Entente (Ivory Coast, Upper Volta, Niger and Dahomey), a much closer association; in a none too certain customs union of all the former members of French West Africa except Guinea; and in another between Ghana and the Upper Volta. The states inherit the differences of colonial days and have often made sharper divides of their boundaries. Nigeria is probably the strongest economically, and has about half the people.

GEOLOGY AND RELIEF

As in most of Africa, the Basement Complex provides the geological base of West Africa, with igneous and metamorphic rocks outcropping over much of the south-west in Sierra Leone, Liberia, the Ivory Coast, northern, western and southern Ghana, most of Togo, Dahomey, western and north-central Nigeria (Fig. 1). These rocks have been severely worn down, have monotonous plateau surfaces mostly 600–1,600 feet in altitude, and are limited by edges along which erosion is active and the rivers fall.

The level plateaux have occasional inselbergs (Plate 4), which are resistant granite masses; or more weathered craggy kopjes, which are heaps of huge boulders. These ancient rocks were folded in Primary times causing north-east to south-west trends, which are reflected in the relief of, for example, the Togo-Atacora Mountains. Gold, diamonds, haematite iron, chrome, tin and manganese are obtained from Precambrian rocks.

During each erosion cycle material was carried away and deposited in fringing seas and gulfs. These sediments were uplifted and sedimentary rocks now cover about one-half of West Africa, lying in varying thicknesses over the Basement Complex; the oldest are probably Cambrian, and occur in the western Sahara and in the Tambaoura scarp of Bambouk near the Senegal–Mali border. Ordovician and Silurian sandstones form the Fouta Djallon of Guinea; the Manding Mountains, Bandiagara Plateau and the Hombori Mountains of Mali; the Sikasso Plateau and Banfora Scarp of the Upper Volta; and the Voltaian Basin sandstones of Ghana, Togo and Dahomey with their impressive erosion scarps. There are also Paleozoic extrusions, of which the half-sunken mass of the Sierra Leone Peninsula is a fine example. Others are the peak of Bintimani (dolerite over granite) in Sierra Leone, Cape Mount in Liberia, and the higher peaks of the Jos Plateau, Nigeria.

Deposits of Secondary or Mesozoic age include the Inter-Calary Continental (Jurassic–Cretaceous) sandstones, conglomerates or clays, so vital for water in North Africa and found in West Africa in eastern Mali, the central Niger Republic and in the Niger–Benue valleys. Terminal Continental (Tertiary) beds, also important for water, occur nearby, and in narrow belts behind most of the Guinea Coast, as well as widely in Senegal, Gambia and Portuguese Guinea. Secondary and Tertiary sandstones form escarpments east of the Niger in Eastern Nigeria, and near Thiès in Senegal. Within Secondary and later rocks are the oil, natural gas, coal and lignite of Eastern Nigeria, and the phosphates of Togo and Senegal.

Whereas movement within the Basement Complex caused the great Rift Valley system and associated volcanic activity in East Africa, there are fewer evident faults in West Africa, except at its western and eastern extremities (Fig. 2). There were volcanoes and lava flows in the east in the Tibesti Mountains, Aïr Massif, Jos and Biu plateaux, Adamawa, Cameroon and Bamenda Highlands, Mt. Cameroon, Fernando Po, Príncipe, São Tomé and Annobon. At the western extremity volcanic activity was limited to the Cape Verde Peninsula and Islands.

In Quaternary times vast sandy deposits accumulated in the interior trough, and there have been alternating wet and dry periods which have affected the drainage. In the present relatively dry phase many valleys are dry, for example in the western Niger Republic.

DRAINAGE AND WATERWAYS

The disruption of a peneplained super-continent with its integrated and mature drainage, by the break-up of Gondwanaland, has been outlined on pp. 21–25. West Africa is a vivid illustration, for the southern plateaux have been uplifted and the interior warped to produce an interior trough. Most rivers flow down the inner gentler slope into the trough occupied by the Senegal and Niger rivers and Lake Chad, and have mature and often winding courses. On the other hand, short rivers from the near-coastal water-shed are cutting down to new base-levels because of the inward tilting of the Basement Complex. Many have rapids, and are gaining head-waters from interior-trough rivers; for example the upper Black Volta and Oti have captured middle Niger tributaries, and the upper Benue might capture the Logone and deprive Lake Chad of most of its supply.

Rivers are highly seasonal, especially those in the higher latitudes. This restricts navigation, even in the flood season, since sandbanks form readily in seasonally-fluctuating rivers (Plate 20). Seasonal flooding also affects settlement. Thus Basse, a trade port on the Gambia, has a permanent high level settlement and lower quayside buildings for handling groundnuts during the trade season.

The Niger

The Djoliba (upper Niger) formerly ended in a lake akin to Lake Chad, and in the same interior trough, in what is now central Mali; while the Nigerian Niger formerly rose in the Aïr Massif. In a wetter period, either one of the western tributaries of the latter cut back into the Inland Niger lake, or the lake overflowed. The Djoliba became the upper Niger of the present river, with an outlet to the sea through the ancient lower Niger breach in the Basement Complex. The interior lake was drained, although relic lakes remain.

The eastern part of the Inland Delta, which had been formed in the lake, is still criss-crossed below Macina by flood-water branches of the river, and is known as the 'live Inland Delta'. The western part was gradually abandoned, and is known as the 'dead Inland Delta'. The latter is the site of the Office du Niger irrigation works which have refilled abandoned channels with water (pp. 230–232). Simple flood-water control for rice cultivation has also been applied to the river in its long course in the dry interior.

What has been an advantage for irrigation has restricted navigation, which has been further hampered by the devious direction of the river, and by its rising in Guinea and flowing on through Mali, Niger and Nigeria. This long course also causes it to have two floods, that of the whole river from June to September, and that of January to June in the lower Niger when it receives flood waters from the upper river delayed by the many channels of the live Inland Delta and the long interior course.

Serious impediments to navigation are rapids at Sotuba (below Bamako, the Mali capital), Labbezenga (on the Mali–Niger boundary), and at Bussa (in Northern Nigeria, where Mungo Park was killed). The river has the following navigable reaches:

(1) Kouroussa (but better from Kankan on the Milo tributary) in Guinea to Bamako in Mali. This has little traffic.

(2) Koulikoro to Ansongo (Mali). Vessels ply between Koulikoro and Gao in full flood, and between Mopti and Gao in lesser flood.

(3) Niamey to Gaya (Niger Republic). This is little used.

(4) Jebba (Nigeria) to the sea. There are flood-water services from Baro (railway branch) between July and September, when the Benue is also open to Garoua, Cameroon (Plate 21). From Onitsha downstream navigation is always possible.

The Senegal

This river has a highly seasonal régime because of its northerly course, and also a dangerous estuary; indeed the St. Louis-Dakar railway, West Africa's first line, was built to provide an alternative outlet to that via the estuary. Since 1924 the direct Dakar–Niger railway has rather short-circuited the river, but vessels provide services all the year between St. Louis and Podor (170 miles) and from early August to late October to Matam (390 miles) or Kayes (580 miles), for trade from northern Senegal and southern and eastern Mauritania.

The Gambia

This and the Congo are the only large African rivers with estuaries, the Gambia Estuary extending 93 miles upstream. Ocean vessels can always reach Kuntaur 150 miles up, now the usual limit of ocean navigation. Because of the very small hinterland within the nearby political boundary, only about a dozen ocean vessels use the river each year, and one local passenger- and freight-carrying steamer. Paucity of traffic has caused deterioration of the river's usefulness, an outstanding example of how the effects of a boundary can reduce a natural advantage.

COASTS

Most beaches are sandy and formed as off-shore bars, creating lagoons on the landward side. Surf and longshore drift are powerful along the Senegal Coast as far south as Cape Verde, and along the Liberian and most of the Gulf of Guinea coasts. These are the most hostile to ports, which have had to be built within mighty enclosing breakwaters at Dakar (Plate 25), Monrovia (Plate 28), Takoradi, Tema (Plate 31), and Cotonou. At Lagos there is a natural (but artificially deepened) inlet to a lagoon, and at Abidjan an artificial one.

The other main type of coast is a shallow drowned one with ria estuaries between Cape Verde and Cape St. Ann (southern Sierra Leone). Since drowning, the land has gained upon the sea through silt brought down by rivers from the Fouta Djallon. Mangrove swamps are extensive but some estuaries are still deep and contain the sheltered harbours of Kaolack, Bathurst, Ziguinchor, Bissau, Benty, Freetown and Bonthe.

CLIMATE

The causation of West African weather and climate has been explained in Chapter 2. The area is always influenced by either the tropical maritime (mT) or the tropical continental (cT) air masses. The Inter-Tropical Convergence Zone (ITCZ) is at about 5°N. in January and between 18°N. and 20°N. in July. Associated with the cT air mass is the dry dust-laden north-easterly Harmattan, and with the mT air mass the wet South-Westerlies.

Along the Guinea Coast and inland to about 7°N., there is a narrow West African projection of the A1 Equatorial climate, with rain in every month and a double maximum. However, several variations are found:*

1 The drier Accra–Togo coastal zone, where annual rainfall is under 35 inches, rain-days are few, and less than 4 months have over 4 inches of rain each. The most likely cause is the terminal upwelling of the cold Benguela Current, deviated here from Cape Lopez (Gabon). These cool waters cause cooler air temperatures, so reducing convection and rainfall.
2 The exceptionally wet area of the Niger Delta and the Bight of Benin, due to the shape of the coast athwart the south-westerly winds, and to high relief on islands and mainland.

North of about 7°N. the A3 Tropical Continental climate occurs, with a rainy season which diminishes and becomes less reliable northward, and which alternates with a dry season which increases in the same direction. This has the following variations:

1 Along and behind the south-western coast, which lies across the path of south-westerly winds, there is monsoonal rainfall reaching 169 inches annually at Conakry.
2 Farther north, along a narrow belt of the Senegal Coast, the cold Canary Current reduces air temperature and convection. Rainfall is lower and comes in a shorter season than inland, but relative humidity is higher because of the sea. Maximum temperatures are not at the end of the dry season but in the wet one. However, ordinary temperatures are more even and lower than inland, and sea breezes are common.
3 Because of the elevation of the Jos Plateau, averaging about 4,000 feet, its temperatures are much lower than surrounding areas.

VEGETATION AND SYLVAN PRODUCE

As West Africa has but a narrow north-western extension of the Equatorial climate, it has only a relatively narrow, less rich, and

* There is a fuller analysis in Glenn T. Trewartha, *The Earth's Problem Climates*, 1962.

interrupted projection of the Western Central African Moist Forest (Fig. 7). Because of the relative proximity of the West African forest to Europe, the greater density of settlement, and more intensive land use and development than in Western Central Africa, substantial in-roads have been made into it by the oil palm in Eastern Nigeria and Sierra Leone, by cocoa in Western Nigeria, Ghana and the Ivory Coast, by coffee in the Ivory Coast, and by rubber in Western Nigeria and Liberia. Yet timber extraction is important in south-western Nigeria and Ghana, and in the southern Ivory Coast. Many timbers are exported; but some are used locally for building and furniture, for firewood, dyestuffs and resins. Logs are mostly floated to mills or ports in Nigeria, some are floated in the Ivory Coast, but movement is mainly by rail or road in the latter and Ghana. All have large and modern plywood and veneer mills.

Inroads of crops and of lumbering have increased the Forest-Savanna Mosaic. Further inland are typical Woodland-Savannas (first moist then dry), Steppes and Desert. Montane Vegetation occurs in the Fouta Djallon, Guinea, Cameroon and Bamenda Highlands. Mangrove is well represented in estuaries of the south-western coast, and in the Niger Delta. Nigeria has all types of vegetation except Sub-desert Steppe and Desert, another illustration of the size and variety of that country.

SOILS

To the general analysis in Chapter Two it should be added that West Africa is characterized by the widespread occurrence of laterite, especially in the south-west. This may be due to the fact that there are many places where rainfall exceeds 40 inches in a wet season followed by an intense dry one, and because there are many poorly drained areas, conditions thought by many to be conducive to the formation of lateritic crusts.

West Africa also has widespread sands, particularly in the interior trough, good clay soils in the *Terre de Barre* of Togo and Dahomey, lacustrine soils in the Inland Niger Delta, alluvial soils being developed for rice along the middle Niger but difficult to use along the lower Niger because of insects and flies, and swamp soils along the coast and inland in the south-west under development for rice.

The Sahara is sometimes said to be advancing as the result of man's activities, yet conservational practices are good in many parts of Northern Nigeria, and elsewhere there is little human pressure on Saharan fringe lands. A graver problem is the rapid retreat of the

Moist Forest in areas of high rainfall, and consequent erosion. This has already caused the poor condition of much land in south-western West Africa and, possibly, in the western part of Eastern Nigeria. It is in such areas that mechanized farming may be dangerous, although it can be a boon in drier areas.

Although conservational practices are rare, there is terracing in the Adamawa Mountains and on the southern edges of the Jos Plateau, and some conservation is practised by the Cabrai people in the Lama-Kara area of north-eastern Togo, the Hausa of Nigeria and Niger, and by the Serer of Senegal. The widespread systems of intercropping and fallow farming are also partly conservational.

PEOPLES

The purest negroes are in the south, and it was these peoples that were largely enslaved in the Americas. Some of the most famous negro peoples are the Ashanti of Ghana, the Fon of Dahomey, and the Yoruba of Nigeria, all of whom formed states in the forest.

The peoples in the Savannas are taller and, though often darker, are more mixed in origin than the negroes of the south, as there are also Hamitic peoples such as the Fulani (French 'Peul'), and a few Semitic ones such as Arabs in the extreme north-east of Nigeria. The Fulani, Moors, Tuareg and Arabs are cattle keepers; most other peoples are crop farmers. West Africa's earliest states were in the Savannas (p. 3), where the groups are larger, for example the Hausa, the Mossi and associated peoples of the Upper Volta and northern Ghana, and the Mande group of ancient and (in part) modern Mali comprising such peoples as the Bambara, Manding, Malinké and Senoufo.

The population density of West Africa is higher than in the rest of tropical Africa or the continent as a whole. This is partly the consequence of early political development, and the long trading connections with North Africa and Europe. Thus there are considerable clusters of population in the Mossi savanna lands of the Upper Volta and in the Hausa political and trading centres of Northern Nigeria such as Kano, Katsina and Sokoto; as well as in the forest ones of Ashanti, Dahomey and Yorubaland.

Yet the slave trades have left their scars, the greatest being the relatively empty 'Middle Belt' which lies between about $7\frac{1}{2}°$ and $10°$N., and was raided by or on behalf of both Arabs and Europeans (Fig. 12). While the slave trades partly explain the usually sparse population, the reduced population was further decimated by the tsetse fly which still prevents easy resettlement, there is much laterite and rather useless moist woodland-savanna vegetation, few minerals, indifferent water supplies and few valuable crops. The belt also has all the disadvantages, pests, and problems of the neighbouring moist forest and dry savanna, with no counter-balancing advantages.

The slave trade encouraged settlement along routes of possible escape like the Senegal and Niger rivers, in walled towns of Northern and Western Nigeria, or in the seclusion of the forest which partly accounts for the Ibo cluster in Eastern Nigeria. This is a striking example of another phenomenon, an apparently irrational concentration on poor soils; the Mossi are another, made possible by political and military organization. By contrast, slave raiding and the tsetse often emptied fertile areas.

Inter-tribal warfare and the tsetse fly have depopulated former battlefields or 'frontiers' such as those between Kano and Bornu, Katsina and Sokoto, the Mossi and old Mali settlements near the Niger River, the Yoruba and Dahomey, Dahomey and Ashanti. The tsetse fly and malarial and yellow-fever carrying mosquitoes prevent occupation of most river valleys south of about 14°N. Other compelling physical factors are water—its rarity north of about 18°N. restricts people to nomadism and oases; elsewhere, however, women often walk considerable distances daily to find water, especially in the dry season. Positive physical factors such as the relatively fertile soils of Yorubaland and Ashanti, or the easily worked soils of western Senegal and Northern Nigeria should not, however, be neglected, and have weighed more with the advent of modern communications and trade.

Tradition kept peoples strictly within their own areas, and is still an influence for the vast rural majority. On the other hand, European contact has brought new coastal clusters as in Senegal, concentrations consequent upon mining as on the Jos Plateau for tin, or in the Ivory Coast for growing coffee and cocoa.

Pressure on the land exists in the Ibo country of Eastern Nigeria, in the Mossi lands of the Upper Volta, and even in many thinly peopled areas of the dry interior. There is considerable emigration by Ibo to the rest of Nigeria (but for political regulation there would be more) and to Fernando Po, and Mossi seek work in the Ivory Coast and Ghana (Fig. 13). Although the population of tropical Africa is not growing rapidly, that of West Africa may be.

Nowhere else in tropical Africa were towns common before Europeans came, but some forty West African towns originated as capitals in the early savanna and forest states, for example Ouaga-dougou (Mossi—Upper Volta), as caravan centres such as Timbuktu (Mali), or as religious centres such as Djenné (Mali). The Yoruba of Western Nigeria have for long lived in large 'urban villages'—towns lived in for protection by people who farmed nearby and whose dwellings were of village type.

Since external contact has been longest with West Africa, and it has a high proportion of tropical Africa's external trade, it is not surprising that there should be more towns resulting from such contact than elsewhere in tropical Africa. Ports typify external contact: such as Dakar (founded 1857, and now with some 250,000 inhabitants); Freetown (first settled by freed slaves 1787); Takoradi (harbour opened 1928) or Port Harcourt (founded 1913). There are mining towns, such as Tarkwa in Ghana, and Jos in Nigeria. Railways created new towns such as Baro and Kafanchan, while there are many administrative creations such as Kaduna, all in Northern Nigeria.

Because of their long contact with the outer world, West Africans have often acquired more education and technical skills than most other Africans, western political and social ideas are better understood, and economic development is more advanced than in many other areas. Nor are there the recriminations and frustrations of multi-racial Africa.

DEVELOPMENT OF THE RESOURCES

West Africa has the most generally developed economy of any equally large division of tropical Africa. Hunting and collecting, whilst supplements to many peoples, are almost nowhere sole sources of livelihood, although the oil, piassava and raphia palm grow more or less wild. Pastoralism, though still essentially for subsistence, has been more touched by commerce than elsewhere. Agriculture is quite often specialized cropping for export or internal trade. Forestry exploitation for export is significant in the Ivory Coast, Ghana and Nigeria, and local needs are met in other coastal lands from Senegal southward. Mining is of major significance to Mauritania, Sierra Leone and Liberia, is important to Guinea, Ghana and Nigeria, and is developing in Senegal, the Ivory Coast and Togo. Industries of many kinds have been introduced, mostly since the early 'fifties; while fish are being caught increasingly off the shores of Mauritania, Senegal, Ghana and Nigeria.

Agriculture

Unlike much of Africa, West Africa has almost no white settlers, there was practically no alienation of land in British West Africa, and it is now significant only in Liberia and the Ivory Coast. Plantations are almost confined to those countries and Guinea, and with them the characteristic plantation crops of coffee and bananas (Guinea and the Ivory Coast), and rubber (Liberia). Guinea's plantations are now state or co-operatively owned.

Elsewhere, crops are grown on small farms by Africans using the simplest methods to produce about two-thirds of the world's commercialized groundnuts (Plate 24) and palm kernels, one-half of the cocoa, and one third of the palm oil (Fig. 16). Senegal and Northern Nigeria are the world's largest commercial growers of groundnuts, and Nigeria of oil-palm produce; while Ghana, Nigeria and the Ivory Coast are the first three producers of cocoa.

In plantation economy, the Ivory Coast is the third world producer of coffee (first in Africa), and its plantations also produce some of the cocoa. Nigeria and Liberia produce substantial amounts of rubber, the first partly and the latter almost wholly on plantations; and several countries have substantial interest in plantations, state farms and co-operative projects, as ways to improve agricultural production. Plantation tree crops are likely to become relatively more important.

In the ex-French countries several crops, particularly coffee, bananas and groundnuts, have enjoyed guaranteed markets at higher than world prices in France, and these greatly stimulated production. Thus, political and economic factors are as important as physical ones in explaining crop locations and developments. This is well illustrated either side of the Ivory Coast–Ghana boundary, where soil and climatic conditions are similar. On the Ghana side cocoa alone is important, because it is easily grown and processed by small farmers. Although cocoa is also grown in the Ivory Coast, coffee is more important because the French permitted large plantations which can process coffee, and high prices could be obtained in the guaranteed French market. Similar contrasts can be seen between the Liberian plantation economy and Sierra Leone small farm production, or between Nigerian small farms and Cameroon plantations.

Rainfall and soil character are the main physical controls of crops. Along the southern Guinea Coast food crops of cassava (manioc), yams, maize and tree cash crops (oil palm, cocoa, coffee, rubber, kola, bananas) prevail to about 7°N., the limit of the A1 Equatorial climate (Figs. 15 and 16). Cassava is tolerant of different climatic and soil conditions, and is found in the other zones, especially as it needs little care, is a prolific yielder, and is in demand as the cheapest food. Yams are found to about 12°N. but are giving way to cassava because they are less tolerant of soil and climatic differences and need careful cultivation. Maize requires richer soils, as well as at least 30 inches annual rainfall. The oil palm, rubber and kola tolerate poor soils, but need quite 45 inches annual rain or equivalent ground water—especially the oil palm. While cocoa, coffee and bananas require rich soils and evenly distributed rainfall (or irrigation), bananas require heavy soils, cocoa well drained ones, and coffee light soils.

On the south-western coast, with its 5–8 months season of monsoonal rain, rice is the main food crop; the same tree crops occur but may need irrigation (e.g. bananas) during the sharp dry season. Rice is being increasingly grown in former mangrove and inland swamps, and in suitable places in the other countries (especially Nigeria), since it is popular as a food, and easy to transport, store and cook.

Inland from the coastal zones the single rainy season becomes shorter and the dry season longer. At first guinea corn (a sorghum more resistant to dry conditions than maize), yams, cassava and groundnuts are the chief crops—all food crops (Fig. 15). North of about 12°N. millet—the most drought-resistant of the cereals—groundnuts and cassava are the main food crops; with cotton for sale from the more southerly areas and heavier soils, and groundnuts from the more northerly areas and lighter soils. North of 14°N. cattle, almost always kept separately, become important, while 18°N. is about the limit of cultivation without irrigation.

Nomadic Pastoralism

This economy and way of life is dominant throughout Mauritania, most of Mali and Niger, and is important in north-eastern Senegal and Northern Nigeria (see Fig. 17). All three basic types of cattle are found in West Africa. The long-horned *Bos taurus* is found near Lake Chad, the local type being known as the Chad or Kuri. The *Bos indicus*, or hump-backed zebu, is the commonest large cattle, represented by such breeds as the White Fulani, Gudale or Sokoto and Red Bororo of Northern Nigeria, Tuareg of Mali, and Maure of Mauritania. They are kept by nomads, the Fulani being the most numerous.

Like other large African cattle, they are highly susceptible to the trypanosoma carried by tsetse flies, and so are mostly found north of

14°N. in the west, or 12°N. in the east. This limit of tsetse is approximate; it varies according to the extent of tree and shade cover, and so advances with the rains. These variations, the aridity of the pastoral environment, and its poor grasses make nomadism essential. Cattle are half-starved for quite six months each year, mature slowly, calve late, give little and poor milk, and yield tough meat. Kept essentially for subsistence, prestige, and as capital, they are marketed only when money is essential; cattle management is rare. Nevertheless, the more numerous coastal peoples with their higher standard of living demand meat, and so there are extensive cattle routes of up to 800 miles to these markets on the hoof, and by road and rail transport.

The small *Bos brachyceros*, which are possibly indigenous to tropical Africa, tolerate the trypanosoma, are found within the tsetse areas, and are well represented in West Africa. These cattle stand about three feet high and are the size of a European calf. They find better nourishment in their wetter environment than do the large cattle farther north, the produce of the small cattle is often of better quality but the amount available is small, and few are kept by crop growing farmers who never attend to animals. The best-known breed is the Ndama of the Fouta Djallon and Guinea Highlands, the main source of meat for Guinea, Sierra Leone and Liberia. Others are the Dwarf-Shorthorn of coastal Ghana, Togo and Dahomey, and the Muturu of southern Nigeria.

Between about 10° and 14°N. are cross-bred humpless cattle, of which the Sanga of Ghana are best known. Cattle zones are more sharply defined than crop zones. There are about 22 million cattle in West Africa, of which some 15 million are large cattle of the dry zone, requiring 300,000 square miles of the poorest grazing to sustain them. Nigeria probably has one-third of the cattle, Niger and Mali another third. The greatest per capita consumption of meat is in Ghana, an indication of its higher standard of living.

Sheep, and especially goats, are more resistant to the tsetse's trypanosoma, and are more widely distributed than cattle. They are kept for the varied produce they yield; mutton is much prized in Mauritania, while goat meat is very widely eaten. The Sokoto or Maradi Red and Kano or Zinder Brown goats are important for glacé kid leather exports to Europe and America.

The spread of Islam has tended to exclude the pig from areas to which it is well suited, but there is a huge pig farm at Kano run by a Lebanese with non-Islamic labour, and many pigs are kept in the southern lands.

Fishing

In view of the shortage of animal protein in the tsetse areas, supplementation by fish is valuable. All types are caught, women usually preparing and retailing the catches. Catching of Niger fish is important in Mali among the Somono people. Trade in dried and smoked fish focuses upon Mopti, from where some 30,000 tons are despatched annually, much far as Ghana. The Niger is also fished by these fishermen in Guinea and Niger, and by others in Nigeria, particularly Ijaw in the Niger Delta. The Senegal River and Lake Chad are also much fished. Lagoon fishing is significant in Togo, Dahomey and Nigeria.

Sea fishing by canoes, sometimes power-driven, is done especially by the Fanti of Ghana, off their own shores and as far afield as Liberia and the Congo. Annual consumption of fish in Ghana is about 80,000 tons, of which 60,000 tons are caught off shore. Larger boats from the Canary Islands and southern Europe visit the Mauritanian coast, and some fish is dried at Port Etienne. Tuna fishing is done off Cape Verde, Japanese fleets even visiting the grounds, and tuna are canned in Dakar. Deep-sea fishing is developing from Freetown, Abidjan, Tema and Lagos.

Minerals

Gold, iron, lead and tin were mined before the arrival of Europeans, the first since about the tenth century. Gold and slaves were the main items in northward-bound trans-Saharan trade, and the first three-and-a-half centuries of maritime trade. Modern mining began in 1878 in the banket gold reefs of Tarkwa, Ghana, and was for long the leading attraction of overseas private investment.

Mining has long been important in ex-British West Africa but elsewhere only since the Second World War. Minerals account for almost all the exports of Mauritania (iron); over one-half those of Sierra Leone (diamonds, iron and a little chrome) and Liberia (iron and diamonds); and more than one-third of those of Guinea (diamonds, iron, bauxite and alumina) and Ghana (gold, diamonds, manganese and bauxite). Percentages are smaller in Nigeria (mineral oil, tin, columbite and coal), Senegal and Togo (phosphates), but are growing fast. It should be appreciated that a high percentage in the small overseas trade of Mauritania is less significant than a low percentage in the large overseas trade of Ghana or Nigeria. While mineral exports are growing rapidly in value and increasing in variety (both as to kind of mineral and country of origin), local use of

Nigerian oil and natural gas is developing, and has long been considerable of its coal.

Gold. Ghana is the only significant producer. Most is from quartz reefs, the Ashanti Goldfields Corporation mine at Obuasi being the best yielder in the world, averaging an ounce of gold per ton of ore.

Diamonds. All West African production is open cast from past or present river beds. At first production in Ghana and Sierra Leone (the leading producers) was by companies, but African panners are now important, far more so in Sierra Leone. There are smaller outputs in the Ivory Coast, Liberia and Guinea. West Africa produces some 40 per cent of the world's gems and 20 per cent of the industrial stones.

Manganese. This is worked open cast at Nsuta in Ghana, which is about the sixth world producer but a leading exporter.

Iron. Although rich haematite iron ore has been worked in Sierra Leone since 1933, other deposits in Liberia and Mauritania were developed much later. Guinea's ore of laterized basic rocks is poorer but there are vast reserves only eight miles from the port of Conakry. West Africa may become a leading ore producer.

Tin. Tin gravels occur in beds of former rivers on the Jos Plateau (Northern Nigeria), and were worked and smelted before the arrival of Europeans, who began systematic mining in 1903, but smelting only in 1961.

Columbite. This is the ore of niobium, much used in steel alloys for jet engines, rockets and gas turbines. It occurs with tin, and Nigeria is a main supplier.

Bauxite. This is a common product of tropical weathering and laterization, but commercial deposits must be near bulk transport. Quarrying began at Awaso, Ghana, during the Second World War, when a mineral line was built to connect with the western railway. Deposits on Kassa, one of the Los Islands off Conakry, Guinea, were opened in 1952. Ores from large deposits 90 miles north-north-east of Conakry at Fria are locally reduced to alumina. Large reserves exist in Guinea, Sierra Leone and Ghana.

Phosphates. Aluminium phosphate has been quarried at Pallo, near Thiès, Senegal, since 1950; and calcium phosphate nearby at Tivaouane, as well as near the coast in Togo since 1960. Although mostly exported, they will improve local soils.

Fuels and Power. Like so many tropical areas, West Africa for long seemed deficient in fuels and power-potential; wood was the main fuel, and still is for cooking. Nigerian coal production began in 1915, and is the sole source of coal. It was formerly used on Ghana and

Nigerian railways, imported coal being used by other lines, but dieselization has greatly reduced demand.

Oil production, also in Eastern Nigeria, began in 1957, and locally refined oil became available in 1964. Natural gas is used in electrical generation and industry in Port Harcourt.

Hydro-electric power development began on the Jos Plateau in the 'twenties to serve the tin mines. The first major development is the Volta River Project (p. 261). Other agreed schemes are the dam across the Niger in Northern Nigeria to generate electricity for general development, and across the Guma Valley above Freetown, Sierra Leone, to provide electricity and water for the Freetown area. These should lead to considerable industrialization and diversification of economies.

MANUFACTURES

Hand-made articles were made throughout West Africa. Many countries still have specialities, such as leather in Mauritania, the coloured blankets of Mali and Niger, embroidered sheep or goatskin-covered bottles and boxes of Guinea and Sierra Leone, Kente cloth of Ghana, and the brassware of Abomey (Dahomey). Crafts have survived best in Nigeria, because of the large population reasonably well served by transport. Some notable centres are Kano (indigo dyeing, leather working, calabashes), Benin (brass and wood carving), and Oyo (calabashes and cushions). More important, however, are the modern crafts of car and cycle maintenance, tailoring and dressmaking (mainly by men).

Large-scale industry has been developed by private and public enterprise. Examples are:

Processing of mineral exports. This began at the end of the nineteenth century with the refining of gold in Ghana. No others were locally refined until 1958, when the reduction of bauxite to alumina began in Guinea. Since then tin smelting (Northern Nigeria) and oil refining (Eastern Nigeria) have started.

Processing of agricultural and timber exports. This began before the Second World War with groundnut oil extraction in Senegal (mainly Dakar), and developed later in Nigeria (Kano) and the Gambia (Bathurst). Others are palm-oil clarification and bulking in Nigeria (Lagos and Port Harcourt); rubber processing in southern Nigeria and Liberia; coffee hulling in Guinea and the Ivory Coast; plywood and veneer making in the Ivory Coast (Abidjan), Ghana (Samreboi) and Western Nigeria (Sapele).

Manufacture of local produce, mainly for national needs. Consumer-good industries producing drinks are widespread, and the large Northern Nigerian textile mills at Kaduna are outstanding enterprises (Plate 32). Cement making (Senegal and Nigeria) provides a vital constructional material (Plate 23).

Manufacture of partly imported goods with local produce. Tobacco factories are in several ports, for example Dakar, and inland towns such as Ibadan.

Assembly or manufacture of imported produce. Trucks are assembled in Ghana (Tema) and Nigeria (Lagos), cycles at the latter, and there are flour mills at Dakar.

Industries are often grouped on estates in ports or major inland towns. Industrial complexes may develop on the oil, natural gas, coal, lignite and iron deposits of Eastern and Northern Nigeria, as well as from the Volta and Niger hydro-electric schemes. Nigeria, with half the population of West Africa, Ghana with the highest standard of living, and Dakar and Abidjan with the greatest concentrations of non-Africans offer the best markets in West Africa.

TRANSPORT

Rivers

These were the means of penetration by slave raiders, who often accidentally spread the tsetse fly to new areas. Because of this, mosquitoes, and the general unhealthiness of river valleys, they are little peopled south of 14°N., so that the lower Niger is of restricted local use (except to and from Onitsha) as distinct from its use for transit trade. Rivers were also important to the early explorers, military expeditions and traders, particularly the Senegal and middle Niger to the French, and the lower Niger to the British. Details of present use for navigation are given on pp. 208–210, where the physical characteristics of rivers are also discussed. Rivers are also important for timber floating in Western Nigeria and the Ivory Coast. As a subsidiary feature of the Volta River Project Ghana will have a 200-mile long waterway—West Africa's first artificial one.

Railways

The first of these were built to overcome deficiencies of rivers, notably, the St. Louis–Dakar line to avoid navigating the Senegal Estuary, the Dakar–Kayes section to avoid using the Senegal for transit, and the Bamako–Koulikoro section around the upper Niger rapids. Railways were also weapons in colonial strategy, as means of securing effective colonial occupation and administration, for example the Kayes–Bamako line—the first section of the Dakar–Koulikoro railway. They were designed for the needs of external rather than internal trade, and for channelling commerce through a colony's ports rather than through those of its neighbours; these aims are well seen in the history of the Guinea and Sierra Leone lines. Different gauges were deliberately chosen, and no international colonial boundaries were crossed.

Some railways were built for sound economic reasons, particularly in Ghana (the western line for mineral exports, the eastern for cocoa). Nevertheless, many are poorly adapted to present needs, especially of internal trade. Routes are devious and speeds slow. Railways are, however, vital to bulk long-distance movement of low-value commodities such as groundnuts and groundnut oil from Northern Nigeria and the distribution of mineral oil (Plate 22). The ex-French West African lines were dieselized by 1954; but partly because of Nigerian coal those of ex-British West Africa only in the late 'fifties.

Roads

Almost all roads were built after the early railways, but again, at first, largely towards ports for the needs of external trade. However, roads were soon built for internal trade as well, while inter-territorial roads, though few in colonial days, are increasing.

Roads and road transport are usually far more important than rail transport. Atlases tend to give the opposite impression, so that Fig. 41 should be studied as a West African illustration of a common phenomenon. Road and road traffic densities are useful indices of development after allowing for alternatives (e.g. rivers in the Gambia and Portuguese Guinea). Road transport is often a great African enterprise, especially in Ghana and Nigeria.

Limiting factors in road development are the costs of construction and maintenance, which are heavy because of the violent character of tropical rainfall. Ferries are still common and cause delays, while bridges are very costly—there are, for example, only five across the Niger.

Air Transport

West Africa was opened up by airlines after the Second World War. In ex-British West Africa internal services were run by a consortium of local governments until independence; elsewhere European companies ran routes. Nigeria, Ghana, Liberia, Sierra Leone and Mali have

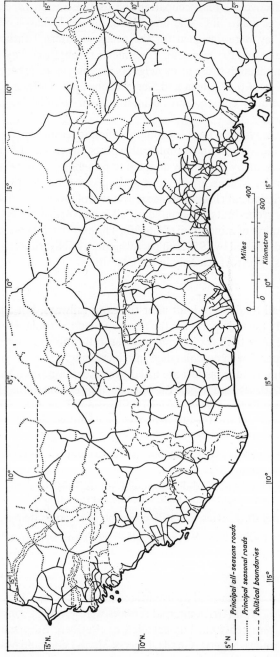

Fig. 41. Main roads of West Africa

airlines, and some of the other ex-French states are associated in *Air Afrique*.

Airways were often the first significant international links, and have fostered co-operation. They have greatly facilitated the movement of administrators and experts. Some 70 airports have regular scheduled services at least once a week, and often much more frequently. Dakar and Kano are major international airports, and Accra a lesser one. North and South America, Europe, North, Central and South Africa can be reached in a day; East Africa and Asia less quickly and directly. European flights terminate on the coasts, sometimes with an intermediate stop at either Port Etienne, Bamako, Bobo Dioulasso, Ougadougou, Niamey or Kano. As planes increase in range and traffic develops, these calls are being reduced.

FURTHER READING

General: R. J. Harrison Church, *West Africa*, 4th ed., 1963; J. Richard-Molard, *Afrique Occidentale Française*, 2e ed., 1952, and *Problèmes Humains en Afrique Occidentale* 1958; Virginia Thompson and Richard Adloff, *French West Africa*, 1956; K. M. Barbour and R. M. Prothero (Eds.), *Essays on African Population*, 1961. *Les Cahiers d'Outre-mer* (Bordeaux) has many useful articles.

Agriculture: Bruce F. Johnston, *The Staple Food Economies of Western Tropical Africa*, Stanford, 1958, and F. R. Irvine, *A Text-Book of West African Agriculture*, 1953.

CHAPTER THIRTEEN

The Dry Lands

THE mainly dry lands of West Africa are:

Country or Province	Area in sq. miles	Population	Density per sq. mile
Cape Verde Is.	1,557	201,549	129·4
Mauritania	419,121	850,000	2·0
Mali	464,752	4,470,000	10·0
Upper Volta	105,811	4,160,000	38·0
Niger	458,874	3,100,000	6·5
Senegal	76,104	3,100,000	39·2
Gambia	4,008	284,000	71·0

THE CAPE VERDE ISLANDS

These ten islands and five islets lie some 300 miles west of Cape Verde and result like it from the same vulcanism; Fogo, 9,279 feet, erupted in the mid-'fifties after nearly three centuries of inactivity. Santo Antão and Sant'Iago are also high and precipitous.

The volcanic soils are rich but water is scarce. Dry north-east trades blow most of the year, and mainly affect Santo Antão, São Vicente, Santa Luzia, São Nicolau, Sal and Boa Vista, which are aligned from west-north-west to east-south-east and known as the Barlavento or Windward group. The moister south-westerly winds blow from August to October, but to a varying degree. They mainly affect more southerly Brava, Fogo, Sant'Iago and Maio, aligned from west-south-west to east-north-east and called the Sotavento or Leeward group. However, the lowest and most easterly islands of both groups—Maio, Boa Vista and Sal—receive least rain.

On the driest islands goats, sheep and the date palm are the main resources; on the wetter ones there is an altitudinal crop succession beginning with coconuts near sea level, and going upwards with sugar cane, bananas (helped by irrigation), maize, oranges and coffee.

Unequal land ownership as well as severe aridity hamper agricultural development, and there is acute population pressure and poverty. Yet São Vicente could have been further developed as a port of call on

* By R. J. Harrison Church.

South American routes, as could the airport on Sal. The capital is Praia on Sant'Iago.

Many Cape Verdians are fishermen, or clerks in Portuguese Guinea. They are dominantly a mixture of Portuguese and West Africans who were taken to these originally uninhabited islands as slaves. The islands thus have geological, historical and cultural connections with West Africa, and so are discussed here; while the Canary Islands, though physically and economically comparable with the Cape Verde Islands are European in population.

THE MAINLAND COUNTRIES

Mauritania, Mali, Upper Volta and Niger have many common features. They are arid or dry and, except for the Upper Volta, extend into the Sahara. They were relatively more important in the days of trans-Saharan trade, but have been on the periphery of economic and political developments in the last three-and-a-half centuries. Irrigation from rivers, well boring to tap deep underground water from the Inter-Calary Continental and Terminal Continental water-bearing formations, and iron-ore mining in Mauritania may do much to help these lands, hitherto largely dependent upon livestock. However, they will always face the difficulty of remoteness, and Mali, the Upper Volta and Niger are severely land-locked.

MAURITANIA

Twice as large as France, this mainly desert country has under a million inhabitants, most of whom are nomads. The only considerable cultivable belt is the Chemama, or Mauritanian half of the seasonally flooded Senegal Valley, on the southern boundary, where rice, millet, guinea corn (sorghum), henna, melons, tobacco and vegetables are grown, and cattle are seasonally pastured. Simple earth dams have greatly improved water control. Agriculture is also found in the Gorgol valleys of the south-east, and in patches where well water from Eocene rocks is available in the low plains of Trarza, Brakna and Assaba.

Most people live in these areas south of 19°N., the approximate limit of Grass Steppe. This supports substantial numbers of livestock, the main resource and export of Mauritania (to Senegal and the Gambia) until the opening of iron reserves. Livestock are especially numerous in the Hodh, which belonged to the French Sudan (now Mali) until 1944. North of 19°N. is desert which occupies two-thirds of the country and in which there are only small oases.

For the latitude, the coastal belt has remarkably modest temperatures, which at Port Etienne range from a mean monthly maximum
of 78° in December to 91° in September, and from a mean monthly
minimum of 54° in January to 69° in September. Sea breezes also
help, and were among the reasons for the choice of Nouakchott
('place of wind') as the capital.

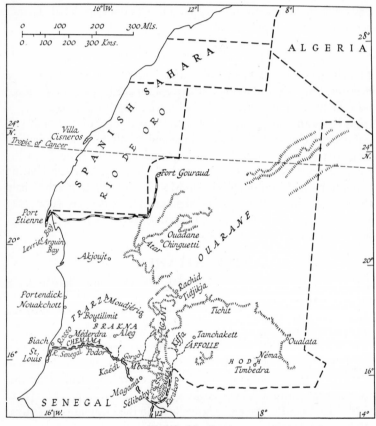

Fig. 42. Mauritania
(From R. J. Harrison Church, *West Africa*)

Port Etienne, lying on the east side of the entirely arid peninsula of
Cape Blanc, began in 1907 as a fish-drying centre, from which fish is
sold in West and Western Central Africa. The town is now more
significant as an iron ore exporter and may become Mauritania's
general port. Devoid of water, it was brought from France by tanker

from 1907 until 1955, when water was first distilled locally from sea water. Since 1962 some supplies have been brought by rail from 75 miles away.

Haematite averaging 63 per cent iron is quarried in the Kédia d'Idjil east of Fort Gouraud. The ore, which is dry and low in phosphorus and other impurities, occurs in Precambrian quartzites on the northern edge of these hills. Water is available, and a mining town has developed in the desert. Export to Port Etienne is by a 400-mile railway that had to be laid across fixed dunes, and may require periodic realignment to avoid active dunes. Spanish terms made impossible a direct route across Spanish Sahara to naturally deep water at Port Etienne; Spanish Villa Cisneros, the nearest harbour, is severely silted. To keep within Mauritania, expensive tunnelling was necessary at Choum, near the south-eastern corner of Spanish Sahara.

This great development by an international company should make Mauritania viable. It will stimulate development of copper deposits at Akjoujt, and may lead to the opening of other but poorer iron reserves south-west of Atar. The independence and transformation of Mauritania by iron ore is comparable with that of Kuwait by oil.

MALI

This state, largely coincident in area with ancient Mali, is the largest in West Africa. Although narrow in the centre, it extends about a thousand miles from west to east and from north to south.

In Mali the Basement Complex has been uplifted in the vivid Adrar des Iforas in the north-east, a region whose many dry watercourses indicate former wetter conditions. Elsewhere, the Basement Complex is covered by Palaeozoic sandstones or Quaternary sands. The former are extensions of the Fouta Djallon, and occur in the Bambouk and Manding Mountains of the west (Figs. 1 and 43), in the Sikasso Plateau, Bandiagara Escarpment and the highly dissected Hombori Mountains of the south-centre. Quaternary sands form the flat plains of eastern Sahel and the Tanezrouft.

North of 18°N. is desert where, after centuries of exploitation, salt is still cut at Taoudenni and brought south by camel caravan (Plate 2). Near the Niger is Timbuktu, where trans-Saharan caravans of the middle ages terminated, but now a miserable shadow of its former greatness (Plate 1).

The Niger is the lifeline of Mali and is navigable from Kouroussa (Guinea) or Kankan (Milo tributary) to Bamako, Mali's well planned capital, main market, and focus of communications. River navigation is broken by rapids below the town but resumes at nearby Koulikoro, from where there is considerable traffic with the irrigation scheme at Sansanding, with Mopti and Gao. The river is also a rich source of fish, which is smoked or dried and marketed through Mopti as far as Ghana.

Fig. 43. Mali
(From R. J. Harrison Church, *West Africa*)

Mali has as many cattle as human beings. Cattle move seasonally between the Sahel, Azaouak and Ioullemedene areas (Fig. 43) north of the Niger, and the river where highly nutritious grasses grow during the floods. There is considerable trade in cattle with Ghana and the Ivory Coast, again through Mopti.

The origin of the Inland Delta of the Niger has been described on p. 209. In the 'dead' upper sector of the delta an ambitious irrigation scheme has been developed by the Office du Niger, which sought to emulate British successes on the Nile. A barrage, completed

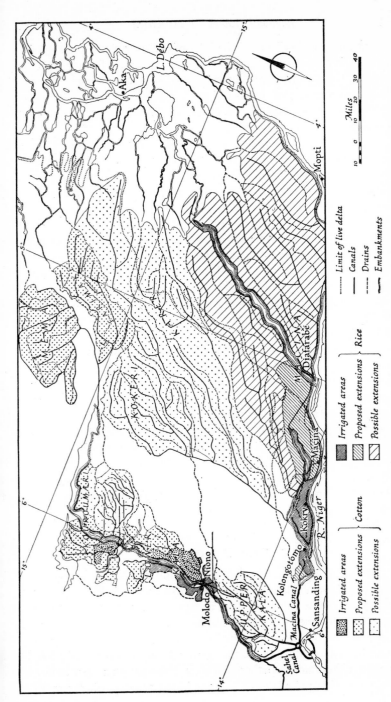

Fig. 44. *The Inland Niger Delta Scheme* (From R. J. Harrison Church, 'Problems and Development of the Dry Zone of West Africa', *Geographical Journal*, 1961, 195, by permission of the Royal Geographical Society)

at Sansanding in 1947, raised the level of the river by an average of fourteen feet, and adduction canals lead water to former Niger channels from which distributaries have been constructed. Some 100,000 acres have been irrigated. Land is mechanically prepared, but the crops are grown mainly by some 30,000 African farmers who live in villages built in traditional styles.

The scheme was intended to produce cotton for French needs but the soils are more suitable and the farmers more apt at producing rice, especially in the Macina area near the river. Sugar and fibre crops are being tried with mechanical cultivation, but all aspects of the scheme have been costly compared with simple flood control works, and much less successful than those in the Sudan and Egypt.

The other significant item in Mali's economy is the groundnut, grown near the railway in the west. Here, and in the south, are the only parts of the country with an adequate rainfall (20–50 inches per annum) for non-irrigated agriculture.

Mali suffers from the length of its transport routes to the sea. After the quarrel with Senegal in 1960, the Dakar–Niger railway was cut at the boundary until 1963, and exports, mainly groundnuts (about one-tenth the Senegal output), a little cotton (two-thirds from ordinary cultivation, one-third from the Office du Niger irrigations), a little shea butter, hides and skins were taken by road to the Ivory Coast railway, by which most imports were received. Trade has since partially resumed through Dakar.

Although overseas trade is difficult and small, there is substantial overland trade in fish and cattle with Ghana and the Ivory Coast, especially from Mopti and east thereof. Much of the economy is a subsistence one (livestock in the north; crop cultivation in the south). There is also considerable periodic emigration for work in the Ivory Coast or Ghana (Fig. 13).

UPPER VOLTA

Less than a quarter the size of Mali, the Upper Volta has nearly the same population. Although rainfall ranges from 25–45 inches per annum, the country is much drier in aspect than these figures might suggest because there is rapid percolation in the sandstone areas of the west and south-east, both part of the Ordovician or Silurian series found in eastern Mauritania, the Guinea Fouta Djallon, and Mali. The rest of the country is either sandy (e.g. Yatenga) where percolation is again quick, or else lateritic (e.g. the Mossi country) where run-off

20. Sandbanks of the Benue River (p. 208) at Yola, Northern Nigeria, in December. The river is navigable as far as Garoua (Cameroon) from July to September, but sandbanks are always a menace, and the channel plainly swings from bank to bank.

21. Transporting merchandise by push-tow unit on the Niger and Benue rivers from Burutu, a Niger Delta port (p. 209), Nigeria.

22. Saddle-bag tanker of Nigerian Railways (p. 223). The outer saddle-bag tanks carry groundnut oil to the coast, the inner round tank carries mineral oil inland.

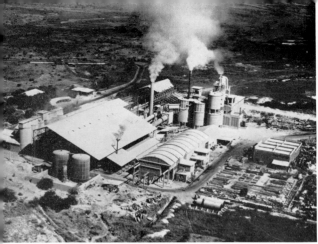

23. West Africa's first cement factory at Bargny (p. 238), near Dakar. Local Cretaceous limestone is used.

24. The leguminaceous *Arachis hypogoea*, or groundnut. It has yellow flowers which, after fertilization, are matured within the soil, which should, therefore, be sandy. West Africa produces two-thirds of all groundnuts entering world trade.

25. Dakar, Senegal, looking south-westward (p. 238). In the foreground are the southern piers, the left-hand one having developed from the first pier of 1861. Immediately beyond is the port-commercial sector. In the centre are buildings around the central Place Protet. Behind again and to the left is the tallest Senegal Government building and Cape Manuel. Gorée is 2 miles east (left) of the piers and invisible.

is also fast. The sandy or lateritic soils are infertile and, although intensively cultivated for groundnuts, guinea corn, millet and beans, poverty and population pressure are severe. Furthermore, water is scarce, except in the swampy Gourma country and along the Volta rivers where tsetse and simulium flies make settlement dangerous or impossible. Given these many disadvantages, it is remarkable that the Mossi states and peoples have a history of sturdy independence and non-conversion to Islam since the eleventh century.

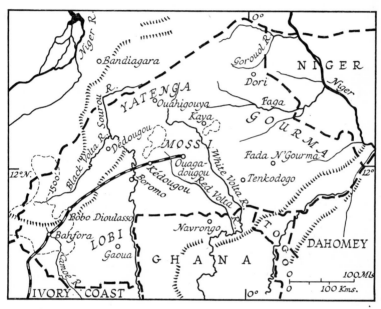

Fig. 45. Upper Volta
(From R. J. Harrison Church, *West Africa*)

The poverty of the soils, the pressure of population upon them, and the 711 mile rail haul to Abidjan from Ouagadougou (the capital), result in there being little surplus for sale beyond livestock, cotton, groundnuts, a little collected shea butter and benniseed. The main marketing centre is Bobo Dioulasso. Large numbers of men—some 150,000 at any one time—work in Ghana or the Ivory Coast. Although so poor, the Upper Volta is important for the transit of livestock and dried fish from Mali to the Ivory Coast and Ghana; and of kola nuts and imports from those countries to Mali. The Upper Volta–Ghana boundary is customs free.

8*

NIGER

Almost as large as Mali but with much more desert, less water and more isolated, Niger is another exceedingly poor country. It lies between latitudes 12° and 24°N. and, although the southern part is farther south than Mauritania, this is somewhat offset by its more continental situation.

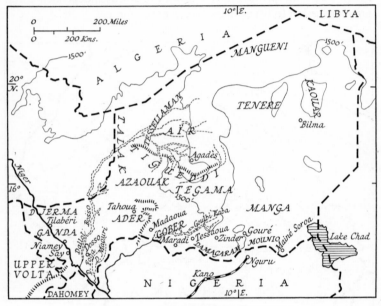

Fig. 46. Niger
(From R. J. Harrison Church, *West Africa*)

As in Mauritania, the cultivable areas are on the extreme southern fringes, where alone annual rainfall is some 20 inches. Most are along the central part of the Niger-Nigeria boundary where Hausa, the largest ethnic group in Niger, live on either side of the boundary. The loose sandy soils are cultivated for millet and groundnuts, the latter sold through Maradi and Zinder. Groundnut oil is extracted in small mills. Cotton is increasingly grown in seasonally flooded valleys near Maradi, where there is a ginnery. These towns also collect glacé kid goat skins.

In the south-west the Djerma cultivate rice in the seasonally flooded Niger Valley, and dry crops such as millet and groundnuts away from it. Tuareg pastoralists seasonally visit the riverine pastures with their livestock. Niamey, the capital, is a focus of road and air routes.

There is a little cultivation in seasonal stream beds of the Precambrian and Tertiary-volcanic Aïr Massif, but this and areas to the south are more important for livestock kept by the Tuareg. Tahoua is a market for cattle traded into Ghana or Nigeria, and of hides and skins for export. Livestock are Niger's greatest resource.

Niger thus has three very dispersed regional, economic and cultural areas. There is no dominant ethnic group as in Mauritania and the Upper Volta; or core area as in the latter and Mali. Unity is elusive; the attraction of the much richer Nigeria immense. Distances to the outer world are long, and Niger lacks a through route like Mali or the Upper Volta. Goods must go by road to or from Kano (Nigeria) or Parakou (Dahomey), and thence by railway. The former involves foreign exchange, the latter a longer and more expensive route ending at Cotonou, to which the Niger and Dahomey governments nevertheless direct much trade.

To Mauritania, Mali, Upper Volta and Niger, West African trade in their cattle is very important. Mali and Niger export small amounts of groundnuts, groundnut oil and a little cotton, and the Upper Volta some shea butter. All involve hauls of 700–800 miles, and are tiny resources for independent states. Only Mauritania is developing significant mineral resources. There is severe population pressure and emigration from the Upper Volta, and some from Mali and Niger.

SENEGAL AND GAMBIA

These countries form a geographical whole, the Gambia being virtually an enclave in Senegal, which surrounds it except on the coast. Both were settled early by Africans, as stone circles in the Gambia and finds of pottery near the Saloum Estuary suggest, and both were early points of European contact. Senegal is the nearest developed tropical country to Europe. This fact, and the moderate character of its coastal climate, have helped to give an almost southern French imprint to St. Louis and Dakar.

The Physical Environment

Senegal, the Gambia and western Portuguese Guinea occupy a sedimentary basin of mainly post-Eocene deposits. Low sandy plains are characteristic, broken only by the wide shallow valleys of the Senegal, Gambia and Casamance rivers, and the usually dry upper valleys of the Ferlo and Sine.

Tertiary and Quaternary volcanism built the Cape Verde Islands and other islands just off the then westernmost point of Africa. The latter have been joined to the shore as the Cape Verde Peninsula and provide a fine environment for Dakar. As far south as Cape Verde the coast is smooth and surf-bound, but thereafter are the navigable rias of the Saloum, Gambia and Casamance.

The rainy season varies from under 20 inches in four months in the north to 60 inches in six months in the south, where relative humidity is much higher. There is a more vivid contrast between the narrow coastal belt where temperatures are lower and breezes common, and the interior which is much warmer by day and drier. Vegetation likewise varies from Grass Steppe as far south as the latitude of Dakar. Dry Woodland Savanna from there to the Gambia, and Moist Woodland-Savanna in Casamance. Riverine forests occur along the Gambia and Casamance rivers, with mangrove in their tidal reaches. Mangrove swamps are being cleared in some areas for rice cultivation, especially along the Gambia river (Fig. 47).

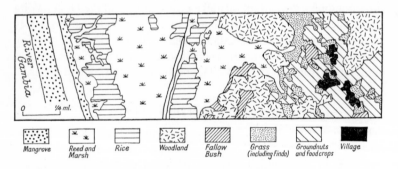

Fig. 47. Land-use transect from the Gambia River
(From the Dunkunku sheet, *Gambia 1: 25,000 Land Use*, Directorate of Overseas Surveys, Crown Copyright Reserved, by permission)

Agriculture

Eastern and north-eastern Senegal are almost uninhabited, as water lies at great depths. By contrast, western Cayor and Nioro du Rip have shallower underground water and are well settled and cultivated. Wolof and Serer farmers grow millet for food and immense quantities of groundnuts (Plate 24) for sale—up to 850,000 tons per annum in Senegal and 65,000 tons in the Gambia. The main areas of production have moved steadily south-south-east from near St. Louis to near

Kaolack (Fig. 48), leaving severely degraded areas near St. Louis and Dakar. However, the Serer, who farm mainly east-south-east of Dakar, are one of the few African peoples who grow crops and keep cattle. This has helped them to maintain the fertility of their soils, despite intensive groundnut production in the main producing district. A typical Senegal farm will have about four acres under groundnuts, five acres under millet, and another acre or two under cassava, sweet potatoes, beans and other vegetables. Ease of cultivation and transport, and high guaranteed prices have led to dangerous dependence upon groundnuts, to the extent that they, groundnut oil and cake, comprise some 85 per cent of Senegal exports and 95 per cent of Gambian exports.

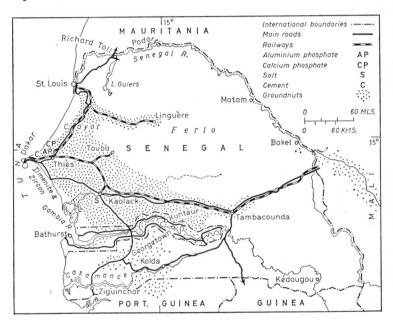

Fig. 48. Senegal and Gambia

Mechanized agriculture has been tried, without marked success, at Richard Toll on the Senegal River, near Kaffrine east of Kaolock, and near Sédhiou, 110 miles up the Casamance. At the first about 11,000 acres are irrigated for rice, which is mechanically sown and harvested. Fertility is maintained with artificial fertilizers. These and pump irrigation are costly, some soils have had to be abandoned because of salinity and wind erosion, and losses to the quelea bird have been enormous. In the other schemes mechanized production of ground-nuts has been curtailed in favour of peasant cultivation with mechanical assistance.

Mining

Aluminium phosphate is quarried at Pallo, north-west of Thiès, the only exploited deposit of the mineral in the world. Assimilable fertilizer is obtained by a simple thermal process. A little to the north-west, at Tivaouane, deposits of calcium phosphate are produced, the kind of phosphate normally used as a fertilizer. This is useful to Senegal groundnut farmers, as well as providing diversification of exports.

Black sands thrown up by high tides and containing ilmenite, rutile and zircon are worked on beaches south of Dakar. Limestone is quarried near Rufisque for use in West Africa's first cement factory nearby at Bargny (Plate 23). Salt is dug, refined and packed at Kaolack.

Industry

This is exceptionally developed for such a relatively small country due to the early encouragement given to groundnut oil extraction through a guaranteed market at high prices in France. Further impetus came during the Second World War when fuel oil could not be imported and groundnut oil was substituted. Industries also came here because Dakar was, until 1959, the federal capital of French West Africa, and the latter their logical market. The large European population (30,000) and a concentrated African population with a higher-than-average standard of living were other inducements, and sustained the industries when their markets elsewhere were imperilled by the break-up of French West Africa. These consumer-good industries are between Dakar and Rufisque.

Towns

Dakar (250,000) now the capital of Senegal alone, was founded in 1857 as a calling-point for French boats on South American services. West Africa's first railway reached Dakar in 1885, which caused it to supplant St. Louis as a port, and to become the outlet for groundnuts grown near the railway. It became a naval base before the First World War, and a northern breakwater then enclosed a harbour of about one square mile. The railway to the Niger at Bamako and Koulikoro, completed 1924, made it the outlet for the French Sudan. The port (Plate 25) has nearly 2 miles of quays with depths of over 26 feet; all quays total 4 miles in length, and some 5,000 ships are cleared annually. They call for water and oil, passengers, groundnuts and especially groundnut oil (conveyed in tankers), and phosphates. Dakar has virtually supplanted St. Vincent (Cape Verde Islands) as a port of call, and rivals Las Palmas (Grand Canary).

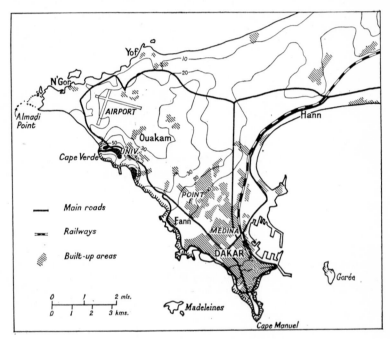

Fig. 49. Dakar and the Cape Verde Peninsula
Heights in metres. Land over 50 metres in black. Cliffs are hachured

Yoff is a leading African airport, a vital point of call on Europe–South America, North America–Africa and some Europe–West Africa routes, as well as being the terminal of many West African services. The city extends some 8 miles north-westward and eastward. The harbour, central business district, industrial estate and many residential areas are impressive, but water is sometimes scarce and the cost of living high.*

* A good study by a Senegalese geographer is Assane Seck 'Dakar', *Les Cahiers d'Outre-Mer*, Bordeaux, 1961, 372–92.

Other urban centres are historic St. Louis, now merely a river–rail or road transfer point for the trade of the Senegal Valley, and a fishing centre. Kaolack is an ocean-river port in the heart of the best ground-nut areas (Fig. 48), and a salt producer. Thiès, a railway and road junction, developed as a railway repair centre and garrison, and is now a commercial centre of the groundnut and phosphate areas. Ziguinchor is another ocean-river port, and serves the Casamance area, par-ticularly as a groundnut exporter and a coastwise shipper of rice to Dakar. It is also linked to Dakar by the Trans-Gambian Highway which has a fast ferry over the Gambia River. Bathurst, capital of the Gambia, has a small pier in the estuary of a deep river, but little traffic because of the long political divorce of the hinterland from the river, and the parallel railway to Dakar. It is a groundnut port and commercial centre. Senegal has a good network of roads, numerous road services, a fully dieselized railway and many local air services.

Senegal and the Gambia are over dependent upon the groundnut, and Dakar's port and airport upon world prosperity, yet diversifica-tion is difficult in this dry environment. Phosphate mining, rationaliza-tion of fishing, and industries seem to offer the best prospects—given greater markets.

FURTHER READING

The most comprehensive sources are listed on p. 225. See also R. J. Harrison Church, 'Problems and Development of the Dry Zone of West Africa', *Geographical Journal*, 1961, 187–204. Parts of René Dumont, *Types of Rural Economy*, 1957, Chapter III, 'The Tropical Savanna of Africa from Chad to the River Casamance', are concerned with these countries.

Gambia: Lady Southorn, *The Gambia*, 1952; H. R. Jarrett, 'Major Natural Regions of the Gambia', *Scottish Geographical Magazine*, 1949, 140–4, 'Geographical Regions of the Gambia', *Idem*, 1950, 63–169, 'Bathurst—Port of the Gambia River', *Geography*, 1951, 98–107, and 'Population and Settlement in the Gambia', *Geographical Review*, 1948, 633–6.

CHAPTER FOURTEEN

The Rainy Lands of the South-West Coast

THE rainy lands of the south-west coast comprise:

Country or Province	Area in sq. miles	Population	Density per sq. mile
Port. Guinea	13,948	544,184	39·0
Guinea	94,901	2,900,000	29·5
Sierra Leone	27,925	2,183,000	78·0
Liberia	37,392	750,000	20·1

Portuguese Guinea, Guinea, Sierra Leone and Liberia have a Tropical climate that is somewhat monsoonal, with rainfall of up to 170 inches in 7 months. This has caused widespread erosion, exposure of lateritic surfaces (especially in the Fouta Djallon), and severe leaching of soils, which, in turn, supported poorer forest than that behind the southern coast of West Africa.

Along the broken coastline, with its shallow rias, is a great tidal range which prevents the occurrence of off-shore bars but encourages the growth of mangrove in the inlets. Consequently, there are few deep inlets (the Rokel Estuary is a notable exception) but many areas are suited to empoldering for the cultivation of rice, here the main food.

PORTUGUESE GUINEA

Less than one-half the size of Scotland, this is a relic of early Portuguese contact with West Africa. Slaves were taken from here not only to the New World, but also to the Cape Verde Islands, some of whose Creoles are now clerks in Portuguese Guinea.

The west is part of the same low sedimentary basin of post-Eocene deposits as Senegal; while the south-east has Ordovician or Silurian sandstone low plateaux of the Fouta Djallon. Rainfall of 80–130 inches in 5 months occurs along the coast, with 70–80 inches in the eastern interior. Relative humidity is always high on the coast.

Mangrove has been extensively cleared, and the land dyked by the Balante and Floup, who are expert rice farmers and grow coconuts,

* By R. J. Harrison Church.

the oil palm and bananas. Cattle are kept mainly for manure to fertilize the land. This is by far the most peopled part of the country.

In the interior the Manding and the normally-nomadic Fulani grow millet, groundnuts, cotton and vegetables in an environment of Moist Woodland-Savanna with riverine forests. Cropping methods are poorer than on the coast, and there are extensive exposures of laterite.

Substantial quantities of groundnuts, palm kernels and coconuts are crushed for oil which, with uncrushed oil seeds, account for most exports. These are brought down the rivers by canoes and lighters to Bissau, the main port and capital. Trade is closely controlled, is overwhelmingly with Portugal, and mainly in the hands of one Portuguese company.

GUINEA

Guinea has contrasted regions and varied resources; dominating it is the deeply trenched Fouta Djallon in which thick Ordovician or Silurian sandstones lie above the Basement Complex. The latter is exposed in the Guinea Highlands and Niger Plains.

The coast, which has an annual rainfall reaching 170 inches at Conakry, is like that of Portuguese Guinea in nature and land use. The Baga have reclaimed mangrove for rice, and the French started some large works. There are also banana and pineapple plantations.

Precambrian outcrops occur at Cape Verga, Conakry, and form the Los Islands. Conakry, the capital, is on an island adjacent to the mainland, and through its very well-equipped port (Plate 27) passes ferruginous magnetite iron ore from quarries 8 miles inland, alumina, and other exports—mainly coffee and bananas. Conakry is partly sheltered by the Los Islands on which a small deposit of bauxite is quarried. A much larger deposit, one of the largest in the world, is at Boké, where an alumina and aluminium plant has been partially built, together with a pier and mineral line.

The Fouta Djallon has varied landscapes and economies. On the level plateaux, with their lateritic surfaces, porous sandstone, and Montane Grassland, the Fulani keep Ndama cattle, which are sold in Sierra Leone and Liberia. This is the only area in West Africa where Fulani keep these small cattle resistant to the tsetse fly, which occurs here. Negro slaves of the Fulani formerly grew food crops for them in the deep valleys; the poorer the plateaux, the greater the number of slaves required, and the denser the valley settlements even today. The Fulani now grow their own essential subsistence crops, usually millet. The trench-like valleys have both river and spring water, far

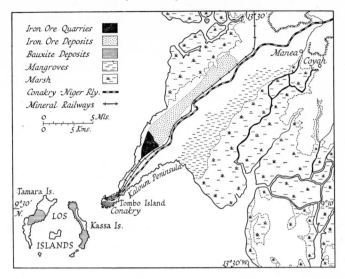

Fig. 50. Conakry
(From R. J. Harrison Church, *West Africa*)

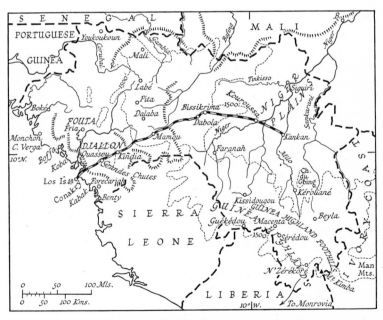

Fig. 51. Guinea
(From R. J. Harrison Church, *West Africa*)

more vegetation and soil, and shade as well as sun; citrus and pine-apple are grown on valley slopes and bananas on the floors.

Industry has started in the Fouta Djallon. At Fria on the Konkouré River 95 miles north-north-east of Conakry is a works (Plate 26) which reduces bauxite from a nearby large deposit to alumina. The plant is one of the largest and most modern in the world. Alumina is sent by mineral line to Conakry, from where it goes to Cameroon for smelting (p. 288 and Plate 33), and to Europe, Canada and the U.S.A. An aluminium factory may be built later at Fria, using power from a hydro-electric power plant which could be built on the Konkouré.

The Guinea Highlands, on the Liberian boundary and part of the Basement Complex, are rounded in form, in contrast to the level plateaux and trenched valleys of the Fouta Djallon. Coffee is the dominant cash crop and a leading Guinea export. Kolas are exten-sively grown for sale in Mali. The area is remote from Conakry, but there is a direct road to the free port of Monrovia, Liberia. Vast iron ore reserves are being worked on the Liberian side, and soon will be on the Guinea side. Diamonds are panned by co-operatives between Macenta and Kérouané, and west of Beyla; some are gems but most are industrial stones.

The Niger Plains have much laterite over the Basement Complex. Rice is grown along the Niger and its tributaries, especially between Kouroussa and Siguiri, but other subsistence crops have poor yields. Kankan, the rail terminus, is important for its roads to the Guinea Highlands and down the valley of the Milo tributary of the Niger, both navigable to Bamako in Mali.

Guinea, a member of the Ghana–Guinea–Mali Union of African States, has socialized its economy. At independence in 1958 France withdrew all personnel and movable equipment, stopped all aid, and closed her guaranteed high-priced market for Guinea's coffee and bananas. Eastern Europe gave aid and provided markets for this produce and some of the iron. Technicians from those countries helped revive or transform mines and farms. Guinea has great poten-tial, particularly if aid and markets are forthcoming, and local power is developed to process the varied minerals and run industries.

SIERRA LEONE

Sierra Leone, like Liberia, was founded as a home for freed slaves. The first settlement was at Freetown in 1787, and the Sierra Leone Penin-sula became a Colony in 1808. Intensive settlement of freed slaves continued around the peninsula in the first half of the nineteenth century in villages such as Wilberforce, named in honour of the campaigner against slavery. African soldiers discharged after the Napoleonic Wars were settled in the equally appropriately-named villages of Wellington and Waterloo.

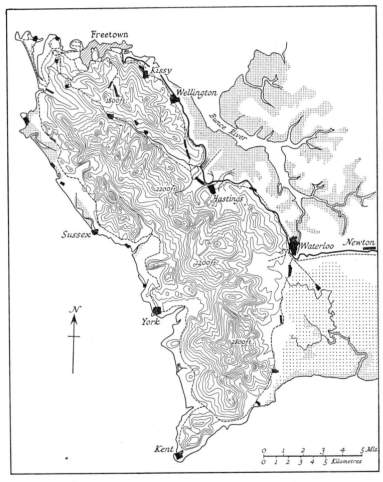

Fig. 52. The Sierra Leone Peninsula
(From H. R. Jarrett, 'The Port and Town of Freetown', *Geography*, April 1955, by permission of author and editor)

These ex-slaves, often of mixed African and European descent, are known as Creoles, and have a non-African culture. This has tended to

estrange them from the Africans of the interior, over whom a Protectorate was declared as late as 1898. The Creoles soon acquired a high
cultural level as the result of missionary activities among them. Fourah
Bay College started university education as far back as 1827, over a
century before such education was available elsewhere in tropical
Africa. Better education brought Creoles into government and private
service in other British West African territories, especially as these
were administered from Freetown during part of the nineteenth
century. All this has changed as the Creoles have ceased to be dominant
in Sierra Leone, education has developed in other areas where they
formerly worked, and Ghana and Nigeria are larger and richer lands.

The Sierra Leone Peninsula is one of the rare mountainous parts of
coastal West Africa. So impressive is it from the sea that it was called
Sierra Leone (the Lion Mountain) by the Portuguese Pedro da Cintra
in 1462. This rugged peninsula is the eastern half of a mass of basic
intrusive rocks; the western half has foundered, so giving the steep
westward face (Fig. 52). Villages around it are no longer distinctively
Creole, but are dormitory suburbs of Freetown and produce vegetables for it.

The Rokel Estuary is wide and deep at the northern end of the
peninsula, and here is West Africa's only excellent natural harbour,
wherein many wartime convoys sheltered. Freetown (128,000), the
capital of Sierra Leone, was the principal anti-slavery naval base;
hence the thousands of freed slaves landed here. Because Nature was
so lavish in providing deep and calm water, and the overseas trade of
Sierra Leone was small, a deep-water quay was not opened until
1953, although a pier for loading iron ore was built up-river at Pepel
in the mid-'thirties.

Until recently many houses in central Freetown (and in Monrovia,
Liberia) were of the white frame-and-board type typical of the southern
states of America. They have a first floor balcony supported on pillars
in front of the ground floor rooms, and dormer windows above.
Because of the steep terrain, the town is mostly spread out along the
lowest slopes. Industries are developing at the eastern end in Cline
Town, near the deep-water quays. Some houses extend up the slopes;
Hill Station high above originated as a European quarter, and Mount
Aureol is now occupied by Fourah Bay College. The airport is
inconveniently across the estuary at Lungi.

As in Portuguese Guinea and neighbouring Guinea, there are
extensive coastal swamps, here some twenty miles wide (Fig. 9).
Mangrove has been cleared for rice cultivation, despite difficulties

with salinity and toxic accumulations. Most reclamation has been along the lower Great and Little Scarcies rivers, and around Port Loko (Fig. 53) usually between 6 and 15 miles upstream. The area of an average rice farm is about 3 acres.

Inland from the mangrove swamps are seasonally-flooded fresh-water grasslands. Some of these along the Little Scarcies and Sewa rivers are mechanically ploughed in government sponsored schemes covering some 16,000 acres; nevertheless, rice—the main food—must be imported to supplement local production. Raphia palms grow extensively along rivers and around lakes near Bonthe and Sulima. Piassava fibres are obtained from the base of the leaf stalks after retting, and are exported for the manufacture of strong brooms and brushes.

The coastal plain lies inland of the swamps for about a hundred miles, averages 400 feet in altitude and is limited eastward by the escarpment of the interior plateaux and mountains. The coastal plain is composed of Precambrian rocks and some granites, and is gently undulating. Interfluves are capped with lateritic crusts, valley slopes are degraded by over-farming, and only the valley floors and swamps are fertile. These are being developed in the same way as the season-ally-flooded freshwater grasslands.

Iron ore is the region's greatest resource, and occurs as haematite in schists at Marampa. The ore has been scraped from two hills since 1933, and the remaining rather poorer ore of 45 per cent iron is concentrated in washeries to 58–69 per cent iron, and taken by a 55-mile mineral line for shipment at Pepel. Iron ore is Sierra Leone's second export. Bauxite mining has started in the Mokanji Hills near Moyamba.

East of the coastal plain are the interior plateaux, akin to the Guinea Highlands, because they are mostly composed of granite. In the Sula Mountains at Tonkolili are further reserves of haematite iron, but diamonds are the greatest resource. Originally worked by a monopoly at Yengema, near Sefadu, they are now won in greater quantities by African diggers along rivers, notably the Sewa and its tributaries. The country produces about 10 per cent of the world's gem stones but only some 4 per cent of the industrial ones. Diamonds are Sierra Leone's leading export, and its main source of revenue, but fears have been expressed that reserves are running out.

Soils are even poorer than in the coastal plain, because of erosion on steeper slopes and over-farming (Fig. 9). The north is especially poor, with mostly subsistence cropping of millet and groundnuts, or nomadic

herding of the small resistant Ndama cattle; in the south-east, however, there is still extensive forest. Cocoa is important between
Kenema and Kailahun, with coffee—more tolerant of seasonal
dryness and poorer soils—on its outer fringes. The oil palm, providing
cooking and other oil, is important throughout southern Sierra Leone

Fig. 53. Sierra Leone; economic

(Fig. 53). The oil palm was Sierra Leone's greatest resource until the
'thirties, and palm kernels are still the leading agricultural export.

Sierra Leone has been hampered by its very narrow gauge and low-
capacity railway and by the formerly numerous time-devouring
ferries on the west–east roads crossing the southward-flowing rivers.
Agricultural produce accounted for all exports until 1930; it only

27. Conakry harbour, Guinea (p. 242). The passenger quay is just off the picture on the left, the first visible one being the general wharf. Beyond is the iron-ore terminal with a dump of dark iron ore behind. On the far right is a third pier for loading alumina.

26. The Fria plant (p. 244) 90 miles north-north-east of Conakry, Guinea, which, alone in Africa, reduces bauxite to alumina.

28. A small part of Monrovia (p. 250), Liberia, with its harbour in the left distance which is one of Africa's two free ports.

29. The Bomi Hills iron-ore mine, Liberia (p. 251).

comprises one-sixth of them now. Minerals, especially diamonds, have transformed Sierra Leone, mostly since 1955. Agricultural advance lies in cheaper rice production, and in co-operative or plantation tree-crops like cocoa, coffee, rubber, bananas and the oil palm.

LIBERIA

The first settlement of freed American slaves was made at Monrovia in 1822, later settlements followed down the coast, and in 1847 they declared their independence. The coast has no deep sheltered estuary

Fig. 54. Relief and regions of Liberia
(From R. J. Harrison Church, *West Africa*)

such as Freetown enjoys, and the settlements lacked the degree of help from America which Sierra Leone has had over a long period from Britain. There was a rift between the Americo-Liberians (the counterpart of the Sierra Leone Creoles) and the indigenous Africans; in Liberia, however, there was no colonial power to defend the Americo-Liberians as there was for the Creoles. Nor was there a colonial power to build railways, roads, provide schools, and so forth. The Americo-Liberians clung on, and Liberia is the only African country which has never been ruled by another power.

Unlike Portuguese Guinea, Guinea, and Sierra Leone there is no continuous belt of coastal swamp, mangrove occurring only at river mouths. Indeed, the coast is more characterised by diorite promontories (like that at Conakry, Guinea), which were seized upon by the Americo-Liberians as being rather higher and so healthier, and capable of defence. Monrovia, the capital, is on Cape Mesurado, one such promontory, and so are Robertsport (Cape Mount), Buchanan, Greenville and Harper.

There is, however, an extensive coastal plain to which government was largely confined for the first century. From here the Americo-Liberians successively exported camwood (a dye stuff) from the forests, cane sugar, coffee, piassava and oil palm produce. Concessions started in 1906 with a British rubber plantation near Monrovia. In 1926 Firestone leased one million acres for 99 years. Rather under 100,000 acres have been planted with 10–11 million trees north-east of Monrovia and on the Cavalla River (Fig. 55), and this is the largest such enterprise in the world. Firestone introduced wage-earning and brought revenue to a penniless and heavily-indebted government. Rubber was almost the only export until 1951, when iron ore exports began, and which now exceed rubber in value.

The strategic importance of the country in relation to Atlantic convoys brought American troops during the Second World War, and they built the central road which now runs into Guinea and, by one spur, serves the Western Province and runs into Sierra Leone and, by another, serves the Eastern Province. They also built the first international airport of Roberts Field, 55 miles from Monrovia, where another airport has since been added. Most valuable has been the American-built deep-water harbour on Bushrod Island (Plate 28), north of Cape Mesurado, Monrovia, opened 1948 and since improved. It is enclosed by breakwaters each about 1½ miles long, and is West Africa's only free port. Through it passes Liberian rubber, much of the iron ore, and imports. Other deep-water ports have been or are being built at Buchanan (see below), at Greenville for the export of the produce of a German banana plantation, and at Harper for general trade.

Behind the coastal plain are low hills, plateaux and mountains, comparable with those in Sierra Leone. These are succeeded on the north and north-eastern borders by the Guinea Highlands. Haematite iron ore, comparable in quality with that first mined in Sierra Leone and now mined in Mauritania, has been worked since 1951 in the Bomi Hills north-west of Monrovia (Fig. 55 and Plate 29). A mineral

Fig. 55. Liberia; economic
(From R. J. Harrison Church, *West Africa*)

line takes the ore to Monrovia, and in 1961 this line was extended to the Mano River (boundary with Sierra Leone) to open another deposit. A much larger one on Mt. Nimba (Guinea Highlands) is served by a 200 mile-long mineral railway, entirely remote controlled, which takes ore to Liberia's second deep-water harbour at Buchanan, opened in 1963. A fourth deposit in the Bong Mountains is being developed by another mineral line to Monrovia. These developments are opening another era in the economic history of Liberia, causing it to be an iron ore exporter rather than a rubber one.

The central road and its spurs have also enabled the interior to be opened up and substantially planted with rubber, coffee and cocoa in concessions granted to non-Liberians. Such tree crops, along with the wild oil palm and piassava palm, are ideally suited to Liberia's heavy rainfall and varied but mostly poor soils.

Liberia has changed fundamentally since 1926, and especially since 1948, but is suffering from an acute labour shortage consequent upon its very small population, believed to be under one million. This affects the evolution of its mainly concessionaire plantation and mineral economy. In great contrast to the ex-British and ex-French countries, there is almost no truly African development, which is almost all by foreign companies whose royalty and taxation payments provide most government revenue.

Liberia is the most southerly of the rainy lands of the south-west coast, and is transitional to the Guinea Coast lands, for in the south-east of the country a double maximum of rainfall appears, and rice gives place to cassava as the dominant food. With poor soils and only moderately productive agriculture, great efforts have been made in Portuguese Guinea, Guinea and Sierra Leone to reclaim coastal and inland swamps for rice production, sometimes at high cost. Guinea, Sierra Leone and Liberia have benefited enormously from increased mineral production, especially from bauxite and alumina production in Guinea, diamonds in Sierra Leone, and iron in all three but especially Liberia. Guinea has socialized its economy and redirected its overseas trade mainly with Eastern Europe, while Liberia is a concessionaire economy.

FURTHER READING

The most comprehensive sources are listed on p. 225. Also:

Sierra Leone: *Atlas of Sierra Leone*, 1953; D. T. Jack, *Economic Survey of Sierra Leone*, 1958. A popular study is Roy Lewis, *Sierra Leone*, 1954.

Liberia: P. W. Porter, 'Liberia', *Focus* (American Geographical Society), September 1961.

CHAPTER FIFTEEN

The Guinea Coast Lands

THE lands of the Guinea Coast in West Africa are:

Country	Area in sq. miles	Population	Density per sq. mile
Ivory Coast	124,471	3,200,000	24·8
Ghana	91,843	6,690,730	72·8
Togo	22,002	1,470,000	64·5
Dahomey	44,684	2,080,000	45·0
Nigeria	356,669	55,670,052	156·0

These five countries, from the Ivory Coast in the west to Nigeria in the east, have an Equatorial climate as far inland as 7–8°N. This is especially well seen in the Ivory Coast, south-western Ghana and southern Nigeria. North of 7–8°N. there is a Tropical climate. These countries, and especially Nigeria, have the most varied physical conditions of all West African lands, and so the most diversified production of crops, livestock and other natural produce. Minerals are important in Nigeria and Ghana, and are being developed in the Ivory Coast and Togo. Nigeria has more people than all the rest of West Africa put together, and Ghana the greatest per capita trade.

THE IVORY COAST

Dense forest and a surf-bound coast east of Fresco delayed the development of the Ivory Coast, which has the richest resources of ex-French West Africa. The forest obstacle was breached when the railway reached Bouaké in 1912 (extended to Bobo Dioulasso, Upper Volta, in 1934, and Ouagadougou in 1954), and the Vridi Canal made Abidjan, the capital, into a deep-water harbour in 1950. Since then progress has been spectacular.

Abidjan (145,000) has been especially prosperous. The administrative core and mainly better residential areas are on the north, on the mainland (Fig. 56). A remarkable bridge (Plate 30), with a road above and railway below in a suspended tunnel, links the mainland with Petit Bassam Island where the port, an industrial area and the suburb

* By R. J. Harrison Church.

of Treichville are situated. Abidjan is well served by roads, the railway into the Upper Volta, and by West African and inter-continental air services.

The coastal plain merges into the interior ones, and these into plateaux. The more basic contrast is between Forest and Savanna, for in the former is concentrated most of the country's peoples and production. As in Guinea, alienation of land was permitted to non-Africans, who established plantations of coffee, cocoa and bananas. Most of the banana plantations, but only one-quarter of the coffee, and a mere 5 per cent of the cocoa areas are, however, owned by non-Africans, and some Africans have large estates.

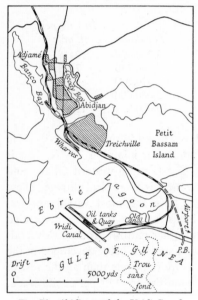

Fig. 56. *Abidjan and the Vridi Canal*
(From R. J. Harrison Church,
West Africa)

Production of these crops has been greatly encouraged by guaranteed markets in France at much higher than world prices; indeed, the Ivory Coast is the third world producer of coffee, and there are 1·3 million acres under it. Yet, across the boundary in Ghana, on similar soils and with comparable climatic conditions, cocoa is alone important; this results from the absence of such guaranteed and lucrative markets for Ghana coffee, and because cocoa is most suited to peasant production.

Most of the coffee is of the hardy robusta variety, and coffee is the leading export, accounting for about one-half of exports. The cocoa areas (600,000 acres) are more restricted to the east (Fig. 57), and are continuations of the Ghana areas. Cocoa is the second export, accounting for one-quarter to one-third of exports. Bananas are only a small item in foreign trade, and are of the small sweet Canary variety, grown on estates with good transport to Abidjan or Sassandra.

Because of the extent of the dense forest, its relative nearness to the European market, and the rivers which can be used for log floating, as well as numerous roads and the railway, timber is the third export (10–20 per cent of the total). Most is mahogany, but many other species are cut.

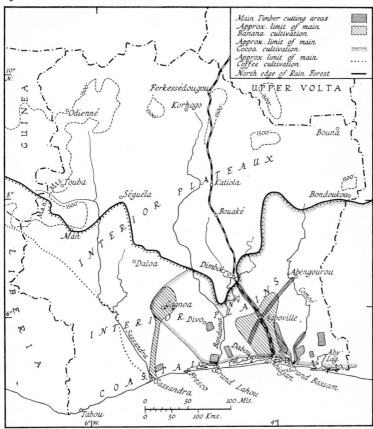

Fig. 57. *Regions and production areas of the Ivory Coast*
(From R. J. Harrison Church, *West Africa*)

Kolas are an important item of overland export to the Upper Volta and Mali as a counterpart to their cattle. These trades are focused through Bouaké at the limit of forest and savanna, well served by road, rail and air services. There is a large cotton mill north of it, which uses cotton from the savanna areas.

Mineral production has become significant. Diamonds are worked on the Bou, a tributary of the Bandama south of Korhogo, and less so north of Séguéla. Increasing amounts of manganese are quarried at

Grand Lahou, and taken by barge along the lagoons to a pier on the Vridi Canal.

Like Liberia and Ghana, the Ivory Coast has a labour shortage, and attracts men from the Upper Volta to work on its cocoa and coffee estates. The railway to the Upper Volta brings transit trade and, following Mali's rupture with Senegal, most of Mali's trade came through the Ivory Coast by road and rail.

The Ivory Coast has been exceedingly prosperous since 1950 and has excellent prospects for the sale of her produce in the European Economic Community. Her agricultural output is more diverse than that of Ghana, and mineral finds have been fortunate. Hydro-electric power from the Bia River at Ayamé has helped industries which, in Abidjan alone, include considerable processing of agricultural and forest products, and metallurgical trades.

GHANA

Of all the countries of West Africa, Ghana has, perhaps, attracted most attention, especially since it became independent in 1957. In part this is due to its substantial resources as the world's leading producer of cocoa, as until 1963 the chief West African producer of minerals, and as the scene of the Volta River Project—one of the greatest hydro-electric power schemes in the world. Other factors have contributed to the favourable situation of Ghana: long contact with the world, its schools, British administrators like Guggisberg and Arden-Clarke, and the drive of Dr. Nkrumah.

Gold has been mined in Ghana for about a thousand years, and it attracted the Portuguese in 1470. The English came in 1553, the Dutch in 1595, the Swedes and Danes about 1640, also attracted by gold, and, in time, still more so by the slave trade. For these trades each trading company built a castle on the coast, the lower floor to keep slaves awaiting shipment to the New World and for storing articles of trade, the upper floor housing the traders. Many of these castles are impressive buildings to this day, for example Elmina, the first castle, built 1481–2 (Plate 3).

Geology, relief, soils and climate are especially significant in Ghana, because physical factors greatly affect the production of cocoa. This needs deep, rich and well drained soils, and an Equatorial climate with at least 45 inches of annual rainfall and no pronounced dry season. Geology and relief are also of great significance in mining. Ghana is very sharply divided into contrasted regions as the result of the inter-action of the above factors.

The Physical Regions and their Economy

The Voltaian Basin is a largely negative region of Ordovician or Silurian sandstones, whose vivid upturned edges are erosion scarps. The soils derived from these rocks are infertile, and it is unlikely that

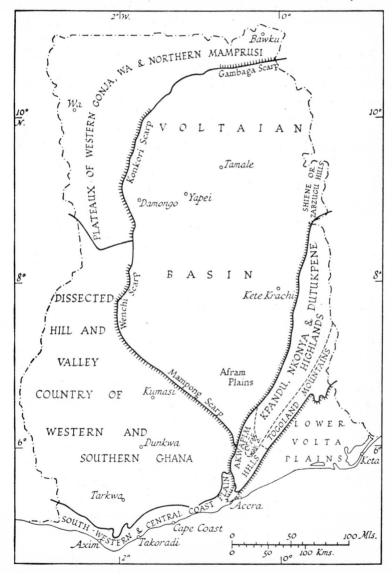

Fig. 58. Physical regions of Ghana

9

minerals will be found. The basin is the problem half of Ghana with only one-sixth of the population, but the 3,275 square mile lake which the Volta River Project will create will be within it. The waterway will require the re-settlement of relatively few people (some 67,000), but will greatly activate development by providing a navigable routeway, fish, and seasonally flooded lands for crops.

The high plains or plateaux of north-western and northern Ghana are similar to the interior plateaux of the Ivory Coast, and are part of the Basement Complex of Africa. They are more fertile but present vivid contrasts in settlement between the dense clusters of the north-east and the sparse population of the west.

In the north-east, in Zuarungu and Bawku districts, settlement is in numerous compounds rather than in villages or towns. The compounds are on interfluves away from rivers (where tsetse and simulium flies are dangerous), but intensive farming has degraded and eroded the soils. Although conservation methods have been adopted, there is pressure on the land and young men emigrate (as from the comparable Mossi lands of the Upper Volta) to southern Ghana. In the west, closer settlement awaits the elimination of the tsetse fly.

The dissected hill and valley country of western and southern Ghana is characterized by a number of north-east to south-west-trending ridges separated by wide valleys. As the producing area of Ghana's cocoa, timber and minerals, it is the economic heart of the country; with one-third the area it has two-thirds of the people.

Cocoa farming, entirely by Africans and mostly on farms of one to three acres, has spread from the south-east to the west-north-west. It is now penetrating south-westward into the area of heaviest rainfall, as north-westward advance is restricted by insufficient rainfall. Almost all of Ghana's output of 300–400,000 tons per annum comes from this region. Cocoa accounts for about two-thirds of exports, and Ghana supplies one-third of the world's cocoa.

Kumasi (221,000) the Ashanti capital, is a great commercial centre for the cocoa lands, and a focus of communications including air services. It has Ghana's University of Technology and growing industries.

Fine timbers are cut in the region, especially near Kumasi, Dunkwa, Awaso, Prestea and Oda. There are many saw mills, and a large plywood and veneer factory at Samreboi in the south-west near the Ivory Coast boundary. Timber accounts for 10 per cent of exports, and Ghana is the leading Commonwealth exporter.

Gold mining is from Birrimian (Lower Precambrian) quartz reefs at Prestea, Obuasi (the most productive gold mine in the world, and

3,600 feet deep), Bibiani and Konongo. Much less productive are the Tarkwaian conglomerates (Middle and Upper Precambrian) of the Tarkwa area, and there is a little dredging at Bremang. Gold mining has become steadily less profitable, many mines have closed, while

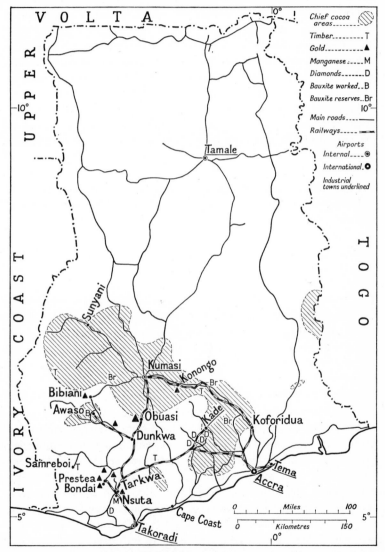

Fig. 59. Ghana; economic
(Partly after *Portfolio of Ghana Maps*)

others have been nationalized. Gold, like manganese and diamonds, accounts for under 10 per cent of Ghana exports.

Manganese ore occurs widely as a capping but is worked only in a vast hill excavation at Nsuta, 39 miles by railway from Takoradi. Ghana, although well down the producing list, is the world's largest exporter. Diamonds are worked by four companies in the Birim Valley at Akwatia, Kade and Oda, and an equal proportion are panned by Africans in the Bonsa Valley south of Tarkwa. Ghana diamonds are mostly industrial stones, of which she is the second world producer, although her output is only one-eighth that of the Congo (Leopold-ville). However, Ghana slightly exceeds her in gem production.

Bauxite occurs as cappings on the Kibi Hills, at Yenahin west of Kumasi, on the Mampong Scarp above Nkawkaw, and at Awaso, but is quarried only at the latter. Ghana bauxite is a minor export.

The coast plain is narrow. In the wet south-west coconuts and rice are grown; and coconuts, cassava and yams in the drier east-centre. Takoradi (121,000 with Sekondi), Ghana's first deep-water harbour, was opened in 1928 and extended in 1953. It consists of one long and one shorter breakwater, and through the port passes most of the cocoa, minerals and timber. The town is served by road, rail and air services and has a number of industries.

The Accra Plains and Volta Delta are covered by Tertiary and Quaternary sands and clays. Soils are generally poor, and the annual rainfall under 35 inches. Water is a limiting factor, and the Black Clays, derived from a gneiss outcrop, are intractable except to deep ploughing. This and irrigation on the sandy soils may be the means of development, but cattle herding, vegetable growing and fishing are the present occupations.

Accra (388,000) the lively Ghana capital, was the capital of the Ga people and an early point of European trade, there being three ancient forts in the town; Christiansborg is now a state residence. Accra has grown with the general development of Ghana, is a great commercial and communications (especially air) centre, and nearby is the University of Ghana. Unfortunately, Accra has suffered from frequent earthquakes due to instability of an offshore deep and, perhaps, of formations in the Akwapim-Togo Mountains. Tema is Ghana's second deep-water harbour (opened 1962) and Africa's largest artificial one (Plate 31). There is an 800 acre industrial estate, an oil refinery, and the aluminium smelter will be here. The town, served by road and rail, has been planned on modern lines.

The Akwapim Hills and Togo Mountains are really two ranges of Precambrian age which extend north-eastward from the coast west of Accra. They rise steeply from the Accra Plains, adjoin the Volta Basin on the west, and continue into Togo and Dahomey as the Atacora Mountains. Cocoa was first planted in the Akwapim Hills, but is now important only in the Dutukpene and Nkonya Highlands east of Kete Krachi.

The gorge between the Akwapim Hills and Togo Mountains is the site at Akosombo of the Volta Dam, now being built. It will create a navigable waterway to the north, provide power for an aluminium smelter at Tema, and for general domestic and industrial use from a grid running from Tema to Takoradi, Kumasi and back to the power station. Initial capacity will be 512,000 kW, rising to 768,000 kW. A small low dam below at Kpong, and a larger one far up river at Bui on the Black Volta west of Kintampo, will ultimately raise capacity to 854,000 kW and 1,044,000 kW respectively. Imported alumina will be used when the power station and smelter are completed about 1966, but Ghana bauxite will probably be used in the mid-'seventies. This project epitomizes the upsurge of Ghana. Power will diversify the economy by introducing aluminium manufacture (initially producing 78,000 tons per annum, expanding to 135,000 tons by 1974), reducing mining costs, activating other industries with cheap electricity, and providing a waterway.

Ghana already has the highest per capita income and overseas trade in West Africa, and these are higher than in many African, Asian, Central or South American countries. Its prospects should be brighter still when the Volta River Project makes substantial changes to the map and economy.

TOGO

Togo is the eastern two-thirds of the former German colony of Togo (1884–1914), the smaller western part having been incorporated in Ghana upon the latter's independence.

Togo and Dahomey have many climatic, regional and economic characteristics in common. Both have the same rather dry conditions near their straight sandy coasts with their heavy surf, sandy ridges and lagoons. The latter often widen into 'lakes', which are former estuaries. Between the lagoons and the sea are dense stands of coconut trees in both countries. The coastal and lagoon villagers prepare copra and coconut oil, keep small cattle, and catch and smoke fish. These figure in internal trade, and copra is a minor export.

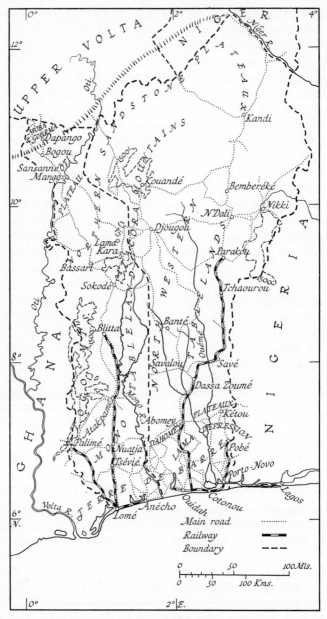

Fig. 60. *Togo and Dahomey*
(From R. J. Harrison Church, *West Africa*)

Lomé, the Togo capital, is adjacent to the Ghana boundary. It has only a pier, to and from which goods must be loaded into lighters which serve ships anchored off-shore, a costly impediment to trade. Thus, available palm oil cannot be exported because ships will call only for minimum cargoes of 300 tons piped directly into holds.

Beyond the lagoons is the *Terre de Barre*, which extends from the Volta River in Ghana through Togo and Dahomey into Nigeria. 'Barre' is a French corruption of the Portuguese word for 'clay', and the region has Tertiary clays which are heavy but fertile, are well settled, and fairly intensively planted with the oil palm, maize and cassava. The latter is locally processed for internal trade, while palm kernels are an export of modest importance. On the southern edge of this region, calcium phosphates are quarried north-east of Lake Togo. A fourteen-mile railway takes them to a concentrator and wharf at Kpeme, east of Porto Segouro. Export began in 1961, and it is hoped that this first mineral production will diversify the economy.

Inland is the poor siliceous Mano tableland, dry and less peopled. Yams, groundnuts and cotton are the main crops. In the rugged Kabrai area the population is oddly denser and cultivation very intensive. Tiny plots are made by terracing, are heavily manured with human, animal and bird excreta, and often irrigated—all rare practices in tropical Africa.

The Togo–Atacora Mountains cross the country from the Ghana boundary in a north-easterly direction. The more southerly and so wetter Togo Mountains are substantially planted with coffee and cocoa, Togo's leading exports. East of a low saddle at Sokode are the dry and poorer Atacora Mountains. These two ranges formerly limited the southern advance of Islamized peoples.

Northward again is the Oti Plateau, an extension of the Voltaian Basin of Ghana, whose Gambaga Scarp is here continued as the Bogou Scarp. North of that scarp lie granitic lands, densely peopled as in Ghana, and again over-cultivated and eroded.

Togo has only modest overseas trade, mainly in coffee and cocoa, with smaller amounts of palm kernels, cotton, copra, groundnuts and phosphates. It is hoped, however, that the latter may become the leading export. After independence strained relations with Ghana hurt Togo, it is still tied economically with France, and the smallness of the population hinders industrial development.

DAHOMEY

Old Dahomey was centred on Abomey, and was frequently at war with the Ashanti and Yoruba. Dahomey also saw the Portuguese slave trade to its bitter end; the last slave ship left only in 1885. When slaves were no longer sold because of the British and French abolition of the trade, political prisoners were put to establishing oil-palm plantations for a new legitimate trade. The oil palm is still the basis of Dahomey's economy, and of her export trade. There are some 30 million palms occupying 1,550 square miles, and four large mills (similar to that of Plate 40) extract high quality oil.

The physical character of the coast and its economy are like those in Togo, but the exceptional dryness gives way to normal rainfall at Ouidah, and the equally important coconut plantations are here owned mainly by non-Africans. Silted lagoons are often reclaimed and heavily cultivated, but the Porto-Novo lagoon is navigable to Lagos. Cotonou's deep water harbour was opened in 1964. Through it passes Dahomey's and much of Niger's overseas trade via the railway to Parakou and the road beyond. Porto-Novo, the capital, is an old African capital and a rare example of a capital that is not a sea port; it lies on the north side of the lagoon.

Beyond the lagoons, the Terre de Barre is more densely planted with oil palms and food crops than in Togo. Unlike there, it is succeeded northward by the seasonally flooded Lama Depression, which could be reclaimed for rice cultivation. North again, are low plateaux, similar to the Terre de Barre, and originally the realm of Old Dahomey and other states, and likewise closely planted with the oil palm.

Most of the rest of Dahomey is part of the Basement Complex, with moderate soils and crops of groundnuts, cotton, guinea corn or millet. In the north-west the Atacora Mountains and the poor Voltaian sandstones extend across the country.

The southern areas are especially productive, internal commerce is considerable, and the people much less poor there than in some countries, despite the narrow export economy and small size of Dahomey.

NIGERIA

Nigeria is Africa's most peopled country, and one in seven of all Africans is a Nigerian. Because of its size and latitudinal extent (4°–14°N.) the country has great diversity. Although the Precambrian Basement is widely exposed, there are also large occurrences of Cretaceous rocks in the north-west and in the Niger and Benue valleys,

The Houphouët-Boigny Bridge, [Ab]idjan, Ivory Coast, looking [sou]th-west (p. 253). The bridge is [nam]ned after the first premier and [has] a four-lane highway above and [a r]ailway in a tunnel suspended [bel]ow. Beyond is Petit Bassam [Isla]nd with the lagoon port and [adj]acent industrial area.

31. Africa's most extensive harbour at Tema (p. 260), Ghana, opened in 1962. On the extreme top right (west) are two large cocoa sheds which can deliver 100 tons of bagged cocoa per hour direct to holds of ships at Quay 1 to their left. Beyond is the general and passenger quay. At the land end of the eastern breakwater (centre) are slipways, a dry dock and a fitting-out quay (which projects west), and at the sea end of the break-water is the oil berth. Fishing and naval harbours are east again at the left base of the photo.

32. One of the cotton mills at Kaduna (p. 271), Northern Nigeria. Floor space covers 400,000 square feet, and annual production is nearly 40 million square yards of cloth.

33. Africa's only aluminium smelter at Edea (p. 288), Cameroon, using alumina from Fria, Guinea, and hydro-electric power from an adjacent station on the Sanaga River.

while Tertiary ones are found in the far north-west, north-east and across the country in the south. Quaternary rocks occupy the north-east (Chad Basin), the coastlands and Niger Delta. Precambrian and Palaeozoic intrusives are important on the Jos Plateau, and Secondary and younger ones in the Biu Plateau and on the Cameroon boundary.

The Jos Plateau rises to over 6,000 feet, and the Cameroon and Adamawa Mountains of the eastern boundary are also impressive. Apart from these high and vivid features, most of Northern Nigeria is between 1,000 and 3,000 feet. There is a west–east range of Precambrian rocks in the south-west, which is the watershed between the Niger and Gulf of Guinea streams, and there are north–south Cretaceous and Eocene escarpments east of the lower Niger in Eastern Nigeria.

The south has typical Equatorial conditions with 120 inches annual rainfall at Calabar and 70 at Lagos. As elsewhere, there are dry months inland, for example two at Enugu which has the same rainfall as Lagos, and three at Ibadan where the total is 48 inches. North of these towns there is a Tropical climate with a dry season increasing to eight months in the north-east. Range of temperature likewise increases inland.

Mangrove and Fresh-Water Swamp Vegetation are well developed on the coast, followed by Moist Forest best seen west of the lower Niger and east of Calabar, where there are important timber exploitations. Central Nigeria has a particularly wide expanse of Moist Woodland-Savanna, followed by the Dry Woodland-Savanna of the more northerly parts of Northern Nigeria.

Physical diversity is matched by human variety, and to accommodate diversity in unity Nigeria is a federation composed as follows:

Region	Capital	Area	Population* 1963	Population per sq. mile
Northern Nigeria	Kaduna	281,782	29,808,659	106
Western Nigeria	Ibadan	30,454	10,265,846	337
Mid-Western Nigeria	Benin	14,922	2,535,839	170
Eastern Nigeria	Enugu	29,484	12,394,462	420
Lagos Federal Territory	—	27	665,246	24,639
Federation of Nigeria	Lagos	356,669	55,670,052	156

In the Northern Region the Islamic Hausa (6 million) and Fulani (3 million) are dominant in the north-west and north-centre, with Fulani and Kanuri (1⅓ million) in the north-east. The more southerly

* These are the figures of the 1963 census, taken after another census of 1962 was annulled. The 1963 figures, like those of 1962, have been disputed as too high, but they are official.

9*

'Middle Belt' has diverse and often non-Islamic peoples of varied cultural levels, for example the Tiv ($\frac{3}{4}$ million) and Nupe ($\frac{1}{3}$ million). In the Western Region the Yoruba (5 million) are dominant. In the Mid-Western Region the Edo ($\frac{1}{2}$ million) are the largest of several peoples. In the Eastern Region the Ibo (nearly 6 million) are dominant in the west, with Ibibio (about $1\frac{1}{2}$ million) in the east.

The greatest cluster of population is of the Ibo east of the lower Niger in Onitsha and Owerri Provinces (Eastern Region), where dispersed compound settlement is the rule, and there is severe population pressure causing periodic emigration even to Fernando Po and Gabon. Another, but very different, cluster is in Yorubaland (Western Region), where there are numerous large towns which originated as urban-villages for defence. The great clusters of Northern Nigeria are again different, and are in and around the formerly walled cities of Kano, Katsina, Sokoto, Zaria and Maiduguri. Here, permanent cultivation is maintained with human and animal excreta from the numerous towns, as in mediaeval Flanders. Between these core areas are thinly peopled areas resulting from past inter-tribal wars and other problems. The largely empty 'Middle Belt' is the result of slave raiding from south and north, tsetse fly, and poor resources.

The export economy of Nigeria is likewise varied, mainly cocoa in the Western Region, rubber, timber and palm produce in the Mid-West, palm kernels and mineral oil in the Eastern Region, groundnuts, cotton, tin, hides and skins in the Northern Region. However, there is extensive and important internal trade, especially in cattle from the north and kola nuts from the west, but also more locally in yams. Nigeria is the only West African country with great forest crops in the south, and large herds of cattle in the north (Fig. 65).

WESTERN NIGERIA

The smooth surf-bound coast line backed by lagoons, so typical of most of the Ivory Coast, Togo and Dahomey, continues as far as the muddy creeks of the Niger Delta. On the coast there is the same three-fold economy of growing coconuts, keeping small cattle and fishing.

Lagos (665,246) the federal capital, is at the only break in this coastline. The oldest settlement is on the lagoon island of Lagos, from which the town has spread on to the islands of Iddo to the north-west and Ikoyi to the east, to the mainland at Apapa (deep water wharves and industrial estate), Ebute Metta (railway shops) and Yaba, and to the beach at Victoria. Lagos has suffered from its low-lying and marshy site (which poses great difficulties to water supply, sanitation and health), and from its dispersion in such separated areas causing traffic congestion on bridges. The airport is twelve miles to the north.

Lagos is also Nigeria's leading port and industrial centre, and the terminus of the western line of the railway which runs to Kano and Nguru in the far north-east. This carries some trade for the Niger Republic, while the Porto-Novo lagoon is used for access to Dahomey. Lagos has a greater value of trade than any other West African port.

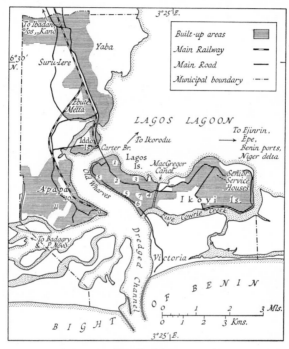

Fig. 61. Lagos
(From R. J. Harrison Church, *West Africa*)

Inland from the coast and delta, southern Abeokuta and western Ijebu are similar to the Terre de Barre of Dahomey and Togo. Again they are intensively cultivated, although with kola, citrus, bananas and pineapple, rather than with the oil palm.

Central Yorubaland lies north of the last two regions and south of the Niger–Guinea Coast watershed. There are fairly fertile loamy soils, which the Yoruba cultivate intensively with the usual forest zone food crops, and with cocoa for cash. There are about 980,000 acres under cocoa belonging to 275,000 farmers, the area extends east-north-east from Abeokuta for 200 miles and is 40 miles across. It is limited by insufficient humidity and rainfall on the north and west, and by leached sandy soils on the south.

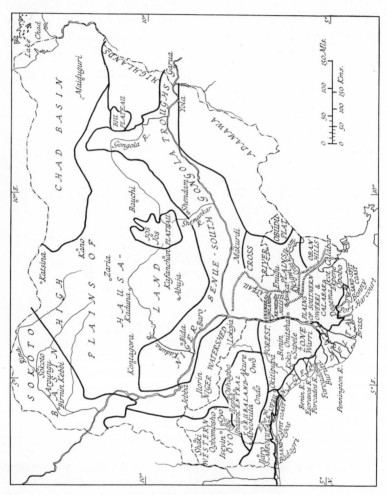

Fig. 62. Regions of Nigeria
(From R. J. Harrison Church, *West Africa*)

The huge Yoruba urban-villages have become progressively transformed; Ibadan (627,379), the largest city of tropical Africa, is the most famous. It is the capital of the Western Region, a great commercial centre, a growing industrial one, and has two universities, one with a superb teaching hospital. It is a focal point of roads, is served by the railway and by air.

In western Oyo soils are lighter, rain less, cocoa does not grow, and yams, other foodstuffs and tobacco are the main crops.

Western Nigeria has some of the richest soils in Nigeria, now mostly planted with the lucrative cocoa tree. Kola, citrus and food crops are also important, so that Western Nigeria is the most productive part of Nigeria.

MID-WESTERN NIGERIA

This was formed from Western Nigeria in 1963, and comprises Benin and Delta provinces west of the Niger River. In the western inlets of the Niger Delta are the ports of Sapele, Warri and Burutu, although Sapele is, strictly speaking, not on a branch of the Niger. It is a timber collecting and exporting port, with a large veneer and plywood factory. Warri and Burutu are ocean ports belonging to private companies where cargoes are transhipped to and from river steamers plying the Niger all the year to Onitsha, and seasonally to Baro (where there is a branch railway). Barges also go seasonally up the Benue to Makurdi, Yola and Garoua (Cameroon). Push-tow barges carry petroleum up-river, and groundnuts, cotton, hides and skins downstream (Plate 21).

Northward is Moist Forest where Nigeria's important timber exploitations are largely concentrated. Logs are floated down rivers, mainly to Sapele, and Obeche (*Triplochiton scleroxylon*) is the main species (Figs. 18 and 65). Nigeria is Africa's major timber exporter and the United Kingdom's main supplier of hardwoods. Rubber is of growing importance in the Benin–Sapele area but towards the Niger, where Ibo have penetrated west across the river, the oil palm is dominant.

The Mid-West is Nigeria's smallest, least peopled and poorest Region. At present dependent upon rubber, timber and palm produce, its hopes lie in mineral oil finds.

EASTERN NIGERIA

The eastern sector of the Niger Delta has most of Nigeria's oilfield. Production began in 1957 at Oloibiri and Afam, and oil and gas are conveyed by pipelines to Port Harcourt where a refinery has been built. Production of crude oil is increasing by about a million tons a year, and within a decade oil could be Nigeria's leading export. Natural gas is used for electrical generation and industrially at Port Harcourt.

Port Harcourt, Nigeria's second port, began when the railway from Enugu was opened to permit the export of coal. The extension of the railway from Enugu to Kaduna and Jos in Northern Nigeria in 1927 made it an outlet for the north, in competition with Lagos and the Delta ports. Like the latter, it lies up a river, the Bonny River, 41 miles from the sea, where mangrove ends and there is deep water.

The plains of southern Owerri and Calabar are formed of Tertiary sands leached by the heavy rainfall. The oil palm, needing heavy and frequent equatorial rainfall but tolerant of poor soils, is the basis of the economy, with food crops grown under the palms. Small oil mills have greatly improved the extraction and quality of the palm oil. About one-half is used domestically, and one-half exported, as are almost all the kernels.

Ibo farmers live in numerous scattered compounds, and population densities are the highest in Nigeria with densities of up to 1,350 per square mile. Onitsha, on the Niger, is a vast market for produce brought by road and river. East of Calabar, an old river port, settlement is much less dense in Ibibio country, and there are some oil palm, rubber, cashew and banana plantations.

North of these plains are the Cretaceous Anambra Lowlands, Udi Plateau and Cross River Plains. The uplands are poor and often severely gullied, and the plains infertile and too dry for the oil palm. Mining of Cretaceous coal began in 1915 on the Udi Plateau from adit mines at Enugu. Production has never exceeded a million tons and the coal has lost most of its markets to oil. It can, however, be made to coke, although it is far more suited to by-product manufacture. Industries should be attracted by it, the oil and natural gas to the south, lignite, brick clays and iron ore to the north, and by lead and zinc to the east. Enugu is the capital of Eastern Nigeria.

On the Cameroon border are the Obudu Plateau and Oban Hills, projections of the Cameroon and Bamenda Highlands. A ranching project is being developed in the former; Moist Forest covers the latter.

For long poor and over-dependent upon the oil palm (much less remunerative than cocoa), Eastern Nigeria now has bright prospects with its mineral oil, natural gas and other minerals for use in industry. Given markets, there seem good prospects for iron and steel and chemical industries, which could alleviate population pressure.

NORTHERN NIGERIA

This is four times larger than Western and Eastern Nigeria put together, but is less developed and has longer lines of communication.

It is basically divisible into the Middle Belt to the south and the Nigerian Sudan to the north.

The Middle Belt

This is especially clear in Nigeria. Although the belt has no accepted definition or sharp limits, it is thinly peopled, afflicted with the tsetse (except on the Jos Plateau) and has few valuable crops.

The boundary with Western Nigeria lies through the Niger watershed, where food crops alone are grown. Illorin is the centre of Yoruba people within Northern Nigeria.

The Niger-Benue troughs have only fair soils, well used around Makurdi by the Tiv for growing benniseed (sesamum) and soya, and for cotton around Lokoja. Alluvial soils are little used, but with flood control are being developed for rice and sugar cultivation.

The southern part of the high plains of Hausaland, north of the Niger–Benue valleys, are part of Africa's Precambrian Basement Complex, lie at 1,000–3,000 feet, but are thinly peopled. Kaduna, founded by the British, is the capital of Northern Nigeria, a railway junction, and the site of a large modern textile mill (Plate 32).

The Jos Plateau, some 65 miles by 50 miles, has an average elevation of 4,300 feet. The granite mass has resisted many erosion cycles, and there have been many volcanic intrusions. Steep bounding edges prevented the ingress of Fulani horsemen, so that the plateau became a refuge for non-Islamic peoples once opposed to the Fulani. Cropping possibilities are few, the smallest grains being grown. Zebu cattle can be kept but pastures are poor.

Tin is quarried, mainly in former river valleys, by cutting away the overburden and washing the gravels either simply or mechanically. For the latter the gravels can be washed out by water jet, cut out by draglines, or dredged. Power is obtained from hydro-electric stations on the edges of the plateau. Local smelting began in 1961. Columbite, tantalite and zircon are produced in association, Nigeria producing most of the world supply of these.

The Adamawa Highlands lie in the east. There is a good deal of terraced agriculture, using human and animal excreta, rotation of crops and the keeping of animals.

The Nigerian Sudan

Compared with the Middle Belt, this is far more densely peopled-better cultivated, and cattle are important as the tsetse is mostly absent. This is the productive north, although water and distance from road or railway are sometimes limiting factors in development.

The northern part of the high plains of Hausaland are similar to those in the Middle Belt but cotton, tobacco and guinea corn are grown around Zaria and northward, with groundnuts and millet around Kano and northward, all on small farms (Figs. 63 and 65).

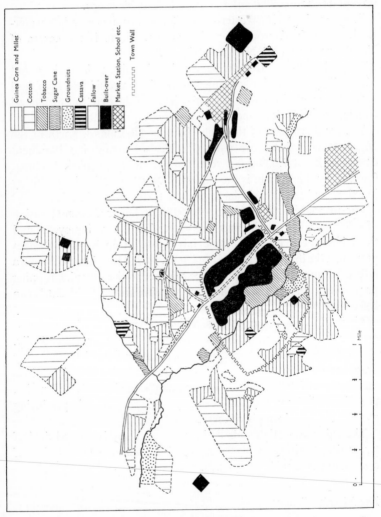

Fig. 63. Land-use at Soba
(From G. D. Watson, *A Human Geography of Nigeria*, p. 21)

Seasonally flooded river valleys (*fadamas*) are used for rice and vegetables; while irrigated plots produce a great variety of vegetables and other crops such as indigo and henna. Around the cities is intensive permanent cultivation using human excreta collected from the cities. The density of population reaches 1,000 per square mile up to 10 miles from Kano, and 400 per square mile up to 30 miles.

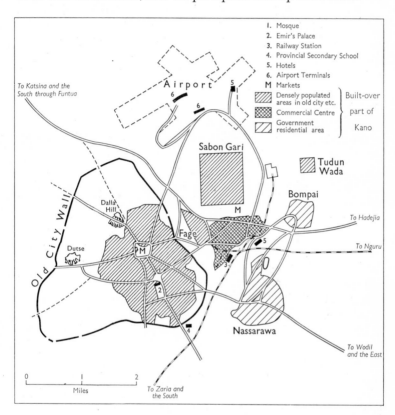

Fig. 64. Kano, Northern Nigeria
(From G. D. Watson, *A Human Geography of Nigeria*, p. 42)

Some 40 walled cities remain and Kano may be taken as a large typical example. There has been a settlement around its two prominent hills for at least a thousand years, and there was a neolithic settlement. Kano was an important trans-Saharan caravan terminal, despatching goatskins across the desert which came erroneously to be known as 'Moroccan' leather. Fields were originally left within the walls to provide food in times of siege; even now, not all the land within the old walls is built over. Outside the walls are settlements for various peoples; Fage is for other northerners, Sabon Gari for southerners, Nasarawa was the first quarter for Europeans who later lived also in Bompai, and around the railway is the commercial township where Lebanese mostly live.

Crafts, especially indigo dyeing, survive within the old walled town, but modern industries are mainly on an estate between Sabon Gari and Bompai. Groundnut oil is extracted and there are diverse consumer good industries. Kano is also a great commercial centre for the rail and road haulage of groundnuts, hides and skins southwards; and for the distribution of imported goods. There is also transit trade with the Niger Republic. North of the city is one of Africa's most important airports, and south of it one of the world's largest piggeries.

The Sokoto Basin occupies north-western Nigeria, where Cretaceous and Tertiary rocks are often severely eroded. Soils are light and porous, so that only occasional poor crops of millet and groundnuts are possible, although the seasonally flooded Sokoto and Rima Dallols are more productive. Sokoto was the Fulani capital, and is another typical walled city.

The Chad Basin, in north-eastern Nigeria, has been filled with Tertiary and Quaternary deposits. Light soils and aridity hamper cultivation of groundnuts, but patches of heavier 'firki' soils are suitable for cotton and guinea corn. Seasonally flooded areas around Lake Chad are cultivated with rice and guinea corn, and fish are caught in the lake.

In the Chad and Sokoto Basins, beyond the few intensively farmed areas and away from the tsetse fly, nomadic herding of livestock by the Fulani is very important. Animals are kept for subsistence more than for commerce, important though the latter is for the large Nigerian market, especially in the south where the standard of living is highest. The famous Sokoto Red and Kano Brown goat skins are exported for glacé kid leather, and hides and skins are a significant export.

Northern Nigeria is varied and undergoing rapid development. Its groundnuts, cotton, hides and skins are important in overseas trade; tobacco and livestock are also vital elements of internal trade.

The strength of Nigeria lies in the diversity of its resources and the large market which its population offers as standards of living improve, points of great contrast with most African states. Each part of the Federation contributes vital exports—palm kernels and oil from Eastern Nigeria; rubber and timber from the Mid-West; cocoa from Western Nigeria; and groundnuts, oil and cake from Northern Nigeria. Each Region contributes other significant items—kola nuts from the West; palm produce from the Mid- West; mineral oil from the East; tin and associated minerals, cotton, hides and skins from the

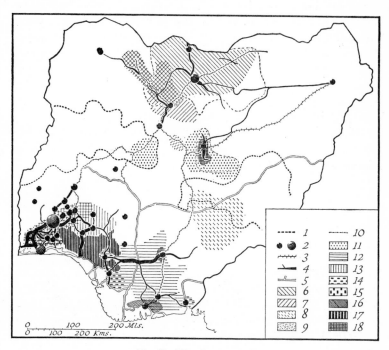

Fig. 65. Nigeria; economic

Numbers refer as follows; 1, areas of very low population density; 2, major towns (spheres proportional to population); 3, railways; 4, traffic flow on major roads (thickness of line approximately proportional to mean daily tonnage); 5, navigable waterways (wet season); 6, major groundnut producing area; 7, export cotton region; 8, benniseed (sesame) area of Benue Province; 9, commercial ginger production; 10, major cattle areas; 11, dairying regions of Middle Belt; 12, major oil palm regions; 13, cacao belt; 14, plantation rubber production; 15, commercial kola production; 16, mineral oil fields; 17, major commercial lumber region; 18, major mining areas. (From K. M. Buchanan, 'Nigeria', *Economic Geography*, 1952, p. 320, by permission of the author and editor, and with amendments and additions)

North. Nigeria is the leading world producer of both palm oil and kernels, the former being enough to make 300,000 tons of soap annually. She is the leading world exporter of groundnuts, and oil from these and palm kernels could also produce 400,000 tons of margarine annually. Nigeria is the second exporter of cocoa, and an important timber and benniseed exporter.

The Federation has varied means of transport. The Niger and the Benue are much used. The railway has main lines from Lagos and Port Harcourt meeting at Kaduna, with several branches, and a new one serves Maiduguri. In most areas road transport is more important, and there is a close network of roads in the densely peopled oil-palm areas of Eastern Nigeria and the cocoa area of Western Nigeria. Nigerian Airways serve the main towns, and many lines link Nigeria with other countries. Nigeria is exceptionally diverse physically, ethnically and economically, and should develop tremendously if it remains federated.

The Guinea Coast lands, and especially the Ivory Coast, Ghana and Nigeria, have the greatest potential in West Africa, and it is in those countries that the greatest developments are likely.

FURTHER READING

The most comprehensive sources are listed on p. 225. Also:

Ghana: E. A. Boateng, *A Geography of Ghana*, 1959; W. J. Varley and H. P. White, *The Geography of Ghana*, 1958; J. Brian Hills, *Agriculture and Land Use in Ghana*, 1962; and W. Manshard, *Die Geographischen Grundlagen der Wirtschaft Ghanas*, Wiesbaden, 1961.

Nigeria: K. M. Buchanan and J. C. Pugh, *Land and People in Nigeria*, 1959; *Economic Survey of Nigeria*, Lagos, 1959; G. Brian Stapleton, *The Wealth of Nigeria*, 1958; J. A. Grant, *The Western Region of Nigeria*, 1961.

WESTERN CENTRAL AFRICA

CHAPTER SIXTEEN

General, and the Islands

THE mountainous border between Nigeria and Cameroon is one of Africa's main physical and human divides. According to the Wegener theory of continental drift, the Brazilian Plateau once adjoined this part of Africa, and it is possible that separation came in Cretaceous times. Faulting developed along north-east to south-west trend lines, followed by mainly Tertiary volcanism. Extinct volcanoes form part or all of the islands of Annobon, São Tomé, Príncipe and Fernando Po; while on the mainland, Mt. Cameroon, 13,352 feet, the highest mountain in Western Africa, erupts occasionally. The Cameroon and Bamenda Highlands, north-east of it, are partly volcanic in origin, though no longer eruptive. These islands and mountains are western African analogues of the East African Rift Valley and volcanic system, and were formed about the same time.

The islands have an Equatorial climate with monsoonal characteristics, are fertile and densely peopled, despite much land useless because of steepness of slope or altitude. They are closely cultivated under a plantation system, use imported labour, and have almost landless and very mixed inhabitants. In their physical character, social and economic conditions, these islands are akin to Réunion and Mauritius, and have considerable social similarities with multi-racial South and Central Africa. The following figures summarize some of their features:

Island	Highest Peak (Feet)	Area in sq. miles	Population	Density per sq. mile
Fernando Po	9,480	785	61,197	78
Príncipe	2,990	42	} 60,159	167
São Tomé	6,313	330		160
Annobon	2,438	6½	1,415	214

Fernando Po alone was inhabited (by Bantu Bubi) when the Portuguese came first in the later sixteenth century. Settlement of São Tomé began in 1485 and Portuguese from Portugal and Madeira, Jews, Spanish, French and Genoese, were soon attracted to plant sugar.

* By R. J. Harrison Church.

To work the plantations, slaves were brought from what are now Gabon and Angola. However, before the end of the sixteenth century cheaper sugar production in Brazil ruined the São Tomé plantations, planters emigrated to Brazil, and for nearly three centuries the islands were slave depots or victualling points on the Portuguese slave route from Africa to the Americas, and from Portugal to India.

Spain resented the fact that, although she was the greatest user of slaves, Portugal was the sole legal and main supplier—the consequence of the Treaty of Tordesillas (1494). However, in 1778 the Portuguese agreed to cede to Spain the largest and smallest islands, Fernando Po and Annobon, as well as rights on the mainland between the Niger and Ogowe rivers, the Spanish in return confirming Portuguese penetration west of the 50°W. line in Brazil.

Having acquired entry to a source of slaves, the Spanish occupied Fernando Po for a mere three years before being forced to leave it because of yellow fever. They were also soon opposed by the developing international campaign against the slave trade and, by an ironical turn of history, had to allow the British Navy to lease bases from 1827–43 at Port Clarence (now Santa Isabel) and San Carlos for the suppression of the slave trade. Freed slaves were landed here, and Sierra Leoneans also came to settle. Pidgin English is still spoken by some people, and is the origin of many local names.

Meanwhile, coffee was introduced to São Tomé in 1800, and cocoa (from Brazil) in 1822. From São Tomé cocoa was taken to Fernando Po, and thence to the Gold Coast, Nigeria, Liberia and other parts of West Africa by returning labourers. Cocoa, grown almost entirely on large plantations owned by companies or absentee landlords, and worked by indentured labour, dominates the economy and the social structure of the three main islands.

FERNANDO PO AND ANNOBON

Fernando Po is separated from Mt. Cameroon by only 22 miles of water. Some 44 miles long from north-east to south-west and 22 miles across, it rises steeply to two main peaks in the north-centre and south-centre. The southern third of the island is deeply trenched by canyon-like valleys, is almost impenetrable, and virtually uninhabited.

Cultivation and settlement are concentrated on the western, northern and eastern coastal slopes. Cocoa grows well up to about 2,000 feet, yields and quality are good, but production depends upon the availability of immigrant labour, mainly Ibo from Eastern

Nigeria, of whom there are some 15,000 on the island. Bananas, grown mainly to shade cocoa saplings, are also exported. Coffee is a minor crop, grown at a higher altitude than cocoa. These occupy nearly 90 per cent of the cultivated land, the rest of the area being under food crops. Some 600 non-African plantations occupy about 90,000 acres (averaging 150 acres per plantation), while 40,000 acres are occupied by some 3,100 African farms (averaging 13 acres per farm).

Above the cultivated area, forest remains on steep slopes, but between 4,300 and 5,300 feet there are pastures supporting European and Canary Island cattle. Temperate vegetables are also grown, the 4,500 Europeans providing most of the market for dairy and vegetable produce. Higher still, are Montane Woodlands and Grasslands; in the latter seven foot high lobelia grows.

Santa Isabel, the capital, on the north coast, has a pronounced Spanish character, and is situated some 200 feet above its deeply arcuate harbour, which is in a volcanic crater breached by the sea. One-half of the island's indigenous and European populations live in it.

Tiny, steep and more remote, Annobon grows the same crops but is over-populated. Many men work as fishermen, often off the other islands.

SÃO TOMÉ AND PRINCIPE

Príncipe, rectangular in shape, is a small Portuguese replica of Fernando Po. Some ten miles from north-east to south-west, and five miles across, it is less settled and developed than either Fernando Po or São Tomé, and the port of Santo Antonio receives less shipping.

The north-eastern part of São Tomé is also most developed, especially above the capital São Tomé, which lies at the head of a fine inlet. On both islands coconuts are more important round the coasts than on Fernando Po, and copra comprises some 10 per cent of exports. Oil palm plantations lie behind most of the São Tomé coast, and palm oil and kernels account for about 15 per cent of exports. Both these commodities are increasing their share of trade.

Up to about 1,400 feet cocoa is dominant. The two Portuguese islands were leading world producers until 1905, but production fell when labour conditions akin to slavery were publicized, and declining fertility and poor methods of cultivation have also contributed. Nevertheless, cocoa accounts for three-quarters of exports. Some 30,000 labourers, mostly from Mozambique, work on the cocoa and other plantations.

Above the planted areas there is forest or grassland, and many peaks are finger-like phonoliths, comparable with those at Le Puy (France).

The volcanic character, fertility and steeply rising terrain of these islands mark them out physically from West or Western Central Africa, and the Spanish and Portuguese mercantilist economic systems keep their economy and trade tightly bound to the metropoles. The plantation system of cultivation has put most of their land under absentee and alien control, and depends upon some 45,000 alien labourers, facts which discourage initiative or energetic development.

THE MAINLAND PHYSICAL ENVIRONMENT

As the western arm of the East African Rift Valley and its adjacent volcanoes tend to separate East Africa from Central Africa (especially the Congo Basin), so the Cameroon and Bamenda Highlands have tended to keep apart West Africa and Central Africa. Except in the narrow lowland gap between Mt. Cameroon and the Cameroon Highlands, they have restricted the spread of plants and animals common in Central Africa but rare or non-existent in West Africa.

These highlands were also a frontier between the Bantu-speaking peoples of Central and South Africa, and the Negroes of West Africa. The former are generally less advanced and less numerous than the Negroes. Furthermore, this highland frontier permitted Fulani horsemen and nomads to penetrate south, so interposing Hamitic people between the Negro to the west and the Bantu to the south-east.

South-east of this vivid divide the Equatorial climate is more widely experienced in both its pure and seasonal variants. Moist Forest is especially well developed, is richer in species than its narrower West African projection, and has denser stands. One especially famous and valuable timber, originally restricted to these Equatorial coastal swamps, is Okoumé (*Oucumea klaineana*); it now grows in former clearings (Fig. 18).

Such is the latitudinal range of Western Central Africa that the south-western coastal fringe of Angola is southern hemisphere desert, while much of northern Chad is northern hemisphere desert. The climatic Equator is about 2°N., and northward and southward from it are Equatorial and Tropical climates—lowland and highland, with their vegetational counterparts. Cameroon in the northern hemisphere and Angola in the southern, have outstandingly varied climates and vegetation.

Oddly enough, the great Cameroon human and floristic divide is not a great drainage watershed (Fig. 4). There are, however, several of

34. View of log train crossing one of the 92 bridges on the Congo-Ocean Railway (p. 295), Congo (Brazzaville). The Leopoldville–Matadi line, Congo (Leopoldville), its earlier counterpart, crosses similar difficult terrain.

35. The 178-mile Comilog mineral line, opened in 1963, taking 40 wagon trains with 2,000 tons of manganese ore from Franceville, Gabon, to Pointe Noire, Congo (Brazzaville). See p. 299.

36. Matadi, head of ocean navigation on the Congo. The view is southward to the Angolan boundary just beyond the last houses. Until 1927 the boundary came much nearer the river (p. 307). The slopes are extremely abrupt, and so acute is the shortage of space for warehouses that goods are stored in barges. Special loading and unloading devices can be seen running across railway lines in the foreground. Compare Fig. 72.

37. Relief and drainage of the Congo Basin.

38. Leopoldville (Congo), showing the port and commercial quarters. See p. 307.

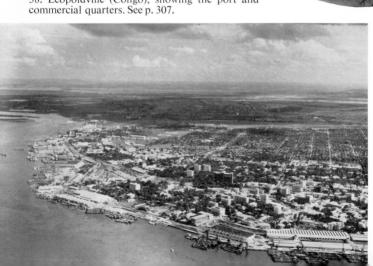

these in Western Central Africa (Fig. 66). The high and largely volcanic Tibesti Mountains are a divide not of surface water, but of the poorest steppe to the south from the arid Libyan Desert to the north. Southward lies the Chad–Nile watershed, forming the eastern boundary of

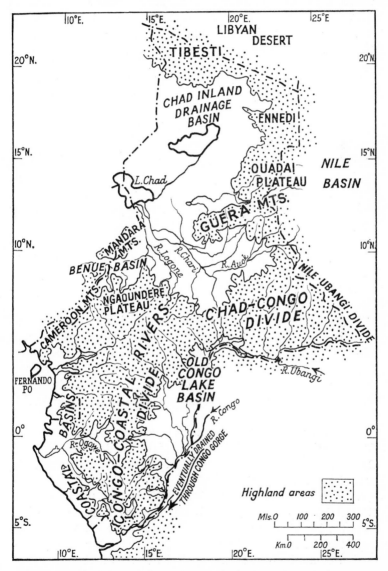

Fig. 66. Physical features (especially drainage divides) of Western Central Africa

the Chad Republic. Much of the Central African Republic is on the Chad–Congo divide, while the central watershed of Cameroon, Gabon and the Congo republics separates the Congo from the coastal rivers. South of the fall-obstructed lower Congo, this divide broadens into the Angolan plateaux, which extend south-eastward into Katanga as the Congo–Zambesi watershed. The Congo Basin is limited eastward by the western arm of the East African Rift Valley system. The Chad Basin is one of inland drainage, and a part of the great trough of Western Africa.

These watersheds are essentially part of the Precambrian Basement Complex of Africa, with vast peneplains and lateritic cappings. The Precambrian rocks are sometimes masked by Primary sedimentaries, mostly of continental origin and composed of sandstone or altered sandstones, for example on the Congo–Chad and Nile–Chad divides. Marine transgressions occurred in pre-Cretaceous times in the Congo Basin, and in Cretaceous and Eocene times behind the present coasts. Volcanic activity on the west has already been described, and the story may be concluded by noting the great expanses of Quaternary sands and clays in the Chad and Congo Basins.

Mineral potential is good, but until the late 'fifties was little developed outside the Congo (Leopoldville) because of the difficulties of exploration and exploitation such as vegetation, climate, length of and obstacles to communications. All these are well illustrated in the problems of exploiting manganese at Franceville in Gabon (p. 299).

The Congo River, though broken by many falls and rapids, is an extensive system of navigation, but most of Angola, Cameroon and Chad are devoid of considerable waterways, much as they need them. Railways have been built to link navigable reaches of the Congo, and with the sea, but railways are few, even by African standards. Nevertheless, the Lobito Bay–Katanga line provides direct access to the rich mineralized heart of Africa.

Hydro-electric power developments have taken place on the upper Congo and its tributaries in Katanga, on the Dande, Catumbela and Cunene rivers in Angola, on the Sanaga in Cameroon, and there is vast potential on the lower Congo and Kouilou rivers.

Less affected by surf than the West African coast, that of Western Central Africa has several broad estuaries between the Cross River (near the Nigerian border) and Cape Lopez (Gabon). South of the latter the coast is affected by the Benguela Current, and has a succession of northward-trending sandspits used in harbour development at Lobito, Luanda, Pointe Noire and Port Gentil.

PEOPLES AND PROBLEMS OF DEVELOPMENT

Separation from West Africa, the enervating climate and dense forest which inhibited closer settlement and kept away Europeans, the widespread occurrence of mosquitoes and tsetse, and the formidable difficulties and length of communications have retarded development, and the peoples of Western Central Africa were always fewer than those of West Africa.

The peoples were further reduced by slave raiding (mainly by or on behalf of the Portuguese) for over three centuries; indeed, this area, the Middle Belt of West Africa, and East Africa were the most afflicted areas. It has been estimated that some 25 million people were thereby lost to Western Central Africa. Where the population was reduced to a critical figure, the tsetse and mosquito killed the survivors, and these pests continue to make resettlement complicated, costly and dangerous. Furthermore, the slavers, travellers and traders also had the effect of spreading the tsetse up rivers and more evenly over the country, a process that continues.

The population map (Fig. 12) shows that the greater concentrations of people are not infrequently in the interior, in remote but easily defended sites, and avoiding rivers because of insects and flies. This is especially true in Cameroon, Chad and the Central African Republic. People remain in these remote and often very poor areas not only through tradition, but also because of the massive difficulties of re-colonizing empty areas; yet the future often lies in the empty or thinly peopled forested lands.

An early attempt to develop this human desert was by the grant of extensive concessions for oil-palm and rubber plantations in the then Belgian Congo and French Equatorial Africa. There was plenty of land, but labour was a formidable problem and transport long and difficult. Plantations are still important, but their area has been greatly reduced. Until the end of the Second World War, forced labour existed everywhere, except in Cameroon. Many crops were introduced as compulsory ones, particularly cotton, often still hated by African farmers.

Thus the states and the Portuguese and Spanish provinces of Western Central Africa are characterized by their low densities of population and, except for the Katanga area of the Congo (Leopold-ville), by their later and lesser economic development than most of West Africa. The following figures show the vast areas with generally low populations. Indeed, with an area of 2,555,000 square miles, nearly one and a half times the area of West Africa and almost that of

China, there are only 27 million people, less than the population of Nigeria.

Country or Province	Area in sq. miles	Population	Density per sq. mile
Cameroon	183,371	3,966,500	22
Chad	496,000	2,580,000	5
Central African Republic	238,000	1,180,000	5
Congo (Brazzaville)	139,000	790,000	6
Gabon	102,290	447,880	4
Rio Muni	10,040	183,377	18
Angola	481,367	4,832,677	10
Congo (Leopoldville)	904,801	13,920,687	15

FURTHER READING

For Western Central Africa as a whole see end of Chapter Seventeen. On the islands of the Bight of Biafra see R. J. Harrison Church, *West Africa*, 4th Ed., 1963, Chapters 27 and 28, and René Pélissier, 'Les Territoires Espagnoles d'Afrique', *La Documentation française*, 3 January 1963.

Cameroon, Chad, Central African Republic, Congo (Brazzaville), Gabon and Rio Muni

CAMEROON

THE name is derived from the Portuguese word *camarões*, meaning 'prawns', which were noticed in large numbers in coastal inlets by early Portuguese navigators. There were many French and British contacts with the area in the nineteenth century but the Germans secured control in 1884. In 1911 they extended their territory to the navigable Ubangi and Shari rivers, and around Spanish Guinea towards Libreville. The First World War saw the return of these French areas, while the country was divided so that five-sixths became a French mandate and one-sixth a British one. These became Trusteeships after the Second World War. The French one achieved independence in 1960, and the Southern Cameroons (part of the small British Trusteeship) rejoined it (as Western Cameroon) in 1961. After 45 years of different systems of administration, currency and monetary areas, tariffs, customs and languages, re-integration is difficult.† The rest of the former United Kingdom Trusteeship joined Northern Nigeria. Eastern Cameroon (ex-French Trusteeship) has an area of 166,790 square miles and a population of 3,223,500; Western Cameroon has an area of 16,580 square miles and 743,000 people. These are the two provinces of the Federation of Cameroon.

Cameroon, while having great natural variety, also has an agriculture diversified in methods and outputs, as well as a considerable aluminium plant. The total area is slightly over one-half that of Nigeria but the population only one-eighth. Although much less peopled than Nigeria, Cameroon is more peopled than its eastern and southern neighbours; in this and other respects it is transitional between West and Western Central Africa.

* By R. J. Harrison Church.

† Compare the similar problems of integrating ex-Italian Eritrea with Ethiopia, ex-British and ex-Italian areas of the Somali Republic, and the problems facing the Ghana–Guinea–Mali Union.

The Physical Environment

Except for the vitally important volcanic rocks of south-western and north-central Cameroon, and some Cretaceous and Eocene limestones, clays and sands of the coast, most of the country has granitic or gneissic rocks of the Basement Complex. The volcanic rocks give the richest soils, those from the Basement Complex are of moderate value, and those derived from the Cretaceous and Eocene series are poor.

The significant aspects of the relief are (Fig. 66), first, the highlands on the western border—Mt. Cameroon, the Cameroon and Bamenda Highlands and the Mandara Mountains—all partly volcanic. Secondly, there is the central watershed, with the partly volcanic Ngaoundéré Plateau in the north-centre and the Yaoundé Plateau in the south-centre being the most important parts. Thirdly, there are the coastal basins, the Benue Basin, the Chad Basin of inland drainage, and the Congo Basin. The highland areas, especially where volcanic and served by roads, offer much greater prospects than the lowland regions except around Douala.

Cameroon has the maximum variety of West or Western Central Africa because of its great latitudinal extension from 2–13°N., its altitudinal range from sea level to 13,352 feet on Mt. Cameroon, and great vegetational variety from Mangrove and Moist Forest in the south to Wooded Steppe in the north. There is more Moist Forest than in Nigeria but less than in Gabon, and much Montane Evergreen Forest and Montane Grassland.

The vital contrasts are between the volcanic and non-volcanic areas; highland and lowland; forest, woodland and steppe; and between areas accessible to road and railway, and those inaccessible. Cameroon is thus sharply differentiated regionally.

The Regions and their Economy

Mt. Cameroon is by far the highest peak in West Africa. Not unexpectedly, its exposed south-western slopes are also the rainiest; Debundscha averages 392 inches a year and Buea 114. While temperature and humidity conditions are equatorial, rainfall totals and wind velocities are monsoonal. In some years there are several rainfall maxima, but broadly there is one very long and rainy period.

Plantations were established on the richer volcanic soils of the mountain and its environs before the First World War by German companies and individuals, predominantly of bananas but also of cocoa, rubber and oil palm. After the war the estates were repurchased by their former owners, but following the Second World War they were leased to the Cameroon Development Corporation which has some 60,000 acres. Other estates, with similar crops, are company-

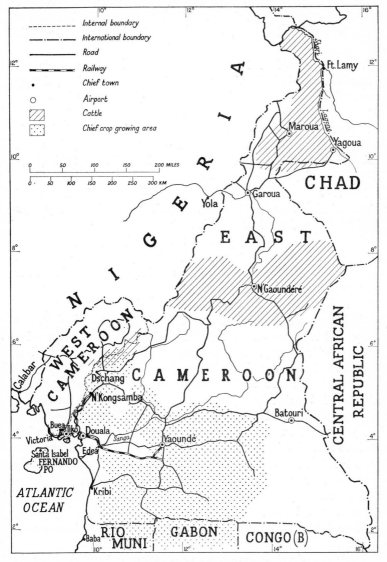

Fig. 67. Cameroon; economic
(Partly after maps by Direction de la Documentation and Ministère de la Coopération)

owned. Storms and disease have affected banana cultivation, so that other crops are being developed.

Buea, with an impressive site and an altitude of 3,000 feet, was the capital of the German colony, and is the headquarters of Western Cameroon. On the coastal edge of Mt. Cameroon lies the port of Victoria, and 17 miles up the Bimbia River is Tiko the loading point for bananas.

Volcanic intrusions into Pre-cambrian rocks have made the Cameroon Highlands bold and beautiful, and most of the villages farm volcanic soils. Timber is cut, and cocoa, bananas and coffee are important cash crops. The Bamenda Highlands are similar to the Cameroon Highlands, but have mostly Montane Grassland with only relict or riverine forests. Cattle are the main resource here, with coffee at lower elevations. Roads would help the development of this potentially important and healthy area.

The central watershed which includes the Yaoundé, Bafang and Ngaoundéré plateaux, rises sharply, and is forested in the south but covered by woodland in the north. In the south are tree crops (cocoa, coffee, oil palm), especially around Yaoundé, the pleasant, hilly, federal capital, where there are more roads and the railway branches. On the Ngaoundéré Plateau cattle are important on the richer pastures of volcanic soils.

The coastal river basins are densely wooded, and tree crops are again important. Douala lies some 20 miles up the Wouri River. The quays and town are on the south side of the river, the town being sharply divided into quarters by streams which have trenched the river terraces. Railways, linked by a bridge, run north to N'Kongsamba and south-east to Yaoundé and M'Balmayo, there is an important airport and some industries. By far the leading port, it also serves the Central African Republic. Edea, on the south-eastern railway and by falls of the Sanaga River, has a hydro-electric power station and tropical Africa's first aluminium smelter (Plate 33) using alumina imported from Fria (Guinea). Power is sent to Douala and Yaoundé, and there is also a very modern rubber processing factory in Edea.

The Congo Basin, drained by the Sanaga and its tributaries, is a densely forested area of the south-east which is gradually being opened by timber extraction, coffee and cocoa cultivation, but it needs more roads.

The Benue–Chad watershed is an area where waters flow either via the Logone to Lake Chad's inland system, or via the Benue to the Atlantic Garoua is served between July and September by push-tow

39. Cotton being grown on a 'paysannat' at Bambesa, Uélé, Congo (Leopoldville). See p. 310.

40. Large palm-oil mill in a plantation at Briga, west of Lisala, Equateur Province, Congo (Leopoldville). See p. 310.

41. Open-cast copper mine (p. 314) at Ruwe, Congo (Leopoldville).

42. Electrolytic copper refinery (p. 314) at Jadotville, Congo (Leopoldville).

43. Train on Jadotville–Tenke electrified section of B.C.K. railway, Leopoldville (Congo).

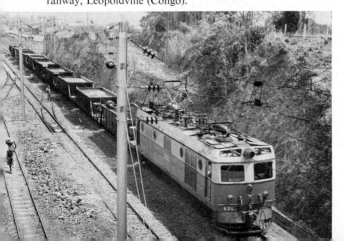

barges bringing petroleum up through Nigeria (Plate 21) and taking out groundnuts, cotton, hides and skins from both northern Cameroon and southern Chad. Otherwise, these basins are remote and poor, and regions of nomadic herdsmen or of poor cultivators of millet, guinea corn, groundnuts, cotton and rice—the last two being more recent developments and grown near watercourses or lakes.

Cocoa comprises about one-third of Cameroon exports, and coffee one-fifth. Most of the coffee by weight is robusta lowland-grown, but the small amount of arabica coffee has a high value. Aluminium accounts for one-sixth the exports, and bananas, timber and ginned cotton are the other significant items. Cameroon is much helped by the European Common Market which absorbs most of the tree crops. Cotton is developing fast and providing money for the poorest peoples. Many areas in and outside the forest are available for development.

Cameroon has good potential but its triangular shape, relatively short coastline and only one good port, lengthen communications. The rugged relief in the richer areas adds to the cost and difficulty of transport, but as this is extended so new areas will be opened to tree crops, timber extraction and mining.

CHAD

Landlocked, remote, and the most northerly of the successor states of former French Equatorial Africa, Chad is larger than the combined areas of the other three—the Central African Republic, Congo and Gabon. Extending from 8°–23°N., it has considerable climatic and vegetational variety within its huge area of 496,000 square miles, one-third larger than Nigeria. Chad's population of 2,580,000 (1958), though small, is much greater than that of most countries to the south, but this is because its remoter areas were places of refuge from the slave trade. The formidable length (1,000–2,000 miles) of its lines of communication, and the scarcity of water are its greatest problems among many others.

The Physical Environment

Chad consists of a vast peneplain, notched by the Logone, Shari and Bahr-el-Ghazal valleys. Lake Chad is the centre of this inland drainage and of a Quaternary sedimentary basin, but it seems certain that it was formerly connected with or replaced at Lake Bodele in the lowest part of the basin north-east of Lake Chad. This greater lake

10

may have dried out when Shari headwaters, cut off by the rising Congo–Chad watershed, were captured by the Ubangi and drained to the Congo.

The vast Chad Basin of inland drainage (Fig. 66) is limited northward by the volcanic Tibesti Mountains rising to 11,360 feet, northeastward by the Ennedi Plateau rising to 4,930 feet and composed of Palaeozoic sandstones, and eastward by the Ouadai Plateau (Nile–Shari–Chad divide) nearly 5,000 feet high. This has a south-westerly prolongation in the Guera Mountains which attain 5,500 feet.

A single rainy season is experienced wherever there is rain in Chad, but there are less than three months of effective rainfall or under ten inches annually (the approximate limit of cultivation) north of about 14½°N. Consequently, fully one-half of the country is, except in rare oases, too arid for cultivation and has revealed no other assets.

South of 14½°N. there is mostly Dry Woodland. In this, around Fort Lamy and Bongor, there are four to five months of rain from June to September with 20–35 inches annually, while towards the southern border at Fort Archambault the rainy season lasts for six to seven months and the annual rainfall is some 40 inches.

The Economy

The greatest human clusters (see Fig. 12) barely attain 25 per square mile. These are found in the cotton-growing areas south of the Mayo Kebbi headwaters of the Benue and west of the Shari in the Fort Archambault area, around the cattle market and expanding groundnut zone of Abeche, south-west of it along the Batha intermittent watercourse, and in Kanem east of Lake Chad where fish are caught, natron dug, cattle watered, and guinea corn and wheat grown on black *firki* soils.

North of 14½°N. there are no more than 50,000 nomads in 231,000 square miles (the area of France). As in adjacent lands, the great human divide is between the Islamic peoples of the north (Tebu, Hausa, Fulani and Arab), and the non-Islamic Bantu of the south (Sara and others). The only considerable town is Fort Lamy, the capital, at the Logone–Shari confluence, a focus of river, air and road routes, especially of the trunk roads from the Sudan to Northern Nigeria and Niger, and south to Bangui and the Congo waterways.

Cotton, forcibly introduced in 1928, is almost the only export crop, and is grown by dry farming on over half-a-million acres by nearly that number of farmers, mainly in the extreme south-west of the country—the Logone-Shari area (Fig. 68). Other crops are almost all

for food. Millet and guinea corn are the dominant ones, but groundnuts have developed a great deal in rotation with cotton, as well as
away from the latter in the drier east towards Abeche. Rice was
introduced just before the Second World War, and Chad is now the

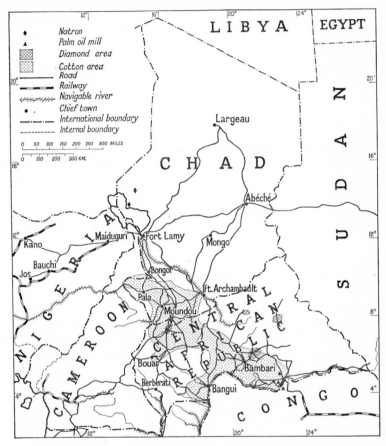

Fig. 68. *Chad and Central African Republic; economic*
(Partly after maps by Direction de la Documentation and Ministère de la
Coopération)

largest producer of the four states of former French Equatorial
Africa. It is grown in seasonally flooded river valleys, especially the
Logone near Bongor and Lai. Further development awaits a change-
over of more people from eating millet to consuming rice.

Nomads of the north and east keep some four million cattle, and
rather more sheep and goats. Although kept mainly for subsistence,

some meat is despatched annually at high cost by air, and about 250,000 cattle and the same number of sheep are driven into Nigeria, which also takes hides and skins. Some 70,000 tons of fish are caught annually; dried fish is sold locally and in Cameroon, and smoked fish in Nigeria. Fishing gives the best return of all economic activities in Chad.

Strenuous efforts have been made to improve communications. Refrigerated meat is sent by air from Fort Lamy and Fort Archambault to Brazzaville, Douala and Yaoundé, high quality cotton from Moundou, and many imports come by air from Europe to Fort Lamy, and are redistributed from there. This is a notable example of the subsidized use of air transport in a country that is remote by surface transport but less so by air. In all the French sphere, only Orly (Paris) handles more air freight than Fort Lamy.

Land routes are by lorry from Fort Lamy or Fort Archambault to Bangui (Central African Republic) some 700–800 miles, than by boat on the Ubangi and Congo rivers to Brazzaville 740 miles, and so by railway to Pointe Noire, Congo (Brazzaville), 319 miles. Some 1,800 miles long, this involves two re-loadings. Alternatively, by lorry from Fort Lamy to Douala (Cameroon) is direct and 973 miles, but this route can be used only for light loads and vehicle imports.

Since the Second World War Nigerian routes have also been used, by lorry from Fort Lamy to Kano or Jos, and thence by railway to Port Harcourt or Lagos, some 1,200–1,400 miles with only one re-loading. The Nigerian branch railway to Maiduguri will so hasten these routes as to make them the most economic outlets. The 3-monthly seasonal route down the Benue from Garoua (Cameroon) is vital for Chad's nearby cotton areas; while salt, cement, steel rods for reinforcing concrete, and petroleum (Plate 21) are brought in that way. These routes, however, require Nigerian currency, a relatively 'hard' one for Chad.

Seasonal and obstructed by sandbanks (Cp. Plate 20), Chad's rivers are, nevertheless, important to such a vast and poor country. The Shari is navigable from July to February (when the road is often flooded) between Forts Archambault and Lamy, and below the latter all the year. Natron and dried fish are brought upstream from Lake Chad by this route. The Bahr Sara is used for floating logs into the Shari, from the Central African Republic.

The aridity of half the country, water scarcity, and distances from the outside world make economic development exceedingly difficult. Chad has problems comparable with those of Mauritania, Mali, Upper

Volta and Niger; and is much affected by the economic attraction of Nigeria and the Sudan, lands with far greater opportunities.

CENTRAL AFRICAN REPUBLIC

Formerly known as Ubangi-Shari, this country is almost as land-locked as Chad, and so has similar problems resulting from long and costly lines of transport. Although less than half the size of Chad and much less varied, the Central African Republic is, nevertheless, as large as France.

The Physical Environment

The north-western part of the country is drained by the Shari to the Chad system, the southern part to the Congo by the navigable Ubangi and its tributaries. The central part of the country therefore lies on the Congo–Chad divide, a rolling plateau averaging some 2,000 feet; much of it is capped by laterite, and erosion has been accelerated by early plantations.

The country lies between 3° and 11°N., so that only the south-western parts have Moist Forest. Most of the country has one rainy season of diminishing extent and reliability in the north-east, and Woodland-Savanna with Riverine Forest is widespread. In climate, vegetation and human distributions, the country has many of the problems of the West African Middle Belt, not least of which are depopulation by former slave raiding, a now-ended concessionary system, and former forced labour.

Population and Economy

The situation on a major watershed, the open character of most of the country, the course of the Ubangi River, and the central position of the republic, have made it a crossroads and meeting point of diverse peoples, yet the average density of population is a mere five per square mile. In the dry and remote north-east and east, within an area of 90,700 square miles, nearly that of the United Kingdom or of Ghana, there are only 71,000 people. The one considerable town in the whole country is Bangui (80,000) the capital, main trading and transit centre.

The country lives from the production of subsistence crops (mainly cassava); and the production of cotton, coffee and groundnuts for export. Cotton, again initially produced as a compulsory crop, is grown in the Kemo, Gribingui and other valleys north of Bangui, thus forming a south-eastern extension of the Chad cotton area (Fig. 68). It occupies rather less land, and yields are much lower than there, partly because physical conditions are less propitious, but mainly because people dislike the crop. Nevertheless, it is by far the leading export. Some is also used in a modern textile mill 50 miles south of Bangui at Bouali, adjacent to a hydro-electric plant. Groundnuts are a more recent and far more popular crop, often inter-sown with cotton. Part of this crop is also processed locally for oil. Sesamum (Benniseed) is a minor crop in the same area.

In the small forest area of the south-west coffee is popular and is the second export crop, more being grown than in any other of these four successor states. Lumber, floated down the Ubangi and Congo rivers, is gaining in importance, especially limbo (*Terminalia superba*). Much timber is also exported to neighbouring Congo (Leopoldville), Cameroon and Chad for local use. Small quantities of diamonds are mined, especially in the Nola area, but these are the third export.

The republic's greatest economic problem is length of transit. The Ubangi, the cheapest link with the outside world, has considerable seasonal variations which prevent its full use throughout the year, as well as rocky sills (e.g. Zinga below Bangui) which, while not now preventing navigation, again restrict its use. Furthermore, transshipment to and from the railway is necessary at Brazzaville in the Congo (Brazzaville), and this river-rail route from Bangui to Pointe Noire is 875 miles long.

Roads are far more developed than in the other three successor states. A more direct outlet than the river-rail one is by road from Bouar or Berberati westward to Yaoundé (Cameroon) and so by rail to Douala. Again, there is a break of bulk and this route, though shorter, is more expensive. Bangui, Berberati and Bouar are served by air, and the first may become more important to general African services because of its central situation. Like Chad, this country is one of the poorest in a very poor continent.

CONGO (BRAZZAVILLE)

Parts of both Congos and of Angola were within the Congo state which reached its climax in the sixteenth century. Some African leaders in the three countries aim to reconstitute that ancient state. Brazzaville is named after the French explorer Savorgnan de Brazza, who made two expeditions in this and adjoining lands in 1875–8 and 1880–2. From 1883–98 he was here as a distinguished administrator. Until French Equatorial Africa broke up in 1959, the Congo (Brazzaville) was its political and economic core.

The Regions

The Congo (Brazzaville) lies astride the equator between 4°N. and 5°S. The coast is smoothed by the Benguela Current, and there are many sandspits blocking mangrove-fringed lagoons, akin to those in the Ivory Coast, Togo and Dahomey. Again, because of this cool current, temperatures are relatively low, and the coastal plain is practically treeless Steppe.

Inland lies the Mayombe Escarpment and a succession of sharp ridges rising to between 1,600 and 2,600 feet, part of the Coast-Congo divide. This is covered by Moist Forest and trenched by many rivers, notably the Kouilou (or lower Niari). This divide is crossed by the Congo–Ocean Railway from Brazzaville to Pointe Noire (opened 1934) to provide a French counterpart to the Leopoldville–Matadi Belgian line (first opened 1898 and later rebuilt). Both lines have spectacular • engineering, but on the 320 miles of the Congo–Ocean line there are no less than 92 bridges and 12 tunnels, the latter being otherwise almost unknown in tropical Africa (Plate 34).

The Niari Basin, like the Ngounie Valley in Gabon, has been etched out of softer Karoo sandstone deposits. It, and all the south-east of the country, has Woodland-Savanna vegetation. The basin has good potential, the more so as it has fertile soil and is served by the railway (Fig. 69).

The Stanley Pool region has many bare hills, giving place to the dry Savanna-covered Batéké Plateaux on the north. These are poor, level, and separated from each other by the deep and forested valleys of northern tributaries of the Congo. The Sangha and other rivers to the north flood widely, and there are vast expanses of swamp vegetation near them.

The Congo Basin has the purest type of equatorial climate, while the greatest seasonality and least rainfall are found in the Bakété Plateaux. The dry periods come as in the southern hemisphere régime.

Population and Economy

Although the average density of population is only six per square mile, the north and north-east is almost uninhabited, while the south has significant clusters. Brazzaville has one-seventh the population of the whole country. It was formerly the capital of French Equatorial Africa, but is now the centre only of some common services of the four successor states, and the capital of the Congo (Brazzaville). It is a rail–river trans-shipment point on Stanley Pool opposite Leopold-ville and, like it, has a good airport. Pointe Noire is the coastal terminus and port for the railway carrying Gabon manganese, Congo timber, and Central African Republic and Chad cotton and groundnuts, as well as lesser exports and imports. The quays are being extended and the town has timber and other works.

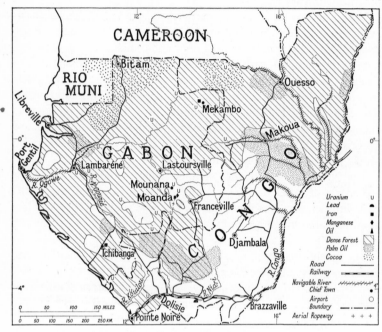

Fig. 69. Congo (Brazzaville) and Gabon; economic
(Partly after maps by Direction de la Documentation and Ministère de la Coopération)

Although most people live by farming, this contributes little to revenue and only a modest part of the exports. Subsistence and export crops are those typical of equatorial regions. Timber is by far the main export and comes from the Mayombe and Sangha regions, especially from near Ouesso. Limbo, mahogany and okoumé are the main species marketed. Palm oil and kernels come from the same areas, mostly from plantations, and thirty large processing mills. Some oil is used locally for soap manufacture.

The Niari Basin is the scene of varied agricultural experiment, public and private, mechanized and traditional, plantation and non-

plantation, African and European, pastoral and arable. A high dam
is planned on the lower Niari or Kouilou at Sounda gorge, some fifty
miles in a straight line from the coast (Fig. 69). In general, conception
akin to the Konkouré (Guinea) and Volta (Ghana) schemes, it would
likewise create a vast lake which could be used to evacuate Gabon
timber. More power would be produced than at Kariba, and could
supply an industrial complex at Pointe Noire using Gabon manganese,
but there is no local bauxite. Lead is mined at M'Fouati, about half
way along the Congo–Ocean Railway. Small amounts of oil are
produced just north of Pointe Noire. There are the usual processing and simple consumer good industries in Brazzaville and Pointe
Noire.

Of the four successor states of former French Equatorial Africa,
this alone has a railway and waterway vital to the other three. Most
of the right bank tributaries of the Ubangi and Congo are also
navigable. Roads link the railway, navigable rivers and adjacent states,
especially the road from Dolisie on the railway to Libreville (Gabon)
and Cameroon. Air services link many towns.

The country is hampered by difficult terrain and climate, by poor
natural resources, and by its small population and market, but because
of its vital role in transit has been fairly well equipped.

GABON

Slaving and general trading posts were first set up by the Portuguese
in the sixteenth century, and they gave the name *gabão* to an estuary
which they thought resembled the outline of a hooded and sleeved
cloak. After 1815 French vessels were active off this coast in sup-
pressing the slave trade, and slaves freed from ships were put ashore
at Libreville which, in name and origin, is identical with Freetown,
Sierra Leone. As in that country, there is a mixed and relatively long-
educated coastal population. Gabon was in the past economically and
culturally supreme in French Equatorial Africa, as was Sierra Leone
in early British West Africa; both have long since lost these roles.
Gabon resents the rise of the Congo (Brazzaville) as a transit route for
the Central African Republic and Chad, and the need to export
Gabon manganese via Pointe Noire.

Like the other successor states of former French Equatorial Africa,
Gabon became independent in 1960. It is the smallest and least
populated, but is compact, being essentially the basin of the Ogowe
River, and is potentially the richest.

10*

The Physical Environment

As far north as Cape Lopez the Gabon coast and coastal plain are climatically and physiographically similar to those of the Congo (Brazzaville). North of Cape Lopez, however, the Gabon coast is indented, easy of access and almost surf-free, being the southern end of a similar coast in Cameroon and Rio Muni.

Behind the coast in the north lie the Crystal Mountains, and in the south the Mayombe Mountains, both the rugged edges of the Basement Complex of the African Plateau, and attaining 2,900 feet in altitude. The rivers cross these mountainous edges with the usual falls or rapids.

Whereas the Crystal Mountains give way to the Woleu-N'Tem Plateau of the north-centre, the Mayombe Mountains are first succeeded eastward by the N'Gounie Saddle eroded in softer Karoo sandstone. This is occupied by the N'Gounie and Nyonga rivers, and is the Gabon counterpart of the Niari Basin in Congo (Brazzaville).

East of the N'Gounie Saddle are the Chaillu Mountains which, though averaging 1,600 feet, reach 5,165 feet in Mt. Iboundji. In the south-east is one of the Batéké Plateaux, the rest being in the Congo (Brazzaville). As there, it is savanna covered—the only extensive savanna area in Gabon, which is otherwise largely covered by Moist Forest, except along rivers where timber cutting has brought Forest-Savanna Mosaic.

Population and Economy

The density of four per square mile is very low and misleading. Areas around towns, lumbering and mining camps, waterways and roads are fairly well peopled, but vast expanses of mountain, forest and swamp are uninhabited.

Libreville, the capital, is a roadstead port in the Gabon Estuary, handling timber brought down the river. Port Gentil, the main roadstead, exports timber from the Ogowe River. It also has the largest plywood factory in the world, and despatches oil from an adjacent field (Fig. 70). Both towns are quite small.

Gabon is outwardly prosperous and, a rare distinction among ex-French states of Africa, has a favourable trade balance. In the past its wealth came mainly from its fine timbers, especially the exquisite and light okoumé. Some 700,000 tons of it are exported annually, and Gabon is the greatest producer. Mahogany, ebony and limbo are also exported, and timber cutting and the plywood and veneer industry dominated the economy of the country until 1962.

The country is now developing its very rich mineral deposits. First in time are petroleum and natural gas, whose exploitation began in 1957 near Port Gentil. This field has very small reserves but the oil is by the sea and is of good quality, and natural gas is used for electrical generation at Port Gentil. The world's largest known deposit of manganese is at Moanda near Franceville, where 48 per cent Mn. is exported, first by a 53-mile aerial ropeway, then by 2,000-ton 40-wagon

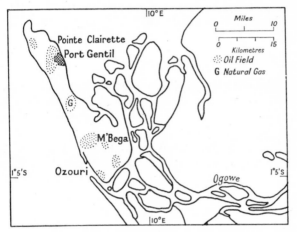

Fig. 70. Port Gentil, and its oil and gas field

trains on a 178-mile mineral line (Plate 35) leading to the Congo–Ocean Railway, on which there is another 124-mile haul to Pointe Noire (Fig. 69) in the Congo (Brazzaville).

In the even more remote north-east at Mekambo is one of the world's largest deposits of rich iron ore. A 435-mile railway would be necessary across the country, but it would also open up new timber areas. A 100 million tons iron ore deposit at Tchibanga is, however, only 30 miles from the coast. Uranium is also being mined at Maunana, 15 miles from Franceville.

The shortage of manpower is acute, and many Gabonese are averse to agriculture, preferring occupations such as timber-cutting or work in towns. The dense forests also hamper agriculture and communications, so that export crops are few and of little importance. Only in the extreme north, in Woleu-N'Tem district, where cocoa and coffee are grown adjacent to areas in Cameroon and Rio Muni, is there a real peasantry.

The density of the forests also hampered the development of roads, and rivers were for long the only means of movement; now only the Ogowe remains important. The main road is that from the Congo (Brazzaville) at Dolisie (on the Congo–Ocean Railway) through the west of Gabon via Lambaréné (site of Dr. Schweitzer's work), to Libreville and Douala (Cameroon). The two ports and Lambaréné are served by air.

Gabon is a mixture of tradition and pioneering, or prosperity despite inadequate transport, and a rare example in Africa of the virtual absence of any significant cash crop.

RIO MUNI

Lying between Cameroon and Gabon, and including the former slave depots of the Elobey Islands and Corisco, Rio Muni is a Spanish Overseas Province. Until recently little development had occurred; what resources Spain could spare in her overseas remnants were concentrated on the far richer Fernando Po. However, vigorous attempts have been made since 1945 to hasten progress, despite pressing needs in Spain. Non-Africans are notably fewer than on the healthier Fernando Po, dominated as this is by a plantation economy which is much less evident in Rio Muni.

Although the coast has a considerable tidal range, surf is largely absent, and ships can be loaded or discharged by lighters at Bata, the capital, and in the Benito and Muni estuaries. As in neighbouring countries, the coast plain ends abruptly at the edge of the interior uplands. These have small areas of Montane vegetation and patches of Savanna, but Moist Forest is dominant elsewhere. With the wettest seasons from February to June and from September to December, the Equatorial climate is a southern hemisphere type, since Rio Muni lies south of the rainfall equator of about 2°N.

Forestry is still the dominant economic activity and over 20 concessions work nearly half a million acres, mainly in the coastal plains near the Campo, Benito and Muni rivers, which are used for floating. Okoumé and mahogany are much exported. There are also some oil palm plantations near the Benito estuary.

Large coffee plantations are in the central uplands east of Bata, but most coffee is grown on African farms, in contrast to the situation on Fernando Po. Liberica is grown below about 1,500 feet and is the main variety; above 1,500 feet robusta is grown. Almost all cocoa is grown by Africans, again in contrast to Fernando Po. It is especially important in the north-east and eastern boundary districts, adjacent to cocoa areas of Cameroon and Gabon.

Despite the recent development of forestry, agriculture and communications, Spanish restrictions on export markets of crops, and insistence upon carriage in Spanish ships hampers progress, and the Fang people, divided by the boundaries with Cameroon and Gabon, are notably poorer than in those countries. Timber concessions and plantations depend on immigrant labourers from Nigeria, and these and the divided Fang may eventually cause political change.

The problems of these countries are essentially those of formidable physical difficulties and obstacles, and a low density of population. One or two have valuable resources, but these are often remote and costly to develop, as in Gabon. Most have the less remunerative articles such as Chad's cotton, groundnuts and livestock produce, which have to move over vast distances to markets. Cameroon is more endowed by nature and with people; her resources are considerable and more accessible.

FURTHER READING

Cameroon, Chad, Central African Republic, Congo and Gabon: E. Guernier, *Cameroun-Togo, Encyclopédie Coloniale et Maritime*, 1951; H. Zieglé, P. Binon and Jean-Claude Froelich, *Afrique Equatorial, Cameroun et Togo*, 1953; E. Guernier, *Afrique Equatoriale française, Encyclopédie Coloniale et Maritime*, 2nd ed., 1960; J. Pouquet, *Afrique Equatoriale Française*, 1954; E. Trezenem, *L'Afrique Equatoriale Française*, 1955; Virginia Thompson and Richard Adloff, *The Emerging States of French Equatorial Africa*, 1960, George F. Patten, 'Republic of the Congo (Brazzaville)', *Focus*, October. 1962, and 'Gabon', October, 1961; D. Hilling, 'The Changing Economy of Gabon-Developments in a new African Republic', *Geography*, 1963, 155–65; William A. Hance and Irene S. Van Dongen, 'Gabon and its Main Gateways; Libreville and Port Gentil', *Tijdschrift voor Economische en Sociale Geografie*, 1961, 286–95; René Dumont, *Types of Rural Economy*, 1957, Chapters II and III, has studies of areas in these countries. There are many articles in *Les Cahiers d'Outremer* (Bordeaux).

Rio Muni: *Atlas Histórico y Geográfico de Africa Española*, Madrid, 1955, with text, and René Pélissier, 'Les Territoires Espagnoles d'Afrique', *La Documentation française*, 3 January 1963.

CHAPTER EIGHTEEN

Congo (Leopoldville)

DESPITE the very difficult environment there were a number of pre-colonial states in this area, such as Baluba (south-eastern Katanga) and Lunda (south-western Katanga and southern Kasai), both founded in the sixteenth century, and the Congo (northern Angola and lower Congo Valley), founded in the thirteenth or early fourteenth century. The latter is well documented in Portuguese records which describe its organization, the smelting of iron and copper, weaving and pottery making.

Portuguese slaving began in 1436 and ended only about 1885, the old Congo state having been conquered in 1665. A study concludes that $13\frac{1}{4}$ million slaves were taken. Many were also captured by Arabs from the eastern parts of the Congo Basin, but numbers are more difficult to assess; they might be more or less than those taken by the Portuguese. Many areas were virtually cleared of able-bodied adults; the rest were ultimately eliminated by sleeping sickness. The small populations of ex-French Equatorial Africa, Angola and the Congo (Leopoldville) remain acute problems to this day.

Leopold II of Belgium was greatly interested in Africa, and wished to see it developed economically and socially, for the benefit of both Africa and his small and then poor Belgium. He organized the International Geographical Conference of 1876 to free Africa from slavery and to bring civilization through legitimate trade; at the conference the International African Association was founded. Explorers such as Livingstone and Stanley had been active in the Congo, and Stanley was the first to descend the Congo, a feat he accomplished from Hyangwe in the east (4°S) to Boma in 1876–7, so proving that the Congo was not part of the Nile. In 1878 he met King Leopold, and, instructed by him, established posts up the river in 1879. By 1884 another body, the International Association of the Congo, had become important, and its recognition by the United States in 1884 was the first step to statehood. In 1885 Leopold II became King of the new Congo Free State.

Everything had to be organized, yet there was no money, and no link to the outer world because of the many rapids and falls on the

* By R. J. Harrison Church.

lower Congo. The Matadi–Leopoldville railway was opened to cir-
cumvent these in 1898 (since rebuilt) and, as there was no currency
and its use was unknown, taxes were payable in local produce—ivory
and wild rubber. Cruel—even sadistic—methods of penalizing tax
defaulters were soon revealed, and ultimately a somewhat reluctant
and ill-equipped Belgium took over the impoverished Congo Free
State in 1908. With its 904,801 square miles it was 77 times the size of
Belgium, and Africa's second largest country.

Again there was a desperate need to secure money for development
and, in a thinly peopled country, the way to do this appeared to be to
grant concessions. The First World War caused delays but large land
grants for oil-palm plantations were made in 1922 to Lord Leverhulme,
through a Belgian subsidiary—Les Huileries du Congo Belge. Mining
leases were granted to large companies able to risk developing ore
fields separated from the sea and non-existent ports by 1,200 miles of
only partly navigable rivers and some of the densest forest in the
world. The concessions have since been reduced in area and their
planting intensified; while mining companies (with partly state capital)
have become immensely rich empires within an otherwise rather poor
and divided republic.

After the First World War Belgium was given a mandate over the
sultanates of Rwanda and Burundi, previously part of German East
Africa. These relatively small areas (20,900 square miles and one
forty-fourth that of the Congo) are, in extreme contrast to the
Congo, over-populated and have as much as one-third its population.
An adequate labour supply was assured to the plantations and mines
of the Congo. Nevertheless, in 1926 a policy of fixed labour supply in
permanent camps near mines was started in contrast to the camps of
migrant labourers typical of South Africa. Since then a vast range of
ante-natal, natal and post-natal welfare and other services has been
provided by Congo mines, so that unkind observers have thought
that not only is the existing supply of labour assured, but also future
supplies.

In 1927 a remarkable exchange of 1,350 square miles of Congo
territory for a mere 1·2 square mile of Angolan territory behind
Matadi (Plate 36 and Fig. 72) permitted the enlargement of that port
and its railway yards. The portion ceded by the Congo now yields
Angola's diamonds, that country's second export, although much of
the field remains within the Congo.

The Belgians provided mainly primary and technical education, and
sought the material rather than the political advancement of the

Congolese. Indeed, the first Congo Parliament met and African ministers took office only ten days before independence, facts which help to explain the formidable difficulties of the present state.

THE PHYSICAL ENVIRONMENT

The Congo extends from 5°N. to 13°S., some 1,250 miles in each direction, and includes most of the Congo Basin. Yet it has 22 miles only of coastline, and the left bank of the Congo Estuary is Angolan below Matadi, the Congo's only important port.

Climate and Vegetation

The climate is largely Equatorial (4°N.–4°S.), or variations of it with one or two dry months on a narrow northern fringe and in a larger southern sector from 4°:10°S. In the south-east there is a Tropical Continental (A3) climate, with a dry season extending to five months. The eastern highland fringe also has a Tropical Continental climate, with the lowest temperatures (Bukavu average 67°F). Frost at night is not uncommon during the four months dry season.

Nowhere else in Africa is Moist Forest so extensive or so rich in species and communities. Forest, either Swamp, Lowland, Riverine or Montane, covers one-half the country, but much is Secondary Forest. Because of the varied species and the length of communications only 5 per cent is exploitable, the areas actually worked amount only to 0·15 per cent of all forest, and the timber is used mainly within the Congo.

More or less wooded savannas largely coincide with the Tropical Continental Climate, but result from burning and farming; they are widely developed in the north. In the areas of High-altitude, Equatorial and Tropical Continental climates, there are different vegetational stages. These are well developed on Mt. Ruwenzori, where grasslands with patches of giant tree ferns occur between 5,400 and 8,000 feet, bamboo to 8,750 feet, tree heathers to 12,350 feet, and giant senecios above that, until an alpine flora grows near the snowfields and glaciers. Those vegetational contrasts, unrivalled elsewhere, emphasize the size and variety of this vast country.

Soils and Geology

Soils are often poor, thin, and eroded after cutting and burning of the natural vegetation. Those of volcanic areas are naturally richest, but as they are usually on steep slopes are often more eroded. Alluvial soils are also somewhat better than average, but again the advantage is nullified because they are infested by mosquitoes and tsetse flies, which make human settlement dangerous.

The varied geology, and closely associated structure and relief, give the basic regional and economic contrasts. The Precambrian Basement Complex constitutes the southern, western and northern margins of the basin (Plate 37). The rocks of the complex, originally sedimentaries, were heavily metamorphosed by heat and pressure to produce highly metalliferous formations in this area. The Lower Precambrian, some 2,600 million years old, is probably Africa's oldest formation, and is the source of gold and manganese. The Middle Precambrian, important in the east-centre, is the source of tin, tungsten, tantalium, niobium, beryllium and bismuth. The Upper Precambrian, of south-eastern Katanga, is the most valuable, since it yields copper (by far the main export), cobalt, zinc, lead, silver, cadmium, germanium and nickel.

The basin also has some Palaeozoic but mostly later sedimentary formations. Poor coal occurs in these, while diamonds, gold and tin are found in beds of former or present rivers which washed these minerals from parent rocks in the rimlands.

The complex was also severely faulted by movements which formed the Rift Valley. Ruwenzori is an uplifted block; while depths of 4,780 feet occur in Lake Tanganyika, depths exceeded only by Lake Baikal. Other mountains originated as volcanoes following the development of the Rift Valley. The Virunga Mountains, north of Lake Kivu and on the Uganda–Rwanda–Congo border, still erupt, and there are other evidences of activity, such as lava vents and thermal springs. The Precambrian rocks and the younger ones of the Rift Valley system together form a mountain rim to the Congo Basin.

The basic regional contrast in the country is, therefore, between the lowland basin, which is enervating, has leached soils and is largely forested; and the mountains or dissected plateaux of the rimlands, which are cooler, have some richer soils and savanna vegetation, and are the sources of almost all the minerals—the main resource of the state. However, these rimlands were only crossed or reached with difficulty, and the metalliferous areas of Katanga had to await railways from far-off Beira, the Cape, and the Rhodesias before they were developed.

THE RIVER CONGO AND ITS USE

The only natural unifying factor has been the river, aided by railways built around its unnavigable reaches or those of its tributaries. The river has undergone an interesting evolution. Several reaches and tributaries originally belonged to at least three drainage areas. At first the main stream flowed north-west to Lake Chad and the Bodele depression, but earth movements contemporaneous with those in the Rift Valley raised the Congo-Chad watershed, and a vast lake accumulated in the basin, of which lakes Leopold II and Tumba are relics.

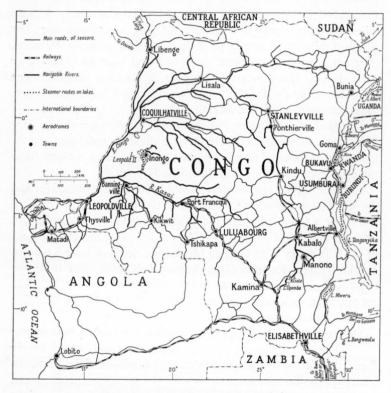

Fig. 71. Congo (Leopoldville); communications

The upper Lualaba once flowed to the Nile but was captured by the lower Lualaba, then flowing into the Congo lake, and now forming the upper Congo. The narrow gorge of the Portes d'Enfer (Gates of Hell) at Kongolo is the site of the capture. An even greater capture took place when a coastal river cut back and captured a river flowing north-eastwards down the inner side of the coastal divide, reversed the flow of the latter river, and created the present outlet to the sea. This has 210 miles of gorges and some thirty sets of rapids or falls, constituting the greatest hydro-electric power potential in the world.

That the upper Congo cuts into and the lower Congo cuts out of the basin, and that the river and its tributaries have numerous falls, are partly the consequences of this drainage history. Falls also occur where rivers pass over the erosion scarps of successively younger geological formations, and because of rejuvenations following Tertiary and later accentuations of the basin rims (Plate 37).

The Congo system is second only to the Amazon in flow of water. For up to fifty miles out to sea fresh water prevails on the surface, and at 300 miles out its olive green waters can be detected. Of the main stream's 2,700 miles, 1,700 are navigable, and the longest navigable reach is 1,082 miles long between Stanleyville and Leopoldville. This is the most important reach for navigation, as it is also joined by the Ubangi River vital to the Central African and Chad republics. Apart from the lowest break of navigation between Matadi and Leopoldville, other breaks occur upstream between Stanleyville and Ponthierville, and between Kindu and Kongolo, likewise rounded by early railways. The latter town has also been linked by railway with Lake Tanganyika (and so by the Tanganyika Railway with Dar es Salaam), and in 1956 to Kamina on the Katanga-Port Francqui line, so that Congo navigation now begins at Kindu.

Two transhipments to railways remain, but against these should be set the fact that the river has a remarkably even flow as it and most of its tributaries flow across the equatorial zone. Indeed, the ratio of minimum to maximum flow is only 1 to 3; for the Nile it is 1 to 48. Regular flow is also an asset for hydro-electric power development and there are some 20 stations on the river and its tributaries (Fig. 74).

The focus of river communications is Leopoldville, the capital (Plate 38). Like all the towns, it is a European creation, sited at the western limit of navigation on the longest and most important reach of the Congo; traffic also comes from tributaries such as the Kasai (served by the Katanga–Port Francqui line). Before independence 1·6 million tons were handled annually by the port. Leopoldville also has important commercial functions, industries such as textiles and brewing, and extends some 7 miles from west to east. Its population grew from 22,000 in 1933 to 380,314 (359,332 African) in 1957.

Matadi is 80 miles from the sea at the limit of ocean navigation. The northern Congo bank is almost vertical, and so Matadi was

developed by the Belgians in the narrow space on the southern bank
between the last rapids and the boundary with Angola (Figs. 72A and
B). That bank also rises precipitously, so that the building of roads

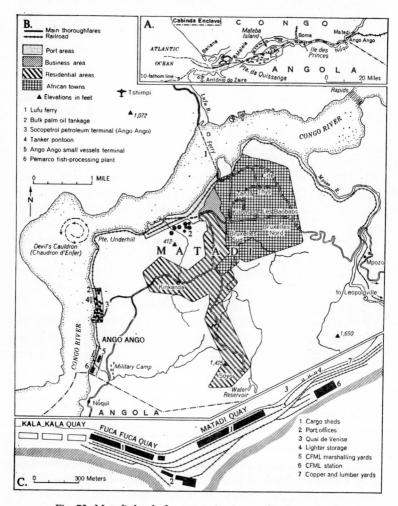

Fig. 72. Matadi, head of ocean navigation on the Congo River.
(From William A. Hance and Irene S. Van Dongen, 'Matadi, focus of Belgian
African Transport', *Annals of the Association of American Geographers*, 1958, p. 43,
by permission)

and houses has been very difficult. Land for wharves and railway yards
has been gained by blasting away very hard rock, and river barges

are used for storage (Plate 36). The 1·2 square mile obtained from Angola in 1927 permitted the construction of installations at Ango Ango (Fig. 72B), below the dangerous Devil's Cauldron (or whirlpool), which prevents the construction of wharves near it. Further down are acute bends, swift currents and sandbanks. Few ports have contended with so many problems.

Economically, Matadi is entirely dependent upon the railway to Leopoldville and the Congo waterways. The Belgians gave every encouragement to this national route, despite congestion and the alternative French Brazzaville–Pointe Noire line north of the Congo. A Franco–Belgian convention even restricted the carriage of the other's goods on these railways. Since 1956 and later independence, with its unsettled conditions, alternative outlets via Dar es Salaam and Lobito have become competitive.

PEOPLES

The historical and physical causes of the low total population of 13,290,687 (1957) have been outlined; the present-day consequences are evident in labour shortage. With an average density of 15 per square mile, there are greater than average clusters in the lower Congo between Leopoldville and Boma, in the east-central part of Leopoldville Province, in central and southern Kasai, north-western Equator Province, south-eastern Uele District in the north-east of the republic, and along the eastern highland fringes. On the other hand, over 10 per cent of the country is almost empty, and two-thirds (mainly the low-lying centre of the basin between 2°N. and 4°S.) has only one-quarter the population. Even Katanga, which provides rich minerals and has considerable towns with sophisticated inhabitants, has a very low rural population.

The Bantu-speaking peoples are the most numerous and comprise nearly two-thirds the total, although they are divided into some fifty groups. They usually live in small compact villages in the forest, or in rather larger ones in the savanna. However, the latter is also the realm of Negroes who comprise about one-third of the total, are divided into 14 tribes, and live in larger villages.

There are no other large groups. The Pygmies number only 150,000; they are found in the dense Ituri forests of the north-east, and in the swampy areas near Lake Leopold II. Not far from the first location there are, by contrast, the very tall Hamitic Tutsi (far more numerous in Burundi), as well as a Nilotic group. Both live in dispersed dwellings or are nomadic.

THE ECONOMY

Modes of life are exceptionally varied, ranging from the Pygmy's primitive hunting and collecting, some almost equally primitive bush fallowing in the centre, improved rotational farming of the *paysannats*, permanent vegetable gardens of a few European colonists in Katanga, and mass production plantation agriculture, to the vast mines, smelters and city industries.

Agriculture

The low density of population and migration to mines and towns have left their marks on farms. Yields are low, because of this and the poor soils. The Belgians introduced paysannats, or cleared corridors in the forest or savanna, with grouped settlement and directed rotational cropping. Fallows of 18–20 years succeed fairly intensive cultivation and 170,000 families were settled by this system (Plate 39). Nevertheless, about 1·7 million families continue to practice traditional shifting and fallow farming. Cassava, maize and bananas are the dominant food crops of the forest, with rice in some river valleys. Guinea corn, millet and groundnuts are the main crops in the savannas, where they are grown intercropped or in rotation. It is reckoned that about one-quarter of these crops is sold in nearby markets.

Four cash crops are overwhelmingly important in export; the oil palm, cotton, coffee and rubber. As the Congo Basin is believed to be the natural habitat of the oil palm, it is not surprising that its oil is both an important food and it, kernel oil, oil cake, and kernels usually constitute the main vegetable export. At first, the wild palm was picked, but this now contributes only about one-sixth the output. Improved varieties have been planted and carefully tended in plantations, which began to bear economically in the 'thirties. They are the only major oil-palm plantations in Africa and extend over 500,000 acres, three-quarters being in full bearing. One-third of the total acreage is owned by Congolese, two-thirds by foreign companies or individuals. In normal times the Congo supplies over one-quarter of the world's palm oil. Congo oil is normally of high quality, because only selected varieties are grown, the fruit is regularly picked, and taken quickly to some 500 highly efficient oil mills (see Plate 40) which produce about 200,000 tons of oil. Clarified and bleached, the oil undergoes several breaks of bulk; at least from plantation to river, river to rail, rail to port bulking plant, and from that to ocean vessel.

On the other hand, palm kernel exports are few, partly because the best trees grown here have fruit with large pericarps containing much oil but only small kernels, partly because Congo plantation mills also crush the kernels, and so export kernel oil and oil cake, rather than kernels. Nevertheless total exports of all oil palm produce from the Congo are valued at only just over one-quarter those from Nigeria.

The indigenous robusta coffee is cultivated up to about 5,000 feet, the introduced arabica between about 3,250 and 8,250 feet. The former

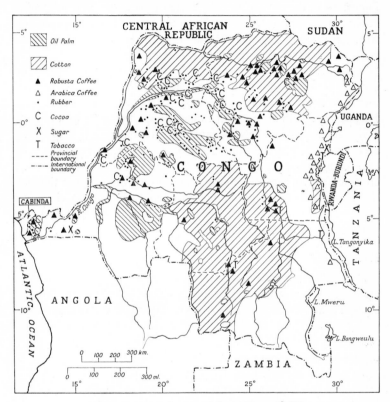

Fig. 73. Main cash crops of Congo (Leopoldville)

is grown by Congolese and European concerns in the lowlands of the north and centre, the latter almost entirely by Europeans in the eastern highlands (see Fig. 73). The Congo is an important African producer of coffee.

Cotton was introduced in 1917 as a compulsory crop to provide African farmers with cash, and local markets with a product which could not then be imported. Cotton is still grown almost entirely by 700,000 Congolese farmers, who have some 825,000 acres under the crop. Although harvesting takes place in the dry season, such a season occurs in one part or other of the country throughout the year; hence the widely separated areas of production. At independence, Congo cotton provided one-sixth of Belgian needs, and another sixth was used in Congo mills.

Indigenous funtumia and landolphia rubber, which were so important in the days of the old Congo Free State, have long since ceased to be tapped, except in wartime. Hevea from Brazil is now widely planted in the equatorial areas of the basin, especially in the west, where it competes for space with the oil palm.

Other cash crops are much less important. Cocoa is a difficult crop because of the need for rich soils and an Equatorial climate—requirements rarely coincident in the Congo. It is mostly grown on large European plantations north of Boma (Congo Estuary), west of Lake Leopold, and around 2°N. Bananas are well suited to the equatorial areas, but the long lines of transport and the many breaks of bulk limit commercial production to the estuary cocoa area, where the crops are grown together. Sugar is also grown there and in the east, on plantations which about fulfil Congo's needs. Tea, cinchona, pyrethrum and tobacco have been considerably developed by European settlers in the eastern highlands.

Fishing and Livestock

Freshwater fish are an important food, as is to be expected with so many rivers, and where large animals cannot be kept in the lowland areas. Yet not all reaches of the rivers are equally full of fish, and some once good have been ruined by over-fishing with poison or explosives. Many rivers and over 122,000 ponds have been stocked with tilapia, a common and excellent freshwater fish. At least 100,000 tons of freshwater fish are consumed annually, the equivalent in meat of 300,000 cattle. Sea trawlers operate from Matadi and normally deliver some 3,000 tons of fish annually to Matadi, Leopoldville and their environs. Dried and smoked fish are also imported from Angola to Katanga.

The tsetse fly normally prevents the keeping of large cattle in the lowland equatorial areas, but on the north-eastern, eastern and southern highland fringes humped cattle are kept by pastoral nomads. Costly ranches have been developed by European companies in the lower Congo, Kwango and in the highlands to produce meat for plantation and mining employees. Hunting of game provides the meat equivalent of 170,000 head of cattle, and is thus over one-half as important as the produce of freshwater fishing.

Mining

Until after the First World War it was the lowland area of the Congo which almost alone provided saleable produce—wild rubber, ivory and, later, palm oil. Now it is the south-eastern and, to a lesser extent, the eastern highlands that yield the valuable minerals which make up two-thirds of Congo exports. They provided revenue for the development of the rest of the country, required the construction of long railways, reduction plants to avoid carrying waste in ores from the

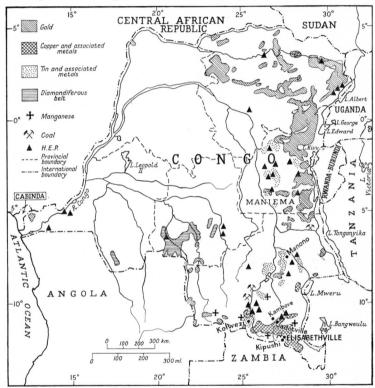

Fig. 74. Congo (Leopoldville); minerals and power

heart of Africa, and the establishment of ancillary industries. The Congo is the leading world producer of cobalt (over one-half) and of industrial diamonds (two-thirds), fourth or fifth producer of copper and tin, seventh of zinc and manganese, and an important producer of tantalium and wolfram.

Copper and cobalt are the most important minerals, and are exclusively worked by the Union Minière du Haut Katanga, one of the world's largest mining companies. The Katanga copper belt lies in the Upper Precambrian on the northern flank of the Congo–Zambezi watershed, the southern flank being occupied by the Copperbelt. The whole zone is 280 miles long from north-west to south-east and 160 miles wide, four-fifths of it lying within Katanga. This belt is the richest area of Central Africa; copper production from both sides accounts for about one-fifth of the world's copper, and for two-thirds the cobalt.

Two types of ore occur on the Katanga side. The original ore is a sulphide, averaging 4 per cent copper, and mined only at Kipushi (west of Elisabethville) where the shafts are 1,600 feet deep. Off-setting the cost of this is the easy concentration done at the pit-head by flotation, which effects a primary separation of copper, cobalt, zinc, lead, cadmium and germanium. The copper concentrate is then smelted in two furnaces to obtain 'blister' copper 99 per cent pure. Electrolytic smelting completes the refining, yielding more cobalt and a little silver. The zinc is roasted and some sent to Belgian manufacturers, while the rest is refined electrolytically in the Congo to 99·99 per cent purity. Sulphur is a by-product, used in making sulphuric acid. Cadmium and germanium are concentrated locally, and in Belgium.

The main copper deposit is, however, an oxidized surface ore, easily worked open-cast at Kolwezi, Ruwe (Plate 41), and Musoni-Kamoto, and contains more copper (6 to 8 per cent) than the sulphide ore. On the other hand, oxidized ore is more expensive to smelt, which is done electrolytically, for example at Jadotville (Plate 42), to produce very pure cobalt and copper. The latter accounts for about 30 per cent of Congo exports (the proportion provided by all exports from lowland Congo), and cobalt for nearly 10 per cent.

Smelting led to the development of the poor coal deposits of Luena; when these were insufficient, coal was imported from Wankie, Rhodesia. Finally, many hydro-electric power stations were built in Katanga, some of which also supplied power to the Northern Rhodesian (now Zambian) Copperbelt before the construction of the Kariba Dam.

Manganese occurs in the oxidized ore of copper, and is also quarried in the Lower Precambrian in south-western Katanga near the railway. Tin and associated minerals are found (as cassiterite) either in the Precambrian or in alluvial deposits. They belong to a vast zone of such deposits extending from Uganda, through Tanzania, Rwanda and Burundi. In the Congo the belt continues south-westward towards the Copperbelt (Fig. 74). The most productive zones are Maniema (west of the northern end of Lake Tanganyika) and Manono (Katanga). Quarrying is by draglines or by hydraulic sluicing. There is an electric smelter at Manono; the Maniema output is smelted in Belgium. Minerals obtained as by-products are tungsten, niobium and lithium.

Gold occurs widely in the Precambrian of the north-eastern Congo, in the same ways and even the same places as tin, so that companies often work both metals. The main producing areas are Kilo-Moto in the remote north-east, and Kivu Province. At first won from alluvial deposits, production is increasingly from quarries and mines. The Congo is only a minor producer.

Diamonds, the only significant mineral worked in lowland Congo, are won almost exclusively in Kasai Province from the northern end of the Angola–Congo field. Two distinct areas are worked: Tshikapa on the Kasai River where one-quarter to one-third are gem stones; and Bakwanga on the Bushimaie stream where, although no more than 2 or 3 per cent are gem stones, the total output is twenty times more important than that of Tshikapa. The Congo is the leading world producer of industrial diamonds, providing over two-thirds of the world output, but is only a minor producer of gems. The value of Congo diamond exports is about three-quarters that from Ghana, and much less than that of Congo oil-palm produce or coffee.

The above are the outstandingly important minerals and those associated with them. The total list is very long and should extend greatly as extraction processes improve, and as the demand for rare metals for special steels and for the aircraft and electronic industries increases. The north-eastern Congo and Katanga are also rich in unworked iron, manganese and cobalt, and have hydro-electric power, so the production of special steel alloys can be expected ultimately. Meanwhile, mineral production is worth about £140 million a year, copper accounting for one-half of this. There are some 300 mines, 300 quarries, and nearly 100 refineries in the Congo. All this is organized by about 60 companies, some among the world's largest. Yet, such is the simplicity of much mining, and the high degree of mechanization, that only 120,000 Congolese and 3,500 Europeans are normally employed.

Industry

The far-inland situation of most agricultural plantations and all mines, whose produce contains much waste, was a powerful incentive to undertake partial or complete local refining. In the case of minerals, this has been much encouraged by the development of cheap hydro-electric power. Likewise, the high cost of importing mining needs, such as explosives and chemicals, soon led to the establishment of industries producing these requirements.

Once there were permanent mining and other towns, simple consumer goods such as soap, cotton clothing, cigarettes, soft and alcoholic drinks, incorporating wholly or mainly local materials, commanded a ready market. Such industries are almost all sited at Elisabethville for the needs of the Katanga mining communities, or at Leopoldville for that city and the rest of the country. A further incentive came with the Second World War, when Belgium was invaded and goods could not readily be brought in from elsewhere, except from southern Africa. Finally, intense development in the 'fifties assisted the establishment of brick and cement works, the assembling of bicycles, cars and lorries, and the construction of barges.

About one-half the industrial needs of the country were met at independence with local goods, whose production occupied some 300,000 people, or two and a half times as many as in mining. Nevertheless, although there are more industries (and more varied ones) than in other tropical African countries except Rhodesia, Congo industries face great difficulties. These are the small population dispersed over a huge area (the Congo has one-third the population of Nigeria dispersed over nearly three times the area), a low standard of living compared with West Africa, long and varying lines of communication, and political instability since independence.

Urban Development

Towns are European creations and their names suggest this, for example those named after explorers (Stanleyville), administrators (Coquilhatville), financiers (Thysville), and members of the Belgian royal family (Leopoldville, Albertville, Elisabethville, Baudouinville). Some towns developed at trans-shipment points on rivers such as Kongolo, Kindu, Ponthierville, Stanleyville, Leopoldville and Matadi on the Congo, Port Francqui on the Kasai, and Albertville on Lake Tanganyika. These have often acquired administrative and industrial functions, for example Stanleyville and Leopoldville. Another group grew up as mining or smelting towns such as Jadotville and Kolwezi; or as focal points for mining areas such as Elisabethville, which has administrative, industrial and commercial functions as well. A third group originated as foci of communications (e.g. Coquilhatville); and a fourth as administrative centres, for example Luluabourg or Bukavu (formerly Costermansville).

About a quarter of the total population lives in towns or mining communities. Yet only two have over 100,000 inhabitants, Elisabethville with nearly twice that figure, and Leopoldville with nearly four times. Both have grown exceedingly rapidly, since the Second World War.

Transport

'The development of Africa may be summed up in one word "transport",'* and this is outstandingly true of the Congo. Its survival requires efficient transport as much as statesmanship. The early significance and present importance of the vast Congo system of nearly 9,000 miles of navigable waterways on which 1,500 diesel-powered boats and push-towed barges operate, and over 3,000 miles of essentially complementary railways is manifest from Fig. 71. The modern port and navigation equipment compares favourably with what may be found in Europe or America. The most vital Stanleyville–Leopoldville and Port Francqui–Leopoldville reaches of the Congo and Kasai respectively are open to barges or boats of up to 1,200 tons, and normally some 400,000 tons are moved annually on each reach.

Three companies run shipping railways and ports on the rivers. Otraco runs services below Stanleyville on the Congo and its tributaries, on the Kasai and tributaries, and on Lake Kivu. It also runs the Matadi–Leopoldville and Boma–Tsela railways, and ports on the rivers. Above Stanleyville another company (C.F.L.) runs river and complementary rail services, as also on Lake Tanganyika. In the north-east another company has narrow-gauge railways linking cotton and gold areas with Congo tributaries.

The most important rail system is run by the B.C.K. Company which linked Katanga with the Rhodesias and Beira (Mozambique) in 1910. It reached Port Francqui on the Kasai in 1927—thereafter the 'route nationale' for Katanga. A link was reluctantly made with the British Benguela Railway to Lobito (Angola) in 1931 but was little used as nationalist policies preferred the 'route nationale'. A branch from Kamina to Kabalo was opened in 1956 to link with the C.F.L. system, whose gauge was altered. The 210-mile section of the B.C.K. railway from Jadotville to Tenke has overhead electric traction (Plate 43).

* Lord Lugard, *The Dual Mandate*, 1922, p. 5.

Road construction is difficult mainly because of wash-outs and much bridging but, as Fig. 71 shows, the 22,000 miles of roads provide essential east-west routes. In 1960 the Congo had the longest internal air network in Africa (22,000 miles) and Leopoldville the world's longest runway. These facts reflect Belgian airline initiative, the size of the Congo, and the long and necessarily slow alternative means of transport with many changes. Leopoldville, Stanleyville and Elisabethville have international airports, from which run many internal services.

CONCLUSION

The Congo is an outstanding example of a country that is huge, diverse, and not easily integrated. It has had a tragic history, not least in independence. The slave trades depopulated it, and the basic problem remains of too few people in such a large area, given the present stage of development. Economic progress requires more people but is held up partly for lack of them. More plantation agriculture, and the further development of power resources and of minerals seem the most reasonable lines of approach, but they cannot begin unless there is political stability and transport is everywhere efficient.

While it is true that Katanga could well support independence, and the rest of the Congo would still be richer and much larger than many African states, it is desirable to retain the unity achieved under colonial rule, since mineral-producing Katanga and the mainly agricultural rest of the country are complementary. Only in unity is there any chance of undertaking the great Inga hydro-electric project on the lower Congo, the capacity of which could be greater than that of all hydro-electric power sites in either the U.S.A. or Western Europe. With it aluminium, special steel and chemical production could be developed using Katangan ores, lower Congo bauxite (not yet worked), and easily imported materials. If this scheme were implemented (and there are no technical impediments) the Congo could seriously change the centre of gravity of world industrialism.

FURTHER READING

Le Congo Belge, Infor Congo, 2 Vols., Brussels, 1959; *Guide to the Congo and Ruanda Urundi*, Office de tourisme du Congo et du Ruanda-Urundi, Brussels, 2ᵉ ed., 1956; F. Dussart and R. Contreras, *Géographie de la Belgique et du Congo*, Brussels, 1955; René Dumont, *Types of Rural Economy*, 1957, Chapter II; W. A. Hance and I. S. van Dongen, 'Matadi, Focus of

Belgian African Transport', *Annals of the Association of American Geographers*, 1958, 41–72 (deals with much more than Matadi); G. Derkinderen, *Atlas du Congo Belge et du Ruanda-Urundi*, Paris and Brussels, 1955; *Atlas général du Congo*, Académie royale des sciences coloniales, Brussels, 1948–58, which also has a very full text.

CHAPTER NINETEEN

Angola

PORTUGUESE Africa came about incidentally to Portuguese efforts to find a sea route to the Orient. Diogo Cão discovered the Congo mouth in 1482–3 and called it 'Zaire', still the Portuguese name. Penetration inland also took place as a means to other ends, the development of richer lands in the Americas with slaves from Angola. To this end Luanda was founded in 1575, Benguela in 1617 and a number of forts up the Cuanza River, and it has been calculated that some three million slaves were despatched in three centuries. In this process, the African Kingdom of Congo was destroyed, and the country so denuded of people that shortage of manpower is still a major problem.

When the Conference of Berlin (1884–5) led to the 'Scramble for Africa', the Congo Free State drove a wedge down the north shore of the Congo Estuary separating Cabinda (2,800 square miles) from the rest of Angola. Furthermore, the Boer treks and British penetration in the Rhodesias thwarted Portuguese hopes of securing territory across Africa from Angola to Mozambique. Reference has been made (p. 303) to the acquisition of territory in north-eastern Angola from the Belgian Congo in 1927.

Little was done to develop Angola until Dr. Salazar came to power in Portugal in 1930. What little was achieved was mainly by concessions or plantations conceded to foreigners, usually Germans or British, who often found their operations restricted by labour shortage.

Since 1930, and especially 1950, very substantial development has taken place through the extension of railways and the improvement of agriculture, mining and industry. Unfortunately, Angola has a population of only 4,832,677 within its area of 481,367 square miles, giving an average density of 10 per square mile. Although a little more than that of the states of former French Equatorial Africa, this is one-third less even than that of the thinly peopled Congo (Leopoldville). However, there are over 300,000 Europeans, most of whom are unskilled and semi- or quite illiterate peasants from southern Portugal, who are re-settled here at the rate of 10–20,000 per year.

* By R. J. Harrison Church.

44. Central buildings and a village of the Cela settlement scheme, Angola (p. 326).
Two villages are just visible in the right distance.

45. Washing plant in diamond field of north-eastern Angola (p. 326).

46. Mt. Baker (15,889 ft.) of the Ruwenzori Mountains. The valley has been glaciated and glaciers remain near the peaks. The Montane plants are groundsels and senecios.

47. The eastern Rift Valley, Tambach, Kenya (p. 345).

Administration is still highly centralized in Lisbon and the economy of Angola and other overseas provinces has been tightly organized around the needs of Portugal. Thus, certain crops (notably sugar and cotton) must first satisfy the needs of Portugal before they may be sold elsewhere and, until reforms in 1961, some crops were reserved for Europeans and *Assimilados* (less than one per cent of Angolan Africans who had accepted the Portuguese way of life and been so registered). Goods must be carried between Portugal and overseas provinces in Portuguese ships, except by special licence. No foreign industries may be established unless Portuguese industries have first been given the opportunity. Whether because of the shortage of labour or because of a belief in the 'dignity of labour', the Portuguese still used forced labour until 1961. Each able-bodied adult male was liable to six months service each year, unless he was already in full-time employment. Africans may live in a town only if they are regularly employed there, an authoritarian proviso that has, however, prevented extensive slums so much a feature of other African towns.

Thus the economic system is not only organized in favour of Portugal; it is also restrictive and contains features rejected decades or centuries ago by other past or present colonial powers, except Spain. The character of the development of Portuguese overseas provinces cannot be understood unless these facts are known.

THE PHYSICAL ENVIRONMENT AND THE ECONOMY

Angola is a large and diverse country, greater than Portugal, Spain, France and Benelux combined, and nearly fourteen times the size of Portugal. The greatest variety is in climate and vegetation, and results from the size and varied relief of Angola, and from the cooling of its coasts by the cold Benguela Current which lowers sea and air temperatures, so restricting convection and rainfall.

The coast from the border with South West Africa to a little south of Benguela is pure Desert; while even to beyond Luanda (9°S.) there is Grass Steppe with giant candelabra-like euphorbia and baobab trees. Yet only 45 miles away in a direct line is the opposite extreme— Moist Forest north of the Cuanza River. Angola is, however, essentially a country of Savanna, which is poorest in the south.

Angola is sharply differentiated regionally into a coastal plain and several plateaux (*planaltos*), each with its own climatic and vegetational characteristics. The coastal plain has post-Cretaceous marine and lacustrine deposits, and is characterized, as in southern Gabon and the Congo (Brazzaville), by northward-trending sandspits (*restinga*)

11

which have deep water on the landward side. As noted already, the plain is cool and dry, and is never wider than a hundred miles. Germans have long developed sisal plantations south of both Luanda and

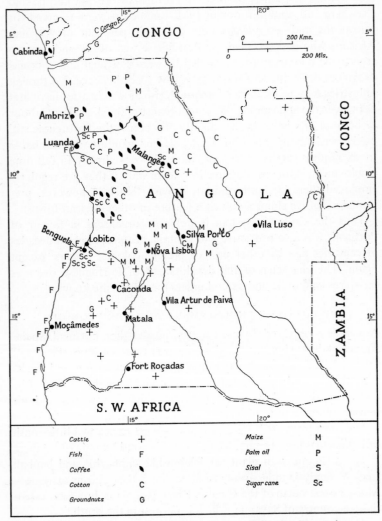

Fig. 75. Angola; cattle, fish and cash crops. (After Van Dongen)

Lobito; while sugar estates, which must have irrigation, are found on the rivers, especially the Catumbela. Salt is evaporated at many places and exported overseas to Portugal, and by rail to Central

Africa, as is dried fish. The important off-shore fishing grounds are a continuation of the South African fisheries in the same cold Benguela Current, and comparable with the Moroccan and Mauritanian fisheries of the likewise cold Canary Current. Both Portuguese and Africans fish off Angola, but mostly the former. There are some ten fish-drying, canning and processing factories between Lobito and the southern border; and fish oil, fish meal (largely exported to the U.S.A.), and fish manure are produced cheaply because of very low wages.

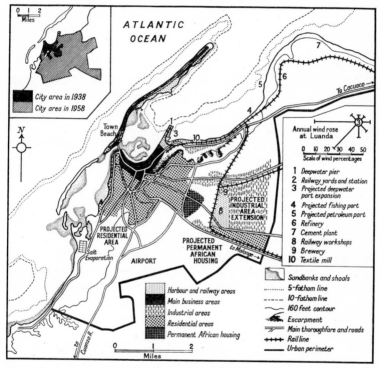

Fig. 76. Luanda, Angola
(After Irene S. Van Dongen, 'The Port of Luanda in the economy of Angola', *Boletim da Sociedade de Geografia de Lisboa*, 1960, end map, by permission)

Luanda, the capital, some four centuries old, was the first permanent European settlement in Africa south of the Sahara. For long it was a rather mean town, but has been elegantly rebuilt since 1938 (see Fig. 76B), some 2,500 buildings having been erected on 250 acres in this period. Now the third Portuguese city, after Lisbon and Oporto, it has a population of nearly a quarter of a million, of which 50,000 are Europeans—probably the greatest urban concentration of Europeans in tropical Africa outside Rhodesia. It has an upper town extending along a spur from the sixteenth-century fort, and a lower commercial town (Fig.76A).

Behind the protective sandspit, which is used for recreation, there is a deep-water pier. Luanda handles more Angolan trade than the other ports, especially coffee brought in by road, and manganese, ferro-manganese and titaniferous iron ore brought by rail. The airport is Angola's largest, and takes inter-continental traffic. There are numerous processing industries, including tropical Africa's first small oil refinery and numerous consumer goods factories—a textile mill employing over a thousand workers.

Lobito (population some 35,000, including 7,500 Europeans) is again protected by a sandspit. In contrast to Luanda, the European quarter is on the sandspit beyond the wharves; otherwise the layout is similar. Lobito was developed as the terminus of the Benguela Railway because of deeper water than at the older town of Benguela. An 838-mile railway connected Lobito with the Congo and Rhodesian railways in 1931; nevertheless, it was only after 1956 that the Belgians permitted much Congo traffic to travel down this British-owned railway to a Portuguese port. Lobito has been even more used since the Congo became independent, as it is the nearest port to Katanga, whose ores are its chief export. It also sends out Angolan iron ore from Cuima and Cassinga south of Nova Lisboa and from Robert Williams (a town 246 miles up the railway named after the Scottish originator of the railway), as well as much maize mostly grown by European settlers on the Benguela-Bié plateaux; while the road north from Vila Luso (on the railway) provisions the diamond fields of north-eastern Angola. Lobito handles greater tonnages than Luanda but their value is less than those from Luanda.

Moçâmedes, originally a fish processing and exporting port, is developing fast as its railway is extended eastward and iron-ore deposits are opened up near the line at Cassinga. There are many minor ports where boats load produce off-shore, for example timber at Cabinda, coffee at Ambrizete and Ambriz, sugar at Porto Amboím and Cuio, and fishing ports south of Lobito.

The rise from the coastal plain is gentle in the north (hence the Dande and Cuanza rivers are navigable for short distances), but is steep in the centre and south, where the granite of the Basement Complex is protected by even harder quartzites and ironstones. Hydro-electric power stations have been established on this and other plateau

edges where rivers have falls. The Benguela Railway originally had a
rack and pinion section here; it now has a normal but very steep track
for five miles which limits train loads to 30 per cent of normal, and
trains must be divided.

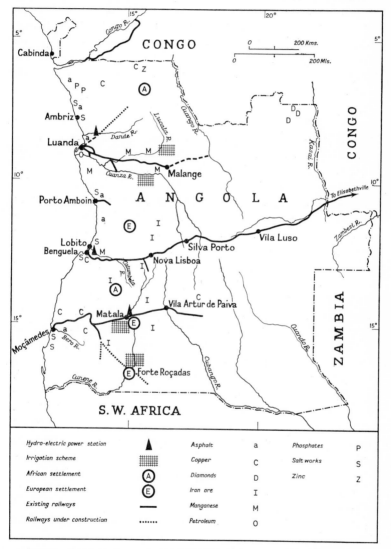

Fig. 77. Angola; railways, minerals, power, irrigation and colonization
(After Van Dongen)

The first plateau averages a thousand feet in elevation, the next two —Malanje in the north and Huila in the south—lie between 3,300 and 4,000 feet, while the Bié or Benguela Plateau rises to the Morro do Moco (8,613 feet) but averages 5,000–6,000 feet; this is another of the continent's great divides, that between the Congo and Zambezi. The plateau edges and the northern (Malanje) plateau are the wettest; the latter is also the warmest, and robusta coffee (by far the greatest export) is grown by European settlers and on estates, especially in the Uige area. Africans also collect oil-palm produce here and grow cotton in the rather drier Malanje area under European supervision.

The central and highest Bié Plateau is much cooler (frosts occur), drier and healthier, and Savanna is dominant. Although there has been some assisted settlement of Portuguese peasants north and south of Malanje, most of it has been in this central zone of the Bié Plateau at Cela north of the Benguela Railway (Plate 44), at Silva Porto and Nova Lisboa on it, and at Sa de Bandeira and Matala on the Moçâmedes line. There are also centres for assisted African settlement under identical conditions at some of these, at Caconda (north of Matala) and Damba (northern Angola), and more are planned. Maize is grown in the rains and is the main crop, although beans are important, especially as a basic food; wheat is grown in the dry season. As the tsetse is absent in the centre and south, large cattle can be kept, so permitting mixed farming by the settlers, providing added income and manure for the rather indifferent soils. In the very dry south livestock are most important, although irrigated crops are developing in schemes in the Cunene Valley especially at Matala, where there is a dam for power and irrigation. Population densities reach 50 per square mile in Angola only in these highland pockets. Malanje, Nova Lisboa and Sa de Bandeira are, respectively, the northern, central and southern regional and market centres for settlers. Nova Lisboa, once intended as the capital, also has railway repair shops, several consumer goods industries, and nearby iron and manganese mines.

MINERALS, POWER AND TRANSPORT

Diamonds are obtained in the Kasai Basin of the north-east from an extension of the Congo fields. Exploitation is again open-cast (Plate 45) and diamonds are Angola's second export. Unlike the Congo, however, more gem than industrial diamonds are produced. Indeed, Angola produces 10 per cent of the world's gems, and these command a much higher price than industrial ones, of which Angola is a very small producer.

One of the many more recent transformations in Angola has been the mining of manganese, ferro-manganese and titaniferous iron ores on the Luanda line, asphalt and phosphates (as well as the older-mined copper) north of that railway, petroleum just south of Luanda, manganese and iron ore on and near the Benguela Railway, and iron ore on and near the Moçâmedes line (Fig. 77). These may greatly reduce the dominance of coffee in overseas trade.

Substantial quantities of electric power are available from the Mabubas hydro-electric plant and from the petroleum oilfield for industries in Luanda, from the Biopio hydro-electric station for Lobito and Benguela, and from the Matala plant for Matala, Sa de Bandeira, and for irrigation and meat packing. The considerable European population offers a larger local market for consumer goods than some African countries.

Roads are poorly developed because the greatest efforts by Portugal have been concentrated on railways. A new railway is being built into the coffee country of the north, which might be linked to the Leopold-ville–Matadi line (Congo), and the Luanda and Moçâmedes lines are being rapidly extended and improved.

Only the northern rivers are navigable, and they are used for carrying sugar, palm produce and coffee. Air transport is important between Luanda and Carmona (Uige), the coffee centre, but otherwise is less developed than in many lands.

CONCLUSION

The consequences of the slave trade, which denuded the country of much of its population, are still with Angola, for it suffers like the other countries of Western Central Africa from a shortage of man-power. The re-peopling of its high plateaux with Portuguese peasants may lead to political troubles from within, or from outside.

Sheer size, steepness of the plateau edges and the aridity of the south have retarded development, especially in the hands of a small and poor governing power like Portugal, particularly with its restrictive economic system. Nevertheless, there have been outstanding developments in almost every sector in recent years, especially in mineral working, the reconstruction of Luanda, and the extension of railways, though more roads are urgently needed.

FURTHER READING

J. H. Wellington, *Southern Africa*, Cambridge, Vol. 1, 1955, describes the physical geography of the southern part of the country. F. C. C. Egerton, *Angola in Perspective*, 1957, Part 2, gives a favourable view of the history and economy, and J. V. Duffy, *Portuguese Africa*, Cambridge, Mass., 1959, and *The Portuguese in Africa* (Penguin), Harmondsworth, 1962, give unfavourable views. Valuable articles are R. J. Houk, 'Recent Developments in the Portuguese Congo', *Geographical Review*, 1958, 201–221; William A. Hance and Irene S. Van Dongen, 'The Port of Lobito and the Benguela Railway', *Geographical Review*, 1956, 460–87; and Irene S. Van Dongen, 'Angola', *Focus* (American Geographical Society), October, 1956, and 'Coffee Trade, Coffee Regions, and Coffee Ports in Angola', *Economic Geography*, 1961, 320–46.

EAST AFRICA

CHAPTER TWENTY

The Environment and Resources

THE countries of East Africa are Kenya, Uganda, Rwanda, Burundi, Tanzania (Tanganyika and Zanzibar). The total area is large, 702,670 square miles, the population small: about 33 million in 1963, including 400,000 Asians and 100,000 Europeans.The density of population is therefore sparse, and the per capita income is very low.

East Africa is considered a geographical whole for the purpose of a regional study of this nature, and so it will remain, despite any political changes of the future. Political boundaries were conceived in Africa by men concerned with external issues, and local opinions were rarely considered. Thus, peoples who by a twist of fate found themselves separated by arbitrary boundaries may in the future desire to opt from their present country and join their brothers elsewhere. Such are the Somali of northern Kenya and the Masai of Kenya and Tanganyika.

There is much backwardness and poverty and although European influence has been limited to the past sixty years, it has been more concentrated than in West Africa, partly due to the suitability of the region for European and Asian settlement. The countries have thus become meeting places for diverse races and groups, resulting in complex social problems, and the area has acquired a British imprint.

HISTORICAL OUTLINE

East Africa was no exception to the general pattern in opening up the interior of the continent. After Vasco da Gama's visit to the coast in 1498, European interest increased, but when the Arabs drove the Portuguese out of Fort Jesus, Mombasa, in 1698, European influence vanished, to be replaced again by Arab traders and slavers. Bagamoyo, forty miles north-west of Dar es Salaam, was the centre of the slave route to the interior, one of the few means of access to the hinterland.

It was not until the nineteenth century that European influence again began to play an active part in East Africa. Pioneer missionaries such as Rebmann, Krapf, Livingstone and Hannington, and explorers such as Stanley, Speke, Grant, Baker and Burton penetrated to the interior and discovered the lakes and the source of the Nile. In 1890,

* By P. J. H. Clarke.

after stopping the slave trade, the British proclaimed a protectorate over Zanzibar.

Tanganyika became a German protectorate (German East Africa) in 1889, and remained so until the end of the First World War. In 1920 most of it was renamed Tanganyika and became a British Mandate, which became a United Nations Trusteeship in 1946 and independent in December 1961. Tanganyika and Zanzibar were united on 27 April 1964, and the new state was renamed Tanzania on 29 October. The small countries of Rwanda and Burundi were together a Belgian Mandate and then Trusteeship until they became independent in 1962. Kenya, at first the responsibility of the Imperial British East Africa Company, was made a British colony in 1905 and became independent in 1963. Uganda became a British protectorate in 1896 and independent in 1962.

THE PHYSICAL ENVIRONMENT

Structure and Relief

The major elements in the physical unity of East Africa are vast undulating plateaux. On the west lies the trough of the western branch of the Rift Valley, while the eastern branch runs from north to south through the plateau. In between these branches and on the plateau surface, where it forms a shallow depression, lies the second largest lake in the world, Lake Victoria. Eastward the plateau slopes uniformly to a coastal plain, broad in the north and south but narrow in the centre. Along both sides of the Rift Valley are volcanoes, culminating in Mts. Kilimanjaro, 19,340 feet, Kenya, 17,058 feet, Elgon, 14,178 feet, Meru, 14,979 feet, and the Virunga (Mfumbiro) volcanoes, 14,786 feet near Lake Kivu. Most of these are extinct and, with the exception of occasional activity from Ol'Donyo Lengai near Lake Natron in Tanganyika, and small steam vents and hot springs in the Rift Valley, the area is at present quiescent. Western Uganda culminates in Ruwenzori (Plate 46) 16,794 feet with the third highest peak in Africa. These moutains are not volcanic but a part of the ancient plateau left upstanding between two down-faulted valleys to the east and west.

The structure of the East African Plateau is similar to that of the peneplained surfaces found elsewhere in Africa. Ancient rocks of the Basement Complex underlie all Kenya and most of East Africa. They are exposed in certain areas, particularly in central Kenya and in parts of Tanganyika and Uganda, where volcanic rocks once covering them have been weathered away. The Basement rocks belong to the

Precambrian period, although their precise ages are unknown. They are for the most part gneisses, schists, sandstones with igneous intrusions associated with them. Minerals are found, including graphite, kyanite, asbestos and mica. Where exposed, the Basement rocks weather to sandy soil which does not hold moisture during the dry season, and to steep-sided 'inselbergs' rising from the plains. Such 'inselbergs' are found particularly in the 'Nyika' areas and in northern Kenya and Uganda. Volcanic rocks of the Tertiary and later periods overlie the Basement rocks in many places, making the discovery of further minerals in these areas problematical. Along the fringes of the coast are many coral outcrops, and the land immediately behind the coastline is thin and infertile.

The Great Rift Valley

The length of this enormous depression amounts to about one-sixth of the earth's diameter. The freshness of geological and relief forms contrasts strongly with the maturity of the lands through which it passes. There is also a distinct climatic contrast; the floor of the valley often showing a marked paucity of rainfall compared with the highlands on either side, which are forested and well watered.

The Rift Valley in central East Africa varies in width from about thirty to eighty miles. Its western side in southern Kenya (the Mau Escarpment, Plate 47) rises gradually and is geologically more mature than the eastern. This is not true in Tanganyika where the Crater Highlands show faulting of a recent date. There the western wall above Lake Manyara is formidable, while slopes are gentle towards Arusha on the eastern side. Steam and hot springs occur in the Njorowa Gorge south of Naivasha and in the Menengai Caldera near Nakuru. Gravity surveys taken in the valley show that materials under the Rift Valley are very light compared with the neighbouring plateaux.

The Rift Valley lakes vary considerably. Those in the eastern branch are (with the exception of Lake Rudolf) smaller than in the western branch; they are much shallower and a number contain large deposits of soda ash. Lakes Nakuru, Elementeita and Magadi are soda lakes. Nakuru and Elementeita contain some water, but Magadi is completely dry and is the source of the world's largest supply of sodium carbonate (Plate 51). The western Rift Valley lakes, nearly all freshwater, contain the vast narrow troughs of Lake Tanganyika and Lake Nyasa, both of great length and with their deepest parts below sea level.

The Recent Volcanic History of East Africa

Volcanoes and volcanic rock have a great importance in the relief and economy of Kenya, Uganda and Tanganyika. Most of the volcanic soils are concentrated near the mountain masses on either side of the Rift Valley. The greatest volcanic area is in Kenya and Tanganyika, although parts of Uganda consist of volcanic areas, particularly near the Virunga volcanoes and the West Nile Hills. In Kenya, most of the country round Lake Rudolf is volcanic, while farther south Laikipia and Loroki are volcanic plateaux between the Aberdare Mountains and Mt. Kenya. The volcanic belt continues southward through Tanganyika to the Southern Highlands in the extreme south-west.

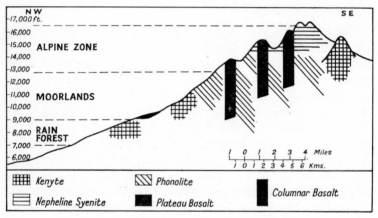

Fig. 78. Section through the western slopes of Mt. Kenya

Eruptions have been going on intermittently throughout the area since Tertiary times, and some of the craters and calderas are extremely large. The caldera of Ngorongoro is twelve miles in diameter, making it one of the largest in the world.

Some of the more characteristic lavas of East Africa are phonolite, basalt (both plateau and columnar), and kenyte, which is a type of phonolite common in East Africa; it has also been found on Mt. Erebus in the Antarctic.

Mt. Kenya is an example of a volcano in an advanced stage of disintegration. Originally its crater was probably some 3,000 feet higher than its present peak. The twin summits of Batian and Nelion, the remains of the original volcanic plug, are composed of hard resistant nepheline syenite, a deep-seated igneous rock now exposed.

The surrounding peaks, many of them as much as 14,000 feet high, are the remains, heavily eroded, of the rim of the old crater.

The existing glaciers were at one time much larger, as evidenced by moraines at about 10,000 feet. The twelve remaining glaciers are receding fairly rapidly, and the mountain itself is much affected by shattering caused by freeze-melt conditions. It is also fairly certain that the Mt. Kenya glaciation was contemporary with the Great Ice Age of Europe, and that the glaciers on Mt. Kenya merely excavated valleys which had been formed previously. Evidence of this is also afforded by the large numbers of perched blocks found on Mt. Kenya, indicating only a small amount of denudation since the maximum glacial period. Gregory gave a geological history of Kenya known as the Kenya succession.

		Period
(1) Doinyan	Eocene	First eruptions of the Kenya phonolite. Later the main eruptive stage of kenyte and olivine, nepheline, syenite.
(2) Nyasan	Oligocene	Probably long interval of quiescence.
(3) Laikipian	Miocene	Third eruptive stage
(4)	Pliocene	Long interval of denudation. Destruction of craters and excavation of existing valleys.
(5)	Early Pleistocene	Maximum glaciation.

The vegetation of the mountain consists of Montane Evergreen Forest at elevations of between 7,000 and 9,000 feet, and of thick tufted grass and moorland above 10,000 feet. At higher levels, for example in the Teleki Valley, there are large numbers of giant lobelias and groundsels found as high as 14,000 feet.

CLIMATE

Rainfall

The climatic belts in East Africa vary with the positions of the two chief wind systems, the south-east and north-east trades. These, in turn, depend upon the movement north and south of the pressure belts and air masses over Africa. From April to October the prevailing south-east trades blow, bringing rain in the earlier months to most of the region; but drier conditions prevail later, as they veer to the south-west and blows across the dry Steppes of Tanganyika. In November the north-east trades establish themselves, later swinging to a more northerly point away from the Indian Ocean and losing their moisture. These winds bring Tropical Continental air from Arabia to Africa.

Most of the rainfall in East Africa falls in the transition periods between the change over from one prevailing wind to the other. The rainfall itself varies extensively, and in East Africa there are many different rainfall patterns. Generally speaking, these can be grouped into two distinct types: the Equatorial, where the rainfall is spread over the year but there are two maxima; and the Tropical Marine which has one wet and one dry season. The areas closer to the equator have two maxima, and those farther away only one. Rainfall in East Africa fluctuates considerably from year to year (Fig. 79). Thus in 1960 a severe drought in the settled areas of the eastern Rift Valley during July, August and September, at a time when some rain could be expected, resulted in the loss of large numbers of cattle from starvation. In 1960 the partial failure of the November short rains in the Kikuyu Highlands resulted in a maize shortage during 1961. By contrast, during October and November 1961 the rainfall was the heaviest ever recorded for the period and created flood conditions in many parts of East Africa. Meru recorded over 50 inches in one month and a fall of 13·2 inches was experienced in one day at Witu, inland from the Kenya coast. Between the years 1923 and 1947 Nairobi had an average rainfall of 34 inches. The highest recorded during the period was 61 inches and the lowest only 19 inches. A similar pattern can be traced throughout East Africa, although Kenya is the most poorly placed for rainfall reliability. Kenya receives a reliable 30 inches per year in only 15 per cent of the country, compared with 25 per cent of Tanganyika, and 75 per cent of Uganda.

The rainfall is convectional or orographic in type, falling chiefly in the form of heavy thunder-showers, particularly in the late afternoon. These storms are often local, and follow certain patterns across the country. As an example, the south-eastern slopes of Mt. Kenya are considerably wetter than those of the west. The prevailing easterly winds deposit a much heavier concentration of rain on the eastern slopes, causing a rain 'shadow' to the west; this is true of most mountain regions exposed to the prevailing winds. Only in the forest on the mountains at altitudes of between 9,000 and 11,000 feet is the reliability of the rainfall at all consistent. Figure 79 shows East Africa divided into a number of zones of reliability. In zone (i) cultivation can be carried on without serious danger to crops. For zones (ii) and (iii) a mixture of cultivation and cattle keeping is most suitable, depending on the area. Zone (iv), where sometimes less than 10 inches

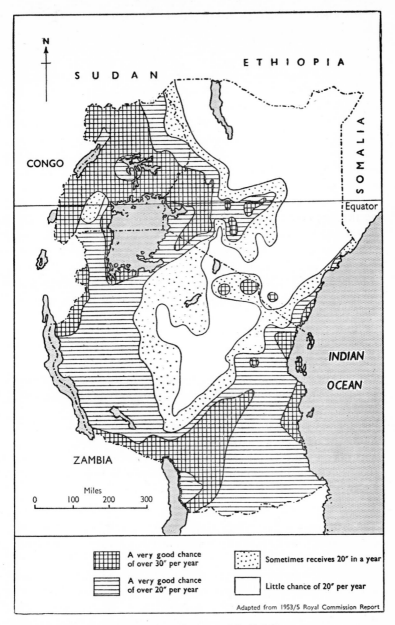

Fig. 79. East Africa; rainfall reliability
(From G. M. Hickman, and W. H. G. Dickins, *The Lands and Peoples of East Africa*, p. 14 by permission)

is recorded, is unsuitable for crops and animals, other than those herded by pastoralists.

Temperature

There is a threefold temperature division for East Africa as follows:

(1) The coastal plain and low valleys are hot in all seasons, having a mean monthly temperature within 3°F of the mean annual temperature of 78°F. Temperatures on the coast are moderated a little by the sea. The highest figure ever recorded in the shade at Mombasa was 98°F and the lowest 60°F, whereas Moshi (2,700 feet), 200 miles inland, has more extreme readings. A maximum of 100°F has been recorded there.

(2) The plateau is much cooler and is pleasant for Europeans, particularly between 4,500 feet and 8,000 feet. The temperature range is still very limited (7°F at Nairobi, 5,500 feet), although the mean is similar to English summer months. The diurnal range is greater, especially during the hot season of January, February and March. The mean daily maximum in March is 78°F and the mean daily minimum 53°F, giving a daily range of 25°F. The plateau of Tanganyika is generally about 1,000 feet lower than that of Kenya, and its daytime temperatures are hotter and nights less cool. Tabora in October, the hottest month, has a mean maximum of 78°F, and that of March, the coolest month, is still 70°F. On mountain summits the diurnal range is greater; warm days followed by very cold nights. Frost is frequent at over 8,000 feet, and snow falls at 14,000 feet and above.

(3) The Lake Victoria region and most of Uganda are too low and humid to have encouraged white settlement. At Entebbe on Lake Victoria the temperature rarely exceeds 85°F or falls below 60°F, and the mean annual temperature of 72°F is only a little less than at the coast.

SOILS

The main soils of East Africa are:

(1) Coastal soils which are mainly alluvial or calcareous, and sandy on the raised limestones.

(2) Nyika soils which are of little use in agriculture. They are porous and sandy, and in the dry season are easily shifted by winds.

(3) Red soils, divisible into 'laterized' and 'non-laterized'. The former, including the volcanic soils of the plateaux and forests, are fine grained and retentive of water, even in the dry season, and support perennial vegetation. Most coffee plantations and highland

farms in Kenya have this type of soil. The non-laterized soils, found more in Central Kavirondo and Ukamba, are well drained, and often developed on Basement rocks.

(4) Black cotton soils which are less fertile from a vegetational point of view, and are a mixture of debris from Basement rocks and from the volcanic areas.

VEGETATION

Most of the plateau land of East Africa is covered by Wooded or Grass Steppe (Fig. 7) and includes large stretches of the uninhabited desolate Nyika bushlands which are at their most infertile in Kenya. The quality of the grasses improves in the Woodland-Savanna of western Tanganyika and Uganda.

The most common types of tree found throughout the Grass Steppe are the acacia and the baobab. The latter is common inland from the coast and up to elevations of about 4,000 feet. In the drier parts of the plateau the acacias follow the watercourses, with bush on the higher levels. North-eastern Kenya is Sub-desert Steppe, with real desert east of Lake Rudolf.

Only about 10,000 square miles out of a total of 700,000 square miles is forested and in most cases this is discontinuous, exceptions being found in parts of Uganda and on mountain slopes. The Montane Evergreen Forest, which usually occurs at altitudes of between 7,000 and 9,000 feet, is very dependent upon rainfall, and the forest areas are denser and extend a greater distance towards the plains on the south-east facing slopes of the mountains where the rainfall is heavier and more reliable. Much has been destroyed by clearing for coffee and tea planting, and also by forest squatters practising a shifting type of agriculture. The lower forests are chiefly Montane Evergreen, but between 9,000 and 17,000 feet camphor, podo and bamboo are found in profusion. Above the forest regions are large areas of Montane Grassland, changing to Alpine flora in the Ruwenzori Mountains and on Mts. Kenya and Kilimanjaro.

On the coast, regions of Forest-Savanna give way to mangroves in the swampy deltas of rivers; while around Lake Victoria, Forest-Savanna is interspersed with Freshwater Swamp vegetation.

DISEASES AND PESTS

Whereas yellow fever has been eliminated by inoculations, malaria is endemic, and only partly restricted, even by vigorous swamp clearance and prophylaxis. In the highlands the incidence is small, as the *anopheles* mosquito does not flourish below temperatures of about 65°F.

Trypanosomiasis is probably as much of a menace today, since the tsetse fly is more difficult to control, and *Glossina palpalis* and *Glossina morsitans*, the types attacking both man and cattle, are often found in adjacent areas. *Morsitans* lives in the large areas of Miombo Woodland in Tanganyika, while *palpalis* likes water and is found particularly round Lake Victoria. Two other types, *Glossina swynnertoni* and *Glossina pallidipes* are common, the former in Nyika country, and the latter almost anywhere. Both these species are extremely damaging to cattle. One of the drawbacks in exploiting the Nyika of Kenya and plateaux of Tanganyika is the high incidence of tsetse; it is almost confined to regions between 2,500 feet and 4,500 feet, but is difficult to stamp out altogether.

Worm diseases, such as hookworm and bilharzia, are common, but can be controlled by improved sanitation. Waterborne diseases, such as the two forms of dysentery, amoebic and bacillary, are common, particularly on the coast. Leprosy, plague and smallpox have also been controlled, and the latter almost eradicated through vaccination. Two of the greatest dangers are tuberculosis and pneumonia, particularly amongst undernourished peoples.

Other major cattle diseases are rinderpest, and foot and mouth disease. While the former has been controlled, the latter is prevalent on many farms in the Kenya Highlands. Plant pests are common, though the greatest threat is undoubtedly the locust, East Africa being within the invasion area from the Red Sea breeding zone. Only diligent efforts by the locust control organization, particularly spraying of swarms from the air, has kept the region relatively free.

THE PEOPLES

AFRICANS

The East African peoples are regarded as descendants of early Hamitic stock which later crossed with Negro. The Africans themselves represent about 98 per cent of the people living in the region, and belong to approximately 220 different tribal groups, each with their own languages and dialects. These tribes show the mixing of several racial characteristics, particularly in the colour of skin and the appearance of face and hair.

Hamites. The people of the north of Kenya, the Galla and Boran, are pure Hamites, and the Rendille and Somali are similar. Although constantly on the move, these people live in huts and keep herds of sheep and goats. Their pastoral customs are suited to the barren wastes of the northern frontier, where soil erosion and land wastage are prevalent.

Bantu, Nilotes, Nilo-Hamites and Semi-Hamites. There are no pure Negroes in East Africa but many people have Negro blood. Even the chief groups are intermixed. The Bantu are the largest group, found throughout East Africa. Some of the better-known tribes belonging to this group are the Kikuyu, Kamba, Meru, Embu, and Luhuya of Kenya; the Chagga, Gogo, Nyamawezi, Haya and Sukuma of Tanganyika; and the Baganda, Soga, Kiga and Toro of Uganda.

The Nilotes are confined almost entirely to the Nyanza Region of Kenya and to northern Uganda. The Luo of Kenya and the Acholi of Uganda are the most numerous. The Nilo-Hamites are mainly Hamitic and are pastoralists, although some of them have abandoned this rather primitive type of economy, now being more influenced by the agriculturalists surrounding them. Such are the Kipsigi and Nandi of Kenya, and the Teso of Uganda. The strongly Hamitic peoples such as the Masai, Suk, Maraqwet, Turkana, Samburu and Karamojong are still pastoral.

There are a number of tribes in East Africa with large populations: 1,500,000 Kikuyu, 1,200,000 Luo, 1,300,000 Sukuma and nearly 2,000,000 Baganda. These contrast markedly with about 120,000 Masai occupying vast areas of bush, and a handful of Wanderobo living chiefly in the forests of the Mau Hills of Kenya. Although the more numerous agricultural peoples have pushed the backward tribes into the forests, a decline in their numbers and those of the pastoralists appears to have been halted.

Distribution of Africans

The mean population density of East Africa at 37 persons per square mile is very low, but also somewhat misleading as the bulk of the population is concentrated in three small areas. These are the shores of Lake Victoria, the highlands and the coastal belt.

The two principal factors concerned with the disposition of population are rainfall and the tsetse fly. In these three regions rainfall is generally adequate (Fig. 79), and they are all removed from the worst of the tsetse infestation (Fig. 17).

Lake Victoria is surrounded by dense populations. In Kenya the Luo and Maragoli country of Nyanza has densities of over 200 persons per square mile. In Uganda the Mengo and Busoga districts, with over $2\frac{1}{2}$ million people, have a high percentage of the total population, while in Tanganyika Lake Province accounts for $2\frac{1}{4}$ million people, or about a quarter of the total population.

Highlands include such regions as the Kikuyu, Meru and Embu reserves in Kenya, Kigezi district in southern Uganda, and the Chagga and Usambara districts of Tanganyika.

The coastal belt is a comparatively fertile region where the growth of ports such as Mombasa, Tanga and Dar es Salaam, together with their associated industries, has induced immigrants to move in from coastal villages.

Probably only about one-sixth of the total area of East Africa falls within these three categories. By contrast, the vast regions of northern Uganda and Kenya and the Masai steppe of Tanganyika, with under 20 inches of rainfall, have population densities of as little as 5 persons per square mile. Here population is restricted as much by the environment as by its traditional means of pastoral livelihood.

THE IMMIGRANTS

Asians. Arabs have as long a history in Africa as many African tribes. Settled particularly on Zanzibar and Pemba, in Mombasa, Malindi and Lamu, they have intermarried with the Bantu to produce a noticeably mixed strain. Indians and Pakistanis came to East Africa with the building of the Uganda Railway, but many have come since to trade and to escape the poverty of India. They are prominent in skilled occupations, in commercial activities and in clerical services, particularly with the government, and in 1964 there were about 220,000 in Kenya alone. The main religious groups of the Indian sub-continent are represented, including the Catholicism of the Goanese communities.

Europeans. These are chiefly of British descent, although most European countries are represented and there are numbers of South Africans. Many are farmers and others have had considerable influence in commerce and in the direction and staffing of government. In 1961 at their peak there were about 4,000 European farmers in the Kenya Highlands out of a total population in Kenya of about 70,000. In 1964 the total European population had fallen to 49,000. In Tanzania the numbers are less, about 22,000 in 1962. They are mostly confined to the highland regions of the country and the large towns. In Uganda, out of a total of 10,000 Europeans in 1962, probably not more than 1,000 were settlers and most of these were engaged in commerce. Neither in Tanganyika nor Uganda has the settler been as well established as in Kenya.

MODES OF LIFE

Hunting and Collecting

Very few people today live by these means. The Wanderobo of Kenya, the Pygmies of western Uganda, and some of the obscure 'click'-speaking peoples of central Tanganyika have no kind of agriculture, pottery or cloth making, and no solid construction for their houses. Mostly they have lost their forest habits, merging with larger tribes close at hand. This is particularly true of the Wanderobo who have become identified with the Masai.

Pastoralism

Pastoralists are few in number but they cover large tracts of East Africa in their search for grazing and water. Two-thirds of Kenya is composed of land so far only suitable to the pastoralist (Plate 48). The principal regions apart from northern Kenya are the Karamoja District of Uganda peopled by the Nilo-Hamite Suk and Karamojong, and the Masai Reserve which includes Kajiado and Narok in Kenya, and large tracts of Tanganyika.

The African pastoralist keeps his cattle largely for the sake of numbers, a symbol of wealth. Such numbers lead to overstocking and soil erosion where the land is already poor. Some tribes, formerly pastoralist, which have developed a tradition of cultivation, also keep cattle. Cattle serve two chief purposes, first, for payment of the bride price, and secondly, for meat and milk. The pastoralist is generally unwilling to sell cattle. The virtual elimination of such diseases as rinderpest means an increase in numbers, but also greater erosion and damage to the land.

European farms in the Kenya and Tanganyika highlands have developed an industry which has sold its products on world markets. Large ranches in Laikipia and Trans-Nzoia have herds of beef cattle, and there is dairy farming in the wetter parts of the highlands.

Agriculture

This is the chief source of wealth to East Africa, even though only about 5 per cent of the surface area is cultivated and most agricultural land is used merely for subsistence crops. In Kenya barely one-fifth of the total land surface has an annual average rainfall exceeding 30 inches. Most of this lies within the African land units with but a small amount alienated to the European. Yet this alienated land has produced about 85 per cent of the agricultural exports of the country, with the remaining 15 per cent coming from the African farmers.

Measures to improve the amount of land under cultivation, include land consolidation, irrigation schemes, and the eradication of tsetse. Land consolidation after the 1952–9 Emergency caused extremely rapid development in some districts with greatly increased production in cash crops. Irrigation schemes on the Tana River are being developed but costs are very high indeed. Tanzania has similar problems to Kenya; irrigation schemes on the Kilombero, Ruaha, Pangani and Rufiji rivers would be costly. At present out of 4,000,000 irrigable acres in the country only 100,000 acres are being irrigated. Despite this, progress has been made in the training of farmers through agricultural colleges and farm institutes in both these countries, and mechanization is slowly replacing the traditional hand implement.

Uganda does not have the same problems because of the absence of disputes over once-alienated land, and the evenly distributed rainfall. The country can be divided into three grassland zones, that of Napier grass near Lake Victoria, the short grass covering most of the country below 6,000 feet, and Kikuyu grass above 6,000 feet. Excepting Karamoja, conditions do not approach the severity of the arid regions of Kenya and Tanganyika and, in consequence, the people have been more prosperous. This is especially so in Buganda and in eastern and western Uganda where the cultivation of coffee, tea and bananas is possible in addition to annual crops.

Forestry

Excepting the driest parts, the whole of East Africa was once covered with forest. This was Moist Forest in the highland areas, and even today traces of the old indigenous forest can be found on the plains and reserves. This type of forest covered only a small part of the country, whereas the Forest-Savanna Mosaic extended over much larger stretches, particularly in northern and eastern Uganda, and in southern and western Tanganyika.

Forests have been protected by reservation as Crown or State forests. Many timber species have been introduced but only a limited number have been able to endure the conditions found in East Africa. The chief value of the forests lies in the protection of water supplies and soils, which would otherwise deteriorate through neglect or misuse. The wood provides construction material (mvuli, podo and cedar are the most common) and cheap fuel. The practice has been to strip the productive forest area of all marketable produce, for sale as building timber, for firewood and charcoal. After this the land is cleared completely and plantations established. At the same time scientific clearing of trees on the edge of forests and the resettling of people goes on, particularly on the mountain fringes. The aim in all three countries has been to reclothe bare and eroded hillsides, to transform seasonal streams into perennial ones, and to prevent destructive floods.

Industry

Much unemployment or underemployment exists in rural and urban areas, the latter being aggravated by the migration of rural unemployed to the towns. The basis of the economy is concerned first with the primary industries of agriculture, and only secondly with industries connected with mining and forestry. Despite this situation, the region is fairly well advanced in the change-over from subsistence to a cash economy, due primarily to the European farmer and the development of estate agriculture for such crops as coffee and sisal. There is a large volume of production for sale, which has industries complementary to it, both primary and secondary. Inter-territorial trade demands have stimulated the growth of a number of local industries. Kenya has the largest amount of such trade, some of which is in machinery assembled in Nairobi. Tanganyika and Uganda have developed tobacco and sugar-cane industries partly as a result of this trade. Uganda has set up a cotton-piece industry using energy from the Owen Falls scheme, which also exports power to Kenya. The proportions of people employed in industry are at the moment small (Kenya 10 per cent, Uganda 12 per cent, and Tanganyika 13 per cent).

Town Life

Towns have grown up in East Africa as market towns, route and administration centres and harbours. Many have developed in proximity to the railways: such as Nairobi, Nakuru, Arusha, Moshi and Dodoma. Despite this, the population is still mainly rural and large towns are rare. Nairobi (300,000) is the largest city in East Africa. While its origin was probably due to chance, its establishment as the leading city of the region is now secure. Many overseas companies find it the most convenient site for their headquarters, and it has become an international air centre. The ports of Dar es Salaam (Plate 55), Tanga and Mombasa have grown up in proximity to breaks in the coral reef where suitable anchorages could be developed. In the case of Tanga the port has become the main outlet for the Tanganyika sisal industry sited a few miles inland, and Dar es Salaam and Mombasa

Regional Studies—East Africa

are now the seaward termini of the two great railway lines to the interior. Zanzibar town has developed on an anchorage suitable for dhows, and has become the centre for the processing of cloves and coconuts. In the interior the lake ports of Mwanza, Kisumu, Port Bell and Bukoba have grown with the increase in lake traffic. Elsewhere, the small market towns and administrative centres have changed little in the last twenty years. Exceptions are Nakuru in Kenya, and Kampala and Jinja in Uganda, which are developing fast. Nakuru is the focus of agricultural industries in Kenya; its position is central, close to Nairobi and within reach of the main farming regions. Jinja is developing as an industrial nucleus (Fig. 87). With available power and water it includes textile mills and copper smelting. Kampala, the capital, is the chief commercial centre of Uganda (Plate 53) and rivals Nairobi as a site for industry and business expansion.

J. W. Gregory, *The Rift Valleys and Geology of East Africa*, 1921; F. Dixey, *The East African Rift System*. The best general but short studies thus far are G. M. Hickman & W. H. G. Dickins, *The Lands and Peoples of East Africa*, 1960, and J. M. Pritchard, *A Geography of East Africa*, 1962. For special aspects see E. W. Russell (Ed.), *The Natural Resources of East Africa*, Nairobi, 1962; L. D. Stamp (Ed.), *Natural Resources, Food and Population in Inter-tropical Africa* (Makerere Symposium), Geographical Publications Ltd., Bude, 1956; K. M. Barbour and R. M. Prothero (Eds.), *Essays on African Population*, 1961; J. K. Matheson & E. W. Bovill, *East African Agriculture*, Oxford, 1950; *Report of the East African Royal Commission*, 1953–1955, Cmd. 9475, H.M.S.O., 1955; V. C. R. Ford, *The Trade of Lake Victoria*, East African Institute of Social Research, 1955; N. C. Pollock, 'Industrial Development of East Africa', *Economic Geography*, 1960, 344–54; Irene Van Dongen, *The British East African Transport Complex*, Department of Geography, University of Chicago, 1954; *Quarterly Economic and Statistical Bulletin*, East African Statistical Department, Nairobi; A. Gordon Brown (Ed.), *Year Book and Guide to East Africa*, London, Annual.

CHAPTER TWENTY-ONE*

Kenya, Uganda, Rwanda and Burundi, Tanzania (Tanganyika, Zanzibar and Pemba)

KENYA

KENYA has an area of 224,960 square miles and a population of 9·4 million people, most of whom live near the railway line in the south of the country. Extending from Lake Victoria in the west to the Indian Ocean in the east, the country can be divided into six regions.

The coastal plain is only about twenty miles in width, with the exception of the Tana Valley where it extends north towards Garissa. The total length from the Somali border to Vanga is about 270 miles. The coast is fairly straight; it has been uplifted in recent geological times to expose flat layers of sedimentary deposits which once formed the ocean bed. The coral reef runs parallel to the coast at distances varying from a few hundred yards to nearly a mile. Rivers such as the Tana and Galana cause breaks in it by depositing silt. Some smaller rivers enter the sea in sunken valleys which form the creeks and harbours of Mtwapa, Kilifi and Kilindini. Behind the coast are marsh and mangrove forest and, in parts, high grass and scattered groups of trees. The rainfall is plentiful (47·5 inches at Mombasa) but decreases inland and northward toward the Somali border.

Two features dominate the highlands east of the rift valley: the faulted block of the Aberdare Mountains, and the volcanic peak of Mt. Kenya. Both these mountain masses include considerable areas of moorland and, in the case of Mt. Kenya, alpine country. Thick forest lies between the moorlands and the intensively cultivated small-holdings of the former African reserves. Rainfall is high in the mountains but decreases towards the plains.

The enormous depression of the eastern Rift Valley, some 50–60 miles wide, is a region of internal drainage responsible for the large number of freshwater and saline lakes which occur on its floor. The eastern and western walls are at their lowest in the high central section, where the floor is nearly as high as the shoulders of the escarpments.

* By P. J. H. Clarke, except for Rwanda and Burundi by R. J. Harrison Church.

Nakuru, for example, is at an altitude of over 6,000 feet, with a rainfall of about 30 inches. To the north and south of this salient, the level of the land drops rapidly. Magadi (2,500 feet) and Baringo both have hot arid climates.

The Cherangani Range (11,300 feet) and the Mau Hills (10,070 feet) are summits of another fault-block to the west of the Rift Valley. In between them the level drops to not more than 7,000 feet and communications take advantage of this. Plateau lands lie to the west, which are the settled regions of the Trans-Nzoia and the Uasin Gishu, and the densely cultivated parts of the Kericho Highlands and the Nandi Hills. To the north-west of Kitale rises Mt. Elgon and the Basement rocks in this region are overlaid by rich volcanic soils. Rainfall is fairly heavy and well distributed (Eldoret, 42·2 inches).

The Lake Victoria Basin is a continuation of the Eastern Province lowlands of Uganda, which it resembles, and to the east it rises gently on the dip-slope of the Mau and Elgeyo-Cherangani fault blocks. Much of Nyanza is composed of Basement rocks but there has been some volcanic activity, particularly in the hills at the entrance to Kavirondo Gulf. This extends in a north-easterly direction towards Kisumu, and is a shallow trough formed by a small rift valley faulted in an east-west direction. Rainfall is spread throughout the year (Kisumu, 44·0 inches) with a maximum in April and May.

The north-east plateau includes both the Nyika hinterland and the scrub and desert of north-east Kenya. Mostly between 800 and 3,500 feet above sea level, it is interrupted only by 'inselbergs' and mountain masses such as Marsabit. It is formed mainly of Basement System rocks overlaid by sedimentary deposits, but there are considerable lava plains, particularly towards the Rift Valley. Rainfall is generally low (Garissa, 10·3 inches) but where mountains occur it is much higher (Marsabit, 31·9 inches).

Agriculture and Agricultural Processing

Because of the variety of local conditions in Kenya, with a rainfall ranging from under 5 inches to over 100 inches a year, practically any crop can be grown in some part of the country. The most productive districts are concentrated in the relatively small regions of the highlands, as the soil is usually too thin near the coast, and the climate in the extreme south and north too arid. European and Asian farmers play a major role in the farming economy but most of the future potential lies in the African lands and in the hands of their farmers now moving into lands previously only farmed by Europeans.

European farming. European farmers can be divided into two groups: the large ranches of up to 20,000 acres, and the smaller mixed farms of 1,500 acres or less. European ranches cover only a fragment of the land suitable for this purpose yet 60 per cent of the produce from the stock industry comes from these ranches. Cattle are sold to the Kenya Meat Commission factory at Athi River near Nairobi, which produces some 30,000 cans per day. Mixed farms have raised the country's livestock products of butter, bacon, pork, mutton and wool to a level where overseas markets are sought. At higher altitudes wheat and pyrethrum (Plate 49) are farmed, with oats and barley for stock feed and brewing. Agricultural processing from the products of these farms has created light industries in many parts of the highlands. Examples are the Lamuria cheese factory at Naro-Moru, the Uplands bacon factory near Limuru, and the Kenya Co-operative Creameries at Naivasha. The improvement in a healthy animal husbandry and the increase in stock has been most marked in recent years.

Figure 80 shows two farms in widely differing districts of Kenya. One is a mixed farm at 6,000 feet on the eastern slopes of Mt. Elgon in the Trans-Nzoia, where the rainfall is about 45 inches with good drainage on volcanic soil. The farm is not a large one (1,261 acres) but is mechanized and scientifically farmed. Machinery is worth £6,000 including 3 tractors, and the labour force is 70, recruited chiefly from local tribes. Maize alternates with wheat or sunflower for four years, followed by four years ley, and maize is never planted in successive years. Pyrethrum and wheat are two other crops well suited to this soil, and to the temperate conditions experienced in the Trans-Nzoia. Livestock consists of large numbers of poultry and pigs, nearly 170 head of cattle, and about 300 sheep. Land not farmed is taken up by forest (cypress) and open grassland, and the labourers have their own paddocks and maize fields to support their families.

The other mixed farm is at 5,700 feet on the edge of the black cotton region of poor rainfall (27 inches) to the west of Mt. Kenya at Nyeri. Drainage here is bad and the land is often useless for crops, being waterlogged in the wet season, and a dust bowl in the dry season. The farm is small, 527 acres only, including about 50 acres of forest on the slopes leading to the Nairobi River. The permanent labour force consists of about twenty Kikuyu and their families, with a fluctuating number of casual labourers. The soil on the plain is black cotton over murrum, which in turn lies above shale to an average depth of three feet. Unforested slopes leading down to the river valley take up 150

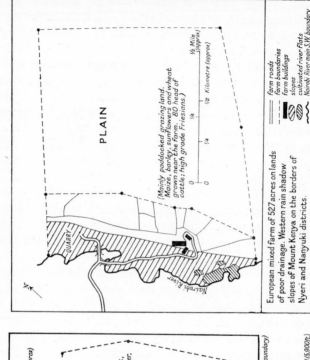

European mixed farm of 527 acres on lands of poor drainage. Western rain shadow slopes of Mount Kenya on the borders of Nyeri and Nanyuki districts.

(Mainly paddocked grazing land. Maize, barley, sunflowers and wheat grown near the farm. 80 head of cattle; high grade Friesians.)

PLAIN

QUARRY

Nairobi River

farm roads
farm boundaries
farm buildings
slopes
cultivated river Flats
Nairobi River main S.W. boundary

½ Mile (approx)

½ Kilometre (approx)

N

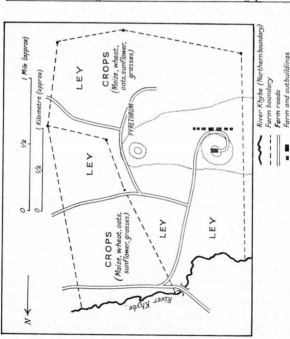

CROPS
(Maize, wheat, oats, sunflower, grasses)

LEY

LEY

LEY

LEY

CROPS
(Maize, wheat, oats, sunflower, grasses)

PYRETHRUM

River Khybe

River Khybe (Northern boundary)
Farm boundary
Farm roads
Farm and outbuildings
Contours of hill on which buildings erected (5,900ft.)

1 Mile (approx)

1 Kilometre (approx)

N

Fig. 80. European mixed farms on Mts. Elgon and Kenya

acres. About 5 acres are riverside flats growing market vegetables, often irrigated by furrow and pipe. Ridging and furrowing are almost essential to cultivation; otherwise these flats are useful only for grazing, the grass being mainly red oat (*Thermida triandra*). Maize, barley, wheat, sunflowers and vegetables can be grown, but no tea or pyrethrum, the altitude and rainfall being insufficient. Little rotation is practised, except on the flats. Most of the plain is paddocked and grazed by a high grade Friesian herd of 80 cattle, upon which the wealth of the farm depends.

African farming. In the past African cultivation concentrated upon growing mainly food crops such as maize, millet, sorghum, bananas, beans and cassava, but land re-development and the lifting of restrictions on African cultivation of some crops have changed the picture by increasing the production of cash crops especially coffee. A steady increase in tea planting by African growers is taking place in central Kenya, particularly close to the forests of the Aberdare Mountains and Mt. Kenya. African farms are mostly in the good rainfall area. Exceptions are the Masai Reserve and the Ukambani in the south; in the case of the latter intensive irrigation schemes are in operation.

Although soil conservation has long been advised by many agricultural officers, the majority of African farmers have little idea of crop rotation and the uses of manure. Not until the veterinary departments established breeding centres did the yield and health of cattle improve. From 1946–55 the Development Plan, aided by the government and enlightened chiefs, sought to enclose the land. Families have been resettled, grazing-management schemes introduced, water supplies increased and, where shortages existed, irrigation schemes have been started. The Mwea-Tebere scheme south of Mt. Kenya has 5,000 acres under crops, with a possible eventual expansion to 12,500 acres. Experiments on the lower Tana may lead to the irrigation of 300,000 acres of semi-desert near Galole.

Land consolidation has helped, especially in the Kikuyu land unit. Small scattered communities have been re-settled in much larger villages (Plate 50). The 'Swynnerton Plan', published in 1954, aims at multiplying tenfold the average cash income of 600,000 African families in the lands of high rainfall. The development of African co-operatives is another factor in the emergence of cash crops grown by Africans. The number of African coffee growers increased to nearly 75,000 at the end of 1958, with 20,300 acres under crops; of this, 14,235 acres were in central Kenya. Similar conditions are true of tea and fruit growing. Despite this, much of the remaining land is held under tenure by inheritance, leading to bad land use and fragmentation. Nevertheless, it is also true that substantial areas of central Nyanza are intensively cultivated and settled, although the traditional systems of land tenure still prevail.

A developing district—Nyeri. The aim in under-developed regions of Kenya is to change from subsistence to cash farming. Cash crops include coffee, tea, pyrethrum, fruit (particularly plums, peaches and pineapples) and wattle, which is now confined to altitudes of over 5,500 feet. African farming of this sort is encouraged by bank loans, self-help groups, co-operative societies, and the Wambugu Farmers' Training Centre near Nyeri. The two examples shown in Fig. 81 are typical. The difference between them is striking, not only in size but

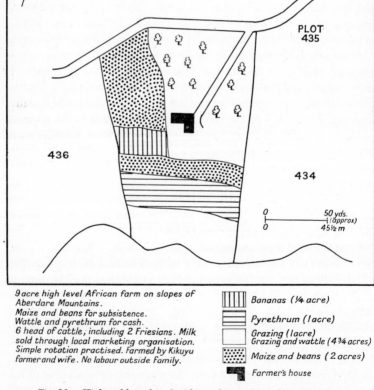

9 acre high level African farm on slopes of Aberdare Mountains.
Maize and beans for subsistence.
Wattle and pyrethrum for cash.
6 head of cattle, including 2 Friesians. Milk sold through local marketing organisation.
Simple rotation practised. Farmed by Kikuyu farmer and wife. No labour outside family.

Bananas (¼ acre)
Pyrethrum (1 acre)
Grazing (1 acre)
Grazing and wattle (4¾ acres)
Maize and beans (2 acres)
Farmer's house

Fig. 81a. High and low altitude African farms, Central Region, Kenya

also in the range of crops and general prosperity. The high level farm at nearly 8,000 feet on the Aberdare Mountains has approximately nine acres, well fenced and maintained. One acre is under pyrethrum, another under maize, and a quarter of an acre under bananas. The remainder is grazing land or under wattle trees. The cattle consist of a few Friesians, Jerseys and local breeds. They are milked daily, and the milk sold on the local market. No real planning is undertaken, although two crops of maize are never planted in consecutive seasons, but alternated with grass for grazing. The farmer counts on his wife and children for labour, and his overheads are negligible. The small low level holding of about 4½ acres is in a primarily coffee-growing area. The single cash crop of such a farm, and its more unreliable rainfall, may lead to considerable hardship in years of drought.

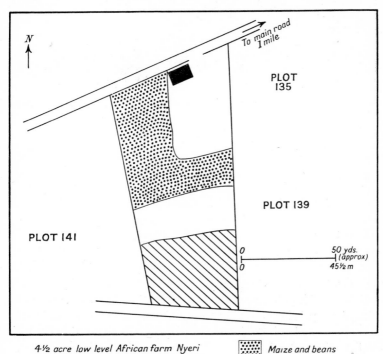

4½ acre low level African farm Nyeri District. A post land consolidation holding. Maize and beans for subsistence. Coffee for cash. Altitude 5,700' Farmed by farmer and his wife.

Maize and beans

Grazing

Coffee

Farmer's house

Fig. 81b

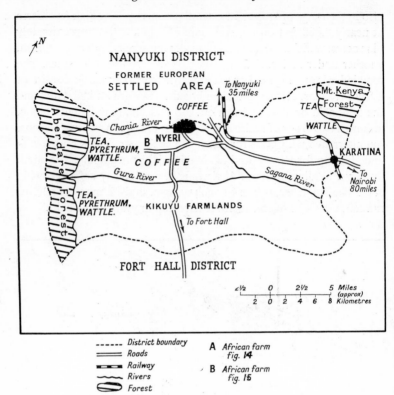

Fig. 81c

Agricultural cash crops in Kenya. Coffee, particularly from European-owned estates near Kiambu, is the chief export. The variety is arabica, which does well on the light dry soils of upland Kenya. Coffee factories are often on or near the estates, and production is being developed wherever the crop can be grown. Tea is mostly confined to the Kericho District, and to a small acreage near Limuru, but there is a large potential from African farms, of the Central Region. Pyrethrum is a high altitude crop, being best suited to altitudes of between 6,000 and 8,000 feet above sea level. Production of pyrethrum is confined to the Rift Valley, Nyanza and the Central Region. Sisal, principally from the Thika and Machakos districts, is also grown in Nyanza, the Rift Valley, and places on the coast. Wattle bark from the Central Region and Uasin Gishu, and cotton from Nyanza are other developing cash crops, while livestock and cereal products are chiefly produced in the Rift Valley and Nyanza. With its diverse climatic conditions Kenya

48. Herds of Masai cattle on the tracks to and from Ol Tukai swamp.

49. Pyrethrum (a kind of daisy producing an insecticide) on a European farm, Kenya.

50. Concentrated Kikuyu village with contour farming (p. 349), Kenya.

51. The soda Lake Magadi (p. 353), Kenya. This contains about 100 million tons of soda. Some 150,000 tons of soda ash (anhydrous sodium carbonate) and 20,000 tons of salt (sodium chloride) are produced per year, the lake being replenished by alkaline springs. The material is dredged, crushed and pumped ashore, where, after cleansing, it is calcined to soda ash.

is yielding a wider range of crops for export, and a considerable increase is expected with efficient farming in the future. An example is the growing of pineapples near Thika, which is making a bid for world markets in competition with the Azores and South Africa.

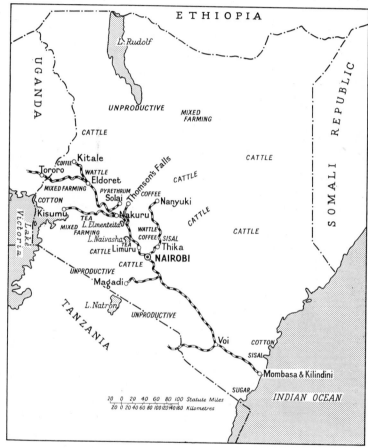

Fig. 82. Kenya; distribution of chief crops and railways

Minerals and Power

There is little mineral production in Kenya apart from sodium carbonate at Lake Magadi (Plate 51). Small quantities of diatomite are mined near Gilgil, kyanite near Taveta, asbestos from Teita, graphite from the Kitui region, and copper from the Macalder-Nyanza mine which also yields a little gold. The export of minerals represents

12

only 5·5 per cent of the total value of exports from the country. Power in inland areas is still obtained from small and costly hydro-electric plants. Such plants are inefficient, due to the need for expensive emergency diesel engines in times of drought. The Owen Falls power line now extends from Jinja through western Kenya to Nakuru and

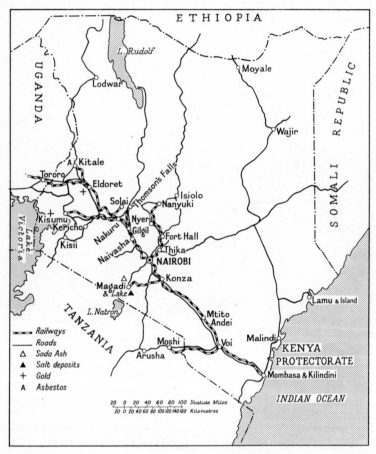

Fig. 83. Kenya; communications and minerals

Nairobi, but not as yet to the coast or to the central areas where the bulk of the population lives. Small plants such as the Tana River and Sagana Falls still serve much of the Central Region, while Mombasa is supplied with power from the Pangani River in Tanganyika. The discovery of further minerals, and the expansion of power lines to isolated districts depend greatly on the state of communications in the country. While the Kenya Highlands are well served by railway branch lines, there is still a paucity of good trunk roads. All-weather roads now serve many districts but their bituminization is a slow and costly process.

Conclusion

Improved land use is the key to the immediate agricultural future of Kenya, as the likelihood of substantial discoveries of minerals is remote. The work done so far by the African Land Development Organization (Fig. 84) needs to be implemented and extended. The cultivation of cash crops (coffee, pyrethrum and tea in African farming

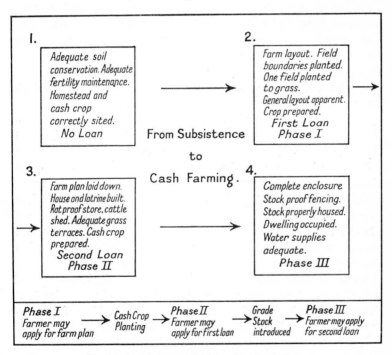

Fig. 84. Development of African farming in Kenya

areas in the highlands), can be increased by better planning and control. Any national agricultural programme must make use of the lands of great potential at present isolated in Masailand and other African areas. It must also follow the principle of a sound use of the land, regardless of race and creed.

The draining of resources during the 1952–9 Emergency and the increasing cost of imports, particularly machinery and other capital goods, require further investment, especially to develop irrigation schemes and improve communications.

The influx of people to the towns compels the establishment of industry to employ them. Nairobi, the largest town in East Africa, has built up a considerable local industry. Light industries such as coach building, light engineering, flour milling, biscuits, margarine, tobacco, clothing and furniture have been established in its growing industrial area. Nakuru has developed as the pyrethrum extracting and chief milling-centre, and Eldoret has wattle-extract factories. Mombasa has a new and important oil refinery, and also produces cement extracted nearby at Bamburi. Elsewhere, smaller factories have been set up in regions of high population. An example is the Bata shoe factory at Limuru; a subsidiary of the European company, the factory has been developed 21 miles from Nairobi but is accessible to it both by rail and road. It is in a region of high population and cheap labour, and produces an article of reasonable quality which finds a market among all sections of the community.

The new populations of these towns, living in overcrowded conditions at below subsistence level, increase the dangers of crime and disease, and there is under- and unemployment. Malnutrition in the African lands is severe, and may increase in the towns. As in other East African countries, there is a high infant mortality; 40 per cent of the children die before 15 years of age, and only about 9 per cent of the population is over 45 years of age. The value of a balanced diet was illustrated in Kiambu in 1958, when 200 tons of dried skim milk were supplied to the children; figures showed that the incidence of clinical malnutrition fell from 20 per cent to 4 per cent in two years.

So far, Africans have contributed little to the material progress of Kenya. Progress now will require the eradication of years of mutual distrust, and will depend on the ability of the African farmer to produce more, and the ability of the new administrators to create the best conditions for continued agricultural expansion.

UGANDA

An inland country, Uganda has an area of 93,981 square miles and a population of 6·8 million people. Smaller than Kenya and Tanzania, its importance has greatly increased since the building of the Owen Falls Dam and the control of the head waters of the White Nile.

Uganda has the most Equatorial climate of all the East African countries, and is essentially a plateau about 4,000 feet in height developed on rocks of Precambrian age. The country may be divided into three regions.

The Western Highlands extend from the Nile in the north to the Lake Kivu volcanoes in the south, with the Ruwenzori range rising to 16,000 feet in the centre. The Western Highlands are the result of the regional folding and warping which also formed Lake Victoria. From them there is a steep drop to the floor of the western Rift Valley, which is generally between 1,500 and 3,000 feet above sea level, and is partly occupied by Lakes Albert and Edward which are on the Ugandan boundary. The rainfall is generally high, with dry months from December to February and in June and July (Fort Portal, 57·0 inches).

The Central Plateau is an area of drained swamps and wooded hills in the Eastern and Buganda provinces, Lake Victoria occupying a shallow basin between the western and eastern Rift Valleys. Immediately to the north of it are large numbers of flat-topped hills, the remains of a former erosion surface. The swamps of Lake Kyoga separate this region from the higher plateau of northern Uganda. The rainfall pattern shows no real seasonal peak close to the Lake, whereas in the north there are distinct dry and wet seasons. The rainfall is heavy (Gulu, 60·0 inches).

Towards the Kenya border, the country is broken up in a series of volcanic ridges, sloping towards Lake Victoria. North of Mt. Elgon, Basement rocks form a wide plateau about 4,000 feet high with occasional higher peaks rising to 10,000 feet in the neighbourhood of Mt. Moroto and Mt. Debasien. Rainfall is high in the south but low in the extreme north-east, with semi-desert in the Karamojong.

Agriculture and Agricultural Processing

The leading agricultural products for export are coffee, cotton, tea and sugar, but of these coffee and cotton predominate. Most crops in Uganda are grown by African smallholding farmers but there are a few European farmers. Robusta coffee is best suited to Buganda and near Lake Victoria, but a small quantity of arabica is cultivated on the slopes of Mt. Elgon in Eastern Province, where conditions are drier.

Cotton is grown in many parts of Uganda and is best adapted to regions unsuitable for coffee and with a marked dry season. Approximately one-half of the total production comes from Eastern Province, about a quarter from Buganda, and a quarter from Northern and

Western Provinces. The cotton is grown on small plots, the cultivated variety being 'American Upland' (Plate 52). Ginning and oil extraction are undertaken locally and the new textile factory at Jinja is marketing cotton piece goods throughout East Africa.

Tea is confined to Western Province, particularly Toro District, and Buganda. Africans are being trained on the tea estates but the

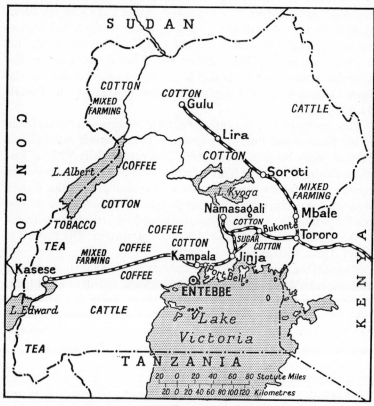

Fig. 85. Uganda; distribution of chief crops

bulk of the crop is still supervised by Europeans. Cane sugar is planted on estates near Jinja, the two largest being owned and run by Asians. Irrigation is not employed, the plantations relying on the even distribution of rainfall close to Lake Victoria.

African farmers produce tobacco and cure the crop on their own farms. The principal areas for this crop are in Bunyoro and Kigezi and in the West Nile Hills.

Away from the rich agricultural regions near Lake Victoria the number of cattle increases. The farms rely on cotton, groundnuts and simsim as cash crops, with the usual subsistence cultivation of maize, sweet potatoes, millet, peas and beans. Apart from the Ankole cattle, mainly owned by the Bahima, the bulk of the cattle are of the Zebu variety and are low grade. Tsetse has limited the number of cattle in many of the lower-lying regions of the country.

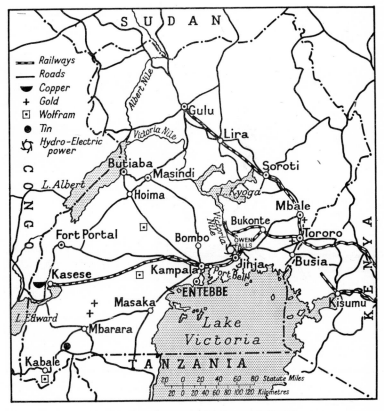

Fig. 86. Uganda; communications and minerals

Food production in Uganda has been supplemented by lake fisheries, particularly on Lakes George and Edward. The Nile tilapia, common in all Uganda's lakes, is caught and marketed through the Uganda Fish Marketing Association in Uganda and beyond.

Minerals and Power

Mineral wealth in Uganda is confined chiefly to copper from Kilembe and cement from Tororo. Mineral deposits are scattered throughout the country but reserves are poor. These range from phosphates and niobium at Tororo to iron, cobalt, tungsten wolfram, bismuth and beryllium in other parts of the country. A £200,000 geophysical survey is planned to determine the actual mineral potential.

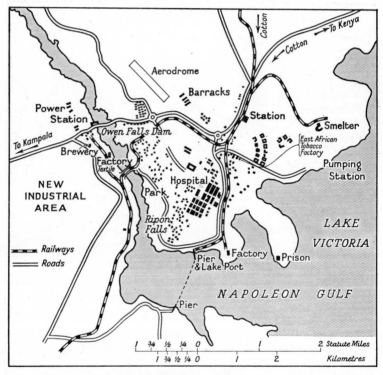

Fig. 87. Jinja; site and industries

Production of copper has risen considerably since the extension of the railway to Kasese was opened. Although the copper content of the ores is low, the new smelting plant at Jinja has made the industry more efficient.

Jinja is the site of the Owen Falls scheme which has ensured virtual control of the Nile headwaters, and established Jinja as Uganda's leading industrial town. So many industries are moving to it that the

52. Cotton picking in Uganda. Over 2 million acres are under this main cash crop.

53. Kampala (p. 361), Uganda, from Kololo Hill, with the Parliament Building in the centre.

54. Sisal estate on the Tanga–Moshi road, near Muheza, Tanzania. Sisal was introduced to Tanzania by Dr. Hindorf in 1893 with 62 plants which survived from 1,000 imported from Mexico via Florida and Hamburg. Sisal cultivation employs almost one-third of Tanzanian workers and accounts for the same proportion of exports.

55. Dar es Salaam (p. 370), capital and chief port of Tanzania, looking north-north-east. In the foreground are the deep water wharves and, beyond, the lighterage wharves, with the Asian trading and residential area. To the right is the more European commercial centre and then, in the trees, are government offices and residences, behind which is the golf course with few trees. Still farther are outer suburbs and, off shore, coral reefs.

industrial area sited on the west bank of the Nile is being constantly extended (Fig. 87). Shortage of capital delays schemes for supplying electricity to remoter parts of both Uganda and Kenya, but negotiations for loans are continuing. Light industry is increasing in Kampala (Plate 53), Jinja, Port Bell, Tororo and Mbale, to cope with the streams of immigrants moving in to the towns from the countryside.

The healthy economy of recent years has brought good communications, especially a fairly adequate network of good bituminized roads to most administrative regions, but the outlying agricultural districts are less well served. A newer branch of the railway runs north-west towards Gulu. The lake steamer services from Port Bell link with Kenya and Tanzania via the ports of Kisumu and Mwanza.

Conclusion

Uganda has been fortunate that stable market conditions have existed for her two major cash crops, coffee and cotton. She and Tanzania have regularly shown a Trade surplus, and this is reflected in the money available to improve public services. These advantages are directly due to geographical conditions of climate and relief not enjoyed to the same extent by the other East African countries. Since independence the picture has somewhat changed; although she is looking for new external markets, the possibility of a new East African trade area has created greater interest in inter-territorial trade with Kenya and Tanzania, and this is expanding. Jinja has not only become the industrial focus of Uganda but also of western Kenya.

Much of the progress in Uganda is due to the activities of the Uganda Development Corporation; their public relations; and the extension of their technical departments and laboratories to serve many important centres in the country have been outstanding. The technical help given to small African-owned industries has taken much of the time of the Corporation. In the future one of its functions may be to assist African farmers in more scientific planting of coffee and cotton. There is land available for further expansion but production can also be increased by better farming.

While the country should move closer towards Kenya and Tanzania in the economic sphere, the same aim does not seem to exist politically. Since October 1962 a stable government has been in power but this has been mainly occupied with internal problems, which are acute.

12*

The country is really a loose federation of small self-governing states, each with its own ruler. One of these wishes to secede and become independent. The Baganda feel that they should be in a position of control in the country due to their overwhelming numbers and healthy economy. It is conceivable that Uganda may in future disappear as a political entity and break up again into a number of small states. An East African federation may have the effect of dissipating this trend but the effectiveness of economic union depends upon political as well as economic identity of views between the three countries.

RWANDA AND BURUNDI

Rwanda (the more northerly of the two) and Burundi probably originated about the fourteenth century with the advent of the tall cattle-keeping Hamitic Tutsi (Watutsi or Batutsi) from Ethiopia via the regions east of the Victorian Nile and the Kitara Kingdom between Lake Albert and the Victorian Nile. The Tutsi, who comprise 15 per cent of the population, are akin to the rulers of other peoples along the western Rift Valley, for example of Bunyoro, Uganda. Two other groups had entered earlier: Twa Pygmies (one per cent) who are hunters, collectors and craftsmen, and the Hutu (Bahutu) who are Bantu and comprise 84 per cent of the population.

German rule began in 1897 and, until Belgian conquest in 1916, this was part of German East Africa, the rest of which is now Tanzania. Ruanda-Urundi became a Belgian Mandate from the League of Nations in 1919, and a Trusteeship from the United Nations in 1946. The countries became separately independent in 1962 as Rwanda and Burundi. They lie east of the western Rift Valley, on the plateaux of East Africa. Only the accident of Belgian conquest, administration, and economic linkage with the Belgian Congo, drew them towards lowland Western Central Africa from 1916 to 1962.

The countries rise sharply from the floor of the Rift Valley to its eastern edge, which is the Congo–Nile watershed. This has an average elevation of 6,000 feet, and a width of 12–25 miles, but broadens and rises northward to 14,660 feet in the volcanic Virunga (or Birunga) Mountains. East of the Congo–Nile watershed most of Rwanda and Burundi consist of a succession of plateaux. Streams flowing across them from the Congo–Nile divide are incised in the upper plateaux, but are wider and shallower in the lower eastern ones. Each of these terminates in an eastward-facing escarpment, at the foot of which are numerous marshes.

The climate, although similar to other areas on either side of the western Rift Valley, is characterized by exceptionally variable rainfall.

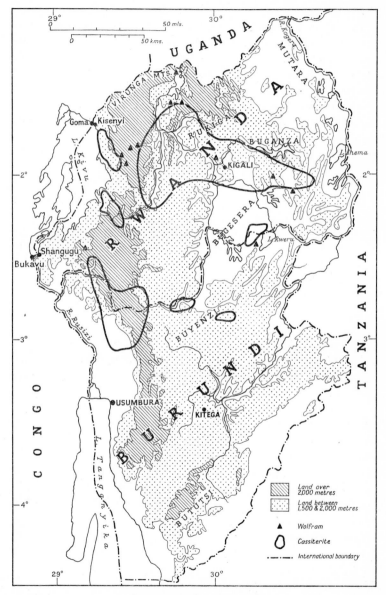

Fig. 88. Rwanda and Burundi

The valley has average temperatures of 73°F and 30 inches annual rainfall, the Congo–Nile divide 63°F and 58 inches (with heavier rainfall in the Virunga Mountains), and the central plateaux 68°F and 47 inches rainfall.

The volcanic soils of the west were originally richer than those derived from basic rocks in the east. Unfortunately, however, they are heavily leached because they lie on steep and exposed slopes; while those of the east, on gently eastward-sloping plateaux, have had gentler erosion. There is thus little to choose between them and erosion is everywhere severe; it is greatly aggravated by population pressure. The Congo–Nile watershed has Montane Grassland, while the eastern plateaux have Moist Woodland, both also degraded by pressure on the land.

The Peoples and Land Hunger

Rwanda and Burundi are the most densely peopled countries of Africa, they are among the poorest, and are the smallest independent ones. These are, in part, the consequence of their situation at the southern end of Tutsi migration. They are in a healthy area, and as they were also shielded by swamps and streams on the east and by mountains and lakes on the north and west, they were for long important refuges from Arab slavers who depopulated so much of the rest of East Africa.

Rwanda has an area of 10,166 square miles and Burundi 10,744 square miles. Their combined area is hardly one-third greater than that of Switzerland, whose population is about the same (5 million). The Congo (Leopoldville) with an area 44 times greater, and with great mineral and agricultural outputs has less than three times as many people. The average density of population equals that of France, which supports her population with many industries; Rwanda and Burundi are without these, have few minerals, eroded soils, are mountainous, and lie far inland on no routeway.

People avoided the hot arid Rift Valley, the steepest and highest parts of the Congo–Nile divide, and the swamps of the east-centre. Instead, they clustered at elevations of 5,000–6,500 feet, distributed from the north-west through to the south-centre in the shape on the map of a question mark. The density in these areas reaches over 500 per square mile, and this intensity—combined with dispersal in scattered family dwellings or amorphous hamlets—resembles northern Ghana, the southern Upper Volta and the Ibo country of Eastern Nigeria.

It is not surprising that, as from those lands, migration and emigration are extensive. The greatest movement is from Rwanda to Uganda, with lesser ones from Burundi to Tanzania and the Congo. Between 1940 and 1954 resettlement was organized from the densest peopled areas to Kivu Province of the Congo. Some of the initially seasonal migrants also stay abroad permanently, and there are 300,000 in Uganda, where they comprise 15 per cent of the employed population.

The Rwanda capital is Kigali, while the Burundi monarch resides in Kitega, both centrally sited in each state, but very small towns. The only considerable one is Usumbura (46,000) which was the capital for both under the mandate and trusteeship, and is now the seat of the Burundi government. The town is a European creation within the Rift Valley at the north-eastern corner of Lake Tanganyika.

The Economy

Given the high density of population, the eroded soils, the unreliable rains, and the interior situation of these lands, it is not surprising that famines were formerly frequent and still threaten. The Hutu grow beans, peas, guinea corn, sweet potatoes, cassava and maize; with subsidiary cropping of cucurbits, groundnuts, tomatoes, yams, onions and red peppers. Around their huts bananas are grown for food and for making beer. For the cattle-keeping Tutsi milk and butter are the main foods, with meat and blood from time to time.

Pastoral Tutsi and agricultural Hutu may live in symbiosis but more commonly an area is occupied by one group. Rukiga District in north-central Rwanda is Hutu and cultivated; Tutsi District in Burundi is upland grassland, good for cattle, and peopled by Tutsi, as are Bugesera, Buganza and Mutara districts of north-eastern Rwanda.

Climate and altitude also exert considerable influence, and up to about 4,500 feet the lowland food crops of Africa are dominant, with robusta coffee, cotton and the oil palm as cash crops. From 4,500 feet to about 6,000 feet, guinea corn replaces rice, and arabica replaces robusta coffee. Above 6,000 feet vegetable crops suited to lower temperatures and shorter growing seasons are common, while wheat, barley, tobacco, tea, pyrethrum and geranium are grown for cash, the last three mainly by a few Europeans. Arabica coffee trees are widely and wisely planted by regulation along the contours or roads as an anti-erosion measure, as well as being the main cash crop and export (75 per cent of the total). Robusta coffee is important only near Lake Tanganyika.

The continued co-existence of the nomadic and self-sufficient pastoralism of the Tutsi with the exclusively-cropping Hutu may be difficult as the human and animal populations grow, cropped areas increase, and pastures become poorer and fewer. It has been said that 'Cattle are murdering Rwanda and Burundi', but the ending of nomadism would involve a drastic social revolution among the formerly dominant yet minority Tutsi, to whom mixed farming involving crop cultivation would be degrading. The change is more likely to come from the agricultural Hutu (already politically dominant in Rwanda) learning to keep cattle.

Fishing is quite important on Lake Tanganyika, which, unlike some lakes, is rich in fish, and from which some 10,000 tons are taken annually, a significant food-supplement.

Rwanda and Burundi lie within the East and Central African tin belt, and tin and associated minerals are worked north of Lake Tanganyika and east of Lake Kivu, and account for one-fifth of the exports.

Most external trade passes through the port of Usumbura. Some goes by boat to Kigoma and then by rail to Dar es Salaam. Another route is by ship to Albertville and then by rail to the Congo or Kasai river routes through Matadi, or by rail direct to Lobito (Angola) or Beira (Mozambique). All are long, involve several trans-shipments, the crossing of several boundaries, and are costly.

Conclusion

These lands are dangerously over-peopled. The rapid increase of the population and the equally rapid deterioration of the soils in a mountainous environment pose formidable problems. The future of the pastoral and once entirely dominant Tutsi is economically and politically obscure. Their virtual enslavement of the Hutu was most severe in Rwanda, where a rebellion in 1959 put many Tutsi to flight, and a republic was proclaimed, but the Tutsi monarchy remains in Burundi. Independence is likely to prove costly for such tiny and poor lands and, though federation with Uganda would seem reasonable in view of kinship ties, the integration of an ex-Belgian type of administration with an ex-British one would be difficult.

TANZANIA: TANGANYIKA

Tanganyika, 361,800 square miles, is nearly as large as Nigeria, yet it has a population of only 10 million people. The coast from near

Vanga in the north to the Ruvuma River in the south is about 500 miles long, and from the Indian Ocean near Dar es Salaam to Lake Tanganyika in the west is a distance of about 700 miles. Most of the country is an undulating plateau nowhere much higher than 4,000 feet and in many cases much less. The eastern Rift Valley divides it into two portions, and the interior is broken occasionally by residual mountains and volcanic peaks.

The coastal belt is fairly narrow in the north but widens appreciably towards the centre, and is similar in origin and character to the coastal plain of Kenya. The harbours of Tanga, Dar es Salaam and Kilwa have been formed by drowned river creeks. There are a number of rivers, including the Pangani, Rufiji, Great Ruaha and Ruvuma, forming deltas into the Indian Ocean, or creeks of varying size and depth. Rainfall is heavy, particularly in the north (Tanga, 49·0 inches) but decreases towards the south (Lindi, 36·8 inches). The scattered forest, bush and coastal grass, so much a feature of the East African coast, become sparser in the south as the rainfall decreases.

Much of the south-eastern plateau is covered by the Miombo Woodlands which suffer intense tsetse infestation. The plateau is chiefly composed of sedimentary rocks, rises gradually towards the west, and has an average height of about 2,000 feet. Towards the coast there are many tors and inselbergs. Rainfall varying between 30 and 35 inches a year falls mainly between November and May. The long dry period inhibits cultivation other than of a shifting character.

The western plateau is separated from the south-eastern one by the spine of highlands running along the rim of the Rift Valley from Babati towards Mbeya. This plateau is higher, rising to 4,000 feet or more in places. Near Tabora the climate is arid, and the region is tsetse infested. Rainfall is unreliable, with a long dry season experienced after the April rains (Dodoma, 23·0 inches).

The Lake Victoria Basin is really an extension of the Western Plateau but, due to the proximity of large expanses of water, rainfall is much higher. The basin has a seasonal maximum in April but rain falls at all times of the year (Bukoba, 80·0 inches).

The highlands are concentrated close to the Rift Valley. They are more broken and isolated than those in Kenya and consist partly of volcanic outpourings, Mt. Meru and Kilimanjaro in the north, the Crater Highlands near the caldera of Ngorongoro further south, the Iringa Highlands of the centre, and the ranges of the far south culminating in the Poroto, Kipengera and Livingstone Mountains, all rising to over 9,000 feet. Rainfall is high, varying between 60 and 100 inches on the mountain slopes.

Agriculture and Agricultural Processing

Sisal, coffee and cotton account for a major share in Tanganyika's agricultural exports, followed by meat, cashew nuts, hides and skins, tea and groundnuts. Unlike Kenya, Africans have long been encou-

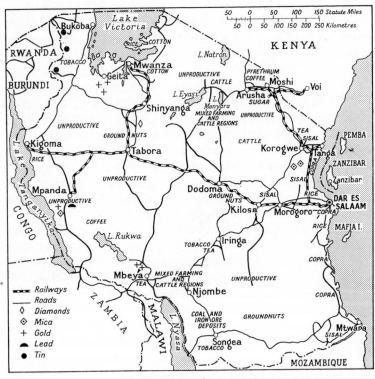

Fig. 89. Tanganyika; economic

raged in the cultivation of coffee and cotton. The Kilimanjaro Native Coffee Union was founded in 1935.

Sisal and tea are grown on plantations; coffee is both a plantation and smallholding crop. Sisal is cultivated at the foot of the Usambara Mountains in Tanga Province (Plate 54) and further south near Morogoro. It is also being planted in Lake and Southern provinces. Sisal fibre is used in the manufacture of rope, upholstery and carpets, but is also a raw material of paper, plastics and the drug cortisone. Sisal plantations occupy many square miles, and are linked to factories by light railways. Processing requires expensive machinery to remove waste from the fibre.

Coffee is mainly an African crop. Arabica can flourish in the dry conditions existing in Tanganyika at certain times of the year, and 80 per cent of it is grown on the slopes of Kilimanjaro, and near Arusha, and Oldeani; it is also being tried out in the Rungwe area of the south-west. Near Bukoba, where conditions are similar to those of Uganda, the crop is robusta.

Lake Province produces over 90 per cent of the cotton grown in Tanganyika, the remainder coming from Eastern Province. Tea is grown in the highland regions of Mbeya, Iringa and the Usambara Mountains. It needs a high rainfall of over 45 inches, and is limited to altitudes of between 4,000 and 8,000 feet. A tradition of skilled pickers has to be created for a crop of this nature. Tanganyika tea is not of the quality of Indian or Ceylon tea but is improved by blending.

Other cash crops are being developed; cashew nuts in Eastern Province and groundnuts in Western and Central provinces are two of the most important. Sugar cane is grown under irrigation of the Ruaha River; and in Northern Province, wheat, seed beans, maize and pyrethrum are being grown for export. A coconut industry is developing on Mafia Island opposite the mouth of the Rufiji, while tobacco, rice and rubber also contribute to the country's cash economy and minor processing industries.

The meat industry is supported by some seven million head of cattle, much of the interior plateau being more suitable for animal grazing than for crop production. About 97 per cent of the cattle are African breeds, although there are a number of imported herds, particularly in the upland regions of European settlement.

Minerals and Power

The mineral resources of Tanganyika are large but widely dispersed. Diamonds are the most important mineral export and about fifty diamond deposits have been exploited in the vicinity of Shinyanga, including the Kimberlite pipe at Mwadui, site of the famous William-son mine (Fig. 89). Gold is extracted at Geita in Lake Province, on the Lupa goldfield in Southern Highlands Province, and at Singida in Central Province. Copper and lead have been mined at Mpanda on a branch of the Central Railway, but the lead deposits are worked out and the mine was closed in 1960. Many other minerals are found in small quantities; among them are gypsum, kaolin, magnesite, salt, tin, tungsten and meerschaum.

Geological surveys have discovered the presence of some 250 million tons of coal in the Ruhuhu Valley near Songea and there are workable quantities near Tukuyu. The poor quality of the coal, and the distance of the deposits from centres of population, have restricted the use of iron ore deposits in the same region.

Hydro-electric power has been produced in the Pangani scheme and transmission lines are being built to Dar es Salaam and Morogoro. Power development is only in its infancy; lack of suitable rivers and their seasonal nature will mean heavy expenditure if further schemes are to be created. However, Tanganyika cannot rely on the use of small wood-burning stations or on the exploitation of her coal reserves to provide the country with cheap electricity.

The slow development of the country is aggravated by poor communications. The two railway lines from Tanga and Dar es Salaam penetrate the interior, and although they are now linked there are few branch lines, and both primary and secondary roads are often non-existent. The southern railway, constructed to serve the ill-fated groundnut scheme and based on the ports of Mtwara and Lindi, has been taken up.

Conclusion

African migration to the towns is less pronounced than in Kenya and Uganda, but is increasing near the centres of population. Morogoro, Dodoma, Tabora, Mwanza and Kigoma are growing. Given political stability and general prosperity, Dar es Salaam can be expected to grow substantially as a cultural, administrative and modest industrial centre, as well as a port. Stability in the Congo would also help the latter (Plate 55).

Tanganyika's problems, only partly similar to those of the other countries, are greater in scope. There are great distances between the centres of economic development in Tanganyika, and these foci are often separated by areas of low or unreliable rainfall and of tsetse infestation. By contrast, little of Unganda is dry, and little of Kenya has tsetse. In consequence, Tanganyika has some special problems. The union with Zanzibar has broadened the economy, but has posed other problems.

TANZANIA: ZANZIBAR AND PEMBA

Formerly a British Protectorate, Zanzibar and Pemba are part of the Republic of Tanzania. Zanzibar, itself 640 square miles in area, is about 50 miles long, while Pemba is smaller—380 square miles. Both islands are formed of coral rock, covered in some places with coconut palms and thick bush. Along the coasts are many inlets and mangrove swamps, interspersed with sandy beaches and low coral cliffs. The land rises to about 300 feet on the seaward side of the islands, evidence of tilting which separated them from the mainland. The land has risen in successive geological stages, and the most recent uplifts have killed

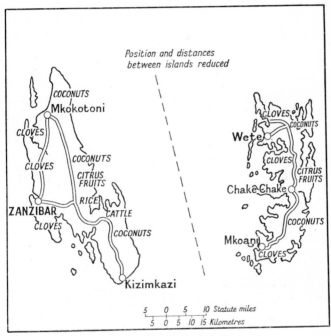

Fig. 90. Zanzibar and Pemba

some of the fringes of the coastal reefs. Evidence of complete submergence in recent geological times is afforded by the discovery of marine limestone on the highest parts of the islands. These are weathered into small ridges, and many streams flow into the western plain where the thin limestone soil merges into more fertile sandy loams excellent for the planting of cloves.

Agriculture and Agricultural Processing

The majority of the world's clove production comes from Zanzibar and Pemba. Introduced from the East Indies, there are about 80,000 acres under cloves in both islands, and over four million trees, bearing an average annual output of about 10,000 tons. Cloves are a planta-tion crop and Pemba is the larger producer, with four-fifths of the total. The towns of Wete and Chake Chake are the chief markets, and Zanzibar town is the selling and export centre. The distilling of clove oil is carried on in factories near the harbour. Over 60 per cent of the cloves are shipped to the East, although there is a consistent yet smaller market in Europe and America. They are used in spices, as a substitute for vanilla, and for cigarettes in Indonesia. The high rainfall of over 70 inches received by both islands is beneficial, most falling during the long rains (Masika) but the heat and humidity of the climate throughout the year precludes any distinct dry season.

Coconuts are the other major crop, particularly near the coast on the lighter sandier soils of Zanzibar. The nut is a basic provider of food to the inhabitants, the husk is used for rope and matting, and copra is the principal coconut export. The average annual production of coconuts is in the region of 13,000 tons.

A wide variety of food crops is a feature of both islands, and although most people live at subsistence level, the diversity of their crops affords them a higher living standard than the peoples of the neighbouring coast. These crops include bananas, tomatoes, mangoes, pawpaw, breadfruit, sweet potatoes, yams and cassava, with maize and millet as grain crops. The diet is varied by fish, which are caught in con-siderable quantities round the islands. Marshland is being used as rice paddy to an increasing extent, and over 25,000 acres of rice are under cultivation.

Zanzibar town (60,000) is an ancient Arab settlement. As a centre of the Arab dhow trade, many varied consumer articles are brought to the town to provision its tourist trade; dates, carpets, perfume, mangalore tiles, basketry, saris and dyes are only a few of these. Dhows take back coconuts, rope, cloth, sugar, soap and poles for building. The trade is strictly seasonal, the boats arriving with the north-east trades, and returning with the south-westerlies. Between these periods the crews make their homes on Zanzibar, and engage in farming or in the clove industry.

Mineral resources and power are non-existent on the islands, but as long as the world wants cloves Zanzibar's future seems reasonably secure. Efforts are being made to broaden the economy; the export of rice and the expansion of cocoa, fruit and vegetable cultivation are possibilities.

Zanzibar and Pemba have a combined population of about 300,000 people, of whom some 60,000 are Arabs and most of the remainder

African. Despite the dense population, standards of life are reasonably adequate, and the islands are almost self-sufficient. Little room exists for a further increase in the population, although the infertile plains towards the west coasts might support more cattle, providing meat which is at present lacking in the islander's diet.

The Future for East Africa

An East African Federation might give greater security to its members, but mutual co-operation is not new. The East African Common Services (formerly High Commission) have controlled a large number of services throughout ex-British East Africa from central offices in Nairobi, and, as a result, those mainland countries are closely associated in common technical and scientific matters.

Communications are poor, and at least Kenya has had adverse trade balances for a number of years. Poverty, malnutrition and disease are common, and aggravated by a general movement from the country to towns which are as yet incapable of absorbing large influxes of population. There exists a clash and cross-current of tribal outlooks; and of African, Asian and European cultures. It is too early to determine whether East Africa will move harmoniously, but all countries have now achieved nationhood and succeeded initially in overcoming many racial and social prejudices on their paths to independence.

FURTHER READING

For general East African studies which may include sections on the countries see p. 344.

Kenya: S. M. Cole, *An Outline of the Geology of Kenya*, 1950; *African Land Development in Kenya 1946–1955*, Ministry of Agriculture, Nairobi, 1956; *Enquiry into the General Economy of the Farming in the Highlands*, 1952, Government Printer, Nairobi, 1953; W. T. W. Morgan, 'The "White Highlands" of Kenya', *Geographical Journal*, 1963, 140–55; R. W. Walmsley, *Nairobi; the geography of a new city*, Nairobi, 1957; *Atlas of Kenya*, Survey of Kenya, 1959.

Uganda: C. C. Wrigley, *Crops and Wealth in Uganda*, *East African Studies No. 12*, East African Institute of Social Research, Kampala, 1959; S. J. K. Baker, 'Buganda—a geographical appraisal' in L. D. Stamp (Ed.), *op. cit.*, p. 344; C. & R. Sofer, *Jinja Transformed*, *East African Studies No. 4*, East African Institute of Social research, Kampala, 1959; B. S. Hoyle, 'The Economic Expansion of Jinja, Uganda', *Geographical Review*, 1963, 377–88; D. N. McMaster, *A Subsistence crop geography of Uganda*, Bude, 1961; *Atlas of Uganda*, Survey of Uganda, 1962.

Rwanda and Burundi: *Le Ruanda-Urundi*, l'Office de l'Information et des Relations Publiques pour le Congo et le Ruanda-Urundi, Brussels, 1959

Tanganyika: Anthony D. Marshall, 'Tanganyika', *Focus*, June 1962; J. F. R. Hill and J. P. Moffett, *Tanganyika; a review of its resources development;* 1958; International Bank for Reconstruction and Development, *The Economic Development of Tanganyika*, Baltimore, 1961; William A. Hance and Irene S. Van Dongen, 'Dar es Salaam, The Port and its Tributary Area', *Annals of the Association of American Geographers*, 1958, 419–35; *Atlas of Tanganyika*, Survey of Tanganyika, 3rd Edn., 1956.

Zanzibar: F. D. Ommanney, *The Island of Cloves*, 1955.

SOUTHERN AFRICA

CHAPTER TWENTY-TWO

Malawi

MALAWI was formerly the British Protectorate of Nyasaland. In 1953 Nyasaland was federated with the Rhodesias, but the Federation collapsed in 1963, and Nyasaland became independent in 1964, at the same time adopting the African name of Malawi.

THE PHYSICAL ENVIRONMENT

Malawi occupies the southernmost part of the Great Rift system, and extends onto the plateau edge to the west. It lies almost entirely upon exposed Basement rocks, with the exception of small areas of Tertiary and Recent sediments in the rift floor. Although the Basement rocks are extensively mineralized, no economic ore body has so far been discovered, and there is no mining in the country.

The northern part of the rift valley floor is occupied by Lake Nyasa, which is 1,565 feet above sea-level and some 2,500 feet deep. The lake is drained by the Shiré River which flows south to join the Zambezi, the valley floor dropping to just over 100 feet where the river leaves Malawi and enters Mozambique. West of the lake there is a narrow lakeshore zone, usually two or three miles wide, and then a sharp rise to the plateau which is about 4,000 feet above sea-level, though heights of 7,000 feet are reached in the extreme north. East of the Shiré in the southern part of the country, Mount Mlanje rises to 8,843 feet, and around its flanks and in the adjacent Shiré Highlands are the chief areas of European settlement (Fig. 91). To the north of Mount Mlanje, the inland drainage to Lake Chilwa constitutes the only drainage system separate from the Shiré.

Although the whole of Malawi falls in Miller's Tropical Marine type, there is little rain in the winter months, over 90 per cent of the rainfall occurring in summer. Most of the country has between 30 and 40 inches of rain per year, but on Mount Mlanje, the Shiré Highlands and parts of the lake-shore zone an average of more than 80 inches is recorded. Mean annual temperatures in the Shiré Valley and the lakeshore zone exceed 75°F, while the plateau areas average about 65°F. October is generally the hottest month, temperatures dropping

* By H. J. R. Henderson.

slightly with the onset of the rains in late October or early November.

The high rainfall tends to give strongly leached soils in most parts of the country, but there are several areas of red and reddish brown soils, mostly associated with areas of Tertiary sediments, and of relatively high fertility. One of these lies just north of Mount Mlanje, and another around Lilongwe; they constitute the only high-quality agricultural soils in the country.

Vegetation consists of Woodland-Savanna Mosaic, mostly of the moist group, though drier types cover the Shiré Valley. Surrounding Lake Chilwa in the south-east of the country is an area of swamp vegetation, subject to annual flooding.

ECONOMIC DEVELOPMENT

Malawi is essentially an African state, over 99 per cent of the people being Bantu negroes. The total population is nearly 3 million, including about 11,000 Asians, 2,000 of mixed blood, and 9,000 Europeans. Very little land is in the hands of Europeans (Fig. 91), for whom the climate is too warm in most parts, while there is no mining to attract them, and soils in the cooler areas are not attractive for commercial farming.

Lack of communications hampered development in the earlier years of British administration, but the building of a railway link to the port of Beira (Fig. 104) in Mozambique, completed by the Sena bridge over the lower Zambezi in 1934, provided a major routeway throughout the length of the country, for Lake Nyasa carries a regular steamer service linking the small ports along its 300-mile length with the railway at Chipoka. Since about 1950 much has been done to improve the main roads, and it is possible to travel on all the trunk roads at any time of the year; previously motoring was extremely hazardous in the wet season.

Farming

Africans are less concerned with commercial than with subsistence farming. Their main crops are millets and maize, rice in the lower areas, groundnuts, and such roots as cassava. The Europeans are chiefly concerned with plantation agriculture producing tobacco, tea and cotton. Virginia tobacco is grown in the Shiré Highlands, covering over 100,000 acres, with a production worth about £500,000 annually. Tea, grown at the foot of Mount Mlanje (Plate 56), in the southern Shiré Highlands, and recently established near Nkata Bay on the west

56. Tea picking at the foot of Mt. Mlanje, Malawi.

57. Kariba dam and lake which at the time was about half-full. The power house is under the south bank (left of photo), and the tail races can be seen emerging near the foot of the dam, which carries the third road crossing so far built across the Zambesi.

58. Spray irrigation of sugar on part of the Triangle Estates, Rhodesia. Regrowths ('ratoons') of cane are growing among old leaves ('trash') of the previous crop, which are left to rot and enrich the soil. They also conserve moisture and restrict weeds, but may harbour pests.

59. The mile-long Victoria Falls, in front of which are dry fall-faces of some of the seven earlier falls. Water from each fall escaped by a narrow gorge through the previous fall-face, and the youngest one is crossed by the international bridge.

shore of Lake Nyasa, covers about 30,000 acres. The tea estates give employment to over 30,000 Africans and produce 30 million pounds of tea annually. Cotton comes mainly from the lower Shiré Valley, where production is rapidly increasing, despite difficulties caused by the variability of the rainfall. Output has reached about 25 million pounds a year from 80,000 acres. Other crops produced for sale include maize and groundnuts, and African farmers have entered this market in recent years, while a few have also attempted to establish the chief plantation crops on a commercial scale. Coffee is grown in the extreme north of the country.

Fishing and Trade

Commercial fishing takes place on Lake Nyasa, where several firms operate motor-driven fishing craft. There is also a good deal of subsistence fishing in the lake, as well as in the streams flowing to it.

Malawi, having virtually no manufacturing industry and no mining, is an exporter of agricultural produce and an importer of manufactured goods, machinery, vehicles, textiles and clothing. Such small industries as there are produce textiles and consumer goods for the local market. Nyasaland's imports in the early 'sixties cost about £18 million per year, roughly 50 per cent more than she earned in exports. Malawi must take steps to correct this imbalance, either by reducing imports or by seeking elsewhere the economic support previously given by the federal government.

Conclusion

During the period of federation with the Rhodesias, Nyasaland was by far the smallest in area of the three partners, but with three million people in her 37,000 square miles was easily the most densely populated. As the population has grown, and pressure on Malawi's land resources has increased, more and more of her people have sought employment in the towns of Rhodesia and even in the mines and industries of Johannesburg. With her newly-gained independence Malawi finds herself with large labour resources, but very little employment to offer within her own boundaries. With the possibility of one or more hydro-electric schemes on the Shiré River, industry can be introduced to the towns, and mining may be initiated if commercial ore deposits can be found. But it seems that for some years to come Malawi will have more labour than she can employ, and many of her people will continue to seek work elsewhere, effectively adding to the country's 'exports' with their labour, for they bring a large proportion of their earnings back with them.

There is the possiblity of political federation with Tanzania and other East African states, but while Malawi has gained political independence, and severed her connections with Zambia and Rhodesia for political reasons, she must for a time remain greatly dependent upon other countries economically. Economic development will depend to a large extent upon her ability to show that she is politically stable.

FURTHER READING

References specifically on Malawi are few, and information has usually to be sought in works covering a wider area. The following may be suggested: F. Debenham, *Nyasaland, the Land of the Lake*, H.M.S.O., 1955; W. V. Brelsford (Ed.), *Handbook to the Federation of Rhodesia and Nyasaland*, 1960; C. H. Thompson and H. W. Woodruff, *Economic development of Rhodesia and Nyasaland*, 1954; A. J. Hanna, *The story of the Rhodesias and Nyasaland*, 1960; K. M. Barbour and R. M. Prothero (Eds.), *Essays in African Population*, 1961.

CHAPTER TWENTY-THREE

Rhodesia and Zambia

IN 1953 Southern and Northern Rhodesia, together with Nyasaland, were linked under a federal government. This Federation lasted only ten years, being dissolved at the end of 1963. Nyasaland became Malawi, and Northern Rhodesia the Republic of Zambia. Rhodesia (dropping the now superfluous 'Southern') remains a British Colony with full internal self-government. Here Rhodesia and Zambia are considered together, for they have much in common; however, their respective economies are also treated separately.

THE PHYSICAL ENVIRONMENT

Geology and Structure

Most of Zambia and Rhodesia lies along the eastern edge of the interior plateau, and most of Rhodesia lies upon exposed Basement rocks, which are seen also in parts of Zambia. These rocks are extensively mineralized, the mineral deposits worked including the gold and chrome of Rhodesia. Zambia, north-west of the line of the Muchinga Mountains, lies on rocks of the Precambrian to Cambrian group, including the Katanga Series in which the copper of the Copperbelt and the lead and zinc deposits of Broken Hill are found.

The Karoo rocks are preserved only where downwarping and rifting have protected them, as in the lower parts of the Zambezi Valley and in the Luangwa Rift. As in South Africa they have an economic importance in that they contain coal seams, which are worked at Wankie in Rhodesia. The only other group of importance is the Kalahari Sand which overlies the older rocks in a large area of western Zambia (Barotseland), and also penetrates Rhodesia along its boundary with Bechuanaland.

The most striking structural features are the faults which bound the Luangwa Valley. The lower Zambezi Valley is probably bounded by major faults too, but these are less evident in the landscape.

* By H. J. R. Henderson.

Relief and Drainage

Most of the area is plateau country lying at 3,000 feet or more. The areas below this level, the Lowveld, are confined to the main river valleys of the Limpopo and the Sabi in the south of Rhodesia, the Zambezi which divides Zambia from Rhodesia, and the Zambezi's northern tributaries, the Kafue and the Luangwa.

In Rhodesia the main core of higher plateau trends from south-west to north-east through Bulawayo and Salisbury, and forms the watershed between the Zambezi and the Limpopo. This area is mostly above 3,500 feet. From Salisbury south-eastwards to Umtali there is another higher area, all above 4,500 feet and reaching 8,500 feet in the Inyanga Highlands and nearly 8,000 feet near Melsetter. These highlands represent the edge of the plateau, which though steep is not as continuously spectacular as the Great Escarpment of South Africa.

In Zambia the main highland area runs, again with a north-east to south-west trend, along the northern edge of the Luangwa Rift. Here are the Muchinga Mountains, and to the north they are continued by a string of isolated areas at about 5,000 feet to the Abercorn Highlands near the southern end of Lake Tanganyika. These lie directly between the ends of Lakes Tanganyika and Nyasa, which are not joined by any through valley, though both are rift lakes. To the west of this line of upland plateaux, the surface drops gently westward towards the Luapula Valley, with much indeterminate drainage, especially in the swamps around Lake Bangweulu. Just west of the 'waist' of Zambia a minor watershed between the Kafue and the Luangwa drainage trends northward from Lusaka to the Copperbelt. From this the plains of the western limb of the country extend westward across the head of the Kafue Basin into the Kalahari Sand plains of the upper Zambezi Basin in Barotseland. Most of this area lies at about 3,500 feet, and is extremely flat and monotonous.

The main elements of the drainage pattern have been mentioned. The Zambezi gathers most of its waters from the north-western parts of Zambia and flows gently south towards the Makarikari Depression. Then, turning east, it covers about 100 miles before plunging from the plateau surface over the Victoria Falls, whence it continues in the Batoka Gorge and then emerges into the great Kariba Lake, the largest man-made lake in the world, 175 miles above the dam (Plate 57) which forms it. From the dam it flows on to Mozambique at the Luangwa confluence. The rest of the drainage is tributary to the

Zambezi, with three exceptions. The area north of the Muchinga Mountains belongs to the Congo drainage, mostly through Lake Mweru. South of the Rhodesian Highveld the drainage is either to the Sabi or to the Limpopo.

River transport has played little part in the development of the country. The Zambezi is interrupted not only by the Victoria Falls (Plate 59), but by several gorges and rapids, and by the Quebrabasa Rapids in Mozambique which form the effective head of navigation. The upper portion is used mostly by African canoes.

Climate

Although the two countries extend 1,000 miles from north to south, and their east-west dimension is almost as great, the whole falls within two of Miller's climatic types. These are Tropical Marine in the east, and Tropical Continental in the west. The distinction is a narrow one, for while a little rain may fall in the winter months in the eastern areas, the whole area receives more than 90 per cent of its rainfall in the summer six months.

Rainfall totals vary from less than 16 inches in the Limpopo Valley in the south to about 60 inches in parts of Zambia. The main valleys have a lower rainfall than the surrounding areas, so that most of the Zambezi and Luangwa valleys have less than 24 inches, while parts of the Limpopo and Sabi valleys receive less than 16 inches. In the drier areas variability of rainfall is a serious problem, but water shortage as a result of poor rains occurs over most of the plateau from time to time.

The rainy season from November to April strongly influences the seasonal variations of temperature. The cool season starts late in May as a rule, with clear skies at night and consequent radiation cooling, which may occasionally give ground frosts in Rhodesia and more rarely in Zambia. August to October are generally much warmer, and constitute the hot season. The influx of shallow layers of mT air at this time increases the humidity and cloudiness, and thunderstorms may occur, especially towards the end of the period and in the west of Zambia. The main rainy season starts in November or December, and is associated with the southward migration of the ITCZ. Rain then occurs on an average of half the days until the rains begin to die out in March. There follows a short post-rainy season with fairly moist air at first, so that convection clouds build up during the day and rain may result, but the generally decreased cloudiness leads to a rise in day-time temperatures, especially in the north, while night temperatures begin to drop. In May, day temperatures begin to diminish too, until the cool season starts again.

Mean annual temperatures are highest in the Zambezi and Luangwa valleys where they exceed 75°F. Only the higher plateau areas have an average below 70°F, and European settlement in Rhodesia is mostly above 3,500 feet, while in Zambia there is little below 4,000 feet. Mean temperatures can tell only part of the story, and it is useful to inspect the monthly means for a few stations. Those quoted are for January, July and October, the last being usually the hottest month.

	Alt. (feet)	Mean temperature (°F)		
		Jan.	July	Oct.
Beitbridge, Rhodesia	1,505	81·1	61·4	77·6
Bulawayo, Rhodesia	4,405	70·1	56·5	71·7
Wankie, Rhodesia	2,567	78·0	66·5	84·6
Ndola, Zambia	4,174	68·9	63·4	73·6

The effects of altitude are easily seen along the traverse from Beitbridge in the south to Ndola in the north, and also between the three stations in Rhodesia. Beitbridge lies in the very dry part of the Limpopo Valley and has a climate more subtropical than tropical, with January the hottest month, not October. The other stations exhibit a drop in temperature at the onset of the rains, and have annual ranges of 12 to 15° compared with the 20° of Beitbridge, except Wankie in the Zambezi Valley which also lies in a drier area, and has a range of 18°.

Soils and Vegetation

High temperatures and moderate to high rainfall usually lead to heavily leached and infertile soils. This is true of those developed on Kalahari Sand in the west, and of the soils of the Zambian Plateau which are lateritic in type, as are most of the soils of the Rhodesian Highveld. The lower parts of the main river valleys usually have reddish or brown soils of higher fertility, for leaching is less active in these areas of rather lower rainfall, and the higher average temperatures cause faster weathering and plant growth, both providing more plant-nutrients to the soil.

Almost the whole area is covered by Woodland-Savanna Mosaic, mostly of the moist group. The dry types are confined to the lower areas of the Limpopo, Zambezi, and Luangwa valleys. Swamp vegetation characterizes a number of areas in Zambia in the Bang-weulu Swamps and the upper basins of the Zambezi and Kafue rivers. Isolated patches of Montane Forest and Grassland top the highlands of Melsetter and Inyanga. Consequently, large-scale cultivation is not easy, and pastoral farming predominates in most areas.

PEOPLES

More than 90 per cent of the peoples are Bantu negroes. The population figures below show that there are very few Coloured and Asian

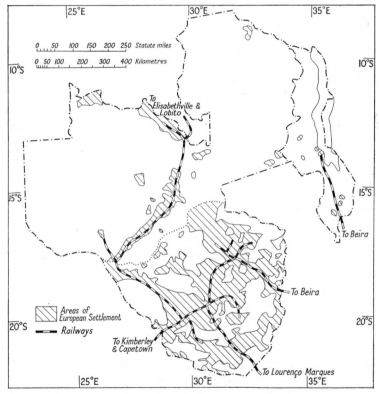

Fig. 91. European settlement areas in Zambia, Rhodesia and Malawi
Most Europeans live in the developed areas near the railways. Only Rhodesia has a large proportion of land in European ownership

people, and Europeans constitute only 5·6 per cent of the population in Rhodesia and 3 per cent in Zambia. Nevertheless, Europeans are important in all forms of economic development.

	Area	Population in thousands				
	sq. miles	European	African	Coloured	Asian	Total
Rhodesia	150,333	221	3,610	11	7	3,849
Zambia	290,410	75	2,430	2	8	2,515

European settlement did not begin until about 1890, when a group of settlers organized by Cecil Rhodes reached the site of modern Salisbury. Before this, few Europeans had entered the area, and these had been mainly missionaries and prospectors. The best-known was David Livingstone, explorer and missionary, who discovered and named the Victoria Falls in 1855, and whose travels took him to Lake Nyasa by 1859. From 1890 onward white settlement took place mainly on the Highveld of Southern Rhodesia, and ten years later mining settlement began to develop in Northern Rhodesia, also chiefly on the higher land. These two areas have remained the chief areas of European settlement to the present.

Figure 91 shows the areas of European settlement to be mainly in Rhodesia, where in 1962 approximately one-half of the country was in the hands of Europeans, although they constituted only one-twentieth of the population. In both countries European settlement is mostly on the higher land and close to the major routeways, as is necessary for commercial activity, but the proportion of land alienated in Zambia is relatively small.

Most Europeans are town dwellers: in Rhodesia, for example, over 150,000 Europeans live in seven large towns, of which Salisbury (84,000) and Bulawayo (50,000) have most Europeans. The respective total populations are estimated at about 300,000 and 200,000. Apart from these two, only Kitwe and Lusaka, both in Zambia, have a European population of over 10,000.

ECONOMIC DEVELOPMENT

As in South Africa, the great majority of the African population depends upon subsistence farming, or upon employment in European enterprises, especially mining and industry. Consequently, the greater part of Zambia and one-half of Rhodesia are not developed beyond subsistence farming and stock rearing.

The interior position of the countries prevented development by Europeans until natural resources were found which would provide the incentive and attract the capital to build railways and open up the interior. The vast mineral resources, first of Rhodesia and

60. The Drakensberg escarpment at the approach to the Natal National Park, near Bergville. The crest of the escarpment is over 10,000 feet high, while the valley in the foreground lies at about 4,500 feet (see p. 403).

61. Effects of different grazing practices upon Karoo vegetation at Middelburg (Cape Province). Both plots grazed by sheep for 6 months per year; the one on left in summer preventing grasses seeding, that on right in winter allowing grasses to multiply. See p. 410.

62. Merino sheep on a farm at Graaf Reinet (Cape Province). The labourers are 'Coloureds'.

63. Vineyards in Hex River Valley, Cape Fold Mountains. See p. 417.

64. Near Umtata, Transkei Reserve, with round huts, garden patches, and most of the land heavily overgrazed. A river valley has cut deeply into one of the erosion surfaces of the marginal zone.

later of Zambia, provided this incentive which started the process of development. The first railway built was that from Kimberley through Bechuanaland to link Bulawayo with the Cape ports, completed in 1897. The line from the port of Beira (Fig. 104) to Salisbury was opened in 1899, and linked to Bulawayo in 1902, while the line north from Bulawayo reached Victoria Falls in 1904 and the Copperbelt in 1909. The only major addition since is the direct line from Gwelo via the Sabi and Limpopo Valleys to the Mozambique port of Lourenço Marques, completed in 1955 (Fig. 103).

With the building of the railways Europeans, mostly of British extraction, began to settle in the country, engaging in farming, mining, and in a variety of small industries to serve local markets. Economic development has in many respects paralleled that of South Africa, though a few years later because of the greater isolation of the area from the outside world. Indeed, a large part of their trade still passes through South African ports, and a growing proportion of their imports comes from South Africa.

ZAMBIA

Mining

By far the most important element in the economy of Zambia is the mining of copper, which is concentrated in the Copperbelt, a continuation of the copper mining area of Katanga. Production could not start until the railway reached the area in 1909, but large-scale development started in the late 'twenties, was interrupted by the economic depression of the 'thirties, stimulated once more by the war needs of the early 'forties, and has since progressed steadily. Electrolytic-copper refining was introduced at the Nkana mine in 1933, and three-quarters of the copper output is now so refined. Unlike Katanga all the ores are mined, although they are at a relatively shallow depth; there are seven mines in operation (Fig. 92), of which the most recent are Chibuluma (opened 1952) and Bancroft (1957).

The impact of mining on the landscape is considerable, for each mine has given rise to a complex urban area, consisting of an administrative zone, shopping and other service areas, as well as separate European and African residential estates.

The chief problems that have faced the Copperbelt are those of transport, fuel and power supplies. While rail contact with the outside world is well established, distances and costs are high. Despite this disadvantage, Zambian copper is the cheapest competing in world

13

markets. The power problem has recently been solved with the completion of the hydro-electric scheme at Kariba (p. 387).

The other important mining centre is Broken Hill, one of the oldest in central Africa. It enjoys good transport facilities, as it lies on the railway from Rhodesia to the Copperbelt. Lead and zinc are the main products, and manganese is also mined in the area. The only other mineral of importance is cobalt, which is a by-product of the Chibuluma and Nkana copper mines.

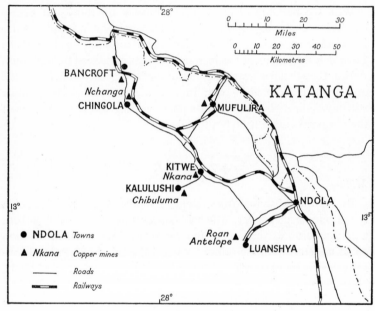

Fig. 92. The Zambian Copperbelt

Farming

The African farming population is concerned chiefly with subsistence economies. In Barotseland cattle herding is the dominant occupation, and cattle are also kept around the Kafue Flats and on the higher plateau on the eastern border with Malawi, but most of the country is affected by tsetse fly, and cattle cannot be kept. Most of the people therefore practice some form of shifting agriculture, using a very wide variety of crops. Indigenous crops include millets and kaffir corn, protein-rich pulses such as cowpeas, and a number of marrows, cucumbers and other vegetables; introduced ones are groundnuts, sweet potatoes and maize, which is rapidly ousting the indigenous grains. As some of the tribal traditions have begun to break down, some Africans have begun to produce crops on a commercial basis, especially maize and groundnuts; this trend has been most notable in the Kafue Basin.

European farming is limited to a few fairly restricted areas, and either produces for the needs of local urban markets, or specializes in high-value plantation crops for export. Cattle are kept for both beef and dairy produce on the Batoka Plateau and the Kafue Flats; both areas are close to the road and railway from Livingstone to Lusaka, and fresh milk is sent by road-tanker to the Copperbelt as well as those towns and to Broken Hill. Maize is grown south of Lusaka. Virginia tobacco is the most important plantation crop, and is grown around Fort Jameson, Abercorn, Lusaka and Broken Hill, while coffee is also grown in the extreme north of the country, in the Abercorn area.

Industry

Manufacturing industry has not made much progress in Zambia, although the refining of copper at the mine is an important industrial activity. Other basic industries include sawmilling at Livingstone, and cement manufacture south of Lusaka at Chilanga. The sawmilling industry is largely concerned with Rhodesian teak, a local hardwood used for railway sleepers, parquet flooring and the furniture industry, as well as producing some constructional timber. Other lighter industry includes cheese making in the south, and brewing at Ndola.

The Kariba Scheme and Power Supplies

Figure 93 shows the great importance of the Kariba scheme in the provision of power to mines, industry and towns in both Zambia and Rhodesia, for its capacity of 600 megawatts is four times as great as that of the largest thermal power stations. Until Kariba came into operation in 1959 the major sources of electricity were the thermal power stations at Salisbury, Umniati and Bulawayo in Rhodesia, and on the Copperbelt in Zambia. All relied upon coal from Wankie which had to be transported several hundreds of miles by rail to the power stations. Broken Hill also drew supplies from two local hydro-electric stations. The more isolated communities still depend upon diesel-driven generating stations, which are more efficient where demand is not continuous, and there are a few small hydro-electric stations in Zambia.

The Kariba dam across the Zambezi is 420 feet high, and holds back the largest man-made lake in the world (Plate 57). It lies between Rhodesia on the right bank and Zambia on the left, a fact which led to difficulties in reaching agreement between the two governments

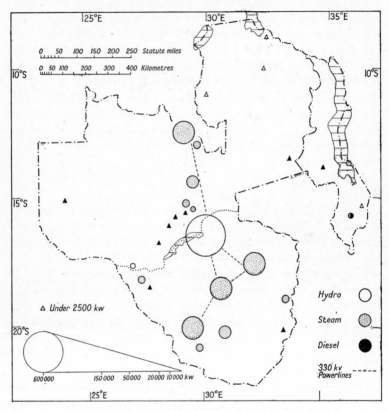

Fig. 93. Power stations in Zambia, Rhodesia and Malawi

and delayed the scheme considerably, It was eventually undertaken by the federal government. Plans for the future include a similar scheme on the Kafue River, entirely within Zambia, and it seems that the example of Kariba may well have brought forward the South African Government's plans to develop the water resources of the Orange River (p. 425). Earlier power stations were built in the main development areas, and thus located upon the major watersheds (Fig. 93). Kariba is symbolic of an awakening to the potentialities of the valleys, and the scheme provides for an African fishing industry, agricultural improvements, and tourism, as well as power generation.

Fishing

Apart from Lake Kariba, which yields over 2,000 tons of fish a year, there are commercial fisheries on Lakes Mwera and Tanganyika, and on the Kafue River. There is also much subsistence fishing by Africans wherever perennial streams allow fish to flourish. Especially noteworthy are the Bangweulu Swamps, the Kafue and the upper Zambezi. Much of the fish caught is dried, the small-scale production of dried fish in Zambia being estimated at 25,000 tons fresh weight per year, of which about 80 per cent is sold in the African markets of towns near the catching areas. The market value of the fish sold exceeds £2 million per year, and the contribution to the diet of the African population is very considerable.

Transport

Apart from the railway already mentioned, which links the Copperbelt southward to Bulawayo, and thus with South Africa and the Mozambique ports of Beira and Lourenço Marques, there is only one other line which gives access to the Atlantic at Lobito via Katanga and Angola, or alternatively through the Congo rail-river link to Matadi. A link from Lusaka to the railhead near Sinoia would reduce the distance to the copper-exporting port of Beira by 400 miles, but is not likely to be built as the Zambezi valley is a major obstacle, and there is already a good road. Politically more attractive is the proposal for a line from Kapiri Mposhi, north of Broken Hill, to link with the Tanzanian railways via Mbeya. A route has been surveyed, but it is doubtful whether the line could pay its way if it were built.

The road system has been greatly improved in recent years, and it is now possible to use the trunk roads at any time of the year. The road from Salisbury to Lusaka, Broken Hill, and north-eastward into Tanzania, is a part of the Great North Road, linking Cape Town with Nairobi. The roads are being increasingly used for commercial transport, as in the conveyance of milk from Lusaka to the Copperbelt.

Trade

Zambia is still a producer and exporter of primary produce, and an importer of manufactured goods, machinery and textiles. Nevertheless, the high value of the copper exports, worth about £110 million a year, far outweighs the cost of imports, and makes the value of tobacco exports at £2 million seem insignificant. Indeed,

Northern Rhodesian copper provided over one-half the total exports of the Federation between 1953 and 1963. This economic strength made secession from the Federation easy. The economic disadvantage of secession is that an economy based on one mineral is extremely vulnerable to any depression in world prices for that mineral.

RHODESIA

Agriculture

In Rhodesia, too, Africans are less concerned with commercial than with subsistence farming. Some, such as the Matabele in the drier south-western parts of the country, were traditionally warriors and cattle herders, and obtained what corn supplies they required by raiding weaker agricultural tribes, such as the Mashona to the north of them. With the coming of European rule and the end of tribal warfare, most peoples have taken to the cultivation of crops as well as cattle herding as increasing pressure on land has forced them into a more sedentary existence. In the lower areas, however, the tsetse fly has prevented the spread of cattle keeping, and the peoples have remained tillers of the soil, living by a number of primitive forms of shifting agriculture, though some are also hunters or fishermen.

Cattle ranching was one of the first activities introduced by European settlers, and in the drier southern parts it still predominates; Crop farming is a risky enterprise in these low-rainfall areas, though recently Turkish tobacco has been introduced successfully in Matabeleland. Most of this cattle farming is for beef, but dairying is important near the towns and along the main routeway across the Highveld from Bulawayo to Salisbury, where road and rail communications give rapid transport facilities to the towns and to dairy processing factories. Nevertheless, Rhodesia is not self-sufficient in dairy produce, and cheese and butter are imported from South Africa and from overseas.

Maize is the most important of the grain crops, being grown mostly in the moister areas of the Highveld, especially on the red soils north and west of Salisbury. Wheat is also grown as a winter crop, much of it under irrigation. However, the most important crops are plantation crops, especially tobacco, tea, cotton, sugar and citrus fruits. Virginia tobacco is grown mostly in the same areas as maize, the moister north-eastern Highveld, and is one of the most important elements of the economy, production being valued at over £30 million annually.

Turkish tobacco is a more recent introduction in the drier south-west, where it appears to be better suited to the conditions than maize, which was previously the only crop grown on most farms, although it is not the main maize-growing area.

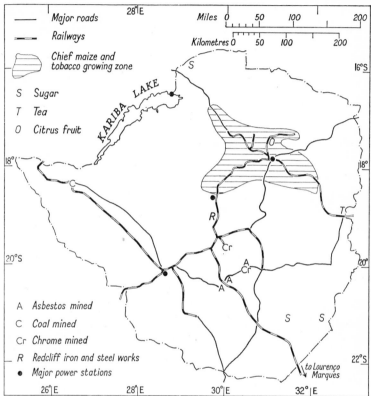

Fig. 94. Agriculture and mining in Rhodesia
Major roads are omitted where they follow a railway line. The Wankie to Bulawayo, and Lourenço Marques lines have no parallel roads

Tea covers 3,000 acres near Umtali in the eastern highlands, citrus fruits are important in the Mazoe irrigation scheme north of Salisbury, and sugar has become important in recent years on the Triangle (Plate 58) and Hippo Valley estates in the south-eastern Lowveld. The sugar is grown under irrigation (partly spray), using water from dams on the rivers which drain south-eastward from the Highveld. In 1963 Rhodesia, which a few years earlier was importing sugar, exported her first consignment of 20,000 tons to Canada as well as meeting all domestic requirements. Sugar has also been grown successfully in the Zambezi Valley below the Kariba Dam at Chirundu. Cotton is another crop suited to conditions in the Lowveld, but it is also grown on the richer Highveld soils around Gatooma and Hartley.

The main agricultural area, therefore, is the north-eastern or Mashonaland part of the Highveld. Elsewhere, intensive farming is limited to a few isolated estates specializing in particular plantation crops. Much European-owned land is either farmed extensively, or virtually unused. Some such land has already been transferred to African ownership to alleviate land hunger in some of the over-populated and over-grazed African areas of Matabeleland. Unless a more intensive use can be found for this land, further transfers will have to be effected in the near future.

Forestry

Timber production is of two main types. Indigenous species are worked in Matabeleland, producing mostly hardwoods (Rhodesian teak) for railway sleepers, mining timber and furniture. But the authorities are attempting to increase the output of exotic trees from plantations, especially eucalypts and tropical pines, as a good deal of constructional timber has still to be imported. These plantations are concentrated in the eastern highlands. Wattles, bark extracts from which are used in the tanning industry, have also been introduced in the eastern highlands, where over 70,000 acres have been planted since 1946. Much of the output, valued at £500,000 annually, is exported.

Mining

Gold, which has been worked in Rhodesia for centuries, was the mineral worked by the early European pioneers, as it was the one ore which could be conveniently reduced to a high-value low-bulk form, and so conveyed by the very limited transport facilities available. The small mines relied on local resources of labour and water, and used wood for fuel. Dreams of developing a mining centre comparable with the Witwatersrand of South Africa came to nothing because of the scattered nature of the workable deposits, and production remains sporadic along the Zambezi-Limpopo watershed. The annual output of over half-a-million fine ounces places Rhodesia seventh among the world's producers, and is valued at more than £7 million.

Gold mining lost its leading place among the mining industries in 1952, when the value of asbestos production first exceeded that of gold. Asbestos is a fibrous mineral widely used for all sorts of heat-proofing, and Rhodesia is the world's leading producer of high-quality asbestos. The mines are at Shabani, Belingwe and Mashaba, east of Bulawayo (Fig. 94), and the annual output of 160,000 tons is valued at £9 million. Chrome is mined at Selukwe and Mashaba, in the same area as the asbestos mines, and copper at Mangula and Alaska northwest of Salisbury. While some of the chrome is used locally in the Rhodesian Alloys works at Gwelo, the majority is exported, and the industry is in strong competition with Russian chrome which first entered world markets in 1963, but it is unlikely that the industry will be severely affected, as it is controlled by American chrome-using concerns.

There are large reserves of coal in the Karoo Series, but the only workings of note are at Wankie, on the main railway from Bulawayo to Zambia, the Congo and Angola. Development is attributable to the railway, for coal is a bulky commodity, and requires good transport links with its markets, which for Wankie are principally in Salisbury, Bulawayo and the other Highveld towns, and on the Copperbelt. Production declined by nearly 20 per cent in the first two years after the hydro-electric power of Kariba became available, and caused the closure of one mine in 1961. Production is about 3·4 million tons a year, valued at over £3 million, and a further decline is unlikely, for coke which is made at the mine-head is vital to the growing iron and steel industry at Que Que. The latter industry has relied mainly on imported ores, but large deposits have been opened up at Beacon Tor, near Que Que, from which ore is shipped to Japan.

Industry

Industrial development has been primarily for the home market, and has relied upon local products being cheaper than those imported, or upon protective duties. Most of the firms are small, though the trend is towards larger ones, and correspondingly the ratio of African to European employees is increasing, as the latter tend to be in managerial or supervisory posts. There are about 125,000 persons of all groups employed in manufacturing industry, while construction industries employ about 150,000 and the mines 100,000. Thus manufacturing has become a larger employer of labour than the mines, while the numbers employed in construction are indicative of the rapid development that is going on.

13*

The iron and steel industry is growing fast, the main centre being Redcliff, near Que Que. Here, three blast furnaces operate, and the works can produce all but the largest items of structural steel; for example, a new factory in Bulawayo required 800 tons of steel, of which 90 per cent was Rhodesian made, and the Redcliff works also supplied much of the steel for the Kariba Dam.

The degree of development of metallurgical industries is shown by the completion in 1953 of Rhodesian Alloys' works at Gwelo, where ferro-chrome alloys are now being produced for export to Britain, South Africa and North America. This has required the training of African workers to work to high degrees of accuracy with hot metals, and has shown the potential of African labour for complex industrial processes. The site of the works near the main railway line was influenced by the presence of local chrome ores and the Umniati power station. The coal for the latter, and high-grade metallurgical coke, both come from Wankie.

The rapid development of Rhodesia has encouraged the production of building materials, of which cement is an example, the output being close to a million tons a year. This comes from three works, and represents a ten-fold increase in production since 1946, when most cement was imported.

The increasing importance of oil as a fuel and as a raw material for industry led to the construction of an oil refinery at Umtali started in 1963, and crude oil is imported by pipeline from the port of Beira. Whereas previously Rhodesia imported all her oil in the refined state, the new refinery will eventually be able to produce all the country's requirements, and there are plans for a petro-chemical plant near the refinery to use the by-products of the main refining processes.

Other industries include sugar-refining at Bulawayo, Salisbury and Ndola, again increasingly using Rhodesian-grown sugar, food-processing, a variety of textile, clothing and footwear factories, together with the production of consumer-goods for the home market. Many requirements of agriculture such as fertilizers, fencing wire, farm machinery, livestock dips and feeding stuffs, and materials for the building industry are also produced, while several British motor manufacturers have assembly plants in the Salisbury area.

Water supply

The watershed location of the major towns and industries has led to difficulties in obtaining adequate water supplies. Water is drawn from the rivers which drain the Highveld, and large storage dams have been essential because of the irregular flow of the rivers. Lake McIlwaine on the Hunyani River was created in 1955 to ensure the water supplies of Salisbury for the next decade at least, and there are several new dams primarily for irrigation water in various parts of the country; an example is the Kyle Dam near Fort Victoria, which provides water for the irrigation of sugar and citrus crops in the Lowveld.

Transport

The development of the railways was outlined on p. 385, and as indicated there, the railways were the key to the development of the country. Nowadays motor transport is increasingly important and every railway except the line to Lourenço Marques is paralleled by a major road. The earlier roads were either gravel-surfaced, or consisted of two tar strips, and they crossed the rivers on low concrete causeways which were often flooded and impassable in the wet season. Many of the causeways have been replaced by bridges, and the main roads are tarred over long stretches, giving an ever-growing network of all-weather roads. The Great North Road enters the country at Beitbridge, and passes through Bulawayo and Salisbury, crossing the Zambezi by the Chirundu Bridge en route to Zambia and East Africa: together with the other trunk roads it gives year-round communication between all the major centres in Rhodesia.

Trade

Although Rhodesia has a more balanced economy than her northern neighbour, she does not have the vast output of minerals to give her a large favourable balance of trade. The total output of minerals is barely worth £30 million a year, and is exceeded by the value of tobacco exported. Thus, while trade figures for the Federation of Rhodesia and Nyasaland showed a credit balance of about £50 million a year. Rhodesia alone barely achieves a balance; this is the main reason why she always favoured the federal concept. Her trade is mostly with Britain, South Africa, the U.S.A. and Germany.

Conclusion

The economic arguments in favour of federation were always put most strongly by Rhodesia for, while she stood to gain by a share in the revenue from Zambia's copper, the Northern Rhodesians were not so firmly convinced that the more broadly-based federal economy was an advantage to them. But the main factor that brought about the secession of Malawi and Zambia was the political one.

Official attitudes to race relations in the Federation were more liberal than in South Africa, the declared policy being that of 'partnership'. But the school of thought which favours white supremacy is strong in Rhodesia, where the return to power of the Rhodesia Front Party in the elections of 1962 convinced the African politicians of the other two countries that their own people would fare better under independent governments. The consequences will depend largely upon the degree of economic co-operation that the independent governments are able or wish to achieve. Zambia will undoubtedly expand the industrial sector of her economy and Rhodesia will continue to develop hers, but must also look carefully to the possibilities of intensifying her agriculture, and alleviating land-hunger among her African population.

FURTHER READING

The only advanced geography text which claims to cover most of the Rhodesias is J. H. Wellington, *Southern Africa*, 1955, a two-volume work in which the first and larger volume covers the physical geography, and the second (now rather dated) the economic and human geography. It has no regional treatment of the subcontinent, and that part of Northern Rhodesia draining to the Congo is excluded. Among official publications, the most valuable is W. V. Brelsford (Ed.), *Handbook to the Federation of Rhodesia and Nyasaland*, 1960, containing 800 pages of articles by experts on a wide range of aspects of the federation. The annual *Economic Report*, Ministry of Economic Affairs, is a useful source of up-to-date information. Other references are: L. P. Green and T. J. D. Fair, *Development in Africa*, Johannesburg, 1962, especially pp. 125–132 on the Copperbelt; W. H. Reeve, 'Progress and geographical significance of the Kariba Dam', *Geographical Journal*, 126, 1960, 140–6; M. M. Cole, 'The Kariba project', *Geography*, 45, 1960, 98–105, and especially 'The Rhodesian Economy in transition and the role of Kariba', *Geography*, 47, 1962, 15–40; J. R. V. Prescott, 'Overpopulation and overstocking in the Native Areas of Matabeleland', *Geographical Journal*, 127, 1961, 212–25; R. W. Steel, 'The Copperbelt of Northern Rhodesia', *Geography*, 42, 1957, 83–92; and K. M. Barbour and R. M. Prothero (Eds.), *Essays on African Population*, 1961, which includes in particular J. R. H. Shaul, 'Demographic features of Central Africa', 31–48, and J. C. Mitchell, 'Wage, labour and African population movements in Central Africa', 193–248.

CHAPTER TWENTY-FOUR

The Republic of South Africa and South West Africa

THE former British Dominion of South Africa, which was declared a Republic and withdrew from the British Commonwealth in 1961, occupies the southern extremity of the continent. It consists of four formerly independent territories which are now the four provinces of the Republic: the Cape Province, Natal, the Orange Free State and the Transvaal. Together these cover 472,494 square miles, or more than five times the area of the United Kingdom. South West Africa is a former German colony and is administered by the Republic; its status as a Trusteeship Territory under the United Nations is not recognized by the South African Government, and although separately administered in most respects, it sends members to the Republican Parliament in Cape Town. The total area is 317,725 square miles, larger than any of the four provinces.

HISTORICAL OUTLINE AND THE PEOPLES

South Africa has many different racial groups among her population, and has become one of the main centres of racial problems in the modern world. The largest group is the African or Bantu people, and the others are the Europeans or 'whites', the Asians, who are mostly of Indian descent, and the Cape Coloureds, who are a very varied group mostly of mixed blood but including relatively pure-blooded descendants of the indigenous Hottentots in South West Africa.

The racial structure of the population is best explained in terms of its historical development. The first European settlement was started where Cape Town now stands in 1652, by Jan van Riebeeck and a party sent by the Dutch East India Company to establish a provisioning station for ships trading with the East Indies. From these people were drawn the first settlers, and in 150 years of Dutch rule, further Dutch, French and German settlers entered, settlement was extended north and east along the coastal zones and, to a limited extent, inland.

Strategic reasons led to the British occupation of Cape Town in 1795, and permanently from 1806. Dissatisfaction over the abolition

* By H. J. R. Henderson.

of slavery, and other aspects of British rule, led to further penetration of the interior by the Boers (that is, farmers) as the Dutch and other early settlers were known. They occupied the eastern parts of the plateau from the 1830s onwards, and established the republics of the Orange Free State and the Transvaal. The first major group of British settlers, numbering about 4,000, arrived through what is now Port Elizabeth in 1820, under a government-sponsored scheme to encourage settled farming along the eastern border of the Cape Colony. They settled mainly in the Albany district, centered on Grahamstown as a regional capital and, with the movement of the Boers inland, rapidly became the dominant group in this area. Other British settlers were established in Natal, which was declared a separate colony in 1856. Thus there are today two distinct groups of Europeans, with separate languages, Afrikaans and English, and different beliefs and customs concerning religion, racial relations and many other matters.

The Bantu are equally immigrants to the extreme south of Africa, and had little or no contact with Europeans during the first century of European settlement, for they were expanding and settling new lands from the north-east while the Dutch expanded from the west. Contact, and in due course conflict, occurred in the region of the Great Fish River in the late eighteenth century; this was the area known as 'The Border' to which the 1820 settlers were introduced in order to stabilize the situation. In the interior the Boers at first had little contact with the Bantu, for inter-tribal war had virtually cleared the plateau at this time, but occasional clashes occurred, with considerable loss of life on both sides.

The first indigenous people with whom the Cape Dutch came in contact in the seventeenth century were the Hottentots. From them the settlers were able to obtain cattle, but their nomadic way of life made them unsatisfactory as labourers, and they were never widely assimilated into the Dutch community, although mixed marriages were not unknown. Soon Malay and West African slaves were introduced, and these, together with the Hottentots and the settlers, formed the basis from which the Cape Coloured population has evolved. These people vary greatly in appearance from almost pure European to pure Negro; the Malays are the only group who have retained their individuality in Cape Town, probably because of their adherence to the Moslem faith.

The Asian population is descended mostly from indentured Indian labourers who were introduced to the sugar plantations in Natal between 1860 and 1913. There were also quite a number of craftsmen and artisans and a few professional men, who entered Natal when, as a British Colony, its shores were open to any Commonwealth citizen. The Indians have retained their identity and remain mostly in Natal, though some have gone to the major towns elsewhere, especially Johannesburg and Port Elizabeth.

Each racial group has a distinctive distribution. European farmers are found throughout the country, but most of the European population is concentrated in the towns. There is a tendency for the rural

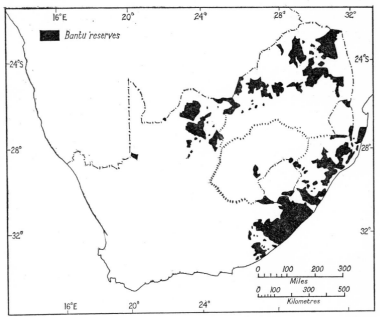

Fig. 95. The Bantu Reserves of South Africa
They are distributed in a horse-shoe pattern around the eastern half of the republic, many of them in the better-watered areas

areas to be Afrikaans-speaking and for the English-speaking Europeans to be concentrated in the towns. The Africans are generally restricted to the eastern half of the country, where the Bantu Reserves are concentrated. These lie in a great horseshoe (Fig. 95) from the eastern Cape through Natal and the Transvaal to the northern Cape, and within them land ownership is reserved to the Bantu. Although their 56,000 square miles is only 13 per cent of the area of the Republic, three-quarters of this has over 20 inches of rain and all lies in the summer rainfall zone. Thus, although some of it is too rugged for agriculture, the land in the Reserves includes much of the best agricultural land in the country. Despite this, the Bantu population is now too large to support itself by farming within them, and employment in industry is a major source of income to the Bantu. Industry is being encouraged to locate in or on the margins of the Reserves, which are intended to become largely independent 'Bantu-stans', with a substantial industrial sector in their economies. The first to be established is the Transkei, which has its own Territorial Authority in which Bantu are playing an increasing part in the administration.

The bulk of the labour on European farms is African, and lives on the farms, being provided with housing, a small amount of land to grow food on, and often the right to run cattle and goats on the farmer's land. Similarly both mining and secondary industry rely largely on African labour, and African townships are set aside in all the towns for the Africans to live in, as well as the privately-run mine compounds in which the mining companies house their labourers.

The western half of the country, though generally more sparsely populated, is the part in which most of the Coloured people live. They find work on farms and in industry as the Africans do in the east, and only in the larger towns (for example Cape Town) do the Africans form a major part of the labour force. The Indians are concentrated in Natal where they still work in the sugar plantations, as well as in many other occupations, but have set up as small traders in many places, especially the larger towns around the coast and in the southern Transvaal. They are prohibited from living in the Orange Free State.

The population figures, divided into racial groups, for the four provinces and for South West Africa are given below:

POPULATION BY PROVINCES (THOUSANDS)
CENSUS OF 1960

	European	African	Coloured	Asian	Total
Cape	997	2,977	1,314	20	5,328
Natal	340	2,156	43	394	2,933
Orange F.S.	275	1,073	26	—	1,374
Transvaal	1,455	4,602	105	63	6,225
S.W. Africa	73	428	24	—	525
Total	3,040	11,236	1,512	477	16,366
Per cent	19·2	68·7	9·2	2·9	

THE PHYSICAL ENVIRONMENT

Geology and Structure

Here, in what was the very core of Gondwanaland, the ancient rocks of the Basement Complex are seen at the surface only around the edges

of the continent, or where other axes of uplift cross the continent. In
the west granites and metamorphic rocks occur near Cape Town, in
Namaqualand and in South West Africa. In the east they stretch from
Swaziland into Rhodesia. Younger Precambrian rocks appear in
South West Africa, and along the Griqualand-Transvaal axis of uplift
which runs from the middle Orange Valley across the southern
Transvaal (Fig. 96). Both groups, therefore, appear only around the
margins of the main basins.

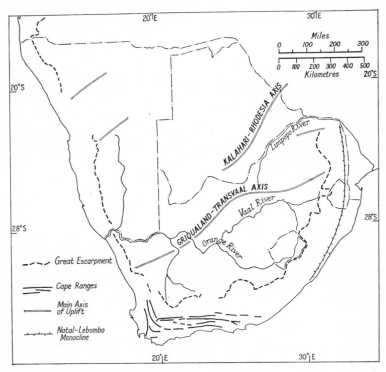

Fig. 96. Main features of the structure, relief and drainage in Southern Africa
(After du Toit and Wellington)

The upper Precambrian is important in that it contains several of
the major deposits of minerals, including the gold of the Witwatersrand. In the neighbourhood of Johannesburg, and beneath a cover of
the Karoo series in the Orange Free State, relatively gently folded
strata of the Witwatersrand series include the resistant quartzites
which form the east-west ridges of the Rand, and the conglomerates
which contain the gold. The gold of Rhodesia, on the other hand,

is found in highly metamorphosed rocks of Archaen age, and this is a clue to the probable source of the gold included in the younger Witwatersrand sediments.

In the Cape Fold belt of the south are sandstones and shales of Silurian to Devonian age, which were intensely folded in the Carboniferous age. Because the upper strata (Bokkeveld and Witteberg series) are predominantly shales they have eroded more easily and are preserved only in synclinal valleys and basins, while the sandstones of the lower Table Mountain series, being more resistant, form anticlinal ranges. The fold trends are parallel to the edge of the continental block, and thus also to the trend of the coast. The two main trends, paralleling south and west coasts, cross in the south-west Cape, and a rugged knot of mountains results, blocking the routes from Cape Town to the interior. The same types of rock are exposed in the core of the Natal monocline, in the coastal belt behind Durban.

The Karoo series takes its name from the Great Karoo of South Africa, although the series covers about 240,000 square miles, or half the republic. The rocks range from Carboniferous to Triassic in age, and stretch from the Cape Ranges to Swaziland, and from Kimberley to the Indian Ocean near East London. Over most of this area there is little or no folding, and the alternation of sandstones and shales gives rise to characteristic escarpments, capped by the harder rocks. Where the processes of erosion have been active at one level for a long time, flat-topped residual hills occur, entirely surrounded by the characteristic scarp. The unfolded Karoo rocks are preserved within one of the downwarped basins of the continent, but on the east of the basin the rocks are bent sharply down in the Natal–Lebombo monocline, a fold associated with faulting of the rift valleys further north and which runs the length of the continental margin from southern Natal to the Zambezi Valley. In this eastern area the upper (Triassic) part of the series contains numerous lava-flows; these rocks are very resistant and besides capping many an escarpment, give rise in the monocline to the spectacular north-south ridge of the Lebombo Mountains which run the length of the Transvaal–Mozambique boundary. Economically, the great importance of the Karoo series is that it contains the great coalfields of South Africa.

Following the break-up of Gondwanaland the sea first washed the shores of the new-born Africa, and laid down the marine Cretaceous beds of the southern Cape where their preservation in a number of basins in the Cape Fold belt is due to later faulting. Tertiary marine deposits are widespread along both southern and western coasts.

In the interior almost the whole of Bechuanaland and the adjacent areas of the Cape Province and South West Africa are covered by wind-blown sands and lake deposits of the Quaternary era. These represent the latest stage in the evolution of the continent, in which the products of erosion have filled the lowest parts of the great basins.

Relief

In this part of Africa the plateau nature of the continent shows superbly. Probably the most significant line in the physical geography of the subcontinent is the Great Escarpment, which separates the plateau from the marginal areas, and runs almost unbroken from the Zambezi in Rhodesia, around the southern edge of the continent and northward until it crosses the Cunene River and continues through Angola. The highest part is the Drakensberg Escarpment of Basutoland which overlooks the Natal coastal belt from a height of 10,000 to 11,000 feet above sea-level; almost everywhere the scarp-crest is above 5,000 feet, and there is a drop of 2,000 feet or more from crest to foot (Plate 60).

The area between the escarpment and the coast is usually about 100 miles wide and is characterized by flat surfaces sloping only gently towards the sea, interrupted by escarpments which divide one surface from the next, and by the river valleys which are cut below them. Such valleys are numerous in the wetter east, but few in the arid west. This is a stepped landscape, in which the erosion surfaces may be likened to the treads of the steps, and the escarpments to the rises. The stepped pattern is interrupted in two ways. In the southern Cape Province the Cape Ranges parallel the Great Escarpment, separating it from the sea, and although the stepped landscape is seen on the seaward side of the ranges, cut across the folded rocks, and the erosion surfaces may be recognized in the Great Karoo between the Ranges and the Escarpment, the Ranges are higher than the Escarpment, and the stepped form is not continuous from scarp-foot to coast. The other form of interruption is provided by the few rivers that break through the Escarpment from the interior plateau to reach the sea. The Cunene, Orange and Limpopo emerge from the plateau to cut straight across the stepped zone; the plateau edge is turned inland to form the valley-side, and the steps also penetrate up the valley.

Thus we distinguish two main physiographic zones; the plateau and the marginal zone. The latter falls into three main areas, which from west to east are: the Western stepped area, the Cape Ranges and the Great Karoo, and the Eastern stepped area.

It is in southern Africa that L. C. King has developed his theory of pediplanation as the mode of erosion in tropical areas, and has recognized the existence today of erosion surfaces which have their origin as far back as the Jurassic era, before the breakup of Gondwana-land. Parts of the crest of the Great Escarpment in Basutoland, South Africa and South West Africa, together with the Kaap Plateau in the northern Cape Province, are recognized as belonging to the oldest, or Gondwana surface; most of the remainder of the plateau, and parts of the coastal belt belong to the African surface, which is dissected by the Victoria Falls and Congo cycles of erosion which are advancing up the main river valleys. The Victoria Falls cycle takes its name from the great falls on the Zambezi which mark the nick-point of the cycle; that is, the farthest upstream that the cycle has so far penetrated (Plate 59).

Drainage

The interior plateau in South Africa is drained by two major exoreic river systems, the Limpopo and the Orange, while a substantial part of South West Africa belongs to the interior drainage of the Kalahari. In contrast, the marginal zones are drained by numerous smaller streams, each running independently to the sea. The characteristics of the main rivers have been described in Chapter 1. Each has a broad upper basin upon the plateau; each falls sharply as it leaves the plateau, the Aughrabies Falls on the Orange being among the world's most spectacular natural phenomena; each has a lower section of more gentle gradient as it runs to the sea. Neither is navigable, and none of the streams of the marginal zones can provide more than a rather limited river-mouth harbour, like that of the Buffalo at East London.

Thus, while the availability of water is one of the major factors in shaping the economic landscapes of southern Africa, water transport has never played any part in the development of the interior. Indeed, it is only quite recently that attempts have been made to harness the waters of the major rivers to serve any useful purpose, except on a relatively small scale.

Climate

Stretching over some 18° of latitude this area includes all the major climatic types of Africa except the Equatorial (A1) type (Fig. 6). Subject to variations caused by altitude and relief, the distribution of temperature conforms to the expected patterns, but the areal and seasonal distributions of rainfall are more complex, and since they provide the major climatic influences upon economic activity in Southern Africa, they merit careful consideration.

Rainfall. The annual rainfall (Fig. 97) is generally greatest in the east of the area, though north of 20° S. the isohyets trend east-west,

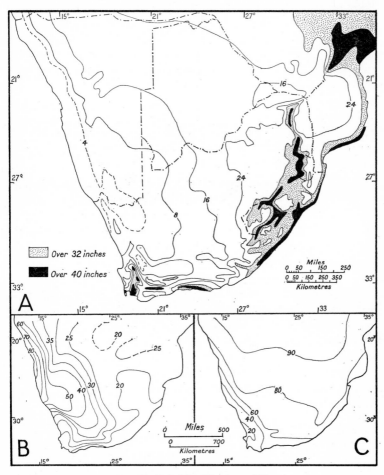

Fig. 97. Rainfall of Southern Africa
A. Mean annual rainfall in inches. Areas with under 32 inches are unshaded.
B. Rainfall variability. Mean deviation of annual rainfall expressed as a percentage of mean annual rainfall. Variability is highest in the drier areas. C. Seasanal distribution of rainfall. The percentage of annual rainfall occurring in the summer six months (October to March).Only the southern margin has reasonably adequate rain evenly distributed through the year. (Based on the official maps of the South African Weather Bureau)

with higher rainfall as the Equator is approached, so that in South West Africa the highest rainfall occurs on the plateau of the north. The outstanding feature of the pattern is the large extent of the drier climates in the west, and especially their eastward extension through the Limpopo Valley. Here the 20-inch isohyet reaches well into the Mozambique Plain, to within 150 miles of the Indian Ocean, and a large part of the valley around Beitbridge has only 12 to 16 inches per annum. In the south-east Cape, too, the main valleys have low average rainfall, and the 20-inch isohyet reaches the coast near Port Elizabeth.

Wherever there is less than 20 inches of rain, water supply is likely to be a problem for crops, animals and man alike; but similar problems are widespread in areas of higher rainfall because of the seasonal distribution of rain. Only the coastal belt between Cape Agulhas and East London has uniformly distributed rain, the area shown in Fig. 97 to receive between 40 and 60 per cent of its rain in the six summer months of October to March, for north of the Cape Ranges the rainfall is so low that the apparently uniform distribution is of no practical significance. Only in the south-west is there a winter maximum of rain (Miller's B_1 climate). Thus, excepting a narrow coastal strip in the east and south, all the areas with over 20 inches of rain per annum receive more than 80 per cent in the summer six months.

Because the rain falls in the warmer season, evaporation losses are high, and plant growth is rapid, but in the dry season ceases completely for lack of moisture. This means that water and supplementary feedstuffs must be found for livestock, and perennial crops can be grown only where irrigation is possible.

The areas of highest rainfall are the coastal belts of the south and east and mostly coincide with relief features that produce a proportion of orographic rain. Indeed, many of the larger river valleys of Natal appear to lie in some form of rain-shadow, although there are no large hill-masses to seaward of them, the valleys being cut into well-marked erosion surfaces. Average falls of over 50 inches are limited to a few coastal districts, the Great Escarpment on the eastern side of the continent, and the higher part of the western Cape Ranges. In other words, the rainfall is plentiful mostly in those areas which through their ruggedness are the least suited to farming activities.

Reliability of rainfall. It is of great importance to any water-user that he shall be assured of an adequate supply at all times; the more uniform the amount of rain from year to year, the easier it is to assure constant supplies. Much of southern Africa has very unreliable rainfall, and drought is one of the greatest fears of farmers, especially in the areas where the average is low, for since the rain falls mainly in isolated showers, the lower the average the greater the variability. If the mean deviation of the annual rainfall is expressed as a percentage of the mean annual rainfall, we have an index of variability, which in southern Africa ranges from 15 along the south coast to over 80 on the Namib coast of South West Africa (Fig. 97). In the drier areas the mean annual rainfall has little significance for the rainfall in any one year is seldom anywhere near the mean, ranging from nothing in a dry year to two or three times the mean in a wet one.

Temperature. Average temperatures reflect mainly latitude, altitude and continentality. In southern Africa the first two tend to counteract each other, for the plateau surface reaches its highest in the Transvaal if one excludes the eastern edge. Thus, temperatures are remarkably uniform over large distances, as the figures for Cape Town, Port Elizabeth, Bloemfontein and Johannesburg show. Comparison of the

	Lat.	Alt. (ft.)	Mean temp. (°F) of Hottest month	Mean temp. (°F) of Coolest month	Mean annual temp. (°F)	Mean diurnal range (°F)
Cape Town	33 °56′	40	70	55	62	17·5
Pt. Elizabeth	33° 59′	190	70	56	63	18·2
Johannesburg	26° 12′	5,751	69	51	61	22·3
Bloemfontein	29° 7′	4,670	73	47	61	27·4
Durban	29° 50′	16	75	62	69	14·9
Pt. Nolloth	29° 14′	23	60	53	57	15·7

figures for Bloemfontein with those for Durban and Port Nolloth illustrates the effects of continentality, all three being in almost the same latitude. The inland position of Bloemfontein raises the summer temperatures almost to the same level as in Durban, thus offsetting the difference in height of 4,656 feet; indeed, day-time temperatures are usually higher in Bloemfontein. But in winter the effects of altitude and continentality are added together, so that the mean temperatures in July differ by 15°F. Both the annual and the diurnal range of temperature are twice as great in Bloemfontein as in Durban. Durban and Port Nolloth are comparable in every respect except one: that all the mean temperature values are about ten degress lower at Port Nolloth which is on the west coast. This is typical of the western coastal belt which, north of St. Helena Bay, has temperatures below the normal for these latitudes.

In winter, the combined effects of continentality and altitude make most of the interior plateau liable to frosts for about three months, and only the coastal fringes can be regarded as frost-free.

The Factors Affecting Climate

The ocean currents washing the eastern and western coasts are partly responsible for the sharp contrasts in climate between the two coasts. The cool Benguela Current parallels the west coast, and there is much upwelling of cold water from depth which keeps surface air-temperatures low, and thus inhibits convection. The east coast is influenced by the warmer Mozambique Current which influences sea-temperatures as far west as False Bay.

Along the coast of South West Africa the surface air is so stable that it is virtually incapable of producing rain, but it is often capped by a layer of stratus cloud at about 5,000 feet, which may produce a light drizzle; convectional rain is a rarity in this coastal area of the Namib. The surface air at the coast is, however, seldom deep enough to over-flow the Great Escarpment so that the cooling effect does not reach far inland.

The understanding of southern African climates has taken a con-siderable step forward with the studies of S. P. Jackson and others of the pressure distributions and winds in the upper air. For example, we now know that at a height of 2,000 metres (6,056 feet) above sea-level, that is, slightly above most of the interior plateau except in Basutoland, the winter subtropical anticyclone weakens in summer, but does not disperse completely as surface measurements suggest; consequently, out-blowing winds prevail throughout the year. The weakening of the high-pressure cell does, however, allow more fre-quent incursions of modified mP air from the south-east, associated with shallow troughs or depressions moving in a north-easterly direction across the country in accordance with the westerly air-stream which prevails aloft. mT air is also drawn into these depressions from the Indian Ocean so that frontal lifting and convection combine to give showery weather in both types of air-mass. A second weather-type which brings rain involves the advection of mE air from the Congo Basin and the Indian Ocean around the eastern side of a low-pressure cell established temporarily in the interior; this, too, pro-duces showery weather. Persistent cloud and rain is less common, and seems to require simultaneously an outbreak of moist cool air from the south-east and a southward movement of mE air which glides up over the cool mP air to give rise to stratus cloud.

The very nature of these weather types which bring summer rain is such that each is likely to affect mostly the eastern part of the sub-continent, thus accounting for the higher rainfall of the east. None involves the onshore action of the South-East Trades which, in any case, are seldom deep enough to penetrate to the plateau. Rain falls as a result of disturbances in the 'normal' situation, not as a part of that normal situation.

These explanations go far to help us understand the rainfall régimes, but there remain many features that are as yet not satisfactorily explained, such as the low rainfall of the Limpopo Valley. It seems certain, however, that only study of the upper air, and not just of surface phenomena, can improve our understanding of these puzzles.

The winter rains of the south-west are better understood, for they affect mostly the coastal belt and have thus found adequate explanation in terms of surface meteorology. Almost all the winter rain of the south coast is frontal, and is brought by the depressions in the westerlies. These have little effect inland as they are deflected away to the east by the well-established anticyclone in the interior. Orographic effects must not be overlooked, however, for the heaviest rain falls on the higher ranges, while part of the lower-lying coastal area north and east of Cape Agulhas, although enjoying winter rain, receives less than twenty inches in the whole year.

Soils

Most South African soils are immature and not especially fertile. In the winter rainfall area soil-forming processes work slowly, and good soils are limited to the basins where the shales weather relatively rapidly into a soil. Lateritic soils predominate in the Lowveld of Natal and the Transvaal, while the rest of the moister summer rainfall areas have podsolic soils. In the drier areas of the Cape Province and South West Africa the soil-profiles do not show any layered structure, except where calcareous or siliceous material has been drawn to the surface in solution, and there deposited to give calcrete or silcrete layers. These are poor agricultural soils, even where water is available, as they are devoid of organic matter and require much fertilization. For this reason there are few areas of soil suitable for irrigation in the drier areas, except where alluvial soils occur in the larger river valleys.

Vegetation

Since pastoralism is important in the farming of both Europeans and Africans, the vegetation plays a large part in determining farming patterns; for example, cattle are grazing animals and can be kept only where grass is available, while sheep and goats can browse on shrubs and bushes. The temperate grasslands of the eastern part of the plateau, and the higher lands of the eastern marginal zone provide the richest grazing in the country. South Africans distinguish between 'sweet veld' and 'sour veld'; the former being superior grazing land because it remains nutritious when it dries off in the winter, unlike the sour veld. The sweet veld is found where the rainfall is lower; the wetter areas where the grass grows more vigorously tend to be sour. The dry Woodland-Savanna Mosaics of the northern Transvaal and coastal Natal are similarly sour, but provide quite good grazing; they are known locally as Bushveld.

To the west of the temperate grasslands much of the plateau is covered by Sub-desert Steppe of the type known as 'Karoo'. Along the margin of the two types the serious effect of uncontrolled heavy grazing has been demonstrated beyond doubt. Acocks has shown that the Karoo vegetation has extended itself eastwards by about 200 miles in the last 300 years or so, at the expense of the more valuable Grassveld. This is because animals will eat the more attractive grasses, which are thus prevented from seeding, while the shrubs of the Karoo multiply unhindered because they are not as palatable (Plate 61). A belt of Sub-desert Steppe also runs northward through South West Africa, changing slowly from the Karoo type to a tropical type in which a few low trees appear. It is mostly below the Great Escarpment and provides poor grazing. South of the Orange, along the west coast, the Karoo Succulent Steppe appears, consisting of succulent plants such as *Mesembrianthemum*, *Aloe*, and *Euphorbia*. Its value as grazing is extremely low, for many of the plants contain juices of unpleasant taste, and only where annual grasses occur is the grazing of much use. Coastal South West Africa and the Orange Valley below Upington are true desert, and bear virtually no vegetation except on the immediate banks of the river, where some small patches of irrigation are established and settlement is possible.

The northern Cape, and most of the plateau portion of South West Africa, are covered by Grass Steppe, and this provides adequate grazing for most of the year, provided that water is available for the stock to drink, though the number of beasts is small in relation to the area. However, it is easily over-grazed and can develop dense patches of bush if the grass is prevented from regenerating, the danger of this being particularly great in a dry year.

In the south-west, and as far east as Port Elizabeth, is a belt of vegetation very similar to some of the types found under comparable climatic conditions around the Mediterranean, and known locally as Macchia. Consisting mainly of low shrubs, it is quite similar in appearance to the Karoo type, but the shrubs have more leathery leaves and are all evergreen. A few species grow to heights of six to ten feet in favourable localities, but much of the flatter land within this zone has been cleared for cultivation. Like the Karoo Steppe, it has tended to extend eastwards under conditions of over-grazing.

Finally, there are a few small areas of temperate and subtropical forests, mapped in Fig. 7 with the temperate grasslands. The natural forests are dominated by slow-growing hardwoods, which were widely exploited in the nineteenth century and earlier, without being replaced. Today the Knysna forests are the only substantial indigenous ones, and these produce relatively little timber, as the Forestry Department has been chiefly concerned to remove dead trees and encourage regrowth.

However, there are large plantations of introduced conifers, especially American and European species of pine, and Australian eucalypts, the former mainly among the Cape Ranges and in the south-east Cape, and the latter along the Great Escarpment in Natal. A sawmilling industry has grown up in these areas and constructional timber is being produced, whereas earlier the principal output was in props and rough timber for the mines of the Rand, which first stimulated the planting of eucalypts in the Transvaal. Paper and rayon industries were established in Natal during the 1950s and draw on local forest resources for their raw material.

There are over half a million acres of black wattle (an Australian species of Acacia) grown at heights of 2,000 to 5,000 feet in the marginal zone of Natal and the Transvaal, in the area known as the mist belt. From the bark is extracted a substance used in the tanning industry, while the timber is used for pit-props. Most is grown on large plantations, but many farmers maintain up to a few hundred acres as a supplement to their farming activities.

THE ECONOMY

In South Africa hunting and collecting economies are virtually absent, the few surviving groups of Bushmen in the Kalahari, mostly in Bechuanaland, being the only people who live in this way. The majority of the African population comprise the Bantu who were traditionally pastoralists or agriculturalists, and who now often combine these types of economy. To these ways of life have been added those introduced by the European; these include further forms of pastoralism and agriculture, but the outstanding contribution of the European is undoubtedly in mining and industrial development, and the urban way of life these bring about. Other innovations are forestry and fishing. All of these have affected the African as well as the European; indeed their impact upon the unadapted African is generally more spectacular than upon the European, whose civilization has produced them. Just as we have seen that the African is usually better adapted to the physical environment of Africa than the European, so is the European better adapted to a social environment of which he is the creator. Nevertheless, the African is becoming increasingly a part of the European way of life, and already the phrases 'urban African' and 'tribal African' are commonly used in contra-distinction, as a substantial number of Africans become severed from all tribal connections and a new generation grows up which knows no environment outside the town. While economic activity is largely controlled by Europeans, it depends heavily on Bantu labour. South Africa's multiracial community has affected economic development in many ways.

By far the greatest proportion of the South African landscape is dominated by farming activity of one kind or another; in the drier areas pastoral farming dominates, and in the more favourable areas mixed farming. The Bantu Reserves are similarly mainly mixed farming areas, but mostly on a subsistence basis; whereas European farming is commercial. But this was not always so, for farming, like industry, could become commercial only when there were markets for its produce. Thus, except in the vicinity of Cape Town, commercial farming did not develop until mining of diamonds and gold brought to the country large numbers of people who had to be provided with food. From this beginning has grown up a highly developed farming industry, with a large production for export as well as for home consumption.

Livestock Farming

Both sheep and cattle play an important part in farming, the former numbering about 38 million in the Republic and 3 million in South West Africa, the latter 12 and 3 million respectively. There are also more than 5 million goats, of which 750,000 are Angoras which produce mohair.

Cattle. These are concentrated mainly in the eastern half of the country (Fig. 98), and both beef and dairy production are carried on, but commercial production has necessitated breeding of suitable animals, for the cattle which the Boers had bred from the animals they bartered from the Hottentots were essentially draught animals and only incidentally producers of meat and milk. European breeds have been introduced, and used both in pedigree herds and for cross-breeding with the Afrikander cattle descended from the Boer herds; the

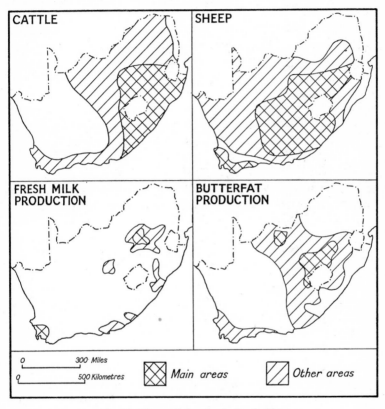

Fig. 98. Livestock farming in South Africa
The upper maps show areas in which cattle and sheep are important, the lower ones the production areas of milk sold for consumption in towns, and of butterfat sold to creameries. The distributions are explained in the text

breeds involved include Jersey, Friesian and Ayrshire for dairying, and Shorthorn and Hereford for beef herds. The crossing of Shorthorn and Hereford with the Afrikander has produced a new breed known as the Bonsmara, which is well adapted to the high temperatures of the Lowveld of the Transvaal.

While cattle farming is generally found only in those areas where grass forms a substantial part of the vegetation, it should not be thought that the physical environment alone determines the type of farming, and the dairy industry well illustrates this point. Milk for sale in the towns as fresh milk is usually produced fairly close to the towns in question, but because the price paid for this milk is higher than for other forms of dairy produce, some producers will send milk as far as 200 miles to the larger towns if adequate transport is available. This gives rise to fresh milk production in the south-east Transvaal (for the Rand), and widely in Natal (for Durban). There is also an important production area around Cape Town, where the market has led farmers to sow pastures because the local Macchia vegetation is not suited to intensive cattle farming. In other words, economic factors have determined the areas of production in this particular type of dairying. On the other hand, dairying for butterfat is much less controlled by the location of a market, for a creamery can be set up anywhere that butterfat can be produced, and its production is consequently much more widespread. Indeed, it has even spread into the margins of the Kalahari, where conditions are not suitable, but where the financial security of a monthly payment from the creamery at Kuruman or Vryburg has led farmers to attempt dairying in an area best suited to the breeding of beef cattle.

Beef farming has become much more important since about 1940 as the increasing use of tractors on farms has caused the abandonment of the ox-drawn plough, and beef is widely produced in all four provinces and in South West Africa. The most intensive production is combined with arable farming on the Highveld of the Orange Free State.

Sheep and Goats. Sheep farming, especially for the production of wool, is important in the Great Karoo and the eastern Cape. The main sheep kept is the Merino (Plate 62), imported in the early nineteenth century, and South Africa ranks with Australia among the world's leading wool producers. Sheep are kept in most areas except the northern Transvaal, and considerable success has been achieved in the breeding of dual-purpose sheep for the more favourable areas, and of sheep adapted to the rigorous conditions of the arid west. The latter include the native Cape sheep and the Blackhead Persian which have no wool, but are kept for meat and for their fat tails, and the curly-haired Karakul which is kept for the pelt of the new-born lamb, known in the fashion trade as Persian Lamb. Wool production has always been primarily for export, Port Elizabeth being the chief export marketing centre. East London and Cape Town also handle some of the exports which go mostly to Britain, though other European countries and Japan entered the market on a large scale during the 1950s. The clip of mohair, almost all from the eastern Cape, is also exported.

Ostriches. The other livestock enterprise of note is ostrich farming in the Little Karoo, which boomed in the first decade of the twentieth century, but declined rapidly when the use of ostrich feathers in the fashions of New York, London and Paris went out of favour in 1913. At that time, there were over a million birds in the country, but despite a slight revival in the industry there were only 56,000 in 1955. The feathers are mainly used for dusters, and Oudtshoorn is the main centre. The one lasting contribution made by the industry was in its financing of irrigation works in the Little Karoo, which now support fruit growing and dairying.

Agriculture

Grains. The principal grain crops are wheat and maize, in the winter- and summer-rainfall areas respectively. Maize is grown over most of the eastern half of the country (Fig. 99), but the chief area is the so-called Maize Triangle on the plateau of the northern Free State and southern Transvaal, roughly delimited by the towns of Mafeking, Middelburg and Bloemfontein. In the early part of the present century maize farming was carried on as a monoculture in this area, and the soils were badly depleted of their mineral content and eroded by wind. On many farms there are banks of the eroded material between the cultivated fields, where the blowing soil lodged among the grass. Crop rotation is now more commonly practised, and such crops as ground-nuts, sunflowers and lucerne are grown.

Maize forms one of the main items of African's diet, and is widely grown in the reserves as well as on European farms. It is also used as a cattle feed, and some is exported. While it is one of the major crops, the yields are not high by American standards; the average for European-owned farms in 1954/55 was only about 790 lb. per acre, and in the reserves a mere 210 lb. More intensive methods could produce better yields.

Most wheat is grown north of Cape Town in the Swartland, and on the coastlands around Cape Agulhas. In recent years much has been done to introduce it as a winter crop in the cooler areas of the high plateau in the east as well, and some new varieties do well under these conditions. While wheat is mostly grown for grain, the other winter cereals, oats, barley and sometimes rye, are more often grown for feeding to livestock in the form of silage, or for grazing.

Fruit Growing. The specialized cultivation of fruit is well-developed in South Africa; started to serve local needs, it has been expanded rapidly to meet the requirements of export markets. The 'Mediterranean' area of the south-west Cape is naturally suited to the vine, and

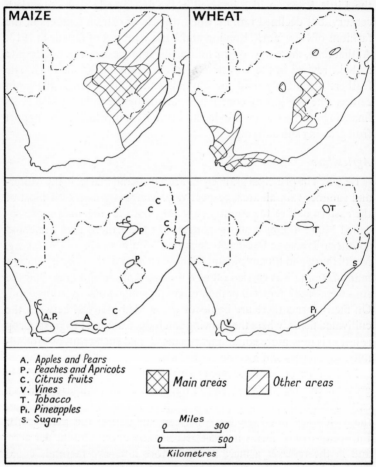

Fig. 99. Agriculture in South Africa

there are about 165,000 acres under this fruit, almost all in the Cape, though small areas are found under irrigation in the Transvaal. Many of the Cape vineyards are also irrigated, especially in the Little Karoo and along the Orange River. The south-western areas are mainly concerned with wine production, which has an annual value of over £5 million, of which £1·5 million is exported—just sufficient to pay for the

65. The central area of Johannesburg. Along the southern side is a line of waste tips from the gold mines, with industrial establishments between them. Beyond stretches the level sky-line of the Highveld.

66. Cape Town (p. 429). The original settlement was on the inland side of the made-ground behind the newer Duncan Dock. Multi-storey buildings are in the central business district, and residential areas on the outskirts. In the foreground are the old docks, in the background Table Mountain.

67. Port, railway station and part of the commercial quarter of Lourenço Marques, Mozambique (p. 441).

68. Multiple sand-bars in Mandrare Estuary, near Fort Dauphin, Madagascar. See p. 451.

annual imports of whisky! In the hotter and drier areas such as the Orange and Breede valleys, the fruit is dried to produce raisins and sultanas, while the Hex River Valley (Plate 63), on the main railway from Cape Town inland, is noted for its table grapes.

Apples and pears are grown in several valleys and basins in the Cape Ranges, where frosts usually occur in winter and there is an annual period of rest for the trees. The basins of Elgin and Ceres are leading areas in the west, and the Langkloof ('Long Valley') further east. Peaches and apricots are grown in the Great Berg Valley, and in many of the valleys of the Little Karoo where some irrigation water is used to grow oats or other crops between the trees for feeding dairy cattle. Deciduous fruits are also grown on the high plateau of the Transvaal and Free State, but are not as important as in the southern Cape.

The production of citrus fruits is significant in certain frost-free areas, most of which are irrigated. The most important areas are the Transvaal valleys draining to the Limpopo, but the south-east Cape has citrus in the Fish and Sundays valleys, and the Olifants valley of the south-west Cape is also a leading area. Over 90 per cent of the crop is of oranges, but grapefruit, lemons and naartjies are also grown. The total crop has in recent years amounted to about ten million cases a year, of which over two-thirds, worth about £15 million, is exported.

A variety of tropical fruits is grown, most of them for the home market, but pineapples in the south-east Cape and coastal Zululand share in the export trade, both as fresh fruit and canned. Bananas, avocados and guavas are among the other tropical fruits grown.

The fruit-canning and jam-making industries are important in such centres as Cape Town, Mossel Bay, and Port Elizabeth, close to the main growing districts.

Sugar. The Natal coastlands have over 500,000 acres under sugar cane which has been grown here for over a century. With modern intensive methods of production, virtually no other farming activity is found in the areas around the crushing mills situated at intervals along the coastal belt from Port Shepstone to the borders of Swaziland. This area is near the climatic limit for the crop, and most of the cane is grown within ten miles of the sea, which moderates winter temperatures and ensures freedom from frost. The bulk of the labour is still provided by Indians descended from those introduced half a century ago to work in the cane fields.

Other Crops. It is impossible here to discuss all crops grown in detail. Many require much capital, intensive farming methods, and

14

irrigation to make them profitable. Examples are tobacco, grown in the Transvaal districts of Rustenburg, Brits and Barberton, and vegetables in the latter two. Barberton, being in the Lowveld, is warm enough to grow vegetables in winter for the towns of the Highveld, fetching a high enough price to cover transport and a higher profit than local growers on the Highveld can secure in summer.

Cotton is grown in the Transvaal, both with and without irrigation, but has not proved ideal for the conditions. An important crop grown on irrigation schemes in the Cape is lucerne, which is made into hay and sold in areas short of animal feed; dairy farmers on the Rand, for example, buy large quantities of lucerne hay from the Little Karoo, Vaal-Harts and Orange River irrigation areas. Elsewhere, there are areas with specialisms, such as the growing of chicory, which is confined to the Alexandria district, east of Port Elizabeth.

Farming in Bantu Reserves

Almost all so far said concerning farming applies largely or wholly to European farms. In the Bantu Reserves traditional customs and methods have survived, often to the detriment of the resources of soil and grazing (Plate 64). Traditionally the land is owned by the tribe, and each man is allocated a homestead and an arable patch; the remainder is common grazing, and since wealth is normally reckoned in numbers of cattle, there is no limit on the number a man may keep. Consequently, overstocking has been frequent.

Cultivation is done almost entirely by the women using the hoe, and seed is usually broadcast. Maize is the chief crop, and although the cattle are allowed on the fields after the harvest, no conscious effort at manuring is made, for the dung is usually collected and used as fuel, since most of the reserves have long ago been stripped of firewood resources.

Men are usually engaged in the migratory labour system that has grown up to provide labour in the mines and factories of the major towns. They spend long periods away from the reserves, but return with their earnings from time to time, partly in order to maintain their claim to their land rights. Usually most able-bodied young men are away, and the task of cultivation falls on the women and older folk. This makes difficult the task of the government in its attempts to improve Bantu farming through education, for those who might be most receptive to new ideas are not in the reserves for much of the time. Nevertheless, there have been some improvements through the introduction of modern machinery, soil conservation techniques such as contour ploughing, and the use of artificial fertilizers. In a few areas livestock numbers have also been reduced, but it is still very hard to persuade the Bantu that quality of cattle matters more than numbers.

Fishing

The fishing industry was mainly a development of the years after the Second World War, government funds having been made available for improved harbours, modern vessels and gear. The continental shelf is extremely narrow, except off Cape Agulhas, and there is relatively little trawling. Most of the fish caught are pilchard and maasbanker, from the inshore fisheries of the west coast. A great deal of fish is canned at such centres as Walvis Bay, Luderitz, St. Helena Bay and Cape Town, but most is processed for fish meal and oil. South Africa no longer participates in the Antarctic whaling industry, but off-shore whaling is based on Durban and Saldanha Bay; one of the products is canned whale meat, sold mainly to the mines for consumption by African employees.

Mining

The most important mining activities are for gold, diamonds and coal, but other minerals which are obtained include iron, copper, uranium and asbestos. Gold and coal mines alone employ over 360,000 Africans, and total employment in mining exceeds half-a-million persons of all races.

Gold. The oldest gold-mining area is on the central Rand, around Johannesburg, where mining was started in 1886. The gold occurs in minute specks throughout beds of conglomerate. Most mines close to Johannesburg are virtually exhausted economically, although rising gold prices in the past made it possible to deepen the mines and thereby prolong their lives. Between the two world wars mining was developed as far west as Randfontein, and eastward into the Springs district.

Gold has also been mined since the end of the nineteenth century in the Klerksdorp area, about 80 miles south-west of Johannesburg. There are thirteen mines in this area, which produced 3·3 million ounces of gold in 1960, out of a national production of 20·9 million ounces. Since the Second World War a new field has been opened in the Orange Free State, where eleven mines work the gold to a depth of about 7,000 feet below ground, the reefs being concealed beneath a cover of Karoo rocks about 4,000 feet thick. The amazing speed with which the field was developed may be judged from the fact that the first mine was started in 1946, and by 1951 twelve mines had sunk 27 shafts. In 1960 production totalled 6·3 million ounces.

The newest development is that of the Eastern Transvaal Highveld Goldfield, another concealed field 40 miles east-south-east of Springs, in the Bethal district (Fig. 100), where three mines are operating. Thus, the gold-mining industry continues to expand both by the deepening of old mines (one on the eastern Rand has exceeded 11,000 feet), and

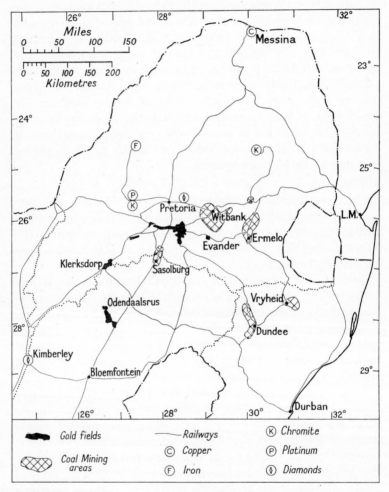

Fig. 100. The principal mining areas and railways of the Transvaal, Orange Free State and Natal

The goldfields lie in an arc from the Orange Free State field through the older mining areas of the Klerksdorp and the Witwatersrand, to the newest field at Evander. For coal, the areas shaded are those where mining is carried on, not the geological extent of known coalfields

by the exploitation of newly discovered fields, but like all mining industries it is expendable, and ultimately must cease operation, as some mines in the older areas have done. Meanwhile, new mines have a very great effect on the landscape. In 1946 the area of the Orange Free State field was almost entirely bare veld, supporting cattle farming and maize growing of rather poor quality. By 1954 the tiny village of Odendaalsrus had become a modern town of about 8,000 Europeans and 16,000 Africans; by 1963 it was expected to reach 13,000 and 27,000 respectively. The whole field, about 30 miles from north to south and 10 miles wide, has three other large new towns in Welkom, Virginia and Allanridge, and a total population nearing 200,000, of whom about one-half are employed in mines. On the Eastern Transvaal field the entirely new town of Evander is growing rapidly. Other landscape features of the goldfields are the great white mine-tips which dominate Johannesburg (Plate 65) and other mining centres, consisting of the crushed rock from which the gold has been extracted.

Diamonds. Diamond mining developed around Kimberley during the 1870s. The diamonds are found in old volcanic 'necks', and consequently their occurrence at the surface is limited. In the early days the necks were excavated as open workings to depths of several hundred feet, and such workings are the 'Big Hole' at Kimberley, and the Premier Mine near Pretoria, which was opened in 1902. Now the mines work by means of shafts driven in the rock beside the neck and horizontal access tunnels to the diamond-bearing rock. The necessity for large-scale methods made mining the monopoly of large concerns, and the De Beers Group has obtained control of all diamond production.

Alluvial diamond deposits were known in the Vaal Valley in the first decade of the present century, and extensive deposits were discovered in the Lichtenburg district in the western Transvaal in 1926. These are now mostly worked out and the main production of alluvial diamonds is from the west coast, where, since 1927, diamonds have been worked in raised beach deposits near the mouth of the Orange River, mainly in South West Africa. In 1962 a vessel fitted with suction-hoses demonstrated that diamond-bearing gravels could be recovered from the sea off the same coast, and commercial production is expected to follow.

Few of the diamonds produced are gems; most are used for cutting or abrasive purposes in industry. In 1961 a factory at Springs was opened to produce industrial diamonds artificially, but being controlled by the same group as the mining of diamonds, it is not a threat to the industry, rather strengthening South Africa's position in the world's diamond trade.

Coal. Many mining and industrial developments that have taken place in South Africa would have been far more difficult had her large resources of coal been absent. Reserves at present known are estimated at about 75,000 million tons, of which over 90 per cent is in the Transvaal. The coal occurs in the Karoo series, is horizontally bedded, and therefore easy to work. Moreover, the seams are mostly between six and fifteen feet thick, and seldom more than a few hundred feet below the surface, so that mechanical methods can be used, and production is relatively cheap.

Coal mined in the Dundee and Vryheid districts of Natal includes the only coking coal in South Africa, but most of the country's coal comes from the Transvaal fields, around Witbank, Springs, Middelburg, and Ermelo; all these are within easy reach of the Witwatersrand industrial areas. The full extent of the Free State coalfield is not yet known, but apart from normal production, there are two mines which were sunk for specific projects. These are the Vierfontein power station on the Vaal near Klerksdorp, and the government sponsored oil-from-coal project at Sasolburg, ten miles south-west of Vereeniging. This produces over 50 million gallons of petroleum per annum, as well as varied by-products, including gas for supply to the Rand.

Other Minerals. South Africa has many other minerals, and can be considered a major producer of uranium, platinum, iron ore, chromite, manganese and asbestos. Uranium is found in small quantities in almost all gold-bearing reefs, and although the content is only about one-quarter of that of North American ores, extraction is worthwhile as the costs of mining are covered by the production of gold. In some cases old waste from the gold mines is being reworked for uranium. Platinum and chromite are worked at Rustenburg, and chromite at Lydenburg in the Transvaal, while extensive deposits of manganese are being exploited in the Postmasburg district of the northern Cape. Copper has been worked since 1852 in Namaqualand, and was exported by rail to Port Nolloth. Production came to a standstill in the 1920s, but was restarted by an American company in 1940, and refining is done at O'Okiep. The other important mine is at Messina in the northern Transvaal.

Iron ore of various types occurs widely, the chief workings being near Pretoria, in the Postmasburg district, and at Thabazimbi, north of Rustenburg. Ore is also obtained near Dundee, in Natal. Large deposits occur in South West Africa, but their development is unlikely unless an overseas market is found, as they are too remote from South African steel-making centres and at present lack a source of power for local refining.

Industry

Not only are manufacturing industries chiefly concentrated in a few major towns to serve local markets, but they have been injected into the economy as factory industry, having few of the roots in domestic industry that European industry had. Until the end of the nineteenth century the people were concerned with the development of a near-subsistence farming economy. The mines provided the first stimulus to the manufacture of articles other than those for the needs of farmers, and often an industry had to rely on imported raw materials, so that the early industries provided a market for further industries.

Thus it came about that the iron and steel industry was established in three localities close to the gold mines—at Pretoria, on the Rand, and at Vereeniging. Pretoria is conveniently situated close to the iron-ore workings of Timeball Hill, has rail links with the Transvaal coalfields, and is conveniently placed to receive iron ore from Thabazimbi. Vereeniging is close to the water supplies of the Vaal, a major consideration since Johannesburg occupies a watershed position and is consequently short of local water supplies. The fourth centre is Newcastle, Natal, which produces only pig-iron, and is the sole plant situated in proximity to both iron ore and good coking coal. Limestone was originally brought from Taungs, 400 miles distant, and now local iron ores are inadequate and ore comes from Thabazimbi and also from Manganore in the Postmasburg district. The iron and steel industry also owes much to the government-sponsored Iron and Steel Corporation (ISCOR), established in 1928 at a time when economic depression made it imperative that the government should take steps to relieve unemployment amongst the 'Poor Whites' (that is, those Europeans who, unable to make a living on the land, left it to seek employment in the towns).

The state-sponsored Industrial Development Corporation has established several new industries since the war. These include the oil-from-coal project at Sasolburg, the exploitation of phosphates for fertilizer at Phalaborwa in the north-eastern Transvaal, the production of wood-pulp for rayon manufacture at Umkomaas a few miles south of Durban, paper manufacture on the Tugela River in Natal, and a textile factory at Kingwilliamstown.

Today the consumer industries are well established in all major centres, and because of the distance between centres, any one industry is usually represented in several of them. Thus, Durban, as a whaling port and importer of vegetable oils is the natural centre for the soap industry, but soap is made also in Cape Town, Johannesburg and East London. Some industries are already more widespread, especially those processing farming produce; creameries, for example, are found in a large number of the smaller towns.

Government policy is committed to some decentralization of industry for two main reasons. One is the shortage of water supplies in major centres. The planning authorities have decided that no major water-consuming industry should normally be allowed to come to the area which relies on the Vaal for water, as the resources of that river are fully used. The other is connected with the racial doctrine of *Apartheid* which requires the development of economically independent Bantu communities to replace the present predominantly agricultural reserves. Thus it becomes necessary to place industry in, or on the edge of, reserves to provide the basis of urban development there. Since most reserves lie in the eastern marginal zone, which is relatively well watered, this is logical in relation to the water-need, but it does not take account of either the location of raw materials or the availability of markets. More important, it ignores the tremendous economic impetus already gained by the major centres, and their pull on new industries; it remains to be seen whether government policy can effectively alter the whole pattern of industrial development in South Africa.

Water Supply

The importance of water supply in affecting the location of industry has been mentioned. The lack of water in the western half of the plateau is one of the reasons for the absence of industry there, for those rivers that do flow have a marked seasonal fluctuation, and the farming community relies largely on underground water obtained through boreholes. The Orange and its tributaries, which include the Vaal, are the only major source of surface water on the plateau south of the Rand.

It was not until 1956 that the right to use river water was transferred from the riparian owners to the state, so that water usage is now controlled by the Department of Water Affairs. Most of the major dams in the country are primarily for irrigation, apart from those built by municipal authorities. The largest storage scheme is the Vaaldam, near Vereeniging, which has a capacity of nearly 2 million acre-feet. It supplied the Rand, the Free State and Klerksdorp goldfields, the oil plant at Sasolburg, Kimberley, and various riparian villages and towns, as well as the major Vaal-Harts irrigation scheme where there are 87,000 acres of irrigable land.

Dams and irrigation schemes are numerous in the Limpopo Basin, and along the smaller rivers of the marginal zones, but several of the larger reservoirs have overestimated the potential run-off of their catchment areas, and have seldom or never filled to capacity. The Orange is the one major river that has not been adequately utilized.

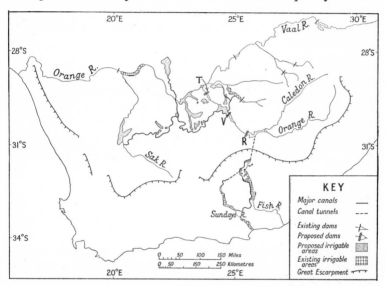

Fig. 101. The Orange River Development Scheme
The project, which was announced in 1962, will consist of three large dams, and will take 30 years to complete. The Ruigte Valley Dam (R) will supply water through the Orange-Fish tunnel under the Great Escarpment to irrigation areas in the Fish and Sundays valleys, and to Port Elizabeth. The Vander Kloof Dam (V) and Torquay Dam (T) will provide irrigation water to areas on the plateau, mostly in the Orange and Sak river valleys. All three dams will incorporate hydro-electric power stations, and others will be built at the outlet of the Orange-Fish Tunnel, and in the Fish and Sundays valleys

There is one dam at Boegoeberg, which provides irrigation water along the banks between the dam and the Aughrabies Falls, 150 miles downstream. In 1962 the ambitious Orange River scheme was announced, providing for the control of the river by three major dams near Douglas, Petrusville and Bethulie (Fig. 101). The storage capacity of these will total a little over 7 million acre-feet, though the site of the

14*

main storage dam is such that the capacity could be increased from the designed 5 million acre-feet to 32 million acre-feet if the height of the dam were raised from 285 to 390 feet. Such a measure is unlikely in the foreseeable future, as the whole scheme is planned in such a way that it is expected to take 30 years to complete, by which time there will be nine other diversion dams and weirs downstream, and about 700,000 acres will have been brought under irrigation.

The planned storage capacity is thus very similar to that of the Snowy Mountains Scheme in Australia. Another feature of that scheme will also be followed in the diversion of water across a major water-shed, from the uppermost dam through a tunnel 50 miles long to the Great Fish and Sundays valleys in the south-eastern Cape, where present water resources are inadequate for industry and irrigation. This diversion from the plateau to the marginal zone reflects the poor development potential of the western plateau, compared with that of the marginal zone. The government anticipates that the scheme will lead to the enlargement of riverside towns, the establishment of new industries using the water and hydro-electric power, and a greatly increased tourist industry. But it is primarily a water-conservation scheme for irrigation and urban supplies; the total power capacity (200,000 kilowatts) will be only one-third that of Kariba, or one-fifteenth of that of the Snowy Mountains Scheme.

Power

With the erratic flow of most of the rivers, South Africa has not developed any major hydro-electric power schemes; those planned for the three main dams of the Orange River Project will be the first. With vast resources of easily- and cheaply-mined coal at her disposal, virtually all electricity is coal-generated. The state-controlled Electricity Supply Commission has a monopoly in all major industrial areas, but many smaller towns have municipally- or privately-owned power stations. Distances are so large that no national grid system has been developed, and only urban areas enjoy a mains supply. Many outlying farms have their own generators, driven by internal-combustion engines or by windmills, and a few more highly developed agricultural areas have generating plant for pumping irrigation water, driving machinery in fruit-packing sheds, or other processing plant.

Gas is available mainly from the steel industry, and from the Sasolburg oil refinery, both of which supply the southern Transvaal. Only five municipal gasworks exist, at Johannesburg, Springs, Cape Town, Port Elizabeth and Grahamstown.

URBAN DEVELOPMENT

Economic activity other than farming is strongly concentrated in a few 'islands' of development. In 1960 there were only eleven towns in South Africa with more than 100,000 people, six of them in the southern Transvaal: Benoni, Germiston, Johannesburg and Springs— all in the Witwatersrand conurbation; Pretoria 40 miles to the north; and Vereeniging-Vanderbijlpark 40 miles to the south. The remaining five were Bloemfontein, capital of the Orange Free State; and the four major ports of Cape Town, Port Elizabeth, East London and Durban. Kimberley had 77,000, and the principal town of South West Africa, Windhoek, only 36,000. Thus, while large towns are few, roughly 30 per cent of the entire population lives in them, despite the high population densities of some of the Bantu Reserves. The reasons for this require examination.

Cape Town grew from earliest times as the administrative centre, market and sole port for the early settlers, and only as settlement was extended did Port Elizabeth, Durban and East London develop as ports. Large towns in the interior developed first as a result of mining activity. Kimberley did not exist before diamonds were discovered there in 1869, from which time it grew rapidly, only to be surpassed by the still more vigorous infant Johannesburg, following the dis- covery of gold on the Rand in 1886. Pretoria already held the seat of government of the South African Republic (later the Transvaal), but did not reach any great size until industries were established there in the 1930s. Vereeniging and Vanderbijlpark are the creation of heavy industry first established in 1913 to use the waters of the Vaal, and to supply steel to the nearby Rand mines. The major towns now possess a variety of industries, which have all been established to serve particular markets within South Africa, rather than because of the presence of raw materials; this is because South Africa is remote from the main industrial regions of Europe and North America, and was encouraged to attempt local manufacture.

Mining is the only industry that is tied to a particular location by physical circumstances; manufacturing industry has been attracted to the markets created by the mines and by the people who work in them. Similarly, industry has been attracted to the ports. Only Pretoria and Bloemfontein among the leading towns achieved importance as administrative centres without developing many industries in the earlier stages, and both have large industrial sectors today.

Because most towns were created as towns from the start, rather than growing from small beginnings, they usually have a rectangular 'grid-iron' pattern of streets. As the towns have grown, land prices in the central areas have soared, and this has caused the construction of multi-storey blocks, which contrast strangely with the lower buildings which survive in places from the late nineteenth century. The newest towns, such as Odendaalsrus, have broad dual carriageway main streets, and are planned for the motor age, contrasting with the narrower streets of Cape Town and Johannesburg. These two cities are now experiencing the problems of conurbations trying to provide adequate transport facilities for the diurnal flow of people to and from jobs in the central districts; in both, urban motorways are appearing, and the cities are in danger of being strangled by the motor car.

The residential, business and industrial areas of the towns are usually well-defined and quite separate. Bantu workers are provided for in separate 'townships', often some distance from the town centre, which are replacing the old shanty towns which grew up during and after the Second World War. European residential areas also commonly consist of independent 'townships', and each tends to provide one type of accommodation for one class of people, so that the urban landscape consists of a number of distinct cells. Only in Johannesburg has there been any development of tall flats near the town centre to allow people to escape from the whirl of a commuting existence. In most towns there is plenty of available land on the periphery, and agricultural land-values are low, so that it is cheaper to build out than to build up, and bungalows are the usual type of residence. At present there are no great pressures to inhibit this outward spread of the towns.

The smaller country towns do not face these problems, but these too have distinct zones within them; usually, there is a business area within the oldest residential area, and on the edge of this the more recent European residences at one side, and the Bantu or Coloured 'Location' at the other.

TRANSPORT

In the early days of European settlement, the standard means of transport was the ox-wagon, traditionally drawn by sixteen oxen. This vehicle served to open up the interior of South Africa and even provided the necessary means of bringing in supplies to the mines in their early days. When diamonds were discovered in 1869 there were only a few short railways around Cape Town and Durban, and it was the mines that both provided the stimulus and attracted the capital for railway development. Kimberley was soon linked to Cape Town and to Port Elizabeth, a gauge of 3 feet 6 inches being chosen to speed construction. The discovery of the Rand gold caused a rapid development of further lines to serve that area, and within twelve years Johannesburg was linked to no less than five ports; Lourenço Marques (Mozambique), Durban, and the three Cape ports. Following the Anglo-Boer war a more complete network evolved, while the network has been enlarged more recently in the principal island of economic development to serve the mines and industrial concerns of the southern Transvaal and northern Free State. The rural areas, however, have always been rather sparsely served by railways, few lines being built specifically to meet the needs of agriculture. However, the railways have been state-controlled from the first and, with the coming of efficient motor transport, the provision of public goods and passenger services was vested in the South African Railways. Today S.A.R. buses and lorries serve all parts of the country, and daily services run in some remarkably remote areas such as the margins of the Kalahari. These provide almost the only transport for the African and Coloured population, and also convey much of the less bulky farm produce, such as cream, to their markets. Europeans, however, almost always travel in their own cars and lorries.

The roads in country areas are all of a loose gravel surface, but usually well-maintained. Until 1945 the only tarred roads were in towns, but since then most trunk routes have been tarred. Thus the country has a good road system, which is not yet used to capacity. Road and rail are supplementary to each other, not alternative, since S.A.R. do not provide road services that would take traffic from the railways.

Overseas communications depend mainly upon shipping, though air services are increasing. None of the four major ports has a good natural harbour; Cape Town (Plate 66) and Port Elizabeth are harbours built out into the bays, and at the former there is a substantial area of made ground on the landward side of the Duncan Dock, which was completed during the Second World War. East London harbour is a very restricted one in the mouth of the Buffalo River, and Durban, although occupying a natural lagoon, had to be greatly deepened, as there were originally only two feet of water over the entrance bar, and tidal ranges are small. Cape Town handles the greatest volume of traffic, closely followed by Durban, as both serve as major ports for the interior. The function of the other two is more to serve immediate hinterlands, and traffic is about one-half that of Durban. Walvis Bay is the only important port in South West Africa, and has a relatively small trade.

The chief international airport is Jan Smuts, between Johannesburg and Pretoria, and others are found in the four major ports, and at Windhoek and Bloemfontein. There are regular services to Europe, Australia, and most parts of Africa.

TRADE

The economy of modern South Africa has developed by the export of primary produce, especially wool and gold. Imports have consisted of manufactured goods of all kinds. Although the country has been rapidly developing manufacturing industry the position is still much the same. Exports in 1961 were headed by gold to the value of £245 million; followed by agricultural produce, including processed items such as butter (£204 million); and then metals, minerals and machinery (£177 million of which only £28 million was accounted for by motor vehicles and machinery). Most of the last group is in the form of refined metals, metal ores, and non-metallic minerals, of which diamonds comprised £30 million.

Imports are led by metals and metal manufactures, valued at £226 million in 1961, almost all in manufactured form. Thus motor vehicles and parts for the vehicle-building industry accounted for £64 million, the largest single item, and the rest included agricultural machinery, electric motors, road-building equipment, refrigerators, radio equipment and sewing machines to name but a few. Textiles and clothing form the next largest group, valued at £81 million.

Despite this emphasis on the export of unprocessed and the import of processed goods, the great natural riches and healthy nature of South Africa's economy is shown by the fact that the imports are practically paid for by exports even excluding gold.

The United Kingdom is still South Africa's leading partner in trade, providing about one-third of the imports and taking one-third of exports. The U.S.A. and West Germany are the next most important in the import trade, but are pushed down the export list by the Rhodesias which receive about an eighth of all exports, a reflection of their less developed economy. South Africa has also gained much export trade to other African countries through her production of tools and other goods designed specifically for African conditions.

CONCLUSION

South Africa differs from most of the other countries of Africa in many respects, the most important being the presence of a relatively large proportion of Europeans who have made their homes and lives there. It is largely due to them or their ancestors that South Africa was the first African country to develop a western industrial economy, and that she is still the most highly developed African country. Nevertheless, there are variations from one part of the country to another, urban and industrial development being concentrated firstly on the Highveld of the Transvaal and Orange Free State, where it is based upon mining, and secondly in those parts of the southern and eastern margins where in favourable climatic conditions the establishment of ports has stimulated the development of the potential. Intensive agriculture tends to be located in the same areas, while the remainder of the country has either an extensive agriculture developed from the traditional Boer subsistence economy, or African farming little changed from the tribal agriculture practised before the influence of the European entered the area.

Over-population of the economically underdeveloped Bantu Reserves has given rise to the continual migratory flow of Bantu labour to and from the areas of development; this is now a basic feature of the South African economy, and while its increase may be checked as the Bantustans are established and industrialized, it is unlikely that the reciprocal needs of the two types of area will decrease to an extent that allows the migration of labour to disappear. South Africa has great economic potential which can benefit the whole of Africa. The realization of that potential depends on satisfactory solutions to her political and racial problems, as well as to the technical and economic problems that have been discussed in this chapter.

FURTHER READING

The two principal works on South Africa are J. H. Wellington, *Southern Africa*, 2 vols., 1955, and M. M. Cole, *South Africa*, 1961; the latter is the easier to use as a reference book, but neither attempts a regional analysis of the whole country. For geology, structure and morphology the following are useful: L. C. King, *South African Scenery*, 3rd ed., 1963, and *Morphology of the Earth*, 1962; A. L. du Toit, *The geology of South Africa*, 3rd Ed., 1954. For climate the best recent account is in G. T. Trewartha, *The Earth's problem climates*, 1962, 138–48, which also gives a comprehensive list of other references. The characteristics of the rainfall régimes are summarized in the South African Weather Bureau's *Climate of South Africa—Part 4, Rainfall Maps*, Pretoria, 1957. Soils and vegetation are covered in the texts by Cole and Wellington, and also in C. R. van der Merwe, *Soil groups and sub-groups of South Africa*, Pretoria, 1941, and J. H. P. Acocks, *The veld-types of South Africa*, Pretoria, 1953.
The historical background to the population composition of the country is comprehensively covered by E. A. Walker, *Historical atlas of South*

Africa, Oxford, 1922 and *A History of Southern Africa*, 1957, or more briefly by A. Keppel-Jones, *South Africa, a short history*, 2nd ed., 1953. N. C. Pollock and Swanyie Agnew, *An Historical Geography of South Africa*, 1963, is an important study of the period up to 1910.

Much information on the Bantu peoples is contained in *Summary of the report of the Commission for the socio-economic development of the Bantu areas within the Union of South Africa* (Tomlinson Report), Pretoria, 1955.

An essential reference on the economic development of the country is L. P. Green and T. J. D. Fair, *Development in Africa*, 1962, which is illustrated chiefly by examples from southern Africa, and treats selected areas from the major urban regions and from underdeveloped areas. The other important reference work in the economic sphere is A. M. and W. J. Talbot, *Atlas of South Africa*, Pretoria, 1960, which contains distribution maps of agricultural and industrial activities. Articles on individual activities are too numerous to list in full here, but may be found especially in the following journals: *Geography, The Geographical Journal, South African Geographical Journal*, and *Optima*, the last being a quarterly review published by the Anglo-American Corporation in Johannesburg. H. J. R. Henderson, 'The dairying industry in South Africa', *Transactions of the Institute of British Geographers*, 1960, 237–52, illustrates the influence of economic factors on the pattern of farming.

There is no readily accessible reference on South West Africa, but much information is included on the territory, as on the rest of the subcontinent, in the *Official Year Book of the Union of South Africa* (no longer published annually; the last was No. 30, 1960) and in *The State of South Africa*, published annually in Johannesburg by da Gama Publications Ltd.

CHAPTER TWENTY-FIVE

Basutoland, Bechuanaland and Swaziland

THESE three territories, each of which is a British Protectorate, are politically independent of the Republic, but are closely integrated with it economically. All are predominantly Bantu territories, and consequently are unlikely to be joined politically with South Africa while the racial policies of the present government are maintained. The areas and populations are as follows:

	Area	Population (*thousands*)				
	sq. miles	European	African	Coloured	Asian	Total
Basutoland	11,716	2	639	0·6	0·3	642
Bechuanaland	275,000	2	292	—	—	294
Swaziland	6,704	9	254	2	—	265

BASUTOLAND

Basutoland is a complete enclave within the Republic of South Africa, enclosed by the three provinces of the Cape, Natal and the Free State. It lies on the rim of the plateau at the highest part of the Great Escarpment, and occupies the headwater valleys of the Orange and Caledon rivers, which are deeply incised in parts and give rise to very rugged country. Because of the altitude, the climate is rather bleak in the higher eastern part, but the lower valleys to the west adjoin the Orange Free State and enjoy much the same climate. Similarly, both soils and vegetation tend to be poorer in the east, though the whole area is covered by temperate and montane grassland, and grazing is carried on to near the crests of the Drakensberg.

The population is almost exclusively Basuto, one of the great groups of Bantu, and no land can be alienated to Europeans or others. Despite this, the country is severely over-populated, and since there is no industry the people are heavily dependent on South Africa for paid employment to supplement their income from farming. The population figure of 642,000 is misleading, being the number actually resident in the country at the 1956 census, for at the same time

* By H. J. R. Henderson.

roughly 155,000 Basuto were temporarily in employment in South Africa.

The chief crops grown are maize, sorghum, beans, peas and wheat. The last two are winter crops in the west, but in the east population pressure has forced people to occupy permanently areas that previously provided merely summer pasture for their cattle, and here the climate is so severe that these crops can only be grown as summer crops, and the others cannot be grown at all. The principal livestock are cattle, sheep and goats, and virtually the only exports are of wool and mohair.

BECHUANALAND

Bechuanaland lies in the very centre of the subcontinent, separating the Transvaal from South West Africa, and with Rhodesia on its northern border. Except in the east, almost the whole country lies on Kalahari sand. Although the southern and western parts are spoken of as the Kalahari desert, they carry a cover of Grass Steppe, which merges in the north and east of the country into Dry Woodland-Savanna, as the average rainfall increases from 6 inches in the south-west to 25 inches in the north-east. The southern portion has many dry river courses tributary to the Molopo, itself flowing intermittently to be lost eventually in the sands of the southern Kalahari, although it once joined the Orange before the lower valley became blocked by sand dunes. The northern part belongs to the interior drainage of the Okovango Delta, Lake Ngami and the Makarikari salt-pan.

Much of the arid interior is virtually uninhabited, except by a few surviving groups of Bushmen. The Bantu inhabitants are primarily pastoralists, for the climate does not permit the cultivation of crops on a large scale. Cattle are the main type of stock, together with some sheep and goats. In the east, and around Ghanzi in the extreme west, are a number of European farms, chiefly concerned with cattle ranching. Formerly cattle were exported on the hoof to Johannesburg, but since 1954 an abattoir has been operating at Lobatsi in the south-east, and chilled carcasses are now exported to the republic. There is little other industry, apart from a creamery at Francistown, and a number of minor mining enterprises, of which the largest produces asbestos at Moshaneng.

The main railway line from Cape Town to Bulawayo runs through the eastern part of the country for nearly 400 miles, having been constructed in 1898, using this route because of hostility between the British and the Boers who occupied the Transvaal. Other communications depend on a few rough tracks passable only in fairly robust vehicles, while there are a few small airstrips, usable by light aircraft. Any future development of the country will depend upon the possibilities of mining where the older rocks outcrop in the east, and of irrigation schemes which might be introduced using the waters of the Okovango, but there is no immediate prospect of either.

SWAZILAND

The smallest of the three territories, Swaziland is also the most highly developed. It straddles the Great Escarpment, includes both high plateau and lowveld, and the eastern boundary follows the line of the Lebombo Mountains. It is essentially a part of the eastern marginal zone of South Africa, and its drainage is eastwards to the Indian Ocean, chiefly through the Komati, Usutu and Umbuluzi rivers, each of which cuts across the Lebombo ridge by a gorge. Extending from over 5,000 feet to under 500 feet in elevation, there is a wide range of temperatures, rainfall and vegetation. The higher parts with a rainfall of 40 to 60 inches are temperate grasslands, and the lower are Dry Woodland-Savannas which receive only 20 to 30 inches of rain.

Unlike the other protectorates, Swaziland had, by the end of the nineteenth century, been divided up and allocated to Europeans, but little of it was settled, being used as winter grazing by sheepfarmers from the Transvaal, who practised a form of transhumance. Much of this land was expropriated and returned to the Swazi nation in 1909, and further purchases and awards of Crown Land have put almost half the country in Swazi hands. This land occurs over the whole country, so that the Swazis own much of the best land as well as some that is poor.

Farming

Until the Second World War Swaziland depended chiefly on cattle farming and a little cotton growing, but in recent years considerable advances have been made and there are now several irrigation schemes. Most, but not all of the cash-crop production is on European farms, the Swazi contributing to production of tobacco and cotton, and also having surplus maize for sale in good years.

There are three major irrigation schemes, of which the Swaziland Irrigation Scheme, started in 1950, is the largest, irrigating 105,000 acres from the Komati. The Big Bend scheme on the Great Usutu (1953) is intended to irrigate 18,000 acres, and the Malkerns scheme higher up the Usutu (1954) covers 10,000 acres. The chief crops grown under irrigation are sugar, pineapples, citrus, rice and a variety of fruit and vegetables. All three schemes provide a part of their water for irrigation farming by Swazi farmers, who are being encouraged to adopt modern farming techniques, and thereby to increase their output of foodstuffs.

Cattle are the chief livestock kept by both Swazi and Europeans, chiefly for sale as slaughter stock; the usual problem of teaching the African to value livestock as a source of cash income has been overcome to a greater extent in Swaziland than anywhere else in southern Africa. Dairying is on the increase, and the sale of cream to the government creamery in Bremersdorp is an important source of income to many Swazi, as well as to Europeans. In the higher areas in the west sheep are kept as well.

Forestry

While there are no indigenous forests, both government and private forests have been established in the area of the Great Escarpment since 1948, and there are over 200,000 acres planted with conifers and eucalypts. Because of the high temperatures and plentiful rainfall, pulpwood can be produced on a fifteen-year rotation system, as compared with 40 years and more in Scandinavia. Several pulp and saw mills have been established. Wattle is also grown by a number of farmers in the higher western areas.

Mining

Asbestos, mined at Havelock in the extreme north-west, and sent by cableway to the railhead at Barberton, twelve miles away in the Transvaal, is the most valuable export product the territory has, valued at over £2·5 million per year. Several other minerals are worked on a small scale, and a new gold mine was opened in 1962 at Forbes Reef, a few miles north of the capital, Mbabane. The future development of the country should be assisted considerably by the mining of the iron ore at Bomvu Ridge, also on the Highveld and close to the western boundary, for a railway is being built via Mbabane and Bremersdorp to link the mines with the Portuguese port of Lourenço Marques.

Industry, Communications and Trade

Industries are at present limited to the processing of the primary produce of agriculture and forestry, but the possibility of developing coal resources in the country may bring further industry in the future.

Exports at present consist of agricultural produce and minerals, either processed or unprocessed and, as in the other protectorates, a considerable income is derived by the Swazi from employment in the mines of the Republic. Communications are entirely by road, the S.A.R. road services covering most parts of the country.

CONCLUSION

Of the three Protectorates, Swaziland alone has any prospect of becoming economically viable, for it is the only one with a wide enough range of resources to support industry as well as producing adequate foodstuffs to meet the basic needs of the population. It also has access to a port through Portuguese territory as well as through South Africa. The other two must continue to rely on economic support from without, and while Bechuanaland might possibly look increasingly to Rhodesia, Basutoland's economy must always be closely related to that of the Republic of South Africa. Both depend exclusively on South Africa for contact with the outside world.

FURTHER READING

The physical geography of the territories is covered in the previous chapter, and by the references on pp. 431–2. *Basutoland, Bechuanaland and Swaziland —Economic Survey Mission Report*, H.M.S.O., 1960; L. P. Green and T. J. D. Fair, *Development in Africa*, Johannesburg, 1962, Ch. 12, 'Swaziland and Bechuanaland'; L. P. Green and T. J. D. Fair, 'Preparing for Swaziland's future economic growth', *Optima*, 1960, 194–206; D. M. Doveton, 'The human geography of Swaziland', *Transactions of the Institute of British Geographers*, 1937; D. Randall, *Factors of economic development and the Okovango delta*, Chicago, 1957.

CHAPTER TWENTY-SIX

Mozambique

(Portuguese: Moçambique)

VASCO da Gama reached what is now Lourenço Marques in 1498, when seeking a route round Africa to the Orient, and in a later voyage he heard of the gold of Monomotapa in the interior (possibly the Ophir and Tarshish of the Bible). Between 1505 and 1520 Portuguese forts were established along the East African Coast, partly to collect gold and ivory, but mainly to defend and provision boats on the route to Asia. Thus the names Algoa (bay of Port Elizabeth, Republic of South Africa) and Delgoa (bay of Lourenço Marques) were given to the points used on outward and homeward sailings respectively.

However, the Portuguese were severely restricted by the Arabs, long established in the slave and other trades on the East African Coast and in the interior, and the forts lost their function as support bases for the Asian trade when the Dutch conquered most of the Portuguese Empire in Asia in the seventeenth century. They languished for two full centuries while Portuguese interests were concentrated in Brazil and in the supporting slave trade from Angola and other coastal points in Western Africa.

The Conference of Berlin's doctrine of the need for effective occupancy to secure territorial title in Africa gave an impetus to penetrate beyond coastal footholds at the end of the last century, but Cecil Rhodes forestalled a link with Angola, although the Portuguese did penetrate to the limit of navigation on the Zambezi—hence the deep westward trend of the boundary. Had Portugal secured what is now Zambia and Rhodesia she could never have found the capital nor would she have applied the economic methods which have made those countries prosperous. Mozambique has, however, taken part in their development, as in that of the Rand, by acting as their importer and exporter. Mozambique has also for long supplied contract labour to the Transvaal, and since the Second World War Lourenço Marques and Beira have become tourist centres for visitors from South Africa, Zambia and Rhodesia.

* By R. J. Harrison Church.

Such was the weakness of Portugal until that war that development in Mozambique was largely by concessions, often to foreign companies. Thus the Anglo-Portuguese Mozambique Company had exclusive rights of trade and government north of the Zambezi until 1942, and it in turn granted concessions to a British company to build the railway from Beira into Rhodesia and to run it and the port. Other concessions were granted for the cultivation of sugar, sisal and other crops. Such features were not unique to Mozambique; there were the British South Africa Company in the Rhodesias, and the Royal Niger Company in Northern Nigeria, and certain rights of these also prevailed until that war, but the concession system dominated Mozambique as nowhere else.

Until 1942 Mozambique was almost an appendage of the Transvaal and the Rhodesias. Since then it has undergone the same kind of transformation described in the chapter on Angola. With an area of 297,654 square miles—three-fifths the size of Angola—Mozambique has more people—6,592,994 in 1960 (22 per square mile), the consequence of its having been less drained of slaves, and of having received many refugees from wars in Central and South Africa.

THE PHYSICAL ENVIRONMENT

Unlike the compact Angola, Mozambique is a Y-shaped elongated land, extending some 1,650 miles (equivalent to the distance from Gibraltar to Innsbruck), and varying in width from 30 to 630 miles. The south lies beyond the Tropic of Capricorn but is still tropical because of the warm Mozambique Current. Mozambique is mainly tropical lowland and less suitable for European settlement than Angola, the more so as it is far more remote from Europe.

Mozambique is almost unique in Africa in its geological variety; indeed from the western and northern plateaux, which reach 8,000 feet and belong to the Basement Complex of Africa, representative outcrops of most geological formations are crossed down to the currently-forming coastal coral.

Land under 600 feet comprises two-fifths of the country, and this is the greatest expanse of coastal plain in southern Africa. Narrow in the north but wide in the south, it includes the deltas of the Limpopo and Zambezi. These and many other areas are mangrove-fringed, but where waters are clearer there is coral. These features, and shallows off-shore, have retarded the development of large ports, except at Lourenço Marques and Beira which serve other countries more than Mozambique.

Behind the coast is a generally featureless and gently undulating plain of mediocre sandy soils of former dunes, with Woodland-

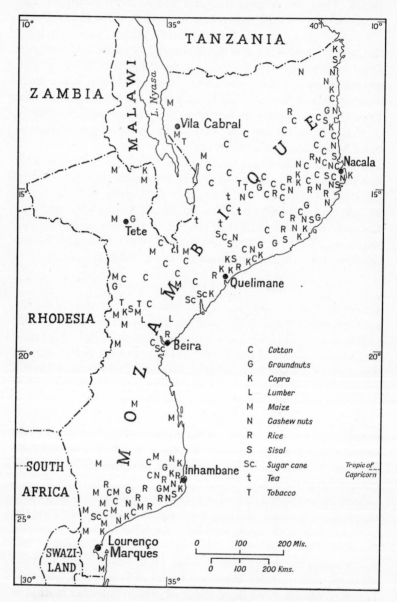

Fig. 102. Crops and timber in Mozambique. (After Van Dongen)

Savanna and heavily infested with tsetse. It is broken only by peaty belts and wide alluvial strips of the several rivers; however, these are also fly-infested, seasonally flooded, and dangerous or expensive to farm, except in certain circumstances by plantations, for example for sugar.

Throughout there is one rainy season, with the greatest falls in the area of Beira. The south-central plains are often dry, not only because of lesser rain but also because of permeable soils.

THE REGIONS AND THE ECONOMY

Coconuts are especially important on the coast between 17° and 20° S.; Quelimane is credited as having the largest coconut plantation in the world, with 50,000 acres and four million palms. Copra, coconut oil and coir comprise one-sixth of exports, over half the produce coming from plantations. Sisal is grown on the coastal plain in the north, and was started by German planters who came here from former German East Africa after the First World War.

Behind the coast maize is the main crop but many other crops are grown, notably groundnuts and cotton (more important in the northern foothills and the most valuable export crop). As in Angola, cotton is grown by Africans, under former compulsion and continued European supervision. Rice is very important between Lourenço Marques and Inhambane, and around Quelimane. Sugar (the second export by value) comes from estates in the alluvial flats of the lower Zambezi, Buzi and Incomati (Komati) valleys, and this crop, like groundnuts and cotton, must first satisfy the needs of Portugal.

In the Limpopo Valley (see Fig. 103) is a comprehensive scheme for flood control and eventual irrigation of 75,000 acres, on which humble peasants from Fayal (Azores), southern Portugal and Africans are being settled. All are treated identically and live together, each with 10–25 acres of irrigated land and 62 acres for dry farming. The area is well served by the Rhodesian–Lourenço Marques railway. Other smaller schemes are developing, and an older settlement, mainly of sugar, citrus and banana planters, is in the Incomati Valley.

Lourenço Marques (93,500 including 20,000 Europeans), the capital, is the best natural harbour of the entire east coast of Africa. It has 10,000 acres of sheltered water and minimum low water depths of 27 feet to the wharves, which are 25 miles from the open sea. The first was opened in 1903 (before that of Durban), and by 1914 the port had already acquired most of its present layout, which makes it possible to accommodate 15 ocean vessels at quayside (Plate 67). The port is the

nearest one (Fig. 100) to the Transvaal mining, industrial and agricultural areas, and is especially well-equipped to load Transvaal
minerals and fruit. The railway and port are guaranteed at least 47·5

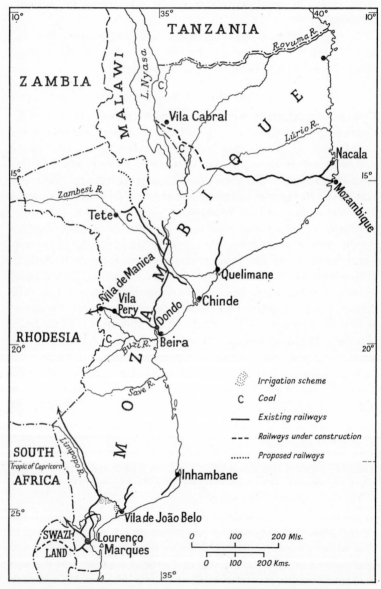

Fig. 103. Irrigation, coal and railways in Mozambique. (After Van Dongen)

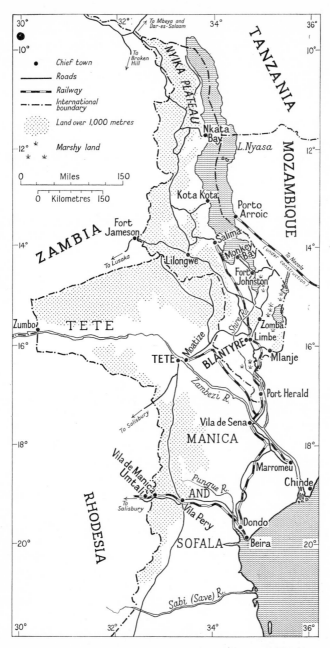

Fig. 104. Communications with Beira. (After Van Dongen)

per cent of all overseas traffic from the Rand. Some six million tons of cargo are handled annually. The railway to Bannockburn, Rhodesia, has made Lourenço Marques a second outlet for Rhodesia, Zambia and Katanga, and one not congested like Beira. A short line to Goba serves (by feeder rail-road services) eastern and north-western Swaziland; it is being extended across Swaziland to Ngwenya for the export of iron ore.

Lourenço Marques is exceptionally spacious, shady and clean, and one of the most attractive cities of Africa. From June to September, during the Rand's 'winter', the town is a holiday resort for the well-to-do of that area, and airlines have encouraged weekend tourism. Nevertheless, Lourenço Marques is badly placed as a capital, the more so as the first through road even to Beira was not completed until 1963, and there is no railway to the rest of the country. Good air services have offset this difficulty to some extent, but coastal vessels provide the main link. Otherwise, isolation from most of Mozambique, emphasizes Lourenço Marques's primary function as an outlet for other lands.

Beira was for long the main outlet for the Rhodesias, Malawi (Fig. 104) and, to a much less extent, for the Katanga Province of the Congo, but it became severely congested after the Second World War; hence the construction of the Limpopo Railway from Rhodesia to Lourenço Marques. Entry to the Pungue Estuary is difficult; the river is very silt-laden and strongly tidal. The town has had to be built on an unstable marsh edged by mangrove swamps. New wharves were added in 1959–60 and the port's capacity enlarged to over five million tons of cargo annually, mainly Rhodesian minerals and agricultural produce. The town has been modernized, and it attracts Rhodesian tourists to its hotels and holiday camp. There are several processing and consumer goods industries.

West of Beira, the railway to Umtali crosses 40 miles of marsh, and speeds and loads are severely restricted. Local traffic is mainly maize, but the railway has also encouraged cement and fibrous-cement industries (using local cement and Rhodesian asbestos) at Dondo, and jute and cotton mills at Vila Pery, both on the railway, Vila Pery having hydro-electric power from the Revué River. On the line to Malawi are many sawmills, selling timber to Rhodesia. Branches from this railway serve the Zambezi Valley, for example Moatize, where coal is mined.

There are a large number of small ports, piers or roadsteads, such as Inhambane, Quelimane, Mozambique (on an island) and Nacala, all of which have railways, as well as others without them but served by river transport, for example Chinde. These handle local produce such as copra, sisal and sugar, either exporting direct or by coastal vessels to Lourenço Marques. Nacala probably has the greatest future, since it possesses a fine natural harbour more spacious even than that of Lourenço Marques. A railway from it is being extended to Porto Arroio on Lake Nyasa and will open new areas in Mozambique, and should be of value to northern Malawi and Zambia.

Inland from the old town of Mozambique, and to the north, the narrow coastal plain is succeeded by a broad belt of broken foothills of the Basement Complex and Karoo rocks. Cotton is very important, as are groundnuts often grown in rotation with it. Cashew nuts, which grow semi-wild, are collected in great numbers, and Mozambique is the second world exporter. Cassava, sorghum (guinea corn) and sweet potatoes are important food crops everywhere, with rice in valleys or swamps.

The mountains east of Lake Nyasa are little developed but this area is being opened up by the railway from Nacala to Lake Nyasa. Settlement of Portuguese is proposed; meanwhile, the region produces some maize and cotton. Further south are the granitic Namuli Highlands, which attain 7,980 feet and, like Mt. Mlanje in Malawi, are being planted with tea.

West of Lake Nyasa and north of the Zambezi are the Angoni Highlands, while south of the Zambezi are the Manica and Sofala escarpments. All are fringes of the Rhodesian Lowveld, while south of the Limpopo, the Lebombo Mountains are the edge of the Transvaal Lowveld. All have pastoral and mineral possibilities but are remote from Mozambique centres and communications, except near the Beira–Rhodesia railway and the Portuguese centre of Manica. These mountainous edges are also steep and eroded, and so costly to farm or ranch. Between them and the coast, and south of the Zambezi, are Karoo lavas where the Jurassic-Cretaceous Malagasy rift occurred.

SOME CONTRASTS WITH ANGOLA

Reference was made earlier to the higher density of population in Mozambique than in Angola. This should not mislead, for the figure of twenty per square mile is still low. Certain areas, notably those between the Limpopo and Save Rivers, and the highlands of the western borders are almost empty, the consequence of tribal wars, of slave raiding by Arabs, and the tsetse. Furthermore, the benefits of the larger population have so far been rather negatived because some

300,000 labourers have for long been sent annually, with varying degrees of willingness or compulsion, to work for several years in the mines of the Republic of South Africa, and on the plantations of São Tomé and Príncipe off the west coast of Africa. Lastly, most of the peoples are more backward than those of neighbouring lands, the consequence of centuries of stagnation after the loss of most of Portugal's empire in Asia, and of being so remote from Portugal, a small and poor power.

Angola has so far played only a minor role as a means of access to or exit from other lands, but in Mozambique this function has been outstanding. The vital importance of the railways from the Transvaal and Rhodesia to Lourenço Marques, and from Zambia, Rhodesia, Katanga and Malawi to Beira, as well as of the ports themselves to those countries, must be evident. Additional to Mozambique's important exports of cotton, sugar, cashew nuts, copra, sisal and tea, there are large invisible ones (for services rendered), such as railway receipts from carriage of foreign produce; harbour, tug and pilotage dues from foreign vessels; the tourist trade; and earnings and remittances by its labourers abroad to their families.

Mozambique, unlike Angola, is not a settlers' country. It has little highland, and what it possesses is remote. Most Europeans in Mozambique are administrators or traders, rather than settlers. They are very much concentrated in the two main ports. The development of the country is being hastened, but its prosperity must always depend very considerably upon that of the far richer Transvaal, Zambia, Rhodesia and Malawi.

FURTHER READING

See further reading on Angola for studies of both countries. Also Irene S. Van Dongen, 'Mozambique', *Focus*, September 1958; William A. Hance and Irene S. Van Dongen, 'Lourenço Marques in Delgoa Bay', *Economic Geography*, 1957, 238–56; and H. C. Brookfield, 'New Railroad and Port Developments in East and Central Africa', *Economic Geography*, 1955, 60–70.

THE AFRICAN ISLANDS OF THE INDIAN OCEAN

CHAPTER TWENTY-SEVEN

The Comoro Islands, Madagascar, Réunion, Mauritius and Seychelles

THE south-west Indian Ocean has a multitude of islands ranging in size from Madagascar (fifth largest in the world) to tiny islets. Madagascar became independent in 1960; the others have varying degrees of autonomy under France or Britain.

Madagascar in part belongs to the Basement Complex of Africa but this has been severely faulted, causing vivid fault scarps on the east and giving rise to former volcanoes there and along associated faults in the Comoro Islands, Réunion and Mauritius. Vulcanism was broadly contemporaneous with that of the Rift Valley system of East Africa, and in Cameroon and its insular projections in the Bight of Biafra, at Cape Verde and in the Cape Verde Islands.

Comparison with islands off the western coast of Africa does not end with geological parallels. Both groups were important to mariners on the route round Africa to South and East Asia. In this and in other ways they are, like North Africa, an African link with Asia, and have for centuries—even millennia—been the meeting place of diverse peoples; they are fascinating places for the study of culture contact.

These islands were of greatest renown from the time of Portuguese voyages of the fifteenth century until the opening of the Suez Canal in 1869. Thereafter, relative isolation from main trade routes and markets, and highly stratified societies became characteristic of them all. They have been somewhat neglected by the world, certainly in British literature. Although marginal to Africa, they deserve inclusion here, if only because of past neglect, and because Madagascar is almost continental in size.

THE COMORO ISLANDS

These steep volcanic islands, totalling only 874 square miles (a little larger than physically-comparable Fernando Po, West Africa), have been given no attention in British literature, yet they have been the focus of peoples from southern Asia and eastern Africa and their respective islands. In the Comoros these peoples are somewhat united

* By R. J. Harrison Church.

in the Islamic faith, and the Swahili or Arab tongues; but they are gripped in a highly stratified and stagnant society. Population pressure, land hunger and soil erosion are acute, land reform is a major issue, and racial and cultural problems are akin to those in many Caribbean and Pacific islands.

The Physical Environment

The islands are the consequence of post-Miocene volcanic activity along a north-west to south-east trending fault, and Mt. Kartala, 7,676 feet, on Grand Comoro, the most rugged island, is still active. The islands consist of black volcanic basalt or white pumice. Finger-like phonoliths of up to 2,000 feet in altitude survive on Mohéli

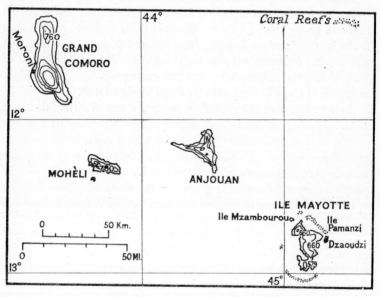

Fig. 105 The Comoro Islands. (After Isnard)

(otherwise the lowest and flattest island), comparable with those on Príncipe, West Africa. Grand Comoro and tiny Pamanzi (off Mayotte) have young porous lavas and pumice, and lack significant permanent surface streams. Water supplies are restricted to wells (sunk near the shore where underground water is near the surface because of hydrostatic pressure between the water table and the sea), to tank storage, to coconut 'milk' upon which people in the uplands often depend, or to brackish water to which some people have become accustomed.

69. A Merina (Hova) woman, Madagascar.

70. Terraced ricefields in a Betsiléo valley, Madagascar. The slopes are under vegetables, pasture and trees, and have the villages (left centre).

71. Tananarive, Lake Anosy and irrigated fields. See p. 456.

72. Tamatave, Madagascar's main port, cut out of a coral reef. See p. 460.

By contrast, the other islands have older lavas, clay-like surface soils, and surface drainage. Soils likewise vary from island to island, both from natural causes and human actions; on the whole, coastal soils are the best because of downwash and admixture.

The Comoros have the same sharply contrasted wind systems, with accompanying wet and dry seasons, as other islands off the East African coast. However, the south-easterly winds are especially dry, since much of their moisture has been left on Madagascar. Relative humidity is, however, high throughout the year. A further characteristic is the sharp variation in climate and, consequently, in vegetation as the result of differences in altitude or exposure, especially on Anjouan and Grand Comoro. Also, even by African and tropical standards, rainfall is exceedingly variable; such variation can be disastrous on Grand Comoro with its lack of superficial drainage, and on poor and lower-lying Mohéli.

There are vivid altitudinal vegetation belts. Mangrove surrounds the coasts; forest—largely cut down for coconut cultivation—extends to 1,300 feet; more truly natural forest follows to about 5,800; while above that are giant heathers.

Peoples

Arabs were probably the first to reach these islands, beginning in the eighth or ninth century; another wave came from Shiraz in Persia in the fifteenth century. Africans were brought in as slaves. As in Madagascar another important group is of Malayan origin, especially evident on Anjouan. In the sixteenth and nineteenth centuries Sakalava from Madagascar raided Mayotte and settled. The Portuguese, Dutch and French have brought European influences; the French introduced French Revolution deportees, Réunionnais, Indians and Chinese.

While the average population density per square mile is 200 (much higher than Madagascar, but comparable with Réunion and Mauritius), this figure means even less than usual because much land is naturally useless, or held in large but thinly-populated and often little-developed estates. There is also great variation even in the average between islands. On Mohéli it is only 50 per square mile, on Mayotte 125, on Grand Comoro 175, and on Anjouan 380. In the last three it is growing fast, land hunger on Anjouan being extremely severe. Migration between islands, seasonal and permanent, has long been typical, and migrants also go to north-west Madagascar and Zanzibar.

15

Urban development began with the Arabs and the numerous towns have a thoroughly Arab character, the several-storied and closely-built houses being built of lava or coral stone. Dzaóudzi, the capital, is on tiny Pamanzi, just off Mayotte, but linked to it by a causeway—the Boulevard des Crabs. This is the only fully sheltered harbour of the group.

Agriculture

This almost alone sustains the economy, and is highly varied in technique and output. On the richer and lower levels the coconut is the basic provider of food, fibre, utensils and building materials. With it are grown the usual foodstuffs of the equatorial zone. On upper or steep slopes the basic food crop is upland rice, and its cultivation has precipitated severe erosion. Cattle and goats are widespread, the tsetse being absent.

Colonial contact and rule brought in plantation agriculture, first for sugar, coconuts, coffee and cocoa; then for vanilla; more recently for plants for essential oils and sisal. Despite severe over-population and shortage of farm land, just short of 200,000 acres (35 per cent of the total land area) are owned by planters or plantation companies. Small farmers have access to just over 220,000 acres, for a population of 176,000, an average of 1¼ acre each. Holdings are highly fragmented and dispersed as a consequence of Islamic inheritance law, the destruction of indigenous society, and competition for land by plantation holders. The latter employ labourers who may farm tiny patches; thus on Anjouan 32,000 labourers grow most or all of their foodstuffs on only 7,200 acres. Nine-tenths of the people of that island have no title to land. Plantations are alone able to produce surpluses, and they produce most of the exports of essential oils, vanilla, cinnamon, cloves, sisal, copra and cocoa—all in competition with Madagascar. Land redistribution would seem inevitable, as well as more intensive use of plantations, and the closer settlement and development of Mohéli.

MADAGASCAR
(The Malagasy Republic)

This semi-continent lies 250–500 miles off south-east Africa, extends a thousand miles from north-south and, at its widest, is 360 miles across. The area of 227,736 square miles, equals the combined areas of France, Belgium and Luxemburg. The population was 5,200,000 in 1961, giving an average of 23 per square mile.

The Physical Environment

Like Mozambique, Madagascar is very varied geologically, with formations from all the great eras, including volcanic rocks. The eastern two-thirds of the island is occupied by highlands which are part of the Basement Complex. They extend 760 miles from north to south, and 260 miles from west to east, with an average altitude of over 4,000 feet. The massif is cut by deep—often canyon-like—valleys, and level areas are rare. Soils are, at the best, clays of very poor quality; when exposed they harden to useless lateritic shell-like surfaces, one of the many afflictions of this island, once called *l'Ile Rouge*.

The highlands are limited by several faults, the most remarkable being the Bongo Lava Scarp of the west, which runs from north-north-west to south-south-east through the south-centre of the island (Fig. 106), and the Angavo and Betsimisaraka scarps which have caused such steep slopes on the eastern side of the island. Between these latter scarps is a relatively level area occupied in part by Lake Alaotra and the Mangoro Valley, a feature which has locally facilitated north-south means of transport. On the south the massif drops fairly sharply to the sea near Fort Dauphin, and in the north high altitudes are continued in the volcanic mass of Ambre, which shuts off the splendid natural harbour of Diego Suarez from easy communication with the rest of the island.

The highest mountains are, in fact, the volcanic outpourings which followed severe faulting of the Archaean massif, and Fig. 106 shows their location. Tsaratanana in the north rises to 9,449 feet. The extensive Ankaratra of the centre rises to 8,047 feet and was the source of lava flows to the west, which gave richer soils. Ankaratra is also the origin of many Malagasy rivers. Faulting led not only to vulcanism, but also to sharp tilting of the island from the east to west, and the longest rivers flow westward.

The eastern coastal zone, under 50 miles in width, has down-faulted strips of the Archaean massif, lava flows and a very young emerging sandy coastline which has cut off river estuaries (Plate 68), so leaving a series of lagoons, like those of the West African coastline. As is the case there, such a smooth coast is inimical to port development; here it is made far worse by coral reefs and cyclones.

The western low plateaux have sedimentary Carboniferous-Quaternary rocks, which were laid down in a syncline between the Highveld of mainland Africa and the comparable highland of Madagascar. Divided by the Mozambique Channel since Jurassic—

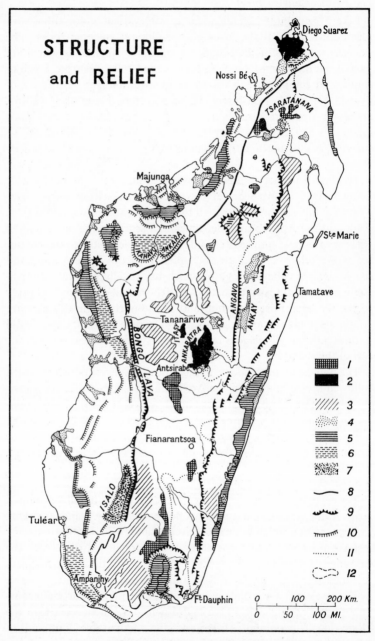

Fig. 106. *Structure and relief of Madagascar*

Cretaceous times, the sedimentary rocks of Madagascar and Mozambique dip toward each other and the channel; in Madagascar they have east-facing escarpments and in Mozambique low west-facing ones. Volcanic intrusions occur, and tropical weathering has covered them with an infertile and compact sandy-clay crust. Alone free from this is the southern but even poorer karstic Mahafaly Plateau.

Although the western coast is not smoothed by sand-spits like the east coast, it is equally sandy, the apparently wide estuaries are obstructed by sand bars, and there are many off-shore coral reefs. To the characteristic of great expanses of infertile laterite on granitic rocks, must be added those of sandy-clay superficial coverings of the western plateaux and the difficult coastlines.

The climate of Madagascar is much conditioned by its north-east to south-west alignment, its asymmetrical relief with steep eastern escarpments, and by the warm Mozambique Current. The south-east trade winds are strong from May to September, causing fine rains on the east coast and eastern highland slopes. Beyond these they become the drier and ultimately drying winds of the highlands' dry season. By contrast, the north-eastern monsoon brings violent storms and heavy rain, and toward the end of their season, between December and March, there are often destructive cyclones. Rainfall is heaviest in the north-west, north, north-east and east, diminishing to the west and south-west.

The east and north-west coasts are always warm, the east always humid as well and has a Tropical Marine climate. The west is drier and subject to great variations of temperature, and so is akin to the Tropical Continental climate of the wetter savannas of the mainland. The south-west is exceedingly hot and dry (as well as being semi-karstic), like the drier savannas or steppes of the mainland. Altitude greatly reduces temperatures, which at Tananarive vary between 75° in the wet season and 54°F in the dry one. Frosts are common at higher altitudes. This High-altitude Tropical climate resembles that of Rwanda and Burundi.

Key: 1. Hard granites, quartzites, syenites, etc. 2. Recent volcanics. 3. Remnants of former peneplained surfaces. 4. Main alluvial plains. 5. Basaltic lava flows, mainly Cretaceous. 6. Karstic limestones. 7. Highly dissected sandstones. 8. Western edge of Basement Complex. 9. Fault, erosion or mixed scarps in or on edge of Basement Complex. 10. Cuestas in sedimentaries or basalt flows. 11. Drainage divide. 12 Closed depression. (From C. Robequain, *Madagascar et les bases dispersées de l'Union française*, 1958, p.17, by permission of author and publisher)

Because of the monsoonal rainfall for half the year, the impermeable granitic rocks of the rainiest areas, and the high and broken relief, it is not surprising that the rivers have steep gradients, are subject to great variation, and flood seriously—especially where they suddenly emerge on level plains. Since these are often intensively used for rice cultivation, embanking and reservoir construction has been needed, for example the Martasoa barrage on the Ikopa near Tananarive to protect the Betsimitatatra Plain, the 'rice bowl' of the capital.

In view of the monsoonal rainfall and the amount of land in slope in the highlands, it is obvious that removal of natural vegetation for fallow farming (*tavy*) may cause serious soil erosion. Forest remains in inaccessible areas of the moist north and east. On the plateaux there are only bare grass savannas or steppes (*tanety*); while on the west coast there is dry forest with baobab and bamboo and, higher up, the lovely but also useless indigenous travellers tree, a species of palm.

The early separation of Madagascar from the mainland has given it a rather special flora and fauna. The travellers tree, shaped like a vast fan, is a floristic example, and the lemur a faunal one. Many African mammals are absent, notably elephant, lion, buffalo, antelope and giraffe, as well as poisonous snakes.

The hostile coasts, steep eastern fault scarps, rugged and laterite-covered highlands, useless—even dangerous rivers, poor soils, cyclones, the dry south-west, degraded vegetation and locust invasions from the south pose great problems. Madagascar has been described as having 'the shape, colour and fertility of a brick'. Its advantages seem to be the moderate temperatures of the highlands, some rich volcanic and alluvial soils, the absence of the tsetse fly, and a population that is young and growing fast (as a result of the virtual elimination of malaria since 1955) which will compel more intensive economic development.

Peoples

The origins of the Malagasy peoples have been hotly disputed but it is clear that they are both African and Asian. It is probable that the bulk of the population is of African Bantu origin, and that they arrived via the Comoro Islands. The coastal tribes of the west seem most akin to Bantu, there are some Bantu and other African words in Malagasy, and the customs and attitudes of the cattle herders are basically African.

The Merina (or Hova) may have first arrived about 2,200 years ago, but most may have come as a consequence of Indian colonization of Java and Sumatra between the seventh and fifteenth centuries. The route to Madagascar may have been straight across the Indian Ocean from the Indonesian islands, helped by the Equatorial Current. This is now considered more likely than the far longer and not necessarily easier route along the Indian, Arabian and East African coasts. There were certainly successive waves of Asian immigrants and, since they probably came from different islands in the East Indies, this would partly account for their varying characteristics and customs. The methods of rice cultivation, associated terracing and water control, the importance of rice as a food, the semi-reverent attitude to cattle, the ancestral cults and excessive interest in death, the facial and other characteristics of some at least of the peoples, and the fact that the sole language is akin to languages spoken in Indonesia point to a second origin there.

There has been considerable admixture, though less among the formerly dominant Merina (Plate 69), who number 1¼ million and live in villages mainly in the central highlands of Tananarive Province. They are the most advanced in agriculture, housing and education, and ruled most of the island until the French occupation in 1895. The Betsiléo, who are closest to the Merina but are darker and more mixed, number 650,000, and are mostly found south of the Merina in hamlets in Fianarantsoa Province. There are some four or five other groups numbering over 250,000. Opinions differ as to the degree of unity among these peoples, but their insular position, common language and consciousness of being Malagasy has made them more truly a nation than many recently-independent African peoples.

Apart from the Malagasy, there are many Creoles from Réunion, Mauritius and adjacent Sainte Marie, Indians from the former French settlements in India and elsewhere, Chinese, Greeks and Arabs, all prominent in commerce and skilled trades, as well as French in the large trading and plantation companies and a few still as advisers.

As Fig. 12 shows, the distribution of population is highly uneven, even by African standards. It is a reflection of the economic development of the eastern fault scarps for tropical tree crops, and of external trade through that coast, the politico-economic development of the Tananarive–Antsirabe–Fianarantsoa areas, and the development of Majunga in the west as a secondary port. About ten per cent of the population is urban.

The Regions and their Economy

Certain things dominate the modes of life of the vast majority of Malagasy and their habitats: the steep slopes of much of the land, mediocre soils, the significance of rice cultivation, and of cattle to highland valley peasants for farm work and to the nomads of the south-west as a sign of wealth.

The highlands are the geographical and, to a large extent, the core area of the country. Despite rugged relief and mediocre soils, two-fifths (or some two million) of the Malagasy live here. Of the very few large plains, those of Tananarive and Lake Alaotra (between the two eastern scarps) are by far the most important, the first being long developed, the latter still in its early stages. Every possible valley floor has been laboriously levelled, every suitable slope terraced, and intricate systems of irrigation channels constructed to push rice cultivation to its utmost extent (Plate 70).

A remarkable diversity of fruits and vegetables, tropical, sub-tropical and temperate, are grown by farmers around their rice fields, but mainly on nearby slopes unsuitable for terracing for rice. This crop variety is achieved through altitudinal zonation, the possibility of growing crops either dry or wet, and in the hot wet season or in the cool (and at night cold) dry one. Moreover, there are some 250,000 people in and around Tamatave to buy the produce. Pigs and poultry find their own sustenance in rice fields, vegetable and fruit plots.

When farm animals are not working, they graze uncontrolled on the steepest slopes, which constitute fully three-quarters of the area. The former dense forests have been destroyed by fires, and the present very eroded grass steppes are poor pastures.

Apart from the peasant areas and system described above, there are also plantation estates producing export crops; for example, the high Fianarantsoa, Antsirabe and the volcanic Lake Itasy area, all important for arabica coffee and tobacco, and the Alaotra Basin and Mangoro Valley for cassava.

Tananarive, the Merina and Malagasy capital, lies around and below a granite inselberg, on the summit of which was the royal palace. On the north the inselberg has two projecting spurs, now covered by suburbs. A formerly marshy depression has been drained and settled, with the market at its inner town end and rice fields at the outer limit. A lake remains (Plate 71), and adds considerably to an already charming site for this city of about 200,000 people.

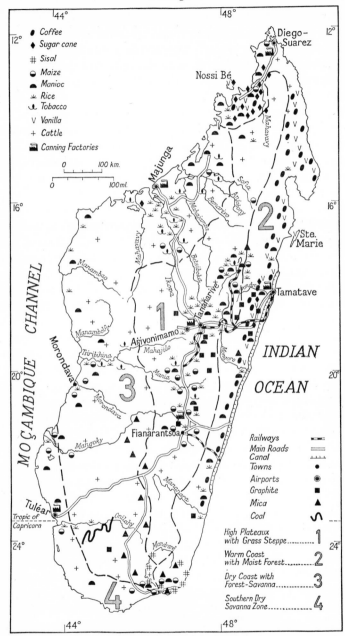

Fig. 107. *Madagascar; economic*
(After maps by Direction de la Documentation and Ministère de la Coopération)
15*

The east coast lowlands are the next most intensively developed area, and their peoples are more concerned with crops for overseas trade. On the gentler slopes of the double scarp, the foothills and alluvial cones of the plain, robusta coffee (a leading export), pepper, cloves, vanilla and sugar are grown, all well suited to the heavy rainfall, but the poor farming methods have caused much erosion. Rice, maize and cassava are grown by Merina immigrants in the valleys.

The lagoons have been joined by the 400-mile long Pangalanes Canal which, though having long detours and limited to very small barges or canoes, provides the cheapest means of transport. Roads are difficult to maintain because of washouts from torrential rivers flowing down the scarps. Tamatave, with some 45,000 people, is the only real port on this inhospitable coast and, not surprisingly, is entirely artificial (Plate 72). As the most important port of the island it is severely congested, but well linked by rail, road and air with Tananarive. Most other east coast ports are open roadsteads, for example Manakara, seaward terminus of the other railway, which serves Fianarantsoa, the Betsiléo centre.

Immediately around the hemmed-in ria of Diego Suarez bay is savanna cattle country. There are some European groundnut and sisal plantations but the small subsistence farms of Réunion creoles are more typical. The north-west is much wetter and Nossi-Bé island, with rich volcanic soils, has long been intensively farmed; among its products are sugar, pepper, spices, vanilla, and plants such as ylang-ylang and lemon grass used for essential oils. On the mainland, the fertile Mahavary valley has a huge modern sugar estate and refinery; while the Sambirano valley produces a diversity of tree crops, especially coffee, cocoa and essential-oil plants. Some are grown by Tsimihety, Betsiléo or Réunion small farmers; some on plantations.

On the western and southern coasts, with their prolonged dry season, the deeply notched valleys are the main cultivated areas. Rice is grown by Merina and Betsiléo immigrants in a share-cropping system. In the richer valleys near Majunga much raphia is grown, near Tuléar vegetables are more important, but sisal again leads in the Mandrare Valley of the south-east. Outside the valleys, transhumant cattle are kept by the Sakalava and Bara peoples, especially in the southern steppes; and some are exported from Majunga and Tuléar.

Majunga is the second port of Madagascar and, though fairly well protected in the Betsiboka Estuary, is essentially a lighterage port. It has a good though heavily graded road-link with Tananarive, and shallow lighters can use the Betsiboka Estuary to Marovoay. Tuléar is sheltered by coral reefs and has deep-water berths. Fort Dauphin is poorly protected, has an immediately precipitous hinterland, and only a small jetty for lighters.

Agriculture

Diversity of climate and terrain, and peoples with differing aptitudes and outlooks, have led to great variety in agricultural methods and crops. An outstanding characteristic is the intensive use of valleys, and the extensive use of most slopes.

Rice occupies over half the cultivated area, is the main crop and food, and a leading export. About 1¼ million tons are produced on 1½ million acres.

Cassava covers over half a million acres, especially in the Alaotra Plain and Mangoro Valley, the highlands and the west, often just above the rice fields and on poorer soils. It is the second most important food and is also fed to animals. Some is exported as tapioca.

Maize is both a food and export crop, and is grown in highland valleys around Fianarantsoa, to the west between Antsirabe and Tananarive, and in the Lake Alaotra Plain. In the west it is confined to valley bottoms.

Coffee occupies about 12 per cent of the cultivated area. Arabica is grown in the highlands south-west of Tananarive; robusta on the north and east lowlands and foothills. Coffee is by far the leading export but many trees are old and its future is uncertain. There is a great variety of lesser crops and agricultural exports, notably vanilla, sugar, tobacco and essential-oil plants, sometimes grown on plantations. In the east and west, a share-cropping system has taken over abandoned plantations, but has led to a stagnant type of farming. A similarly depressing situation is found on the small farms of Réunion and Mauritian creole immigrants who, in growing numerous crops for subsistence and as an insurance against failure of some, grow none well.

The cultivated area is less than three per cent of the whole, but pastoral areas comprise 68 per cent. Cattle number over six million, but are unselected and poorly fed. Nevertheless, some are exported to Réunion and Mauritius. Forests occupy only ten per cent of the country and twenty per cent is waste.

Mining and Industry

Many ores have been located but few are worked because deposits are mostly small and scattered, and the island is remote from markets for heavy ores whose local refining is difficult. Consequently, there has been a concentration on minerals valuable in relation to their weight and needing little refining. Graphite is the main resource, and is worked in the highlands and south of Tamatave at Vatomandry. Madagascar is a leading world producer but world demand is small, as it is for mica, mined in the south. Minerals comprise about five per cent only of exports, and they have played a very minor role in local economy.

The chief industries process rice, cassava, sugar and sisal for export. There are the usual consumer goods industries, but development is hampered by cost of transport and the small market dispersed over a huge area. The high potential of hydro-electric power has been little developed—there are only about ten hydro-electric plants, and the Sakoa coalfields in Tulear Province are scarcely worked.

Transport and Trade

The physical features of the island have greatly discouraged external contact and internal movement. The dangers of the east and west coasts have been described on pp. 451–3. Only at Diego Suarez is there excellent natural shelter, but land access is difficult and the town is excentric to the island. Yet because of the difficulty and cost of land transport, goods are often moved coastwise in sailing dhows, and this, and the variety of goods coming from relatively isolated yet contrasted regions, accounts for the 18 ports, of which 14 are open to international trade. Tamatave, Diego Suarez and Tuléar only have deep-water quays, Tamatave alone is modern but is under-equipped (Plate 72). It handles about one-half the overseas trade, because of its links with the heart of the country. Nevertheless, as Majunga develops, it is likely to attract relatively more traffic.

The Tananarive East Coast railway links the capital with Tamatave and there are branches to Lake Alaotra and to Antsirabe. The only other line connects Fianarantsoa with Manakara. Since both lines descend the eastern scarps they have difficult profiles, were costly to build, and are expensive to run. The terrain is exceedingly inimical to the construction of roads and washouts are common. The highlands are best served, and from them are links to coastal points. Lorry and bus services are fairly well developed.

The difficult terrain, which hampers land transport, has been a spur to the development of air routes. There are about 60 airports with scheduled services, and some areas depend upon air transport, for example Andapa in the north-east which exports coffee and vanilla and brings in foreign goods by air. Tobacco is widely collected by air.

Madagascar has varied exports but their diversity has not helped her. Coffee accounts for 40–50 per cent by value of the exports. Rice, tobacco, vanilla and cloves (with clove oil) each account for about five to ten per cent. Ten more products (including graphite and mica) each occupy about one to five per cent of the total value. Thus coffee is overwhelmingly important and, as elsewhere in ex-French lands, was stimulated by high guaranteed prices in France. Malagasy products are expensive because of inflation, high cost of production, and remoteness of the island from world markets. Despite their even greater isolation and dependence upon sugar, Mauritius and Réunion, small as they are, together have a greater overseas trade than Madagascar.

Conclusion

Is Madagascar African or Asian? Or neither? Or is there a mixture of both in this 'Indian Ocean Continent'? Its affinities with Africa are considerable in the Archaean and Precambrian rocks of most of the island, highlands with steep eastern scarps like those of southern Africa, widespread laterite, natural erosion made worse by man and his livestock, rivers useless for navigation, obstructed estuaries, and forbidding or dangerous coasts. Most of the peoples are regarded as of African origin, their fallow farming or nomadic pastoralism are widespread, and economic development is patchy. In all these respects Madagascar is typically African. On the other hand, although the influx of Asian peoples may have been numerically small, they have given an Asian physiognomy to most of the diverse peoples. Rice cultivation with animals dominates the life of the more advanced groups, made possible here by the absence of the tsetse fly.

There is a unifying language, nationalism rather than tribalism, a much greater degree of literacy and a higher standard of living, in general, than on the mainland. Malaria has been virtually eliminated, the population is increasing faster than in most tropical African lands, and this may bring new attitudes and help the introduction of better techniques.

RÉUNION

This entirely volcanic island lies 400 miles south-east of Madagascar and 120 miles south-west of Mauritius. With the latter, Rodriguez and some small islands it comprises the Mascarenes, and lies on a submarine ridge at the northern end of which lie the Seychelles. Réunion, with an area of 980 square miles and nearly 400,000 people, is an overseas *département* of France.

The Physical Environment

The island lies on another north-west to south-east trending fault, along which volcanoes have successively developed. One on the south-east, Piton de la Fournaise (or Brûlant), is active. Those to the north-west are extinct and their craters have been eroded into three cirques or basins (Mafate in the north-west, Salazie in the north-east and Cilaos in the south) ringed by almost overhanging ramparts, one of which rises to over 10,000 feet. Towards the sea are gentler slopes, which are the outer edges of the craters and akin to the *planèzes* of the French Cantal. Rivers have cut back into the former craters, and are also deeply trenched in the outer slopes. These torrents have brought down huge quantities of pebbles, the Rivière des Galets having built up a stony delta like the *Crau* of the French Durance.

Réunion has the same wind systems as Madagascar, and so its windward side is the north-east with 60–160 inches of annual rain, while the leeward south-west has under 60 inches. Temperatures are greatly modified by altitude, and dry season frosts are common in the high interior.

Sequent Occupance and Economy

Uninhabited by man but the home of many animals when discovered, Réunion was occupied by some French in 1638 and later named *Ile Bourbon*. The French East India Company established victualling bases, settlers providing vegetables and meat for ships. Slaves were introduced from Madagascar and Africa. In the first half of the eighteenth century coffee became dominant, far more slaves were introduced, villages developed round the coast, and escaped slaves established settlements in the interior.

When coffee prices fell spices became most important until about 1835, when sugar took the lead. Following the French abolition of slavery indentured labour was brought in from Indo-China, India, French Somaliland, the Comoros, Mozambique and Madagascar. By 1860 sugar occupied two-thirds of the arable land, and the recent immigrants one-third of the population. As in Mauritius, malaria was introduced by Indian immigrants.

Enlargement of estates for sugar cultivation with immigrant labour tended to squeeze out the poorer white farmers, who initiated a second penetration into the uplands. They planted geranium and temperate vegetables on the lava slopes between 2,200 and 3,300 feet, and kept livestock higher up. Lastly, came the colonization of the upland basins, first in forest clearings for self-sufficient farming, later for vine cultivation. With the construction of roads and the introduction of cars, thermal sources have been opened up, and summer holiday homes established. There is thus an historical, ethnic, social, and agricultural zonation, far clearer spatially than on the tiny and scattered Comoros.

On the coastal plains sugar is the main crop, except in the dry north-west where little will grow, and in the south-east where sugar gives way to vanilla in the forests which survive despite the lava flows from the active volcano. On the dry south-west, sugar is absent on the sea margins which yield only poor pasture, and is found first at 1,000 feet. It extends up to 2,600 feet on the leeward side (to secure sufficient moisture), and up to 1,600 feet on the windward side. Grown for the most part on large estates, the crop accounts for 80 per cent of exports. Although by far the most valuable crop, it is not as exclusively so as on Mauritius where, however, more than twice as much is grown and a far better quality produced. Archaic land and social systems make progress even more difficult on Réunion.

The coastal peoples include very diverse Europeans in commerce and government, African ex-slaves, varied Asians, and mixed peoples. Densities exceed 250 per square mile, and standards of living are low. There are numerous small compact rectilinear towns, houses being of wood with verandas, as in so many ex-slave towns of the world. St. Denis is the capital, but the port is in the pebble delta.

On the high slopes people are either negro, mixed or white, live in small hamlets, and grow geranium and other flowers for essential oils, arabica coffee and tobacco on the leeward side; and vegetables, maize and fruit trees almost everywhere. Geranium cultivation has pushed back the forest some three to four miles and up to 4,000 feet, but at the price of much soil erosion.

In the upland hollows settlement is dispersed. Poor whites grow the vine on trellises, the rather acidic wine being processed and marketed by Chinese. Salazie basin is wet; the other two dry, and all also produce vegetables and fruits. The peoples are poor, were very isolated until recently, are inbred and degenerate. Mafate basin has no road, but visitors to the other basins have brought in new ideas and money.

There is considerable land hunger in coastal Réunion (some fifty plantations have over 1,000 acres each), and there is much useless highland. Although Réunion is larger than Mauritius, has more varied crops, is less Indianized, and has less population pressure, it nevertheless is over-dependent upon sugar, and has a rigid social stratification.

MAURITIUS

Lying north-east of Réunion, likewise volcanic and once French, Mauritius is otherwise radically different, especially in its human geography. The Mauritian population is dominantly Indian in origin, unlike the Malayan and African origins of the Malagasy, or the mainly European and African ones of Réunion. Like the Comoro Islands, Mauritius is experiencing a population 'explosion'; yet while the former have plantations and small holdings with varied crops, Mauritius has virtually a plantation monoculture of sugar.

The Physical Environment

With an area of 720 square miles (about the size of Fernando Po or Surrey), the island was built in three volcanic phases between the mid-Tertiary and the Pleistocene. As on Réunion there was one large cone, but on Mauritius erosion has reduced it to fragments which attain 2,700 feet. However, most of the bold uplands consist of 20 well preserved craters aligned from north-east to south-west, and forming the main watershed some 2,000 feet high. Lava flows from these have weathered to fertile soils now used for sugar cultivation. Vulcanism has thus extended over a longer period and been more diverse than on Réunion, and in Mauritius the scenery is more mature.

In partial contrast to Réunion, most rain comes from south-easterly trades, but cyclones are a menace to both islands. The basic contrast in Mauritius is between the southern and eastern windward coasts with 40–60 inches of rain, rising to some 200 inches on the watershed, and falling to under 35 inches on the leeward western coast. As in the other islands, there are sharp contrasts consequent upon situation and slope, notably in the south-west.

The Peoples

When discovered by the Portuguese between 1505 and 1528, the island was, like Réunion, uninhabited. It was conquered by the Dutch in 1598, who thereafter maintained a port of call on the south-east coast for vessels trading with Asia. The French followed, founding Mahébourg in 1715, and later Port Louis which was their port of call on the Indian route until taken by the British in 1810.

In the eighteenth century about 150,000 negro slaves were imported from East and West Africa to grow sugar on the windward coasts. The abolition of slavery in the nineteenth century caused most of them to resettle on the leeward coast as small-holders or fishermen. Labourers for the sugar plantations were then secured from the Indian subcontinent, China and Madagascar. From 1834 to 1925 the Indian immigration was nearly 300,000.

Two-thirds of the present population of 650,000 are mainly of Indian origin. Nearly three-quarters of these are Hindus, mostly living on the windward side as labourers on the sugar estates. Nearly another third of the whole population are mainly African or of mixed African and European descent and so termed 'Creole'. They are usually on the leeward side, still as small-holders, fishermen or labourers. The Moslem Indians and Chinese are predominantly on the same side but engaged in commerce or administration. The relatively few Europeans are mainly the old French or British aristocracy and a few British officials or traders. Most people speak French or a patois and are Roman Catholic, but five Indian languages (especially Hindi), Chinese and English are also spoken.

Elimination of malaria and good prices for sugar are probably responsible for a 50 per cent population increase since 1944, so that the population density is some 900 per square mile, so exceeding any other island studied in this book.

The Economy

Mauritius has as near a monoculture as any country could have, and sugar has dominated it for a century and a half. Sugar (some 600,000 tons per annum) and its by-products, account for about 95 per cent of the exports, most going to the United Kingdom.

The crop occupies 85 per cent of all arable land, and 40 per cent of the island. Most sugar is estate-produced by permanent cropping with long ratoons (regrowths). The wet eastern and southern coasts, and volcanic soils are ideal; the leeward side requires irrigation. Large estates occupy 70 per cent of the sugar area, some having 5,000 acres or more.

Other than the company estates, there are large and small planters, and share-croppers, but 87 per cent of the land owners have under five acres of land. Nevertheless, there are few subsistence peasants, unlike the French islands, and cheap foodstuffs are mostly imported in Mauritius. All the same, there is an economic and social rift between large and small growers. Sugar crushing is done by estate mills; these

16

are smaller than those in Natal or on the Caribbean isles, although the quality of the sugar is high.

Tea was first introduced by the French in the eighteenth century, when many other crops were brought to their islands from Asia, but sugar has remained most profitable here. Really significant tea cultivation dates only from 1945 as a means of diversification.

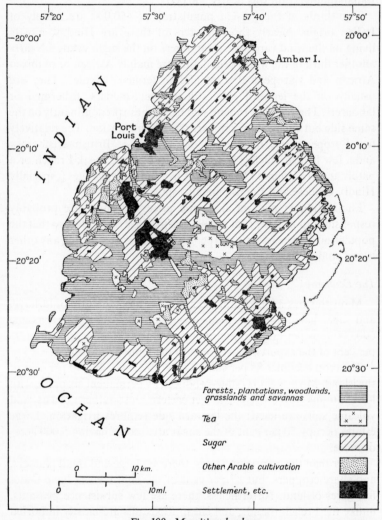

Fig. 108. Mauritius; land use
(Simplified from 1 :300,000 approx. *Land Use of Mauritius*. Directorate of Overseas Surveys, Crown copyright reserved, by permission)

Cultivation is usually in high and little-peopled areas where the vital skilled labour is scarce and competes with labour for the sugar harvest. Alternatives to sugar are difficult to find, although the Comoro Islands and Réunion provide suggestions.

Port Louis is dominant commercially. It has an excellent harbour, an Indian character, and is hot and oppressive; indeed, many of the richer commercial and administrative personnel live at Curepipe, 1,600 feet up. The excellent harbour and airport on the route between Africa, Ceylon and Australia, give the island strategic importance. Mauritius has a formidable dependence upon sugar, and a grave population problem.

MAURITIAN DEPENDENCIES

Tiny volcanic islands, often ringed with coral, extend east and north from Mauritius, the best known being Rodriguez twelve miles by four. The Aldabra group lies north of and parallel with the Comoro Islands, while the Admiralty Isles are west-south-west of the Seychelles. Some 16,000 people live on these islands, almost all mixed African-European, Catholic in faith, and more comparable with the Seychelles, Réunion and the Comoros than with Mauritius.

SEYCHELLES

These comprise some 90 islands between 4° and 10°S., and are the emergent granite bosses of a submarine plateau. Some are high, others small, barely-emergent knobs, others again mere sandspits, but almost all are ringed with coral. The south-east trades are here at their weakest, and only July and August are really wet. From November to March north-west winds prevail, and there are sudden storms.

The islands were settled by exiles from the French Revolution and by others from Mauritius; like the latter and its dependencies, the Seychelles became British in 1814. Later on, liberated slaves from East and West Africa came to work on copra plantations. Copra is still the dominant export and those human groups the main ones, the British element being small and mainly official. Workers on plantations keep cattle and poultry and grow their own food crops; fishing also provides food.

Mahé, some forty miles from north-west to south-east and ten miles across, rises to 2,993 feet. Above the coconut areas cinnamon, vanilla and palms are grown. On the north-east coast is the capital, Port Victoria. Praslin, the only other permanently-inhabited island, is less developed, but is famous for its so-called double 'coconut'. Other islands often have coconut plantations, but are not permanently inhabited. Some 42,000 people live on Mahé and Praslin.

FURTHER READING

Madagascar: this is well documented, but mainly in French, e.g. C. Robequain, *Madagascar et les bases dispersées de l'Union française*, 1958, which has a full bibliography. A short study is O. Hatzfeld, *Madagascar (Que Sais-Je?)*, 1952. W. A. Hance has many articles in English, especially useful being Chapter 8 in his book *African Economic Development*, 1958; 'The Economic Geography of Madagascar', *Tijdschrift voor Economische en Sociale Geografie*, 1957, 161–172, and 'Madagascar', *Focus*, May 1958. For the physical relationships with southern Africa see J. H. Wellington, *Southern Africa*, 1955, Chapter 15.

Comoros: C. Robequain, *op. cit.*, and H. Isnard, 'L'Archipel des Comores', *Les Cahiers d'Outre-mer*, 1953, 5–22.

Réunion: H. Isnard, 'La Réunion', *Les Cahiers d'Outre-mer*, 1950, 1–22.

Mauritius: H. C. Brookfield, 'Problems of Monoculture and Diversification in a Sugar Island: Mauritius', *Economic Geography*, 1959, 25–40, 'Pluralism and Geography in Mauritius', *Geographical Studies*, 1958, 3–19, and 'Population Distribution in Mauritius', *The Journal of Tropical Geography*, December, 1959, 1–22. Also *Bi-annual Report*, Colonial Office, H.M.S.O. F. D. Ommanney, *Shoals of Capricorn*, 1959, is a delightful popular book on Mauritius and the Seychelles.

CONCLUSION

CHAPTER TWENTY-EIGHT

Political, Social and Economic Characteristics and Trends

POLITICAL CHARACTERISTICS AND TRENDS

EUROPE, Asia and Africa all meet in this old continent, now in its second youth. In the lifetime of some, Africa has been transformed from a mosaic of usually small tribal areas, through colonialism, to mostly independent states. Some of the larger peoples are still assertive, most notably the Somali, but, in general, African nationalism has been moulded within boundaries defined by the colonial powers.

Except in the Congo, independence has been achieved peacefully in countries where there are or were few white settlers. Indeed, in many African countries there remains considerable respect and even affection for former rulers as has been shown on the visits by the Queen. The bitter fighting and disputes have been in countries with settlers, such as Algeria, and the prospects for other such countries are not happy.

The Balkanization of Africa

Some of the larger colonial units broke up at independence. Thus ex-French West Africa split into eight independent countries, and ex-French Equatorial Africa into four, the Federation of Rhodesia and Nyasaland has fallen apart (though on the issue of white domination), and tiny Rwanda and Burundi have insisted upon separate freedom. Africa is not unique in this, the same thing happened in Central and South America and in Asia, but in Africa it has led to some very small and often also little peopled countries achieving a precarious statehood, usually dependent upon aid from others. Thus Rwanda, Burundi, Togo and Sierra Leone are all smaller than Scotland; while these, Mauritania, Niger, Senegal, the Ivory Coast, Dahomey, Cameroon, Chad, the Central African Republic, the Congo (Brazzaville), Gabon, Malawi, the Somali Republic and Libya each have under four million inhabitants. The attractions of separate independence include an individual vote at the United Nations, their own voice with

* By R. J. Harrison Church (Political and Economic) and John I. Clarke (Social).

which to seek aid, and more posts in ministries at home and embassies abroad.

One-Party Rule

One-party rule has become usual in most countries but is rarely a dictatorship. Rule by a strong personality is understandable in a continent used to the rule of chiefs, is necessary where so much has to be done quickly, where there is a shortage of educated people, and where opposition can mean delay or seem to be colonialist or seditious. Moreover, there is usually very free discussion in village and district gatherings, parties, the press and in parliament.

African Re-integration

The new countries have inherited from former rulers some of their ideals and methods and, though these will gradually change, they limit co-operation between the new states. Official languages and currencies differ, states belong to separate trading and currency zones, their legal systems are contrasted, and they seek different advisers. Nevertheless, there have been some political re-groupings. The ex-Italian Trusteeship of Somalia and the ex-British Protectorate of Somaliland united in the Somali Republic; while part of the ex-United Kingdom Trusteeship of the Cameroons joined the ex-French Trusteeship in the Federation of Cameroon. The Gambia will almost certainly join Senegal eventually, while Malawi (Nyasaland), Rwanda and Burundi might join an East African Federation.

Inter-African co-operation short of political unity or reunion already exists in many fields such as the Benin–Sahel Entente linking the Ivory Coast, Upper Volta, Niger and Dahomey; the East African Common Services used by Kenya, Uganda, Tanzania and, partly, by Zanzibar; the Afro-Malagasy Union grouping almost all the ex-French states of tropical Africa, and most of these have formed the airline *Air Afrique*. Co-operation is also sought by political unity, and has been forcefully urged by Ghana, Guinea, Mali, Morocco, Algeria and Egypt; technical co-operation is more favoured by other countries. The distinction is less acute than it was, and what limits co-operation is more the division between states formerly French, Belgian or Italian-administered that are associated with the European Economic Community, and those that are not.

The dominant themes throughout Africa are Pan-Africanism, Negritude and the African Personality. Essentially, these seek political unity or co-operation, the development of Negro or general African culture in such things as literature, music and art, and the revival of the dignity, confidence and self-respect of Africans.

SOCIAL CHARACTERISTICS AND TRENDS

Most social groups are traditionally small in Africa and are a reflection of the small-scale economic organization of the continent, the predominance of production for subsistence, and the rarity of production for exchange. The idea of the community is basic in African society, and the individual is an integral member of a group. Group existence has prevailed throughout the continent, but is under great strain as social mobility and intercourse increase. Until they came into contact with Europeans (and very often even now) the typical African tribe—or kinship group within it—was self-contained, self-regulating and self-sufficient. Land was held communally, families being allocated plots according to need. Families were very extended, comprising many relatives, all bound to help each other. Capital was dispersed, and the personal acquisitive spirit had no place; nor had the individual except as a vital member of the community. Individual initiative was all but impossible, and so experiment or innovation could hardly come from within; and as these societies were shut off from the outer world innovation could not come from without. The wheel, written languages and paper were unknown, except in areas of Arab control or influence.

The social changes now experienced in Africa resemble those which took place in Western Europe when peasants and craftsmen were replaced by agricultural labourers and factory workers. In Europe, however, the changes arose from internal forces; in Africa they are the result of the impact of European civilization upon African societies, the contact of widely disparate levels of technical advancement, administrative organization and codes of conduct. African social changes therefore tend to be more rapid.

Africa is a continent of contrasts, and social changes have not been everywhere equal; they have varied according to the extent of colonial influence, economic development and urbanization. Africans have also been selective in their acceptance of European innovations, ideas and techniques. In Kenya, for example, the Kikuyu have been receptive while the Pakot have been resistant. European innovations have not necessarily replaced African cultural elements, but frequently became additional elements. It is often said that Europeans have superimposed themselves upon African society; thus it is wrong to suppose that African cultures will disappear in face of the modern world.

The Family

African families and households are too varied in size and composition to permit generalization, but certain features warrant mention. Monogamy is more or less confined to the Berbers, the Monophysitic Christians of Ethiopia, and scattered hunting peoples; the remaining peoples of Africa are partly polygamous. Polygamy is supported by Islam and has an economic motive. In most parts of Africa women perform much of the daily work; not only does the wife prepare the food, fetch water and firewood and make utensils, but also works in the fields and rears many children. In these circumstances a wife is often glad of the assistance and company of the second wife. But wives have a well-defined status and are frequently individually endowed with livestock and land. The Christian attitude of repugnance to polygamy is therefore not easily understood by Africans.

Bride-wealth or bride-price is another institution which is widespread in Africa and incompatible with Christianity. Payment to the bride's parents in livestock, currency or services is made to ensure a valid and stable marriage. It is also associated with limited personal preference in the choice of partner, which is often regarded by Europeans as a form of female slavery, reducing marriage to a commercial transaction. On the other hand, bride-wealth in its present form has been considerably influenced by colonialism; payment for educated wives has now reached such astronomical proportions in some territories that governments have vainly tried to limit the bride-price.

By tradition, marriage in Africa is almost exclusively exogamous, that is to say between members of different social groups. The exception are the Arabs. In the towns, however, marriage is becoming a more personal arrangement, and women are gaining greater independence, largely because men outnumber women—by as much as seven to one in Salisbury, five to one in Nairobi, and two to one in Mombasa, Kampala, Brazzaville and the Rhodesian Copperbelt. In West African towns, where women are often traders, the sex-ratio is far less abnormal. Elsewhere, women in towns perform a far smaller economic role than in rural areas. Polygamy is a luxury which few urban men can afford, especially with current housing difficulties.

The social position of women is generally low, and their marital and legal rights are few. In towns they remain subject, with some modifications, to the sanctions of tribal life, although many engage in petty trade, brewing and prostitution to achieve a higher economic status. A movement for the emancipation of women is growing, and some new nations, notably Moslem Tunisia, are giving it great encouragement.

Kin and Local Groups

The kin group is a body of people who feel united by common descent. Kinship ties are the integrating force of community life in Africa. *Unilinear descent* is most common, descent which affiliates individuals through relationships on either the male side (*patrilineal descent*) or the female side (*matrilineal descent*). The latter is less widespread than patrilineal descent and is found in three main areas only: a zone across Central and East Africa, the southern Ivory Coast and among the Berbers of the central Sahara. Kin groups may be of various dimensions from small and compact lineages to larger and less geographically distinctive sections of societies. Amongst Arab peoples there exists a hierarchy of kin groups in which the descendants of different ancestors form separate groups.

The clan develops as a compromise between the rule of descent and the rule of residence. Unilinear descent is associated with *unilinear residence*, which is almost universal in Africa and means that the married couple live with or near the relatives of one of them (usually the husband, that is, *patrilocal residence*). The clan gives the individual a dignity, status and code of conduct to which he must conform.

Clans are essentially characteristic of rural societies with limited outside contacts. Throughout Africa large well-integrated units based on kinship are breaking down into smaller units, in particular the family. Long-distance migrations and urbanization naturally weaken kinship ties, although many Africans moving into towns use them to enter employment and social activities. Kinship relations persist, especially in towns where housing is built by African private enterprise, such as Leopoldville, Brazzaville and most West African towns. In towns which have restricted numbers of migrants and which provide official housing, such as Salisbury, Nairobi, Mombasa and in the Copperbelt, the scope for kinship is limited by the incomplete range of kin present. The same is true on plantations where the labour force usually contains many bachelors.

In Europe we are accustomed to associations of people based more on locality and occupation than on kinship; in Africa kinship has a much stronger role. Nevertheless, the village community and the nomadic or semi-nomadic band have an important place in African society. Both may be identified with single kin groups in some parts of Africa, but in general the peoples of villages and nomadic bands are of varied origins. In fact, the village has greater general significance than the clan, as it is a geographic and economic unit as well as a social unit in which mutual assistance is a traditional feature of life.

The Tribe and the Chief

The tribe is an agglomeration of groups and individuals who may not be related, but form a cultural and political unit. It also has territorial associations, a chief, a common language and common customs. The size, effectiveness and territorial extent of a tribe is influenced by the environment, mode of life, military strength and power of the chief. In some areas true national states emerged from tribal organization. Among the best organized were the Zulu, Tswama and Basuto in southern Africa, the Somali of East Africa, and the Lozi and Ngoni of Central Africa; but they are rare and many stages of tribal aggregation may be found in Africa. The political role of tribes varies greatly, but is weakened by the influence of towns, where local government and the police prevail.

The principal function of the chief is the administration of justice and the perpetuation of the social order. Bound by custom and tradition, he preserves the unity and prestige of the tribe, and is to some extent a sacred person in that he is the receptacle of the magical powers of his ancestors. Because of this, tyrannical rulers have been permitted to plunder and establish hierarchies based on briberies and rewards. Freedom, in the sense of civil liberties, may be utterly lacking, but this situation is often preferred to one in which obeisance must be paid to outsiders.

Chieftainship was greatly affected by the advent of European rule. By its policy of Indirect Rule Britain supported chiefs, while the French, with Direct Rule in mind, adopted wider administrative units. In both cases, the chiefs lost much of their power, such as the ability to organize warfare and to inflict severe punishments. Even the Belgian system of paramount chiefs was not very successful, as these chiefs had no hold over the allegiance of subordinate chiefs. Many chiefs who accepted responsibility under European rule have been attacked by nationalists for supporting colonialism, or for being out-of-touch with the modern world.

Towns

While it is true that labour migrations inevitably weaken the tribal structure, urbanized Africans are not beyond the influence of the tribe. Tribal associations are frequently found in towns and are often the basis for common action. Some towns are so closely connected with certain tribes (for example Kampala with the Ganda, Lagos with the Yoruba) that the tribal structure is maintained. In towns where privately constructed houses occur, tribal quarters often arise.

Towns contain a high proportion of recent arrivals and temporary residents, as well as a wide variety of social and cultural groups. Europeans, Asians and Africans of diverse origins, classes, cultures and occupations work side by side but tend to live in separate groups, influenced by the traditions and customs of their homelands. The result is often a lack of mutual co-operation, most marked in South Africa, where, by the philosophy of apartheid, an African is considered as a rural being and the town as the creation and prerogative of the white South African.

Africans, many of whom intend to return to their own societies, take occupations in towns and live in conditions for which their early upbringing gave them little training. They are faced by impersonal relationships, labour contracts, wage incomes, cash transactions, national laws and state police. Kinship and family relationships suffer, and poor people sometimes lack the protection of a unit larger than the family. The evolution of urban classes has been held back by the fact that trading is primarily in the hands of Europeans, Asians and Levantines, while European administrations have tended to lump Africans into one social class. Yet towns are centres of change and are producing new cultural groups and political parties. In many ways they are the portent of the future Africa.

Education

Undoubtedly one of the most powerful forces of social change in Africa has been the spread of modern education. Instrumental in this work were the numerous missionary societies who established a network of schools all over tropical Africa. Education for Africans has varied widely even within a colonial empire. In later years educational systems were integrated with metropolitan systems, so that there were marked differences in the types of education received, for example, by Algerians, Nigerians, Angolans and Congolese. Though in theory there were plans for compulsory education, inadequate finance and numbers of teachers delayed their fruition. Most new states are faced with problems of massive illiteracy and of the social gulf between the literate and illiterate. They are making great efforts to increase educational facilities and speed up social change.

Health and Nutrition

The health and nutrition of most African peoples are poor, and are main causes of the high mortality and sickness rates. Inadequate diets are responsible for deficiency diseases such as kwashiorkor (lack of protein) and goitre (lack of iodine). Although pastoral peoples usually secure more proteins and fats than most agricultural peoples, their diets are often monotonous and deficient in some vitamins or minerals; on the other hand, agricultural peoples often lack meat and milk. On occasion deficiencies are remedied by consumption of local delicacies such as dried fish and local brews.

Health services in Africa vary considerably in their density and efficiency according to the development of the territory and the finance available. The task is enormous, and the approach has been one of compromise. On the whole, while British and Belgian medical services have provided elaborate treatment for the few, the French provided simpler treatment for the many. The new states are striving to increase their medical services, but there are still many Africans who never see a doctor.

Standards of Living

Standards of living are notoriously difficult to evaluate, particularly among African peoples of different races, economies and conditions. Purchases of cycles, radios and western clothing are indicative of the increase of goods and services available to Africans, but not always of a rise in general standards of living. Modern monetary economies have brought new values and a redistribution of wealth, though in some societies there has been little net gain. Individuals have benefited fabulously, while others have remained attached to their traditional ways of life. It is not true to say that town-dwellers have gained most; urban amenities are available, but the cost of living is high and housing conditions often poor. Furthermore, the wage-packets of workers in Cairo, Casablanca and Cape Town have to sustain large families and numerous hangers-on who are jobless and have broken their attachments to the land. Many town-dwellers live a more precarious and unhealthy existence than country folk.

Despite the emergence of a small, educated and prosperous African middle class, the bulk of Africans suffer from poverty, illiteracy, malnutrition and disease. Their social and economic progress is a constant challenge to the new states and to the world.

ECONOMIC CHARACTERISTICS AND TRENDS

Agriculture, Livestock and Forestry

Africa is essentially an exporter of raw materials, the development of which has been sporadic according to the availability of cheap transport to the coast. Africa produces three-quarters of the ground-nuts entering world trade, over two-thirds of the cocoa, two-thirds of the palm oil and palm-kernel oil, nearly two-thirds of the sisal, and over two-fifths of the olive oil. These commodities have been subject to the vagaries of world prices, but commodity boards, mainly in ex-British countries, have sought to pay more stable prices to growers and, in general, have been very successful. Development has not been restricted as critics feared, inflation has been controlled and producers have been content. In ex-French countries high guaranteed prices have encouraged production but at the cost of inflation, and the need to buy imports from France often more costly and less varied than from elsewhere.

The future development of African agriculture must also lie in its ability to produce greater outputs of food crops for Africans. To emulate the intensive cropping of Monsoon Asia it would be necessary to reform land tenures, eliminate or push back mosquitoes and the tsetse fly, effect water control, and apply cheap natural or artificial fertilizer. Work on the land would have to be given a higher status. Irrigation schemes with peasants are costly and require disciplined and energetic participants, but can be the nuclei of great economic and social revolutions, as the Gezira has shown. Co-operatives for peasants have met with only fair success because of the scarcity of educated and dedicated officials to run them. State-initiated or state-run farming schemes have rarely been successful. They vary from purely mecha-nized farms with paid labour, to mechanized schemes with peasants. State-run plantations appear to be more promising.

Africa is only a small exporter of livestock and meat because of the poverty of the environment, disease, and because cattle in tropical Africa are kept more for subsistence and status than for commerce. To change this attitude among the nomadic pastoralists would require a major social revolution, but this may come. More likely, however, is the improvement of the small but resistant cattle of the forest zone, so that they could supply more of the great local meat needs and be kept on mixed farms to the advantage of crops, animals and farmer.

Although Africa has over one-fifth of the world's forests, two-thirds are inaccessible, and her output of wood products is only one-twentieth of the world total. Although some fine wood is exported, for example from the Ivory Coast, Ghana, Nigeria and Gabon, Africa is a net importer of forest products.

Minerals, Power and Industry

Africa is renowned as a mineral producer, producing almost all the world's gem and industrial diamonds, three-quarters of the gold, one-half the cobalt, two-fifths the chrome, nearly one-third the copper, antimony and phosphates, and substantial amounts of the manganese asbestos, tin and lead. Gold and copper comprise over one-half the value of Africa's mineral output. Africa is rapidly increasing its output of mineral oil, rich iron ores and phosphates. Mineral production is mainly in the Republic of South Africa (about two-fifths), Zambia, Rhodesia, the Congo (Leopoldville), Ghana, Morocco and Algeria. East Africa produces very few minerals. Unlike many agricultural products, minerals are almost entirely exported, but the future will see much more local use of oil, natural gas, iron, phosphates and limestones (for cement).

Energy production is very low, although hydro-electric power potential is greater than the figure of power already developed in the world, half the potential being on the lower Congo. Several large schemes are in progress, notably on the Volta and Niger. Most coal reserves are in South Africa; most mineral oil ones in North Africa.

Industry is little developed, and mostly consists in the processing of primary produce for export, or the production of simple consumer goods. Industry is really important only in the Republic of South Africa, which probably produces two-fifths of all African industrial output, but a modest range is found in North Africa, the Congo (Leopoldville) and in Rhodesia. The major difficulties are paucity or non-availability of local capital and skills, and small markets.

Trade

Most African countries are dependent upon a few articles for export, usually to Europe or the U.S.A., though increasingly to Japan, Russia, Eastern Europe and China. While diversification of exports is desirable, it is very difficult to achieve in a short time. More inter-African trade is sought, but it is so far slight because trade is overwhelmingly in similar goods to outside Africa, and local markets are small and poor. It is growing, especially in food crops, livestock, fish and some industrial products, but only Rhodesia and the Republic of South

Africa have more than 10 per cent of their external trade with African countries. Too many of the newly-independent countries have established the same industries—textiles, shoes, soft drinks, furniture and cement—and so restrict markets and the opportunities for large-scale production. Boundaries have become sharpened since independence with more controls, quotas and financial restrictions, and most new states have adopted their own currencies which has further complicated trade.

Africa changed from being mainly colonial in 1955 to mainly independent in 1961—a remarkable change of a continent's political structure. A parallel revolution is called for in its social and economic organization to bring it to world standards.

FURTHER READING

Only a modest selection of the vast literature can be given and, as books in these fields date so quickly, emphasis is on recent ones.

General: Those most geographical are P. Gourou, *The Tropical World*, 2nd ed., 1958; R. Dumont, *L'Afrique Noire est mal partie*, 1962; and Peter R. Gould (Ed.), *Africa, Continent of Change*, Belmont, California, 1961. Other studies are: John Hughes, *The New Face of Africa*, 1962; Guy Hunter, *The New Societies of Tropical Africa*, 1962; Colin Legum (Ed.), *Africa: a Handbook to the Continent*, 1961; Arnold Rivkin, *Africa and the West*, 1962; and less up-to-date, Lord Hailey, *An African Survey Revised 1956*, 1957.

Political: G. Hamdan, 'The Political Map of the New Africa', *Geographical Review*, 1963, 418–39; James Cameron, *The African Revolution*, 1961; Sir Andrew Cohen, *British Policy in Changing Africa*, 1959; John Hatch, *Everyman's Africa*, 1956; Thomas Hodgkin, *African Political Parties*, 1961; Hugh Wynn Jones, *Africa in Perspective*, 1960, Chapter 11; G. W. Kingsworth, *Africa south of the Sahara*, 1962; Melvin Lasky, *Africa for Beginners*, 1963; Vernon McKay, *Africa in World Politics*, 1963; Ezekiel Mphahlele, *The African Image*, 1962; Ndabaningi Sithole, *African Nationalism*, 1960.

Social: A. Southall (Ed.), *Social Change in Modern Africa*, 1961; S. and P. Ottenberg, *Cultures and Societies of Africa*, New York, 1960; W. R. Bascom and M. J. Herskovits, *Continuity and Change in African Cultures*, Chicago, 1959; M. J. Herskovits, *The Human Factor in Changing Africa*, 1963; G. P. Murdock, *Africa: Its Peoples and their Culture History*, New York, 1959; International African Institute, *Social Implications of Industrialization and Urbanization in Africa South of the Sahara*, UNESCO, 1956; *The Sociological Review*, New Series, July 1959, Special number on Urbanism in West Africa; D. Forde (Ed.), *African Worlds*, 1954; W. M. Macmillan, *Africa Emergent*, 2nd ed., 1949; D. Westermann, *The African Today and Tomorrow*, 3rd ed., 1949; L. P. Mair, *Studies in Applied Anthropology*, 1957; B. Malinowski, *The Dynamics of Culture Change*, New Haven, 1945;

W. O. Brown (Ed.), 'Contemporary Africa: Trends and Issues', *Annals of The American Academy of Political and Social Science*, 1955, 1–179. For an admirable résumé, see L. P. Mair, 'Social Change in Africa', *International Affairs*, 1960, 447–56.

Economic: Arthur Hazlewood, *The Economy of Africa*, 1961; H. Wynn Jones, *Africa in Perspective*, 1960, Chapter 10; United Nations, *Economic Survey of Africa since 1950*, 1959; United Nations, *Economic Bulletin for Africa*, 1961 to date.

INDEX

Index